Buster Keaton's C

Buster Keaton's Crew

*The Team Behind
His Silent Films*

LISLE FOOTE

McFarland & Company, Inc., Publishers
Jefferson, North Carolina

LIBRARY OF CONGRESS CATALOGUING-IN-PUBLICATION DATA

Foote, Lisle, 1963–
    Buster Keaton's crew : the team behind his silent films / Lisle Foote.
    p.   cm.
    Includes bibliographical references and index.

    ISBN 978-0-7864-9683-9 (softcover : acid free paper) ∞
    ISBN 978-1-4766-1806-7 (ebook)

    1. Keaton, Buster, 1895–1966—Criticism and interpretation. 2. Motion pictures—Production and direction. I. Title.
PN2287.K4F66 2014
791.4302'8092—dc23   2014038283

BRITISH LIBRARY CATALOGUING DATA ARE AVAILABLE

© 2014 Lisle Foote. All rights reserved

No part of this book may be reproduced or transmitted in any form or by any means, electronic or mechanical, including photocopying or recording, or by any information storage and retrieval system, without permission in writing from the publisher.

On the cover: Buster Keaton in the 1924 film *The Navigator* (Metro-Goldwyn Pictures Corporation/Photofest)

Printed in the United States of America

McFarland & Company, Inc., Publishers
  Box 611, Jefferson, North Carolina 28640
    www.mcfarlandpub.com

For David
who inspired my interest
in cameramen

Acknowledgments

Ray Cannon wrote in the preface to his first book *How to Fish the Pacific Coast,* "The author had no idea that answers to the hundreds of questions involved could be so elusive and that he would spend six years finding them; if he had, he never would have started this book." Now I know what he was talking about. Luckily, I had a lot of help.

I'd like to thank the following people for all of their assistance: Patricia Eliot Tobias, for editing my manuscript and for everything she'd done to advance Keaton scholarship. The Daughters of Naldi always shared research tips, especially Kelly Brown who found Donald Crisp's first wife, Marilyn Slater for the Elgin Lessley article, Joan Myers for her Eddie Cline theory and Rebecca Eash for Cline's birth certificate. Federico Magni helped me find the "old man's" draft registrations. Chris Mankovsky scanned and gave me the Static Club Minutes. The Damfinos were kind enough to read some of the early versions of my research. Buster's Gals on Facebook, particularly Susan Buhrman, Valerie Collins Billingsley, and Christina Dunigan, helped me with my hunt for photos. The staffs of Margaret Herrick Library, the New York Library for the Performing Arts, the Los Angeles Public Library and the UCLA Library were all helpful, particularly my co-workers at the SRLF (especially my boss Tin Tran, who let me use the microfilm reader at lunchtime). Several relatives of the crew members shared family history with me, particularly Fred Gabourie, Jr., Helen L. Zink, Karla Everett and Michael Peters. Finally, I want to thank my family for putting up with me: my brother Bill Foote and my husband David Mullen.

Table of Contents

Acknowledgments vi

Preface 1

THE CAMERA AND ELECTRICAL DEPARTMENTS 5
*Dal Clawson 7 • Elmer Ellsworth 12 • Bert Haines 15 •
Wayne "Denver" Harmon 18 • Byron Houck 21 •
Dev Jennings 25 • Gordon Jennings 33 •
Reggie Lanning 38 • Elgin Lessley 40 •
William McGann 48 • William Piltz 51*

CO-DIRECTORS 54
*John Blystone 57 • Eddie Cline 61 • Donald Crisp 75 •
James Horne 84 • Charles Riesner 90 • Malcolm St. Clair 97 •
Edward Sedgwick 106 • Assistant Directors 112*

WRITERS 122
*Al Boasberg 124 • Clyde Bruckman 131 •
Raymond Cannon 142 • Bryan Foy 148 • Tommy Gray 152 •
Carl Harbaugh 156 • Jean Havez 159 • Lew Lipton 164 •
Joseph Mitchell 169 • Lex Neal 171 • Charles Smith 175 •
Paul Gerald Smith 179*

THE REST OF THE CREW 182
*Lou Anger 183 • Harry Brand 189 • Chrystine Francis 194 •
Fred Gabourie 197 • Bert E. Jackson 202 • J. Sherman Kell 205 •
Ernie Orsatti 207 • Costume Designers 215*

ARBUCKLE'S CREW 222
George Peters 223 • Joseph Anthony Roach 225 • Herbert Warren 228 • Frank D. Williams 229

Source Notes 237

Bibliography 297

Index 299

Preface

Buster Keaton didn't make his movies by himself, and he was the first one to say so. He was unusually honest about the collaboration on his films compared to other filmmakers. He wrote in his autobiography, "The greatest thing about working in a small studio like ours was having the same bunch of men going with me as a team on each new movie. The director, two or three writers, and myself would figure out the story. But the others—the prop man, the unit manager who found our locations, the two cameramen, the cutter—all sat in with us."[1] This book is about the people who worked with him during his years as an independent filmmaker, 1920 to 1928.

There's no way to untangle exactly who was responsible for what. That's why I think there's enough room in Keaton studies to remember these people, too. I've also included some of his co-workers with Arbuckle, and some of the crew from his first film as an MGM studio employee, *The Cameraman*.

They were so important to Keaton's life and films, yet not much was known about them. Men like Lou Anger, who introduced Keaton to Roscoe Arbuckle, which began his career in film. Frank Williams, who first showed him a camera, then let him take it apart. Elgin Lessley, the cameraman who told him that *Sherlock Jr.* had to be a projectionist's dream. Eddie Cline, who Keaton said came up with his funniest gag, at the end of *Hard Luck*. They deserve to be remembered.

Keaton's crew was a diverse group. They were sons of a doctor, farmers, dry goods and liquor merchants, vaudevillians, an architect-watercolorist and a bank president involved with organized crime. They came from all over the United States and abroad. Some had little formal schooling and some attended college. Most of them did some other kind of work before they went into film, from civil engineering, songwriting, and train conducting to professional baseball.

Keaton couldn't have made the films without them. As he said in 1965, "As a rule, when I'm working alone, the cameraman, the prop man, the electrician, these are my eyes out there. I'd ask, 'Did that work the way I wanted it to?' and they'd say yes or no. They knew what they were talking about."[2]

It's impossible to improve on what Luke McKernan wrote in his blog, *The Bioscope*:

> And why research someone so obscure? *You have to ask?* Is there any nobler activity out there than to recover a life? Certainly it is always excellent when anyone recovers a corner of history that has been lost or ignored, however small it may seem. It's a contribution to knowledge, and telling us something that we didn't know before is a whole lot better way to spend your time as a researcher than re-telling that which we already know. So go out and do likewise—and then tell the world about it.[3]

A note about my sources: In the text, there are references to four different draft registrations. Not unlike the registration scene in *The General*, this was how it worked: All American men between particular ages had to report to their draft board on an appointed day. On June 5, 1917, during World War I, all men ages 21 to 31 had to present themselves, and the boards gathered information on their addresses, occupations, dependents, and physical disabilities. One year later, June 5, 1918, they held a registration day for all the men who had turned 21 since the previous event, and on September 12, 1918, they had a supplemental draft for all men ages 18 to 45 who hadn't already filled out the form. The fourth draft in the text, held during World War II, was sometimes known as the "old man's draft": All American men ages 42 to 64 had to register with the Selective Service on April 27, 1942, not for active duty but in case they were needed for national service on the home front. The rest of the draft information for the Second World War isn't available yet.

At the end of individual sections there are further notes on research and citations to census data, where that information is available. These are in addition to the source notes at the back of the book. Because this material broadly informs each section, it is included at the end of the corresponding profile, rather than attached to specific sentences as notes.

Opposite: Some of the crew on *The General*. Most have not been identified, but behind the cameras left to right: Dev Jennings (wearing a tie), Byron Houck, Dal Clawson, Buster Keaton. (*From the collections of the Margaret Herrick Library, Academy of Motion Picture Arts and Sciences.*)

The Camera and Electrical Departments

It seems simple enough: Cameramen operate the camera. But there's more to it than that. Someone has to decide where to put the camera, what kind of film stock to put into the camera, which filters to put onto the camera, and how to light the scene in front of the camera. This is where the difference between directors' and cameramen's responsibilities gets muddy.

The camera department was headed by the chief cameraman, also known as the cinematographer or the director of photography. Beneath him was the second cameraman, who operated a second camera when they needed to make a second negative for foreign prints. Subordinate to them were the camera assistants, who carried equipment, helped set it up, and kept the cameras loaded with film.

In a 1965 interview[1] Keaton was asked if he chose the camera setups himself. He answered,

> Always, when it was important for the scene I was going to do. If I had an incidental scene—someone runs in, say, and says, "Here, you've got to go and do this"—the background wasn't important. Then I generally just told the cameraman that I had these two characters in the scene, two full-length figures, and asked him to pick a good-looking background. He would go by the sun. He'd say, "I like that back crosslight coming through the trees. There are clouds over there right now, so if we hurry up we can still get them before they disappear." So I would say "Swell," and go and direct the scene in front of the cameraman's set-up.

During his career as an independent, Keaton had two chief cameramen, Elgin Lessley and Dev Jennings. He had worked with Lessley on the last three films he made with Roscoe Arbuckle: *Backstage*, *The Hayseed* and *The Garage*. Lessley stayed with Keaton when Arbuckle moved on to make features; he was the chief cameraman on all of Keaton's shorts and the features from *Three Ages* through *Go West*.

Then Lessley left to work on Harry Langdon's films and Keaton needed to find a new chief cameraman. Dev Jennings had as much experience as Lessley, having shot more than 50 films including *What Price Beauty* (1924) and *Cobra* (1925). He became Keaton's camera chief on his next four features: *Battling Butler, The General, College* and *Steamboat Bill, Jr.* Then he and Lessley switched places; Lessley came back and shot *The Cameraman*, and Jennings shot Langdon's *Heart Trouble*.

A camera assistant's responsibilities at that time were simpler than the chief cameraman's. During Karl Brown's job interview in 1914, Billy Bitzer (D.W. Griffith's cameraman) boiled it down: "Look, kid. All I require of an assistant is a strong back and a weak mind, and you just don't strike me as being the type. Sorry."[2] (Brown got the job anyway, and he went on to become a cinematographer, director and screenwriter.)

Many men worked as camera assistants on Keaton's crew. The credits aren't always clear on who did what, and this list is probably incomplete because they weren't credited. The first camera assistant for whom there's a record is Byron Houck. As Byron's career in professional baseball with the Vernon Tigers came to a close, his brother-in-law Lou Anger probably helped him find work at Arbuckle's studio in 1919, and then he transitioned to Keaton films in 1920. He stayed with Keaton until 1926, usually credited as the still photographer and later as the second cameraman for *Sherlock Jr.* and *The Navigator*.

Bob Parker was listed in *Camera!* magazine's "Pulse of the Studio" as a camera assistant in August and September 1922.[3] There isn't much information available about him; his first name was published once because he pitched in a Keaton indoor baseball game against the team from Fillmore in 1924.[4] He was a good pitcher, striking out twelve batters and leading the team to a 9–2 victory.

When Keaton started making features, he needed a second cameraman to shoot the foreign negative. Fortunately for latter-day researchers, the names of these men usually do appear in the film credits. William McGann joined the crew briefly for *Three Ages*. Harry Thorpe, McGann's co-cameraman on Douglas Fairbanks' films, was announced as the second cameraman on *Our Hospitality*, but it seems as if he had a short tenure with Keaton[5]; instead, Gordon Jennings (Dev Jennings' younger brother) got the credit. Jennings returned as a camera assistant on *Sherlock Jr.*

Bert Haines had worked on Keaton's crew since 1921, and he became the second cameraman for the next five films, *Go West*, *Battling Butler*, *The General*, *College* and *Steamboat Bill, Jr.*

The General was such a huge production that Keaton needed additional crew members. To supplement his regular crew of Haines and Houck, Dev Jennings hired old acquaintances Dal Clawson and William Piltz to operate the cameras, as well as newcomer Elmer Ellsworth to carry and set up equipment.

After Keaton's contract was sold to MGM, Reggie Lanning, a studio employee, was assigned to be the second cameraman on *The Cameraman*. He became the chief cameraman for *Spite Marriage*.

The camera department can't function without the electrical department; a 1922 *American Cinematographer* article called the electrician "the cinematographers' right-hand man."[6] The writer pointed out that the electricians didn't just string wires and flip switches—they had to know about each light's properties and how it photographed (mercury lights emit more blue-green light, tungsten arc lights are full-spectrum), as well as how to do effects such as lightning.

Credits are even less complete for the electrical crew than for the camera crew. We do know that Wayne "Denver" Harmon was the chief electrician on five films, from *Our Hospitality* to *Go West*. He went along with Lessley to work on Harry Langdon's *The Strong Man*, but came back to shoot special lighting effects for *The General*.

Although two other names appear in credits as chief electricians: Ed Levy, on *Battling Butler* and *The General*, and Jack Lewis, on *College*. It hasn't been possible for me to find background or biographical information on either of them.

So how did this group of camera and electrical professionals come together? It's far too late in the game to ask the principals that question—they are all long gone—but many of these people did crisscross each other's paths before they wound up at the Buster Keaton studios. It's certainly not impossible that they recommended former co-workers to the boss. And as simply as that, the team behind some of the greatest comedies in history might have come together.

Dal Clawson

Dal Clawson's career was full of firsts. He shot the first feature film directed by a woman, the first feature made in Thailand and the first sound

8 THE CAMERA AND ELECTRICAL DEPARTMENTS

Dell Clawson
Member Static Club
Cinematographer

Phillip Smalley Company
Universal Films

J. D. Jennings
Member Static Club

CINENAPOGRAPHER

Francis Ford Company
Universal Films

Two advertisements taken out by members in *Souvenir: Picture Player Camera Man's Ball Under the Auspices of the Static Club of America*, January 16, 1914. At that time, directors of photography had not yet settled on what to call themselves; in the booklet it was evenly divided between "cinenapographer" and "cinematographer."

nature documentary. His trip to Cottage Grove, Oregon, to help his old friend Dev Jennings shoot *The General* seems a little tame in comparison.

Lawrence Dallin Clawson was born in Salt Lake City, Utah, exactly ten years before Buster Keaton, on October 4, 1885.[1] His father, a dentist for 57 years, was Stanley Hastings Clawson and his mother was Mary Ann Jones Clawson.[2] The third child of a large family, Dal joined Stanley (1879) and Elliott (1883), and then his parents had six more children: John (1888), Freddy (1889), Paul (1892), Edmond (1895), Rebecca (1897) and Clarence (1900). Dal didn't lack for aunts and uncles either—he had a total of 56.[3] Dal was named Dallin after a family friend, Cyrus Dallin, a respected sculptor best known for his monuments to Native Americans.[4]

The family was active in the Church of the Latter-Day Saints, and his grandfather was Hiram B. Clawson, Brigham Young's business overseer. In fact, Hiram's third and fourth wives were Young's daughters. Dal's grandmother, Margaret Gay Judd, was Clawson's second wife. Dal Clawson's maternal grandfather, Nathanial Very Jones, also had four wives. His maternal grandmother, Rebecca Maria Burton Jones, was Jones' first wife.

In 1905 Clawson was employed by the Salt Lake City Engineers as a tapeman, the member of a surveying crew who measures distances with a tape.[5] By 1906, he had become a civil engineer. In 1910, he changed careers and became an electrician. He also ran a small photographic studio and film laboratory.[6]

When he was 25, in 1910, he married 21-year-old Hazel Olivette Hanson. Two years later, the young couple left Salt Lake City and moved to Los Angeles.[7] One of his earliest jobs as a cameraman was for the short-lived *Argus Weekly* newsreel.[8] He joined the Static Club, the first cameramen's social organization, in April 1913.[9] According to his 1918 draft registration, at age 32 he was tall and stout, with blue eyes and light hair.[10]

His older brother Elliott was also in Los Angeles, working as a screenwriter. In 1913, Elliott wrote a scenario for Lois Weber called *Shadows of Life*. Elliott went on to adapt *The Phantom of the Opera* (1925) and was nominated for four Oscars. He may have introduced Dal to the director, because Dal Clawson's first film credit was for Weber's version of *The Merchant of Venice* in 1914,[11] the first full-length feature film directed by a woman.

Throughout his career, Clawson worked for a variety of studios, but for the next seven years, he continued to collaborate with Weber and her husband, Phillip Smalley, shooting 14 of her features.[12] Concurrently, he worked for Thomas Ince's company, Kay-Bee, and was one of eight cinematographers, along with Dev Jennings, on Ince's big-budget spectacle *Civilization*. Made in 1916, this anti-war film starring Howard C. Hickman and Enid Markey was a hit with audiences and may have helped get Woodrow Wilson re-elected in 1918 with its pacifist message. In demand as a cameraman, Clawson shot films for Raoul Walsh at Fox, including *The Conqueror* (1917) and *The Pride of New York* (1917), and for Sessue Hayakawa at Haworth Film Company, including *The Temple of Dusk* (1918) and *Bonds of Honor* (1919).[13] When he was hired by Oliver Morosco to photograph one of his brother Elliott's screenplays, *The Yankee Girl*, in 1915, the *New York Dramatic Mirror* wrote that "his salary will surpass any other man in the business in like position."[14] At this point in his career, he'd shot eight feature films.

Unlike most of his contemporaries, Clawson wasn't glued to the Los Angeles area. In 1919, he traveled to Canada, where he shot the most successful Canadian silent film, *Back to God's Country*,[15] co-written by and starring Nell Shipman. Then in 1923, he went with Henry MacRae to Thailand, shooting the first feature made there, *Nang Sao Suwan* (*Miss Suwanna of Siam*). The *Los Angeles Times* reported that they ran into trouble while shooting in China. The local people were frightened by the camera, and tried to throw the crew out of the village. Instead of just leaving, Clawson photographed the people there, quickly developed the film, and then showed the end result to the anxious residents. Once the locals saw the resulting footage, they liked it, thereafter allowing the crew to record anything they wanted to.[16]

Despite his hectic work schedule, Dal found time in 1919 to co-found, along with Dev Jennings and 13 other cameramen, the American Society of Cinematographers, still in existence today. In 1922 when the organization's magazine, *American Cinematographer*, ran short biographies of its members, he refused to give an interview.[17]

Suddenly, in July 1920, Hazel Clawson died of a heart attack while the couple was in New York City.[18] She was buried in the Hollywood Memorial Park Cemetery (now called Hollywood Forever).

Soon thereafter, Clawson remarried. His bride was Irene Marie Boylan,[19] born in Fort Lee, New Jersey, in 1896. Little more than a year later, on July 20, 1921, she gave birth to a son, Lawrence Dallin Clawson, Jr., in Englewood, New Jersey. It isn't known how long the marriage lasted, but in 1928, Clawson and his son would travel to New York from Southampton, England, without her.[20]

In the summer of 1926, after a two-year break since his last feature

Another Scandal (1924), Clawson was ready to go back to work when Dev Jennings went looking for a larger crew to film *The General*.[21] He joined the team in Cottage Grove for just the one film for Keaton.

Once his duties were completed, he continued his freelance career, shooting a few sound films, including one that involved a trip to India: *Hunting Tigers in India* (1929) was billed as "the first all-talking nature picture."[22] By 1929, he was definitely single again and apparently had relocated to New York. At 3 a.m. on March 20, 1929, he and 25-year-old Charlotte Mary Schuer, born in New Orleans, rousted a Rye, New York, justice of the peace out of bed to marry them.[23]

In the 1930s, he mostly worked on industrial films in New York, including a series on dog breeds for Pedigree Pictures.[24]

At the age of 51, Clawson died on July 18, 1937, in Englewood, New Jersey, of "an intestinal malady," according to the *New York Times*. For some reason, the actual cause of death was blanked out on his death certificate.[25] He was cremated, and his ashes were buried in the Salt Lake City Cemetery.

His son, Lawrence Dallin Clawson, Jr., tried being a cinematographer briefly; he shot one film, *Louisiana Territory*, in 1953, for RKO Studios. He died in Tucson, Arizona, in 2002.[26]

Census Records

1900 U.S. Federal Census (Population Schedule), Salt Lake City Ward 4, Salt Lake, Utah, ED 39, Sheet 6, Dwelling 83, Family 105, Stanley H. Clawson household, jpeg image (Online: The Generations Network, Inc., 2007) [Digital scan of original records in the National Archives, Washington, D.C.], subscription database, http://www.ancestry.com, accessed 3 August 2007.

1910 U.S. Federal Census (Population Schedule), Salt Lake City Ward 4, Salt Lake, Utah, ED 132, Sheet 4B, Dwelling 70, Family 73, Stanley H. Clawson household, jpeg image (Online: The Generations Network, Inc., 2009) [Digital scan of original records in the National Archives, Washington, D.C.], subscription database, http://www.ancestry.com, accessed 10 October 2010.

1910 U.S. Federal Census (Population Schedule), Salt Lake City Ward 4, Salt Lake, Utah, ED 133, Sheet 9A, Dwelling 64, Family n/a, Robert W.H. Hanson household, jpeg image (Online: The Generations Network, Inc., 2009) [Digital scan of original records in the National Archives, Washington, D.C.], subscription database, http://www.ancestry.com, accessed 2 February 2013.

1920 U.S. Federal Census (Population Schedule), Los Angeles Assembly District 63, Los Angeles, California, ED 166, Sheet 1B, Dwelling 30, Family 31, Dallin Clawson household, jpeg image (Online: The Generations Network, Inc., 2007) [Digital scan of original records in the National Archives, Washington, D.C.], subscription database, http://www.ancestry.com, accessed 3 August 2007.

1930 U.S. Federal Census (Population Schedule), Orangetown, Rockland County, New York, ED 29, Sheet 6A, Dwelling 33, Family 33, Dallin Clawson household, jpeg image (Online: The Generations Network, Inc., 2007) [Digital scan of original records in the National Archives, Washington, D.C.], subscription database, http://www.ancestry.com, accessed 3 August 2007.

Elmer Ellsworth

For every Hollywood success like Buster Keaton, there were hundreds of Elmer Ellsworths, aspiring to be in the film business. At various times, he tried writing and cinematography, finally getting his chance when Dev Jennings hired him as a camera assistant for *The General*. But after only a month on location in Cottage Grove, Oregon, he broke his arm while playing in one of Keaton's famous baseball games and got sent back to Los Angeles. Despite this, he was luckier than most. In 1930, he found his true vocation: film costuming. He went on to a long and successful career.

Elmer Emery Ellsworth was born on January 4, 1900, in Johnson City, Tennessee.[1] He was the fourth child of Elmer Ellis and Carrie Kennedy Ellsworth, joining Joseph (1895), Elizabeth (1896), and Kennedy (1897). The Ellsworths had three more children after Elmer: Phillip (1902), Carrie Eleanor (1904) and Theodore (1906). Elmer Ellsworth, Sr. operated two flour mills.[2]

In 1913, when Elmer was 13, the family moved to Los Angeles, where Ellsworth Sr. had a variety of careers, working as a mineral miller, manager at a paint manufacturer, theatrical manager and in the wholesale chemical business.[3] The family first lived near the Fairfax district, later moving to 5552 Carlton Way, right in the center of Hollywood.

Elmer Ellsworth Jr. was still a student at Hollywood High when he registered for the draft in 1918.[4] He was of medium height, medium build, with brown hair and blue eyes. Fortunately for him, the war ended before he could be drafted into service.

Young Ellsworth was apparently fascinated by the movies. In 1919, he sold a feature script to the Universal Film Manufacturing Company. *The Weaker Vessel* was the story of a small town girl who moves to the big city, becomes a waitress, reforms an alcoholic actor and later marries him. That year, he also played a bit part in Charlie Chaplin's short *A Day's Pleasure*.

His film aspirations can be followed by the way he listed himself in the *Los Angeles City Directory* from 1920 to 1934.[5] Even though he still lived with his parents, he maintained a separate listing. In 1920, he was apparently a scenario writer. Then, between 1921 and 1926, he called himself a cameraman, but the *AFI Catalog* lists only one credit during those years, as an assistant on *Thundering Dawn* (1923), a J. Walter Kerrigan-Anna Q. Nilsson melodrama made at Universal Studios.[6] During those years, he might have worked on short films with credits that haven't been compiled yet.

Then, in 1926, he got his big break: He was hired to assist on *The General*. After traveling with the rest of Keaton's crew to Cottage Grove, Oregon, at the beginning of June, he worked for a month before the disaster struck. While playing a friendly after-dinner baseball game, he fractured his arm, according to the *Cottage Grove Sentinel*.[7] (Forty years later, he told costumer Stephen Lodge that he broke it when he was knocked off of a moving train while they were filming.[8] The newspaper account written at the time is probably more accurate, although Keaton did organize at least one baseball game on top of one of the trains used for the film.) Dispirited, he returned to Los Angeles, and the next occupation he gave to the City Directory was chauffeur,[9] although he might not have been giving up on his ambitions entirely; occasionally, as in the case of Reggie Lanning, drivers became cameramen.

Around this time, he also finally moved out of his parents' house, but his brief attempt at independence lasted for one edition of the directory, and he moved right back to his parents' place, now deciding to become a photographer.[10] Or maybe a writer. When he sold another script, he was listed again as a writer[11] for the shipwreck melodrama *Sea Fury*, released in October 1929.

The following year, at age 30, he became a costumer. Over the next four decades, he did costumes for some of the major studios, including RKO, Warner Bros., Selznick International Pictures and Paramount. Career highlights included wardrobe supervisor (i.e., overseeing the day-to-day use and maintenance of costumes) on *The Adventures of Robin Hood* (1938), associate wardrobe supervisor for *Gone with the Wind* (1939) working under head designer Walter Plunkett, and designing costumes for films like *Davy Crockett, Indian Scout* (1950) and *Escort West* (1958). Ellsworth probably met Keaton again when the two worked on Chaplin's *Limelight* (1952). His final costuming credit was for the television series *The Fugitive* in 1965. Following this active and distinguished career, he became research director for the Western Costume Company, which provided many of the costumes for Hollywood's films and television shows. (Coincidentally, this was the same company that provided the costumes for *The General* back in 1926.) Western Costume was (and is) famous for its world-class research library and care for historical accuracy in costuming.[12]

Costumer Stephen Lodge, who worked with him on *The Fugitive*, described meeting the man: "He was a slightly built, red-faced man in his middle sixties, with well-groomed, wavy white hair and a small, well-manicured mustache. He was dressed immaculately in an expensive suit and tie. I would find out later suit and tie was Elmer's usual attire—even when he was using oiled rags and dust bags to dirty down an actor's outfit or when aging an old wool jacket."[13]

Ellsworth became quite active in the IATSE Motion Picture Costumers Union, Local 705, helping to found the organization in 1949, and serving six terms as its president as well as three terms as its business representative.[14] He was also a member of the negotiating committee, executive board and the chairman of their constitutional, budget and welfare committee.

After he had made the switch to costuming, he married an actress, Carmen La Roux, on March 24, 1934, and moved for good out of his parents' place.[15] La Roux was born Carmen Maria Roux in Durango, Mexico, on September 4, 1909. Her family moved to Los Angeles when she was nine years old, in 1918. Unless one was a star, like Dolores del Rio or Lupe Velez, it was difficult for Mexican-American women to find work in Hollywood. La Roux mostly played small parts in low-budget Westerns. Her most memorable role was as Senorita Rita in the Three Stooges' short *Saved by the Belle* in 1939. La Roux was a stand-in for del Rio, who attended the Ellsworth–La Roux wedding.

The couple had one daughter, Dolores, no doubt named after the actress, in 1934. Ellsworth adopted La Roux's son Robert (by her first husband Mr. Ybarra), born in 1927.[16]

La Roux's final role was as one of Xanadu's maids in *Citizen Kane*. When she was only 32, on August 24, 1942, she committed suicide by eating ant poison.[17] The *Los Angeles Daily News* reported that ill health was the impetus for her actions.[18] She was buried at Hollywood Memorial Park Cemetery (now Hollywood Forever).

Never remarrying, Elmer Ellsworth lived on for 26 years after his wife's tragic death, dying of a heart attack on April 4, 1969,[19] after suffering from hypertension for several years. He was buried next to his wife at the Hollywood Memorial Park Cemetery.

Robert Ellsworth followed in his stepfather's footsteps, working in the costume department on films like *Jaws* (1975) and *Family Plot* (1976). Also like Elmer, he was active in the Costumer's Union, serving as Secretary/Treasurer of Local 705 in the mid–1980s.[20] Dolores Ellsworth briefly worked as an extra in the mid–1950s, then retired from the film industry.

Census Records

1900 U.S. Federal Census (Population Schedule), Johnson City, Washington, Tennessee, ED 150, Sheet 17, Dwelling 330, Family 350, Elmer Elsworth [sic] household, jpeg image (Online: The Generations Network, Inc., 2009) [Digital scan of original records in the National Archives, Washington, D.C.], subscription database, http://www.ancestry.com, accessed 3 November 2010.

1910 U.S. Federal Census (Population Schedule), Johnson City, Washington, Tennessee, ED 199, Sheet 13A, Dwelling 249, Family 268, Elmer E. Ellsworth household, jpeg image (Online: The Generations Network, Inc., 2007) [Digital scan of original records in the National Archives, Washington, D.C.], subscription database, http://www.ancestry.com, accessed 30 April 2007.

1920 U.S. Federal Census (Population Schedule), Los Angeles Assembly District 63, Los Angeles, California ED 160, Sheet 14A, Dwelling 269, Family 290, Elmer E. Ellsworth household, jpeg image (Online: The Generations Network, Inc., 2007) [Digital scan of original records in the National Archives, Washington, D.C.], subscription database, http://www.ancestry.com, accessed 30 April 2007.

1920 U.S. Federal Census (Population Schedule), Los Angeles Assembly District 65, Los Angeles, California ED 234, Sheet 36B, Dwelling 564, Family 568, Antonio Roux household, jpeg image (Online: The Generations Network, Inc., 2007) [Digital scan of original records in the National Archives, Washington, D.C.], subscription database, http://www.ancestry.com, accessed 4 August 2007.

1930 U.S. Federal Census (Population Schedule), Los Angeles Assembly District 55, Los Angeles, California, ED 55, Sheet 19B, Dwelling 247, Family 520, E.E. Ellsworth household, jpeg image (Online: The Generations Network, Inc., 2007) [Digital scan of original records in the National Archives, Washington, D.C.], subscription database, http://www.ancestry.com, accessed 30 April 2007.

1930 U.S. Federal Census (Population Schedule), Los Angeles Assembly District 64, Los Angeles, California, ED 404, Sheet 6A, Dwelling 94, Family 143, Antonio Roux household, jpeg image (Online: The Generations Network, Inc., 2007) [Digital scan of original records in the National Archives, Washington, D.C.], subscription database, http://www.ancestry.com, accessed 4 August 2007.

1940 U.S. Federal Census (Population Schedule), Beverly Hills Judicial Township, West Hollywood Tract, Los Angeles, California, ED 19–61, Sheet 6A, Family 133, Elmer E. Ellsworth household, jpeg image (Online: FamilySearch Historical Collections, 2012) [Digital scan of original records in the National Archives, Washington, D.C.], https://www.familysearch.org, accessed 8 July 2012.

Bert Haines

Although his name didn't appear in the credits of a movie until 1925, Bert Haines played on Keaton's studio baseball team as early as 1921. He apparently worked for the Keaton Studio throughout the 1920s.

Herbert Marcus Haines was born on December 14, 1896, in Dayton, Ohio, the son of David M. Haines, a cabinet maker, and his wife, Ida May Shank Haines. He had an older sister, Edith (1888), and two older brothers, Glen (1891) and Irvin (1894). The Haineses had two more children, Ross

(1899) and Dorothy (1902). Around 1908, the family moved to Los Angeles,[1] and David Haines became a carpenter.

Bert Haines was a few months too young for the 1917 draft registration, but he is listed on the June 5, 1918, supplemental registration.[2] At the time, a slender man of medium height, with gray eyes, brown hair, unmarried, with no disabilities, he worked for the Sunset Film Laboratory at 6100 Sunset Blvd. After he was conscripted, he served as a private from September 3, 1918, to February 21, 1919, in Company A of the 32nd Infantry Division.[3] During that time, the Division served on the Western front in the Meuse-Argonne offensive, the battle with the highest casualty rates that American forces fought in. It was the final push that won the war for the Allies.[4] Haines served in combat, for which he was awarded a Victory Medal with Battle Clasps after the war.

After the war, he returned to Los Angeles, where he married 22-year-old telephone operator Dorothy (Theodora) Vidou on July 31, 1919.[5] From the listings in the Los Angeles City Directory, it appears that the marriage lasted only about four years, and the two broke up some time in 1923 or so, after which Haines moved back in with his parents.[6]

When he returned from war, Haines resumed his budding career as a film technician. It's unclear when exactly Keaton might have hired him, but he certainly was a pitcher for the studio baseball team on January 18, 1921,[7] when he led them to a crushing victory over the Los Angeles city team, 12–4, in an indoor match. The *Los Angeles Times* reported that "the pitching of Burt [sic] Haines for the victors featured the contest. With his speed ball breaking well, the defeated nine had about as much of a chance as a lame horse in Detroit."[8] Haines must have been a pretty good pitcher, because it was him on the mound rather than the former professional pitcher Byron Houck, who also played in the same game.

When he was first hired, he was a camera assistant, carrying the heavy equipment, loading the cameras, and helping out with whatever needed to be done. In 1925 he got promoted to second cameraman. In the silent era, most films were shot with two negatives simultaneously, one for domestic and one for foreign prints. As a result, they needed two side-by-side cameras ... and two camera operators. He worked alongside of Elgin Lessley on *Go West*, then Dev Jennings on *Battling Butler*, *The General*, *College*, and *Steamboat Bill, Jr.* Somewhere along the way, he acquired the nickname "Boots," and he remained one of the strongest players of Keaton's baseball team, the Keaton All Stars, according to the *Cottage Grove Sentinel*.[9]

Although the 1930 census still lists him as a motion picture cameraman, I could find no additional credits as a cameraman.[10] Once sound arrived in the late 1920s, Haines became a sound technician at MGM, where he worked for 30 years.[11] Because he wasn't a department head, his name wasn't in film credits, so documentation is scarce. In 1936 he played in Metro's golf tournament,[12] and almost a year later, director Robert Z. Leonard thanked him for his able assistance on the Jeanette MacDonald-Nelson Eddy musical *Maytime*, which came out in March 1937.[13]

In 1939 or '40, he married again, this time to Olga McCoy, who had also been married previously. Her first marriage was in 1911, and it prompted a *Los Angeles Times* article called "Gumshoe Cupid Pulls the Wool O'er Dad's Eyes"[14]: When she was 17, Olga eloped to Santa Ana with Charles Gummerson, who was 19. While the groom's parents did "not even suspect the existence of more than a bowing acquaintance," her mother knew, "having gone along to see that no hitch other than the desired one occurred in the matter." Gummerson worked as a broker and later in a title insurance firm where Olga did office work. They had one daughter, Marjorie, in 1913. All was well until 1924, when they once again generated newspaper copy. According to an article in the July 30 *L.A. Times* called "Divorces Mate Who 'Worked at Night at Office,'"[15] Mr. Gummerson told her he went back to the office to work nearly every night. One evening Olga telephoned to tell him something important, and the night watchman informed her, "Nobody ever does work here nights except me." Needless to say, she stayed up late that night to question her husband about the situation, later telling the judge, "His story wouldn't stand investigation, so he just got mad and left me." The judge granted her a divorce decree on a desertion charge, and the caption under her photo said, "Now she wears that free-again smile." The free-again single woman then went to work as a stenographer for the county recorder's office.

Bert and Olga Haines stayed together until she died on May 9, 1966, from generalized lymphosarcoma.[16] Her ashes were buried at the Chapel of the Pines, Pierce Brothers Mortuary, in Westwood, California.

Bert Haines would live longer than any other member of Keaton's crew, dying at age 94 following a heart attack on June 19, 1991.[17] He was also the last crew member to pass away, two years after Harry Brand. His ashes were interred next to his wife's.

Census Records

1900 U.S. Federal Census (Population Schedule), Dayton Ward 5, Montgomery, Ohio, ED 51, Sheet 9, Dwelling 195, Family 231, David M. Haines household, jpeg image (Online: The Generations Network, Inc., 2007) [Digital scan of original

records in the National Archives, Washington, D.C.], subscription database, http://www.ancestry.com, accessed 9 May 2007.
1910 U.S. Federal Census (Population Schedule), Los Angeles Assembly District 71, Los Angeles, California, ED 179, Sheet 4A, Dwelling 63, Family 93, David M. Haines household, jpeg image (Online: The Generations Network, Inc., 2007) [Digital scan of original records in the National Archives, Washington, D.C.], subscription database, http://www.ancestry.com, accessed 9 May 2007.
1920 U.S. Federal Census (Population Schedule), Burbank Township, Los Angeles, California, ED 18, Sheet 11A, Dwelling 228, Family 270, Charles W. Gummerson household, jpeg image (Online: The Generations Network, Inc., 2007) [Digital scan of original records in the National Archives, Washington, D.C.], subscription database, http://www.ancestry.com, accessed 8 August 2007.
1920 U.S. Federal Census (Population Schedule), Los Angeles Assembly District 63, Los Angeles, California ED 169, Sheet 10A, Dwelling 250, Family 251, David Haines household, jpeg image (Online: The Generations Network, Inc., 2007) [Digital scan of original records in the National Archives, Washington, D.C.], subscription database, http://www.ancestry.com, accessed 9 May 2007.
1930 U.S. Federal Census (Population Schedule), Los Angeles City, Los Angeles, California, ED 229, Sheet 13A, Dwelling 261, Family 335, Olga Gummerson household, jpeg image (Online: The Generations Network, Inc., 2007) [Digital scan of original records in the National Archives, Washington, D.C.], subscription database, http://www.ancestry.com, accessed 8 August 2007.
1930 U.S. Federal Census (Population Schedule), Los Angeles Assembly District 57, Los Angeles, California, ED 126, Sheet 109A, Dwelling 107, Family 107, David M. Haines household, jpeg image (Online: The Generations Network, Inc., 2007) [Digital scan of original records in the National Archives, Washington, D.C.], subscription database, http://www.ancestry.com, accessed 31 March 2007.
1940 U.S. Federal Census (Population Schedule), Los Angeles Assembly District 59, Los Angeles, California, ED 60–867, Sheet 61B, Family 264, Herbert M. Haines household, jpeg image (Online: FamilySearch Historical Collections, 2012) [Digital scan of original records in the National Archives, Washington, D.C.], https://www.familysearch.org, accessed 8 July 2012.

Wayne "Denver" Harmon

Like many other members of Keaton's crew, electrician and lighting technician Denver Harmon found continued success after leaving Keaton. He eventually became an executive at Columbia.

Wayne Lowell Harmon was born three years and one day before Buster Keaton, on October 3, 1892, in Columbus, Ohio. The family consisted of his parents, Henry L. and Jessie Irene Fermin Harmon, and an older brother, Ollie, who was born in 1878. Henry Harmon was a policeman and Ollie worked for the railroads, starting out as a train flagman and then moving up to brakeman, then conductor.[1]

The 1910 census found him still living in Columbus, but only with his widowed mother, who earned her living as a dressmaker while he worked as an assembler in a local railroad yard. In 1913, they moved to California. Four years later, when he registered for the draft, Harmon, tall, of medium build, with gray eyes and light hair, recorded that he was married and had a child, but no other documentation of that marriage or child has surfaced.

Because film credits of the time usually didn't include electricians, it's only possible to piece together a partial list of his credits. Around the time he registered for the draft, Harmon was working as an electrician at the Lasky Film Company.[2] Years later, cinematographer Arthur C. Miller (*How Green Was My Valley*, *A Letter to Three Wives*) wrote that Denver Harmon, then a chief electrician, showed him around the Universal lot when he arrived in 1918.[3] By August 1919, Harmon had become the lighting chief for Astra, Miller's company, on *The Third Eye*, a 15-part Warner Oland serial directed by James W. Horne, who would go on to direct *College* for Keaton and *Way Out West* with Laurel and Hardy.[4] His next job seems to have been as chief electrician on the Astra feature film *The Beloved Cheater* (aka *The Pleasant Devil*), which starred Keaton's good friend Lew Cody, and was released in December 1919.[5] Two years later, in 1921, he seems to have still been working for the same company; he told the Los Angeles City Directory that his employer was Robertson-Cole, which distributed Astra's films.[6] While there, he may have run across future Keaton cameraman Dev Jennings, who also worked for Robertson-Cole at that time. In the 1922 member roster of the Electrical Engineers Illuminating Society, he's listed as being employed by King Vidor Productions.[7]

Harmon joined Keaton's crew in 1923. Although he wasn't listed in the credits for *Three Ages*, his name does show up in the film itself, on the football team list, which used the names of Keaton crew members as football players. On *Our Hospitality*, *Sherlock Jr.*, *The Navigator*, *Seven Chances* and *Go West* he was the electrician. In 1926, he and cameraman Elgin Lessley left Keaton to work for Frank Capra and Harry Langdon at Columbia where he became the electrical supervisor on Langdon's *The Strong Man* and *Long Pants*. But he returned to Keaton later in 1926 to become the chief lighting technician on *The General*. He's not mentioned in any of the *Cottage Grove Sentinel*'s coverage of the filming, possibly because he only worked on the interior scenes shot in Los Angeles.[8]

Harmon spent the rest of his long career at Columbia, working his way up the ranks. By 1929, he was the chief studio electrician, and he was a great manager of those who worked for him.[9] Columbia sound recordist Edward Bernds remembered Harmon as "a gentleman encased in a hard shell ... a rough-hewn man whose career began in Hollywood's earliest days. Electricians, whether they install conduit in high-rise buildings or wrestle heavy lighting units into place on a move set, tend to be a hard-bitten breed, but when Denver Harmon spoke to his electricians, often at the top of his voice, they listened, respectfully. They knew that their boss often argued, loudly, nose to nose, with Harry Cohn in defense of his men."[10] Bernds also mentioned that Harmon was great in a crisis, thinking quickly and acting accordingly. During the 1933 Long Beach earthquake, which was strongly felt in Hollywood, Harmon didn't even wait for the shaking to stop before he ran to shut off the high-voltage transformers that were "swaying like a cornstalk in a high wind."[11]

At some point, Harmon's older brother Ollie joined him at Columbia, becoming a property man. The brothers lived together in a house at 1556 La Baig Avenue that gave them a great commute every day—their house was just a few blocks from the studio.[12]

Years after his mystery marriage and child during World War I, he married for a second time on March 23, 1929.[13] His bride was Bird M. Claypool Zerble, who came from Mason City, Iowa. Both were 37 years old, and she brought along her 16-year-old son from a previous marriage, William Charles Zerble, who was adopted by Harmon.[14]

In 1943, he was promoted to plant supervisor,[15] which was his job until he retired in July 1958.[16] Following a heart attack at home, he died on February 1, 1959, seven years to the day before the death his former boss.[17] He was buried in Forest Lawn Memorial Park, in Glendale, California.

His widow, Bird Harmon, lived many more years, dying of heart failure, although she was also afflicted with colon cancer, on November 23, 1982,[18] at the age of 91. She was buried next to her husband.

Further Information

Just in case you're planning on doing more research into this gentleman, you need to know that there were *two* Denver Harmons living in Los Angeles, circa 1920–1950. Denver Dudley Harmon was an interesting man, too. Just two years younger than the electrician, he also grew up in Ohio. After a lifetime of working as a potter and kiln fireman, he went into show business. He managed The Educated Chimps, a traveling group of trained chimpanzees. He died June 24, 1957, also following a heart attack.

Census Records

1910 U.S. Federal Census (Population Schedule), Columbus Ward 12, Franklin, Ohio, ED 0007, Sheet 44A, Dwelling 252, Family 340, Irene Harmon household, jpeg image (Online: The Generations Network, Inc., 2008) [Digital scan of original records in the National Archives, Washington, D.C.], subscription database, http://www.ancestry.com, accessed 31 January 2009.

1920 U.S. Federal Census (Population Schedule), Los Angeles Assembly District 63, Los Angeles, California ED 169, Sheet 7B, Dwelling 189, Family 191, Wayne Harmon household, jpeg image (Online: The Generations Network, Inc., 2008) [Digital scan of original records in the National Archives, Washington, D.C.], subscription database, http://www.ancestry.com, accessed 31 January 2009.

1920 U.S. Federal Census (Population Schedule), Mason City, Cerro Gordo, Iowa, ED 33, Sheet 11B, Dwelling 228, Family 235, I.T. Fellows household, jpeg image (Online: The Generations Network, Inc., 2008) [Digital scan of original records in the National Archives, Washington, D.C.], subscription database, http://www.ancestry.com, accessed 31 December 2008.

1930 U.S. Federal Census (Population Schedule), Los Angeles Assembly District 55, Los Angeles, California, ED 54, Sheet 11B, Dwelling n.a., Family n.a., Mayne [sic] L. Harmon household, jpeg image (Online: The Generations Network, Inc., 2008) [Digital scan of original records in the National Archives, Washington, D.C.], subscription database, http://www.ancestry.com, accessed 31 December 2008.

1940 U.S. Federal Census (Population Schedule), Los Angeles Assembly District 57, Los Angeles, California, ED 60–127, Sheet 8B, Family 231, Wayne L. Harmon household, jpeg image (Online: FamilySearch Historical Collections, 2012) [Digital scan of original records in the National Archives, Washington, D.C.], https://www.familysearch.org, accessed 8 July 2012.

Byron Houck

Buster Keaton loved baseball … and baseball players. Among several ballplayers hired to work with Keaton over the years was Byron Houck, who had an unusual career trajectory, from pro baseball player to Hollywood cameraman to salesman. He spent seven years with Keaton, from 1919 to 1926.

Byron Simon Houck was born on August 28, 1891, in Prosper, Minnesota, to farmers Arthur and Ida Call Houck, who already had three older sons, Herbert (1880) George (1885) and Jesse (1886), and a daughter, Blanche (1888). Two years after Byron was born, they had another daughter, Dot.

For whatever reason, the family gave up farming, and by 1910 they had moved to Portland, Oregon, where Arthur had become a plaster contractor. Also in 1910, Byron, age 19, became a student at University of Oregon in Portland.[1] He was a pitcher on their baseball team, the Ducks, and he played two seasons with them.[2] He abandoned his studies when a more interesting opportunity arrived.

In 1912, the Philadelphia Athletics (or the A's, as they were known—now the Oakland A's) recruited him to play professionally. He must have been a very good prospect, because the A's were then one of the top American League teams, winning the World Series in 1911 and 1913. Now known as "Duke," Houck was a six-foot-tall right-hander, weighing in at 175 pounds, and he made his major league debut on May 15, 1912.[3] According to baseball historian Norman L. Macht, Houck seems to have been an inconsistent player: "[W]ith the Athletics, Houck was sometimes unbeatable, and sometimes walked every batter he faced."[4]

Less than a year later, on April 13, 1913, Houck got married in Delaware. His bride, Kittye Issacs, was a year older than he was, and came from Philadelphia. Her older sister was Sophye Barnard, a noted vaudeville singer who had married another vaudeville performer, Lou Anger, the man who may have introduced Buster Keaton to the movies. Houck's brother-in-law would later influence his career as well.

Houck was with the Philadelphia A's for two years, before they sent him to the then minor league Baltimore Orioles on May 20, 1914. Houck refused to play in the minors.[5] Instead, he jumped over to the Federal League, debuting with the Brooklyn Federals (aka the Tip-Tops) only two days later. The *New York Times* reported "[A]lthough his work as a pitcher was not very impressive, his hard hitting made him look like a decidedly valuable addition to the Tip Tops' offensive strength."[6] Valuable he may have been, but the Kansas City Packers beat them that day, 6–2.

He played with the Federals only for one season; the Federal League folded in 1915. On March 23, 1916, a sportswriter reported, "Houck had a sad experience with the Feds. He thought he had an iron-clad contract, but it was repudiated and he had to settle on a cash basis calling for about half of what he had contracted for."[7] In March 1916, he joined the Portland Beavers of the Pacific Coast League.[8] Although it was the minors, the League was the predominant West Coast baseball organization—in fact, no major league team existed west of St. Louis. The Pacific Coast League also included a team that would play a prominent role in Houck's future: Roscoe Arbuckle's Vernon Tigers.

Houck was still playing for the Beavers when he filled out his draft registration on June 5, 1917.[9] At the time, he was 25 years old, tall, of medium build, with blue eyes, brown hair, and no disabilities, but he claimed a draft exemption because he was married.

Things seemed to be going Houck's way. In 1918, he returned to the majors, spending a season with the struggling St. Louis Browns.[10] However, he didn't have a good season, playing in 27 games and getting credit for winning two and losing four.

It was back to the minor leagues for Houck: The Vernon Tigers bought his contract in February of 1919.[11] By this time, Lou Anger had given up performing and was now managing Roscoe Arbuckle's business affairs, including his baseball team, the Vernon Tigers, which Arbuckle bought the following May. Anger may have had something to do with a newspaper reporter discovering "noted baseball pitcher Byron Houck" during a tour of Arbuckle's studio in November 1919.[12] The reporter doesn't say what Houck was doing at the studio, but he may already have been part of the camera crew. Later, when sportswriters wanted to rib him, they called him the "camera chauffeur and movie idol."[13]

Houck continued to both play baseball and work at the studio for another year, but then he ran into trouble: His best pitch, the spitball, was outlawed in 1921. When the spitball prohibition was announced, Harry A. Williams, the *Los Angeles Times* sports editor, wrote, "[O]ne of the most severe spine shivers was experienced by Byron Houck, who has a 'spitter' that is hardly out of swaddling clothes. Byron started out as an arid pitcher, but was not wholly successful. He began bringing home the bacon regularly only after he had learned to juice up the ball. In short, he entirely revised his pitching system. Only his last season was he at his best."[14]

Houck got to play one last "wet" season. From all accounts, his spitball really was something. On September 3, 1920, one of the *L.A. Times* sportswriters commented, "Byron wields a flicker spitter that is a blurring to the eye at times as is the old celluloid at third speed.... Every time Byron faced a firing squad and a handkerchief was about to be placed over his eyes, what does he do but put an extra veneer of cleverness on the old satsuma and twist the visitors into a few infield Roman candles. [Satsuma is a type of mandarin orange.] Houck's work in the pinches yesterday was the niftiest seen here this year."[15] The Tigers beat the Seattle Rainiers that day, 3–1.

At the end of the season, Williams reported, "Byron is now irrevocably wedded to art as typified in the deaf and dumb drama [i.e., he's going to work in silent movies].... Any contract sent him this spring will be purely a formality to be chronicled as a matter of record. [i.e., the Tigers might send him a contract, but they don't expect him to sign it]"[16] The Vernon Tigers didn't officially drop him until July 10, 1922,[17] so Houck played in a few more Tigers games[18] and then occasional exhibition games,[19] as well as playing with Keaton's studio baseball team. But his professional baseball career was over.[20] The *Oakland Tribune* reported in 1923 that he tried to stage a comeback, but "he found difficulty getting back into shape."[21]

Kittye Houck died on March 26, 1923,[22] after four years of suffering with chronic encephalitis, brain inflammation that causes progressively worse dementia and physical disability. Around this time, Houck went to work for Keaton full-time, shooting still photographs and helping with the camera crew. The still cameraman didn't only shoot photographs used in advertising, he also took pictures of the sets to keep track of where the props and furniture were placed.[23] Credits for assistants aren't complete, but he received second cameraman credits on *Sherlock Jr.*, *The Navigator* and *Seven Chances*. In the summer of 1926, The *Cottage Grove Sentinel* reported that he shot stills for *The General*.[24]

The Navigator was a particularly difficult shoot for the camera crew. Along with Keaton and Elgin Lessley, Houck froze at the bottom of Lake Tahoe to get the underwater shots.[25] They also had to deal with the Pacific Ocean. Harry Brand, Keaton's publicist, used one adventure for a press release, giving us a glimpse of Houck's dark humor. As the cameramen were shooting in a small boat, it sprung a leak. "Hey, come and get us, we're sinking," shouted Lessley and Houck. "Don't get those cameras wet," megaphoned Lou Anger, now the Keaton business manager. A rescue party was launched as the boat quickly took on water. "Hurry up," shouted Lessley, "there's sharks around here, and I think I see a couple of swordfish." "Save those cameras," pleaded Anger, "and don't give up the ship." "Don't worry, Mr. Anger," shouted Houck, "if the worst comes to worst, we'll go down with the ship. You'll find our bodies on the ocean bottom with a lens in each pocket and a tripod clasped in our arms."[26] Odds are good that this was a cleaned-up version of the events. After all, who calls his former brother-in-law "Mister"?

In 1925, Arbuckle was banned from appearing on screen but directed whenever he could, always under the name William Goodrich. He gave Houck the chance to be the chief cameraman on four two-reelers, three starring the talented Lupino Lane (*His Private Life*, *Fool's Luck*, and *The Fighting Dude*) and one starring Lloyd Hamilton (*The Movies*).

Houck seems to have quit the film business in late 1926. He left at the same time that Lou Anger was promoted away from the Keaton studio, so perhaps his connection with Anger prompted his retirement from the movies. In 1928, his City Directory entry recorded his profession as a manufacturer's agent.[27]

On October 26, 1927, he married for the second time.[28] His bride was Rose Johnson Carr, who was born in Utah on October 11, 1892.[29] It was her second marriage, too.

Occasionally his name cropped up in the *Los Angeles Times*, when he played in golf tournaments or when he went to baseball old-timers games.[30] In those articles, he was still referred to as a Hollywood cameraman, and he doesn't seem to have corrected that mistaken designation. In the City Directory he was listed as a salesman for the Hersee Paper Box Company,[31] and he later worked for the Flintcote Box Company.[32]

Rose Houck worked for the Pacific Telephone Company for 30 years,[33] beginning as an operator and later as part of the public relations department.

He and Rose retired to Aptos, California, near Santa Cruz, in 1956.[34]

He died on June 17, 1969, aged 77, of septicemia after five years of acute and chronic kidney infections (pyelonephritis). Rose died seven years later, on February 16, 1976, of congestive heart failure.[35]

Census Records

1900 U.S. Federal Census (Population Schedule), Canton, Fillmore, Minnesota, ED 19, Sheet M, Dwelling 212, Family 214, Arthur Houck household, jpeg image (Online: The Generations Network, Inc., 2007) [Digital scan of original records in the National Archives, Washington, D.C.], subscription database, http://www.ancestry.com, accessed 14 April 2007.

1900 U.S. Federal Census (Population Schedule), Philadelphia Ward 20, Philadelphia County, Pennsylvania, ED 436, Sheet 6, Dwelling 109, Family 116, L.E. Issacs household, jpeg image (Online: The Generations Network, Inc., 2010) [Digital scan of original records in the National Archives, Washington, D.C.], subscription database, http://www.ancestry.com, accessed 2 April 2010.

1910 U.S. Federal Census (Population Schedule), Chicago Ward 6, Cook County, Illinois, ED 0344, Sheet 4B, Dwelling 40, Family 20, Max J. Liebenstein household, jpeg image (Online: The Generations Network, Inc., 20010) [Digital scan of original records in the National Archives, Washington, D.C.], subscription database, http://www.ancestry.com, accessed 26 March 2011.

1910 U.S. Federal Census (Population Schedule), Portland Ward 8, Multnomah, Oregon, ED 321, Sheet 1B, Dwelling 19, Family 19, Arthur J. Houck household, jpeg image (Online: The Generations Network, Inc., 2007) [Digital scan of original records in the National Archives, Washington, D.C.], subscription database, http://www.ancestry.com, accessed 12 April 2007.

1920 U.S. Federal Census (Population Schedule), Los Angeles Assembly District 63, Los Angeles, California, ED 160, Sheet 5A, Dwelling 134, Family 141, Byron S. Houck household, jpeg image (Online: The Generations Network, Inc., 2007) [Digital scan of original records in the National Archives, Washington, D.C.], subscription database, http://www.ancestry.com, accessed 12 April 2007.

1930 U.S. Federal Census (Population Schedule), Los Angeles City, Los Angeles, California, ED 636, Sheet 10A, Dwelling 317, Family 317, Byron S. Houck household, jpeg image (Online: The Generations Network, Inc., 2007) [Digital scan of original records in the National Archives, Washington, D.C.], subscription database, http://www.ancestry.com, accessed 12 April 2007.

1940 U.S. Federal Census (Population Schedule), Los Angeles Assembly District 42, Los Angeles, California, ED 60-36, Sheet 62A, Family 225, Byron S. Houck household, jpeg image (Online: FamilySearch Historical Collections, 2012) [Digital scan of original records in the National Archives, Washington, D.C.], https://www.familysearch.org, accessed 8 July 2012.

Dev Jennings

In a 1926 interview, Buster Keaton laid out his hiring criteria for a chief cameraman: "For a big picture the chief cameraman must be one who has proven his ability. As films are seldom made under ideal conditions, he must be one who can put action and feeling into a picture taken under the difficulties of changing light and shade."[1] Dev Jennings had certainly proved his ability by the time Keaton hired him in 1925, having shot over fifty films. Jennings was in charge of the camera department for four of Keaton's best features, including *The General*. He went on to have an important post–Keaton career, shooting films like *The Public Enemy* (1931). He finished his career working with his brother Gordon in the Paramount Studios effects department. They shared the first Oscar ever given for special effects, for *Spawn of the North* in 1939.

Like cameraman Dal Clawson, Dev Jennings came from Salt Lake City, Utah, and he was a member of the Church of the Latter-Day Saints (aka the Mormons). All of his grandparents were pioneers; they came from England as part of a church-sponsored emigration. Both grandfathers were poor boys who worked hard and made good. Paternal grandfather William Jennings was a merchant, tanner and cattleman (and the mayor of Salt Lake City from 1882 to 1885). Polygamy was part of Mormon life at the time, and William had two wives, Jane Walker and Priscilla Paul. With his two wives, he fathered 14 children. On October 26, 1858, Priscilla gave birth to Dev and Gordon's father, Joseph Arthur, who worked first as a miner and later as a missionary in London, England. After he returned to the United States, he attended the University of Vermont and became a medical doctor.[2]

Dev Jennings' maternal grandfather, Henry Dinwoody, was also successful. He built the Dinwoody Furniture Company of Salt Lake City into a prosperous business, and he would serve on the boards of directors for several other companies, as well as the city council in Salt Lake. A leader in the church's administration, he had three wives: Ellen Gore, Anne Hill and Sarah Kinnersley. When the United States got serious about enforcing anti-polygamy laws, Dinwoody got into legal trouble; in 1886, he pled guilty to unlawful cohabitation, paid a $300 fine, and served six months in the federal penitentiary.[3] (Jane Walker Jennings died in 1871, so William Jennings didn't run afoul of the law.) Jennings' grandmother was his second wife, Anne. She gave birth to their mother, Ellen Louisa, on July 24, 1862. Ellen was the first of Anne's nine children.

Jennings' parents married on October 25, 1883, and Joseph Devereux ("Dev") was born 11 months later, on September 22, 1884. Four more children followed: Helen Kittie (1887), Clifford (1891), Henry Gordon (1896) and Ruth (1904).

Dev Jennings studied at the University of Utah.[4] He became a civil engineer (a profession Keaton himself aspired to as a child),[5] and soon got a job as the chief maintenance engineer for the Americana Smelter and

Refining Company in Salt Lake City in 1906.[6] In 1910, the family moved to Los Angeles. For many years, Ellen Jennings had suffered from depression, so Dr. Jennings hoped that the climate might improve her health.[7] He was wrong. On December 6 of the same year, she sent her family off to school and work, went into the bedroom, and slashed her throat. Her husband found her still alive, and took her to Clara Barton Hospital in downtown Los Angeles where she died.[8] At this point, most of the family moved back to Salt Lake, with the exception of Dev.[9] Dr. Jennings gave up medicine as a career, and in 1912 he founded an insurance agency, the Jennings Insurance Agency.[10] In 1928, he retired and moved back to Los Angeles, where he died on June 29, 1943, after falling into a diabetic coma.[11]

During the family's time in Los Angeles, Dev got a job as a manufacturers' agent for the Southern Pacific Railroad and he stayed put.[12] According to the *Salt Lake Tribune*, he had been bitten by the movie bug "after seeing a troop [sic] on location near Provo one day."[13] In 1908, he had bought himself a camera and began experimenting on his own, eventually getting professional work in film between 1911 and 1913. In 1926, he told the *Cottage Grove Sentinel* that he "was induced by a friend to get into the movie camera game 15 years ago and has never regretted that he did so."[14] The "15 years ago" seems to have been imprecise, however, because in his 1928 *Salt Lake Tribune* interview, he said that he made his career change in 1913, starting as an assistant cameraman for Universal Films.

Dev married Cleo Wells on July 4, 1914,[15] and they settled down near Hollywood, along with her mother Minnie. The couple separated in the early 1920s.

Dev was an early member of the Static Club, which had been founded on February 13, 1913, establishing "primarily and essentially a social organization devoted to the betterment of technical work as applied to cinephotography."[16] He joined before the organization held its first dance on January 16, 1914. At that time he was still at Universal Films with the Francis Ford Company and the MacDonald Powers Comedy Company, but he had advanced from an assistant cameraman to a higher-level position as a cameraman.[17] By January 1915, he had gone to Thomas Ince's New York Motion Picture Company (NYMPC), which was soon to become part of the Triangle Film Corporation.[18] From 1915 to 1919, Triangle (formed by Ince, D.W. Griffith, and Mack Sennett) employed the biggest stars, including Roscoe Arbuckle, Mary Pickford and Douglas Fairbanks, and produced some of the most memorable films of the era, from *Birth of a Nation* (1915) to the Keystone Cops shorts.

By contemporary accounts, Dev was a gregarious guy. In its February 20, 1915, issue, the Static Club's magazine, *Static Flashes*, called him "the entertaining cameraman ... Mr. Jennings is one of the active and popular cinematographers who believes in the future of the cameraman, and he is ever alert and responsive to the wishes of his director, aiding in the best of his ability in securing proper photographic results, and always appearing with a cheerful smile."[19] In May of that year, he invited Static Club members to attend the Century Theatre to see a burlesque show as the NYMPC's guests.[20] The next month, it was reported that he "threatens to make a speech at the Stag banquet of the Statics Saturday night at the Bristol, and his advent is awaited with much expectancy. Jennings is some speechmaker and when he says anything, it is interestingly projected."[21]

Static Flashes also praised his work as a cinematographer: "Jennings has the remarkable asset of being able to detect possibilities of the camera that frequently are passed by the average cameraman. His association with Hunt [Jay Hunt, a director-actor at NYMPC] has brought him face to face with many difficult problems, such as the filming of big battle scenes, balloon ascensions, and the like, yet he has always emerged victorious." Of particular interest to Keaton scholars is the next sentence: "Retakes are virtually unknown to Jennings, for the great care he takes in his work usually results in flawless photography."[22]

His earliest feature credit with Triangle was *Matrimony* (1915), a drama about marital fidelity starring Julia Dean and Howard Hickman. Jennings shot 12 films for Ince's company over the next year. He was also one of the eight cameramen on the epic *Civilization*. In 1916 he moved to the Fox Film Corporation, where his credits include Tom Mix Westerns, crime melodramas and adventure films such as *The Scarlet Pimpernel*. The closest he came to a funny movie was *Cowardice Court*, a 1919 comedy-drama about feuding families in the Adirondacks.

Along with Dal Clawson and 13 other cameramen, he helped to found the American Society of Cinematographers on December 21, 1918.[23] The ASC is an honorary society; members still meet regularly to discuss their work. Jennings was also a Mason and a Shriner, belonging to the Al-Malaikah Temple.[24]

His 1918 draft registration card reveals what could be a serious problem for a cameraman: Dev Jennings was partially blind in his right eye,[25] probably caused by an accident that occurred when he was seven years old and playing with gunpowder and matches.[26] In the explosion, he was badly burned and it was feared that he might lose one of his eyes. But this physical disability doesn't seem to have hindered either his career or reputation as an outstanding cameraman.

After shooting more than 20 feature films in only three years, Jennings left Fox in 1920 when Samuel Goldwyn hired him to work with the highly regarded Broadway actress Pauline Frederick, known for *La Tosca* (1918) and *Smouldering Fires* (1925). (She was also the good sport who laughed and fed them breakfast when Keaton, Lew Cody, and Roscoe Arbuckle dug up her expensively manicured lawn one Sunday as a practical joke.[27]) Their first collaboration was *The Woman in Room 13*. He went on to shoot eight more films for Frederick over the next two years, continuing to work for her even after she left Goldwyn and went to Robertson-Cole Pictures. At Robertson-Cole, he got to work with Henry King, who went on to direct *Tol'able David* (1921), *Twelve O'Clock High* (1949) and *Carousel* (1956). When Frederick left Robertson-Cole to go back to Broadway in 1922, Jennings briefly returned to Fox for six films. The pay must have been good—or perhaps he was careless or didn't trust banks—because when he got mugged in July of that year, he had $406 in his pockets.[28] In 1923, he became a successful freelance cinematographer, shooting *What Price Beauty* in 1924 with Nita Naldi and *The Eagle* (as co-director of photography with George Barnes) and *Cobra* with Rudolph Valentino, both in 1925. One shot that Dev Jennings pulled off for *Steel Preferred* (1925) was so frightening that it was reported in the *Los Angeles Times*:

> Shades of Dante were recalled when Jennings was called upon to photograph a scene for the picture during a location trip to Pittsburgh steel mills. A "drag" of steel ladle cars, each containing tons of molten iron en route to Bessemer, was upturned on the side of a hill.
> Jennings stood at the bottom of the hill, directly in the path of the seething flood. The crank was kept turning until the boiling fluid was within a few feet of the tripod when a hasty retreat was made.[29]

Plainly he had proven himself up to the challenges of filming a Buster Keaton movie. When Elgin Lessley left Keaton to work for Frank Capra and Harry Langdon in 1926, Jennings was hired as Keaton's first cameraman, with Bert Haines as his second. During the next two years, he shot *Battling Butler*, *The General*, *College* and *Steamboat Bill, Jr.*

The General was a challenging job for a cameraman, partly because so much of it was filmed from moving vehicles—either on the trains themselves, on other trains running on parallel tracks or from automobiles. According to Kevin Brownlow in his influential film history *The Parade's Gone By*, "A great deal of the chase was shot, not from the engine, but from a vehicle, tracking alongside from the road. The tracking shots are perfectly timed so that the engine is held center of frame, and there is no vibration. Keaton fitted Westinghouse shock absorbers on the automobile and used a road scraper to smooth the surface down before shooting. 'We were pretty fussy about that,' Keaton says."[30] Jim Kline, in *The Complete Films of Buster Keaton*, has estimated that as much as 70 percent of *The General* is made up of tracking shots.[31]

Years later, Jennings' achievement was still appreciated. In 1999, *American Cinematographer* readers voted for the 50 best-shot films from 1894 to 1949. *The General* came in at number 22.[32]

Jennings made another important contribution to the film, but one that was uncredited. He played the general who orders the Texas (a train) to cross the burning trestle, and it plummets into the Row River below.[33] His reaction to the disaster he has created is one of the funniest gags in the film.

On June 6, 1925, just before he began working for Keaton, Jennings married divorcée Adele Camille Badarous Davis.[34] Born in San Francisco on February 16, 1888, she had previously been married to John J. Davis, owner of Coffee Dan's, which had gone from being a 24-hour restaurant best known for its ham and eggs to a speakeasy when Prohibition went into effect in 1920.[35] (The place was also known for its entrance: It was located in a basement, and customers slid down a slide to get in.) The couple separated in 1922 and she moved to Los Angeles, where she eventually met and married Jennings.[36]

The marriage ended only a few years later. While visiting San Francisco in December of 1928, Adele was hospitalized with gallstones, and she died there a few months later, on March 10, 1929, five days after undergoing surgery.[37] She was buried in Woodlawn Cemetery in Colma, California. Dev Jennings never married again.

Professionally, before his wife's illness in 1928, Jennings traded places with Lessley, shooting Harry Langdon's feature *Heart Trouble* while Lessley shot *The Cameraman* for Keaton, now at MGM. Then he became a director of photography under contract at Warner Bros. While there, he shot 14 films, including *Vamping Venus* with another Keaton alumnus, director Eddie Cline, and *The Public Enemy* with William Wellman (which ranked number 45 on the ASC's best-shot list in 1999).[38]

In 1932, Jennings joined his brother Gordon at Paramount, which is where he finished his career planning and executing special effects. He had already dabbled in effects work in 1925 on *The Lost World*, where he was credited as "additional technical staff." For his first five years at Paramount, he alternated effects work with regular camera assignments until

1937, when he went to work solely on special effects, specializing in miniatures and composite effects. Composite shots combine elements from different sources into one image. His article "How Miniatures are Photographed" for *American Cinematographer* is clear and well-written enough that even non-professionals can appreciate it today. The man who filmed *The General*'s Texas crash (often credited as being the most expensive single shot in the silent film era) wrote: "[M]any scenes [that] would be prohibitively expensive or actually dangerous to film in the normal manner are made safely, economically and—which is more important—satisfactorily, by use of miniatures."[39]

The brothers' work was noticed by the industry. A special Oscar was given to the Paramount team in 1939 for *Spawn of the North*,[40] the first Academy Award ever given for effects. The film "dealt with Canadian deep sea fishermen and featured a great deal of process and miniature work. The rousing climax—incorporating models and actual location footage—had an iceberg crumble and destroy one of the trawlers."[41]

The following year, the effects Oscar became a regular award, and Gordon Jennings and his department would go on to get nominated for it nine times, winning won four more: *I Wanted Wings* (1941), *Reap the Wild Wind* (1942), *When Worlds Collide* (1951) and *The War of the Worlds* (1953).

Dev Jennings died at his brother's house on March 12, 1952,[42] of bone cancer in his left leg which had been discovered five months earlier. He was cremated, and his interment was private.

Further Information

"Devereaux" was also the name of his grandfather William Jennings' house. It was the first mansion in Utah, and the name came from "Jennings' ancestral home in England" according to Kate B. Carter (*Heart Throbs of the West*. Salt Lake City, UT: Daughters of Utah Pioneers, 1939, p.42). The house is still used for weddings and receptions.

Census Records

1860 U.S. Federal Census (Population Schedule), Great Salt Lake City Ward 14, Great Salt Lake, Utah Territory, Page 58, Dwelling 360, Family 134, William Jennings household, jpeg image (Online: The Generations Network, Inc., 2006) [Digital scan of original records in the National Archives, Washington, D.C.], subscription database, http://www.ancestry.com, accessed 28 June 2006.

1870 U.S. Federal Census (Population Schedule), Salt Lake City Ward 16, Salt Lake, Utah Territory, Page 19, Dwelling 11, Family 11, William Jennings household, jpeg image (Online: The Generations Network, Inc., 2006) [Digital scan of original records in the National Archives, Washington, D.C.], subscription database, http://www.ancestry.com, accessed 1 July 2006.

1880 U.S. Federal Census (Population Schedule), Salt Lake City Ward 16, Salt Lake,

Utah Territory, ED 148, Sheet 2, Dwelling 12, Family 19, William Jennings household, jpeg image (Online: The Generations Network, Inc., 2006) [Digital scan of original records in the National Archives, Washington, D.C.], subscription database, http://www.ancestry.com, accessed 1 July 2006.

1880 U.S. Federal Census (Population Schedule), Salt Lake City Ward 7, Salt Lake, Utah Territory, ED 136, Sheet 19, Dwelling 173, Family 199, Anne Dinwoody household, jpeg image (Online: The Generations Network, Inc., 2009) [Digital scan of original records in the National Archives, Washington, D.C.], subscription database, http://www.ancestry.com, accessed 7 September 2010.

1881 England Census Record, Islington, London, England, Folio 82, Page 43, jpeg image (Online: The Generations Network, Inc., 2006) [Digital scan of original records in the National Archives, London, England], subscription database, http://www.ancestry.com, accessed 28 June 2006.

1900 U.S. Federal Census (Population Schedule), Salt Lake City Ward 4, Salt Lake, Utah, ED 43, Sheet 11, Dwelling 314, Family 225, Henry Dinwoody household, jpeg image (Online: The Generations Network, Inc., 2009) [Digital scan of original records in the National Archives, Washington, D.C.], subscription database, http://www.ancestry.com, accessed 9 September 2010.

1900 U.S. Federal Census (Population Schedule), Mayfield, Santa Clara, California, ED 53, Sheet 2, Dwelling 52, Family 52, Sidney Badarous household, jpeg image (Online: The Generations Network, Inc., 2009) [Digital scan of original records in the National Archives, Washington, D.C.], subscription database, http://www.ancestry.com, accessed 1 January 2011. 1910 U.S. Federal Census (Population Schedule), Los Angeles Assembly District 64, Los Angeles, California, ED 109, Sheet 3B, Dwelling 68, Family 71, Joseph A. Jennings household, jpeg image (Online: The Generations Network, Inc., 2006) [Digital scan of original records in the National Archives, Washington, D.C.], subscription database, http://www.ancestry.com, accessed 28 June 2006.

1910 U.S. Federal Census (Population Schedule), San Francisco Assembly District 42, San Francisco, California, ED 282, Sheet 3B, Dwelling 42, Family 95, John J. Davis household, jpeg image (Online: The Generations Network, Inc., 2009) [Digital scan of original records in the National Archives, Washington, D.C.], subscription database, http://www.ancestry.com, accessed 1 January 2011.

1920 U.S. Federal Census (Population Schedule), Los Angeles Assembly District 63, Los Angeles, California, ED 147, Sheet 6A, Dwelling 154, Family 160, Joseph D. Jennings household, jpeg image (Online: The Generations Network, Inc., 2006) [Digital scan of original records in the National Archives, Washington, D.C.], subscription database, http://www.ancestry.com, accessed 28 June 2006.

1920 U.S. Federal Census (Population Schedule), Salt Lake City Ward 4, Salt Lake, Utah, ED 141, Sheet 1, Dwelling 12, Family 13, Joseph A. Jennings household, jpeg image (Online: The Generations Network, Inc., 2006) [Digital scan of original records in the National Archives, Washington, D.C.], subscription database, http://www.ancestry.com, accessed 1 July 2006.

1920 U.S. Federal Census (Population Schedule), San Francisco Assembly District 28, San Francisco, California, ED 272, Sheet 5A, Dwelling 90, Family 114, John J. Davis household, jpeg image (Online: The Generations Network, Inc., 2009) [Digital scan of original records in the National Archives, Washington, D.C.], subscription database, http://www.ancestry.com, accessed 1 January 2011.

1930 U.S. Federal Census (Population Schedule), Los Angeles Assembly District 63, Los Angeles, California, ED 56, Sheet 19A, Dwelling 367, Family 555, Minnie M. Wells household, jpeg image (Online: The Generations Network, Inc., 2006) [Digital scan of original records in the National Archives, Washington, D.C.], subscription database, http://www.ancestry.com, accessed 28 June 2006.

1940 U.S. Federal Census (Population Schedule), Los Angeles Assembly District 56, Los Angeles, California, ED 60–1064, Sheet 3B, Family 91, Jos. D. Jennings household, jpeg image (Online: FamilySearch Historical Collections, 2012) [Digital scan of original records in the National Archives, Washington, D.C.], https://www.familysearch.org, accessed 8 July 2012.

Gordon Jennings

Buster Keaton had a knack for hiring smart and talented people who often went on to have important careers. Gordon Jennings advanced from being the second cameraman on *Our Hospitality* to distinguished special effects work at Paramount Studios. He and his older brother Dev Jennings shared the first Oscar ever given for special effects, for *Spawn of the North* in 1939. As a special effects expert, he did everything from recreating Egypt on the cheap in *Cleopatra* (1934) to blowing up the Los Angeles City Hall in *The War of the Worlds* (1953).

Henry Gordon Jennings was born 12 years after his brother Dev, on June 25, 1896. Their family history is covered in Dev Jennings' entry.

In August of 1917, at age 21, Gordon Jennings was just the right age to leave his mechanical engineering studies at the University of Utah and volunteer as an ambulance driver with the Eighty-Sixth Division in France during World War I.[1] He served for almost two years. During a leave on September 15, 1917, he married Mary Genevra McClellan, daughter of the Mormon Tabernacle Choir's organist John J. McClellan.[2] Soon they had two children, Genevra (Jedda) in 1918 and John Douglass in 1920. By this time, both his brother and fellow Salt Lake City native Dal Clawson had written to him about the "easy money" to be found in Hollywood.[3] Gordon was convinced. When he moved to Hollywood to try his luck in film, he left his wife and children with her parents in Salt Lake.

Because silent films credits tend to be incomplete at best, it's hard to document his early career. In December 1947 he told *American Cinematographer* magazine that he moved to Los Angeles in 1919 to take an assistant cameraman job with Lois Weber.[4] His first credit was on Weber's most artistically and financially successful film *The Blot* (1921), which was about genteel poverty and social class. His second credited film was *Our Hospitality*. Harry Thorpe was originally announced as the second cameraman.[5] It's possible that Jennings got a promotion when Thorpe quit.

In the '20s, the camera crew, working with the prop department, was also the special effects department. On *Our Hospitality*, Jennings had the chance to learn a lot about miniatures and matte shots; the film is full of subtle special effects. For example, the Canfields' Southern Plantation house was a matte painting. But the most complicated effects shots were for the scene where Virginia Canfield is saved from going over the waterfall. The sequence was filmed in Hollywood, not on location, although shots of the actual Truckee River and a real waterfall were intercut to add suspense.[6] Keaton's crew built the waterfall over a studio swimming pool, and the valley in the background was a miniature. A net was strung right below the area captured by the camera, just in case Keaton lost his grip and fell.

Now that Jennings had proven himself on *Our Hospitality*, he continued working for Keaton. *Sherlock Jr.* generated this creative bit of between-picture publicity in the *L.A. Times* name-dropping Gordon and two other Keaton cameramen:

> *Inventions to Revolutionize Cinema Making*
> Four cinematographic inventions which [it] is conservatively estimated will save the motion-picture industry $28.75 in the next 10 years have been perfected by Byron Houck, Elgin Lessley and Gordon Jennings, Buster Keaton's three cameramen.
> Reading from left to right the inventions are a film stretcher for making enlargements, a dark lens for night effects, hot points to keep tripods from slipping on polished floors, and a rubber lens for shooting around corners.
> "I consider the rubber lens the most valuable of all," declares Buster Keaton. "In scenes where cops are hiding around a corner of a house, barn, or other detached building this rubber lens will enable the photographer to shoot what he can't see. It also will enable audiences to see things that were heretofore invisible."[7]

While Jennings forgot to invent the rubber lens, he went on to create other innovations after he left Keaton. Later in the 1920s he invented scrolling titles for Thomas Ince by painting the words on glass sheets that he then slid upwards over a painted background. "They kept the other fellows in the business fooled for a long time," he said in a 1947 interview.[8] Years later, he won two Scientific or Technical Award Oscars.[9] The first was in 1944 for the design and construction of the nodal point tripod. A standard tripod pivots around its head, causing the camera mounted above it to slightly shift in physical position when tilting or panning; this shift in the camera's position (parallax error) is more noticeable when shooting very close objects like miniatures—the small scale makes a camera shift of a fraction of an inch look like a movement of several feet if the miniature were an actual large-scale object. A nodal point tripod pivots around the camera itself, reducing this parallax error as the camera is tilted or panned.

He won the second in 1951 with S.L. Stancliffe (a former Navy radar engineer) for the design, construction and application of a servo-operated repeating device, which enabled the camera to repeat movements precisely when needed, as it did when making matte shots. Over a 20-year period, Jennings also received three patents: the first in 1934 for a tilting and panning tripod head, the second in 1936 for a special-effects printer, and the third in 1953 for his and Stancliffe's repeating device.[10]

Because he spent much of his time on special effects, and because credits for special effects assistants at that time were as rare as those for camera assistants, it's nearly impossible to trace his career. *Variety* reported that he was at Cecil B. DeMille's studio in 1925,[11] and in 1928, he became the head of Paramount's film laboratory.[12] He also played in their golf tournament that year.[13]

In 1931, Jennings was appointed head of the Paramount effects department, and the department head's name appears on every film that has a special effect whether he worked on it directly or not. As a result, the *AFI Catalog* lists 188 films to his credit.[14] He knew better, though, writing in 1934, "When it is remembered that this diversified work was accomplished simultaneously with the production of similar special-effects scenes for several other films in production at the same time, it can clearly be seen that this could not be a one-man achievement, but was necessarily the result of perfect team-work on the part of a large and efficient staff."[15] His best-known work was for Cecil B. DeMille; Jennings supervised everything from the Battle of Actium in *Cleopatra* in 1934 to the train wreck in *The Greatest Show on Earth* in 1952.

In a 1934 article he wrote for *American Cinematographer*, he described the way his team made two miniature galleys look like 35 (they used mirrors to multiply the images), then detailed the responsibilities of the effects department for *Cleopatra*:

> [I]n addition to providing all of the necessary fades, dissolves, wipes and other transitions, and executing a number of important miniature shots, designed, constructed and supervised a great number of "set-miniatures" and "hanging miniatures" completing several of the impressive setting, collaborated with the studio's Transparency staff in making many of the projected-background scenes, and conceived, photographed and assembled the entire montage-sequence depicting the Battle of Actium, which is one of the dramatic highlights of the film.[16]

Science fiction films gave him and his crew their most showy opportunities, particularly on *The War of the Worlds* (1953). One point four million dollars of the film's $2 million-dollar budget went to special effects.[17] Those effects included not only flying Martian war machines but also everything they blew up, such as the Los Angeles City Hall (which so impressed the *Los Angeles Times* that it sent a reporter to cover that day's filming).[18] The effects department worked on all kinds of films: fantasies like *Alice in Wonderland* (1933), comedy-musicals like the Hope-Crosby Road pictures, comedies like Bob Hope's *The Paleface* (1948), Westerns like *The Virginian* (1946) and straight dramas like *Sunset Blvd.* (1950), in which Keaton played a small role. An interviewer summed him up as "a big, genial man with a photographic eye for detail and a talent for deceiving motion picture audiences."[19]

In his autobiography, DeMille described him as "a big, athletic, but soft-spoken and almost diffident man, the best special effects man I have ever been privileged to work with. A director could say to Gordon Jennings that he wanted a volcano to obliterate a city teeming with people or Niagara Falls to roll back and expose a dry cliff. A few weeks later Gordon would come around and say, 'Well, you might as well come and look at this. I've spent a lot of money and it's probably not what you want, but, well, come and see it anyway'; and the effect would be so realistically perfect that the director himself could hardly believe it."[20]

Not all the effects work were done in the safety of the studio, and Jennings occasionally confronted danger. While on location in Big Bear Lake on March 4, 1937, he slipped and rolled off a cliff and into a tree,[21] breaking his back. He was in the hospital for more than two months, until mid–May; when he finally returned to work in August, he was still using crutches.[22] But he was back on the golf course by June 1938, when he shot an 88 in his club's tournament (tying with cinematographer Karl Struss).[23]

It's obvious that golf was his second love. From 1928 on, he regularly appeared in the *Times* golf columns. A member of the Lakeside Country Club, along with many other Hollywood employees like Bing Crosby, Humphrey Bogart, and Johnny Weissmuller,[24] he proved that he was a pretty good golfer. At the first annual American Society of Cinematographers Golf Tournament in 1934, he was ranked with the first flight of players,[25] and he won a leather golf bag. His brother Dev, also a golfer, was down in the fourth flight, and he won a whiskey barrel set.

Not too surprisingly, Gordon's long-distance marriage fell apart during the 1920s. An "intention to marry" to an unusually named woman appeared in the *Los Angeles Times* on June 13, 1929 ("H. Gordon Jennings, 33; Prairie Stock, 34") but nothing seems to have come of that engagement.[26] In October of 1933, he eloped to Yuma with Florence Anderson.[27] Born on November 5, 1898, in Iowa, Florence was also a golfer, telling the *Times* golf reporter when she broke 100—it was a 99.[28]

The brothers' work was noticed by the industry. A special Oscar was given to the Paramount team in 1939 for *Spawn of the North*,[29] the first Academy Award ever given for effects. The film "dealt with Canadian deep sea fishermen and featured a great deal of process and miniature work. The rousing climax—incorporating models and actual location footage—had an iceberg crumble and destroy one of the trawlers."[30] The following year, the effects Oscar became a regular award, and Gordon Jennings and his department would go on to get nominated for it nine times, winning won four more: *I Wanted Wings* (1941), *Reap the Wild Wind* (1942), *When Worlds Collide* (1951) and *The War of the Worlds* (1953).

Jennings was invited to join the American Society of Cinematographers in 1935, and served on the Board of Directors in 1946 and '47. Both Jennings brothers were Masons and Shriners, belonging to the Al-Malaikah Temple.

On January 11, 1953, Gordon Jennings was stricken with a heart attack doing what he loved, playing golf, on the twelfth hole of the Lakeside Country Club.[31] He was buried at Forest Lawn in Glendale. Cecil B. DeMille delivered the eulogy at the Mormon funeral service.[32]

After her husband's death, Florence Jennings stopped appearing in the newspaper's golf pages and started appearing in the community service pages. A busy woman, she served as the president of the Los Angeles Area Camp Fire Girls and was program chairman for the Westwood Hills Congregational Church, among many other activities.[33] On July 21, 1982, she died at age 83 of pneumonia, two months after suffering a heart attack, and was buried next to her husband.[34]

John Jennings, Gordon's son, attended Black Foxe Academy with Keaton's two sons.[35] When he grew up, he became a Brentwood, California, dentist but he also took an interest in art. In 1950, he produced a short Oscar-nominated film, *The Face of Jesus*, which showed sculptor Merrell Gage modeling a clay head of Jesus.[36] John died on January 1, 1992.[37]

Census Records

1920 U.S. Federal Census (Population Schedule), Los Angeles Assembly District 63, Los Angeles, California ED 147, Sheet 9A, Dwelling 165, Family 174, Henry G. Jennings household, jpeg image (Online: The Generations Network, Inc., 2006) [Digital scan of original records in the National Archives, Washington, D.C.], subscription database, http://www.ancestry.com, accessed 28 June 2006.

1920 U.S. Federal Census (Population Schedule), Salt Lake City Ward 4, Salt Lake, Utah, ED 141, Sheet 1B, Dwelling 13, Family 14, John J. McClellan household, jpeg image (Online: The Generations Network, Inc., 2006) [Digital scan of original records in the National Archives, Washington, D.C.], subscription database, http://www.ancestry.com, accessed 1 July 2006.

1930 U.S. Federal Census (Population Schedule), Salt Lake City Ward 6, Salt Lake, Utah, ED 93, Sheet 14B, Dwelling 279, Family 328, Mary McClellan household, jpeg image (Online: The Generations Network, Inc., 2006) [Digital scan of original records in the National Archives, Washington, D.C.], subscription database, http://www.ancestry.com, accessed 28 June 2006.

1940 U.S. Federal Census (Population Schedule), Los Angeles Assembly District 42, Los Angeles, California, ED 60–52, Sheet 10B, Dwelling 10146, Family 330, Gordon Jennings household, jpeg image (Online: FamilySearch Historical Collections, 2012) [Digital scan of original records in the National Archives, Washington, D.C.], https://www.familysearch.org, accessed 22 June 2013.

Reggie Lanning

Reggie Lanning was a journeyman cinematographer: He never won an Oscar, but he made a living just like hundreds of other craftsmen. He happened to be a second camera operator at MGM when he was assigned to work on Keaton's last two silent films, *The Cameraman* and *Spite Marriage*. He went on to a long career as a director of photography.

Reginald Thomas Lanning was born in Congress, Arizona, on October 6, 1893. His parents Nathaniel and Bessie Harris Lanning were both from Northern Ireland. At the time of his birth, Congress was a booming gold mining town; the mine played out in the 1930s and today Congress is a ghost town.[1] For some reason the Lannings eluded the Federal census takers in 1900 and 1910.

In 1911, father and son Nathaniel and Reggie Lanning moved to Los Angeles where they opened a bicycle repair shop called N & Son.[2] In 1914, Reggie dropped out of the repair business, at which time his father teamed up with a Mr. Corbin.[3] Reggie next listed his occupation as a driver in the *Los Angeles City Directory* in 1917[4]; when he registered for the draft on June 5, 1917, he said he was supporting his father by working as a chauffeur for Morris and Company.[5] According to his draft registration, he was 24 years old, with blue eyes, dark hair, of medium height and build and no disabilities. The National Personnel Records Center has no record of his service, so he may have gotten a deferment.[6] His father died on March 6, 1920,[7] and Lanning became a border with John Christensen, a grocer originally from Denmark, his wife and two daughters. The older daughter, 21-year-old Eileen Juanita, worked at Christensen's Grocery, and before long she and Lanning married on September 23, 1923.[8] In 1936, they had a daughter, Sharon.[9]

Lanning told the 1920 U.S. Census taker that he was a photographer at the studios, although he had worked as a property boy for a time.[10] In

1948, *Variety* reported that he celebrated his 30th anniversary in the film business, which means he would have gotten his start in 1918.[11]

It might seem unusual for a chauffeur to become a cameraman, but according to film writer Rob Wagner, it was not that uncommon: "[I]n early days, when companies went out on location, the driver of the car acted as an assistant to the camera man, packing the tripod, giving him focus, and so on. Through this friendly intimacy, the chauffeur would learn to load and thread a camera, and occasionally shoot a few feet of test film."[12]

In his new role, Lanning got a job as a second cameraman for Paramount/Famous Players Lasky.[13] He had moved to MGM by the time Keaton arrived in 1928. Lanning became the second operator on *The Cameraman*, and after Elgin Lessley retired from feature filmmaking, Lanning got promoted to chief cameraman on *Spite Marriage*.

MGM didn't let him continue as a chief cameraman. After one more film in that capacity (1929's *China Bound*, directed by Charles Riesner), he went back to being a second cameraman until 1934. Then he went to work for low-budget Monogram Pictures. It was less prestigious than MGM, but at least there he got to be a director of photography. In addition, he managed Monogram's baseball club.[14] In 1935, Monogram merged with Mascot Pictures and Liberty Films to become Republic Pictures. Republic was known for its B-movies (primarily Westerns) and serials. He shot more than 100 features and serials for the studio, including its big-budget war film *Sands of Iwo Jima* (1949), starring John Wayne in an Oscar-nominated performance.

Working for Republic had its own difficulties. When a new studio head, William O'Sullivan, complained that Lanning had lit only the actors and not the space under a table, Lanning replied, "Bill, on these schedules you can have light on the actors' faces or under the table. If you want both, add five weeks to the schedule."[15]

The cinematographers who shot serials are rarely noticed, but Lanning's contributions to *Spy Smasher* (1942) has been praised. The authors of *The Great Movie Serials* said, "The cinematography of Reggie Lanning is not merely adequate, as was the case with most chapterplays, but atmospheric and often artistic."[16] Roy Kinnard, another film serial historian, commended his split-screen photography in the same show, saying it "could have easily been ruined or shot in a cruder and more obvious manner, but Lanning pulled it off without a hitch."[17]

Like a few other Keaton cameramen, Lanning was also a good golfer—he ranked in the first flight at the ASC's first golf tournament, along with Gordon Jennings.[18]

Lanning remained at Republic until 1955. He then moved over to television production and ended his career on *Alfred Hitchcock Presents*, shooting 55 of the 268 episodes.

After he retired in 1958, he and his wife moved to Camarillo in Ventura County, California.[19] He died of emphysema on December 6, 1965, at the Motion Picture County House and Hospital in Woodland Hills,[20] at the age of 72. He was buried at Oakwood Memorial Park in Chatsworth, California. His wife Eileen stayed in Ventura, and she lived until December 29, 1991,[21] when she died of septic shock several weeks after breaking her hip at age 93. She was also buried at Oakwood.

Census Records

1920 U.S. Federal Census (Population Schedule), Los Angeles Assembly District 73, Los Angeles, California, ED 402, Sheet 2A, Dwelling 31, Family 32, John Christensen household, jpeg image (Online: The Generations Network, Inc., 2007) [Digital scan of original records in the National Archives, Washington, D.C.], subscription database, http://www.ancestry.com, accessed 12 April 2007.

1930 U.S. Federal Census (Population Schedule), Los Angeles Assembly District 16, Los Angeles, California, ED 143, Sheet 26B, Dwelling 474, Family 500, Reggie T. Lanning household, jpeg image (Online: The Generations Network, Inc., 2007) [Digital scan of original records in the National Archives, Washington, D.C.], subscription database, http://www.ancestry.com, accessed 12 April 2007.

1940 U.S. Federal Census (Population Schedule), Los Angeles Assembly District 42, Los Angeles, California, ED 60–1307, Sheet 6A, Family 167, Reggie Lanning household, jpeg image (Online: FamilySearch Historical Collections, 2012) [Digital scan of original records in the National Archives, Washington, D.C.], https://www.familysearch.org, accessed 8 July 2012.

Elgin Lessley

Buster Keaton considered Elgin Lessley "one of the best cameramen in the business"[1] and maybe one reason is that Keaton put Lessley through his paces; cameraman did not have it easy keeping up with Keaton. Lessley did it very well, though, filming Keaton through the busy city streets of Los Angeles and New York, in the rushing waters of the Truckee River, and at the frigid bottom of Lake Tahoe. Lessley shot all of Keaton's silent shorts and seven of his features, as well as Harry Langdon's best films. But after *The Cameraman* in 1928, he never shot another feature.

Elgin Lessley was born on June 10, 1883, in Higbee, a small town in central Missouri. His father, Shelton Lessley, was a dry goods dealer and a veteran of the Confederate Army. Lessley's mother, Orpha Jane Brooks, Shelton's second wife, worked as a milliner. Elgin had three sisters: Bindy

(1881), who died in infancy, Ora Ethel (1886) and Annette Lee aka "Nettie" (1888).

At the time of the 1900 census, 16-year-old Elgin was working for the telephone company and his family was still in Higbee. However, by 1904, they had moved to Colorado Springs, Colorado.[2] Shelton Lessley opened a department store where his 20-year-old son worked as a window trimmer.

He may have made money as a window trimmer, but he had discovered his real love: the camera. Six years later, in January 1910, he joined the International Photographic Association, describing his interests as "5 × 7 and enlargements to 10 × 12, on developing and bromide papers, of landscapes and mountain scenery; for landscapes, water scenes, and animal pictures."[3]

Soon he was entering amateur photography contests. *Photo-era Magazine* ran several of his images, and in July of 1910, Lessley won second place in its "Snow Scenes" (beginners) category with the photograph he called "A Fresh-Broken Trail." According to the magazine, "[W]e have an exceptionally artistic conception of the theme.... The lines are graceful and the whole scene expresses a chord of perfect harmony. The technique is admirable and evinces a masterly hand. Data: R.R. lens, f/8; Cramers 3-times Isos Ray filter; November; bright sunlight; 1–2 second exposure; Seed L Ortho plate; pyro and soda developer; enlarged with a home-made enlarging camera from a 5 × 7 negative on Special Rough Velox paper."[4] These must have been encouraging words for a beginner. The rules said that participants had to do all the work themselves, from exposing the plate or film to the completed print. His prize brought him five dollars, plus his photo got published.

Later that year, he got two honorable mentions: one from *American Photography* for his picture "A Foggy Morning" in August,[5] another from *Photo-era* for "Early Morning Shadows" in September.[6]

Following his father's death in 1910, Lessley, his mother and sisters moved to Los Angeles,[7] where he became a clerk at Bullock's Department Store.[8] He had blue eyes, brown hair and no disabilities, according to his World War I draft registration.[9]

The following year, Lessley began his moving picture career in the camera department of the Melies-Star Company,[10] the American branch of French filmmaker Georges Melies' company. Run by Georges' brother Gaston, the company moved to Santa Paula, California, in May 1911, making primarily one-reel Westerns such as *The Great Heart of the West* and *The Outlaw and the Baby*.[11]

Although he was now a professional cameraman, Lessley continued to send his still work to photography magazines. His photo "A Breaking Wave" appeared in the November 1912 issue of *Popular Photography.* It illustrated a story on how to take a good shot of moving water, something Lessley would soon have plenty of experience doing. According to the magazine:

> [T]hat 1–25 second is an excellent exposure to render water in motion is shown by Mr. Lessley's picture. There is just enough blurring in the print to give a good suggestion of the rush of the water. The viewpoint was well chosen and the exposure was made at just the right moment to secure the most pleasing result. If it were not for the catching of the foam flecks from the retreating water in just the right position to break up the foreground, the arrangement would have been too much one of parallel lines. The three principle lines of the picture are the diagonal mass of the rocks, its parallel diagonal of the breaking wave, and the upward slope of the distant headland. The composition, however, is saved by the good definition of values and the strong foreground interest. The picture was made with a 5 × 7 Century fitted with 8¼ inch Zeisse Tessar lens. The exposure of 1–25 second was made with a stop *f*: .8 at 3 p.m. November on a standard Orthonon plate in bright sunshine. The plate was developed with pyro, and the print is an enlargement from a portion only of the negative.[12]

In the summer of 1912, Gaston Melies left to make documentary films in the South Seas and Asia.[13] Lessley joined them near the tour's end, in Yokohama, Japan, arriving in early April 1913[14] and replacing camera operator Hugh McClung, who was promoted to director. While there, he worked on the short documentary *Japanese "Judo" Commonly Known as Jiu Jitsu* and a fiction film, *The Yellow Slave.* The exposed film was sent back to the United States by slow freighter, and most of it was ruined by heat and humidity. Lessley didn't stay in Japan very long; Melies was exhausted, the tour was falling apart and finally he sent everybody home on May 10, 1913.

On November 17, 1914, Lessley married Blanche May Olmstead Schultz Maxwell.[15] She'd been married twice before. Originally from Denver, Colorado, she had a son, Leonard Wheeler Schultz, from her first marriage.[16]

Lessley found work as a cameraman at Mack Sennett's Keystone Studios[17]; Sennett soon joined with Thomas Ince and D.W. Griffith to form Triangle Studios. In late 1915, Lessley traveled to Fort Lee, New Jersey, and worked on *He Did and He Didn't* with Roscoe Arbuckle and Mabel Normand.[18] According to the January 8, 1916, payroll report from Triangle Productions, he earned $55 per week. In early 1916 writer Wil Rex, who found him working with the same stars in the same place, called Lessley "the intrepid camera man who has the reputation of turning out the clearest films of any Keystone crank turner."[19]

In October, he was back in Los Angeles, attending a Static Club business meeting,[20] and in December he shot *A Royal Rogue*, a Raymond Griffith short.[21] He also made some one-reel comedies with Al St. John, including *Grab Bag Bride* and *Her Caveman*, as well as Ben Turpin's first starring short, *A Clever Dummy*.

By 1917, Lessley had graduated to feature films; his first was *A Phantom Husband* starring Ruth Stonehouse (Joseph Anthony Roach's wife). In 1917 and '18, he shot 12 films, including mystery, war, crime and Western films, as well as three Gloria Swanson melodramas.

At a time when cameramen were rarely mentioned in reviews, *Variety* singled him out for praise. In its review of *High Stakes*, a Raffles-inspired story of a jewel thief set in England, a writer called "Ibee" wrote, "Elgin Leslie [sic] aided with good camera work." The review for *Her Decision*, a tale of female sacrifice, also remarked on his camerawork as well as his lighting.[22]

Triangle stopped making films and Lessley went to work full-time for Arbuckle's Comique Film Company. He shot the three shorts that Arbuckle and Keaton made after Buster returned from his World War I service: *Backstage*, *The Hayseed* and *The Garage*. He was also the studio's chief still photographer. When Arbuckle moved on to features, Lessley stayed with the Keaton company. They would make 19 two-reel comedies together. Out of all of them, Lessley's greatest challenge was *The Playhouse*. The first reel was set in a theater run entirely by Keatons, and at times there were anywhere from two to nine of them in the frame at once, dancing, joking and playing musical instruments. Clyde Bruckman told biographer Rudi Blesh that to record multiple Busters, Lessley put a lightproof black box over the camera with multiple shutters in front of the lens. He masked part of the lens, shot one Keaton—remember that this was all hand-cranked—and then rewound the film by hand, masked another part of the lens, and hand-cranked another Keaton—as many times as was needed for a given shot.[23] As Keaton observed later, "[I]f he were off the slightest fraction, no matter how carefully I timed my movements, the composite action could not have been synchronized. But Elgin was outstanding among all the studios. He was a human metronome."[24] In his autobiography, Keaton wrote, "[I]t was considered a scientific miracle."[25] The results still astonish people.

When Keaton moved on to features in 1923, he took his crew with him. Lessley was the lead cameraman on seven of these longer films, including *Sherlock Jr.* In a 1958 interview, Keaton said that he showed Lessley some of the gags and tricks they'd worked out, and Lessley had said,

> You can't do it and tell a legitimate story, because there are illusions, and some of them are clown gags, some Houdini, some [Ching-Ling-Fu]. It's got to come in a dream. To get what we are after, you've got to be a projectionist in a projecting room in a little small-town motion picture theater, and go to sleep, after you've got the picture started. Once you fall asleep, you visualize yourself as one of the important characters in the picture you're showing. You go down out of that projection room, go right down, walk up on the screen and become part of it. Now go tell your whole story.[26]

Although the end result is still astonishing, Lessley might not have known how much trouble he was making for himself. After Keaton climbs up into the film, the background scenes change abruptly several times, showing Keaton in a snow bank, on a rock surrounded by water, etc. These shots were a particular challenge. As the locations changed, Keaton and Lessley had to match Buster's position exactly for the scene to work. According to Keaton, "every cameraman in the business went to see that picture more than once, trying to figure out how the hell we did some of that.... As we did one shot, we'd throw it in the darkroom and develop it right then and there—and bring it back to the cameraman. He cut out a few frames and put them on the camera gate. When I come to change scenes, he could put me right square where I was."[27] In 1924, Mordaunt Hall, the critic for the *New York Times*, called it "one of the best screen tricks ever incorporated in a comedy."[28]

The location shoot for the snow scene inspired one of Harry Brand's better bits of publicity, which refers to Lessley, although not by name:

> **Keaton's Bill for Expenses Rouses Anger**
> Here's real studio economy!
> Buster Keaton and his entire production staff left this week for Sonora, Cal. The staff consisted of one movie cameraman. Buster claims that this is the smallest studio staff that ever went on location.
> On the way to Sonora Buster played pinochle with his cameraman. When they tired of that the cameraman brought out a pocket checkerboard with stick-in pawns. Then they reminisced for a while, bought oranges from the train butcher and finally went to sleep on each other's shoulders.
> Upon arriving on location, Buster stood while the cameraman shot him. After this was done they came back to Los Angeles. Upon his return Buster said, "We had a great time."
> Lou Anger, general manager of the Keaton studio, nearly collapsed when Buster and the cameraman put in a joint expense account of $7.84.

"Save it, Buster," advised Anger, "and show it to von Stroheim and Mr. DeMille."[29]

Sherlock Jr. also contains one of the best examples of Lessley's skill at seeing the gag and getting the laugh: When the crime-crushing criminologist is ready to escape the thieves' house, the wall blocks the audience's view of the interior. Then the wall dissolves in-camera, and we can see Keaton leap through the window directly into a disguise as an old woman, all in one continuous take. It's perfectly framed so the audience can see that Keaton has dived through the window straight into the costume; a cut would have made the shot look like a trick, something Keaton had an aversion to. The dissolve was done in the camera: Lessley gradually faded out the wall image by closing the shutter as he cranked the film, then he rewound it, the crew removed the wall, and he gradually reopened the shutter as the film went through the camera for a second time. It required precise cranking and shutter manipulation.

Keaton's films often involved stunts and gags that were dangerous for both the star and his camera crew. The cattle stampede in *Go West*, Keaton's wild ride on the handlebars of a driverless motorcycle through the Los Angeles streets in *Sherlock Jr.*, and the river sequence of *Our Hospitality* were all difficult to shoot. But the most uncomfortable sequence was the underwater scenes in *The Navigator*. In the film, Keaton must put on a deep sea diving suit and underwater to repair his ship. Initially, Keaton and Lessley considered shooting it in a tank, but the weight of the water forced out the bottom of the pool. Then they tried shooting it near Catalina Island off the California coast, but the water wasn't clear enough. So they traveled to Lake Tahoe, where the water is very clear, but also very cold. A watertight wooden camera box just big enough to hold two cameras and two cameramen was weighted down with an extra thousand pounds, so it sat at the bottom of the lake, 20 feet under. To keep the glass from fogging up, the temperature had to be the same inside the box as outside. To keep the temperature stable, 300 pounds of ice were packed in the box. Keaton, Lessley and second cameraman Byron Houck could stand the cold for only 30 minutes at a time. As Keaton said, "You want to get up and get out of there."[30] It took a month to shoot the sequence.

In 1926, Lessley was tempted away from Keaton's crew to go to work with Harry Langdon and Frank Capra. According to Langdon biographer William Schelley, "Langdon scored a major coup by signing veteran cinematographer Elgin Lessley. Lessley was reckoned to be the best comedy cameraman in the business, and was noted for his knack of getting tricky shots with a minimum of fuss."[31] Lessley shot all five of Langdon's major features, including *The Strong Man* and *Tramp, Tramp, Tramp*. He was even briefly interviewed during this time in *Moving Picture World*, which reported how Lessley filmed a particularly difficult opening shot for *Long Pants*. At the time, camera movement of the kind described was rare in Hollywood films: "[T]he audience will get the photographic effect of looking for a book in a big library. They will swing from the bottom shelf to the top row before they pick out a well-known romantic tale. This effect Elgin Lessley, Harry Langdon's chief cameraman, obtained by laying out a track some 14 feet long in front of the library set in *Long Pants*. Upon this track, he placed a movable platform where he perched his camera. From this position Lessley could secure the thousand and one angles for this unique shot which could not have been obtained had his photographic apparatus remained stationary on the studio floor."[32]

Unfortunately, there's some evidence that Elgin's home life wasn't happy. In the 1925 Los Angeles City Directory, Mrs. Blanche Lessley lived in a separate residence.[33] Then on March 10, 1926. Lessley appeared in Municipal Court to answer charges. The day before, police answered a call from neighbors about noise from a party. Alcohol was found, and Mrs. Lessley had two black eyes. For possessing liquor, he was fined $150. The *Los Angeles Times* reported, "Lessley declared the party had not been as bad as it sounded. The noise, he said, was made by a radio and the black eyes were accidental."[34] Discreetly, he kept his connection to the film industry out of the paper, giving his profession as "laborer." The Lessleys reconciled and bought a two-bedroom bungalow on Edinburgh Street in the Fairfax district of Los Angeles in 1928. (The house is just a few blocks from the Silent Movie Theater. The theater opened in 1942 but it closed quickly, because the owner, John Hampton, was soon incarcerated for conscientious objection to the war. I suspect that Lessley never got to see his films there.)

Lessley left Langdon that year (Langdon's final feature, *Heart Trouble*, was shot by another Keaton alum, Dev Jennings) and went back to Keaton, who was now at MGM. Together they made *The Cameraman*, Lessley's last credited film. He didn't work on Keaton's final silent comedy, *Spite Marriage*. It's possible that he might have taken time off to care for his wife, who died September 28, 1931, of Wernicke's disease, a brain disorder usually caused by alcoholism.[35] Symptoms include loss of muscle coordination, vision changes, loss of memory, and mood and behavior changes. She was only 46 when she died. She was buried in the Olmstead family plot next to her son Leonard Wheeler Schultz (who'd died in 1916) in the Littleton Cemetery near Denver, Colorado.[36]

It's also possible that his own health issues kept Lessley from continuing what had been a notable career up until then. In 1934, he was diagnosed with chronic myocarditis, an inflammation of the heart muscle.[37] The symptoms include chest pain, fever, joint pain and rapid heartbeat. However, according to *The History of Cardiology*, "chronic myocarditis" was an all-purpose phrase for the ill effects of both hypertension and coronary artery disease.[38] Whichever was the true diagnosis, doctors at that time weren't able to do much for heart patients. Surgery was still experimental, and effective hypertension drugs weren't available until 1950.

Even though his name wasn't in the films' credits, Lessley continued to work, apparently sporadically. He appeared as a second cameraman in the 1930 union membership list.[39] On the 1930 and 1940 censuses, he said he was a cameraman in the motion picture industry. Every year, when the canvassers for the city directory came around, he gave his profession as "cameraman" or "studio worker."[40] When he registered for what was called the "old man's" draft in 1942, Lessley was working for special effects cameraman Alfred Schmid at the Samuel Goldwyn Studio.[41] Until his death, he remained a member of the cameraman's union, the Local 659.[42]

Lessley died on February 8, 1944, aged 60,[43] and was buried in Forest Lawn Cemetery, Glendale. He was survived by his sister Nettie Lee Hesse and her daughter, Evelyn Velma.

Relatives of Lessley continued to work in the film industry. His niece Evelyn married Donald Ehlers, an assistant process cameraman at RKO, and she filled in for him at the studio while he was fighting in World War II,[44] becoming the only female assistant camera operator in the industry. After her husband returned from the war, he became a film producer and she later worked as a film editor at RKO in the 1960s. They had a daughter and a son, Donald "Corky" Ehlers, who also became a film editor, working on *Lonesome Dove*, *Gettysburg*, *Gods and Generals* and *South Dakota*.

Because of his unique perspective, his long tenure working with Keaton, and his ability to handle Keaton's special effects and comedic needs, Elgin Lessley was one of the most important members of Keaton's team. In *Keaton*, biographer Rudi Blesh summarized his contribution:

> No estimate of *Our Hospitality* is complete without mention of Elgin Lessley's camera work. Its clarity and beauty, altogether exceptional then, are uncommon even by today's standards. Shots such as the views of the locomotive silhouetted on a mountaintop against the towering summer clouds are of particular beauty. Among the many things that keep Keaton's best silent films modern—despite the lack of sound, color, and widescreen—Lessley's photography must be included.[45]

Census Records

1880 U.S. Federal Census (Population Schedule), Higbee Township, Randolph, Missouri, ED 113, Sheet 27, Dwelling 223, Family 232, Shelton Lessley household, jpeg image (Online: The Generations Network, Inc., 2009) [Digital scan of original records in the National Archives, Washington, D.C.], subscription database, http://www.ancestry.com, accessed 29 August 2010.

1900 U.S. Federal Census (Population Schedule), Higbee City, Randolph, Missouri, ED 132, Sheet 9, Dwelling 177, Family 150, Shelton Lessley household, jpeg image (Online: The Generations Network, Inc., 2009) [Digital scan of original records in the National Archives, Washington, D.C.], subscription database, http://www.ancestry.com, accessed 29 August 2010.

1900 U.S. Federal Census (Population Schedule), North Littleton Precinct no. 11, Colorado, ED 145, Sheet 7B, Dwelling 144, Family 146, Chauncy Olmstead household, jpeg image (Online: The Generations Network, Inc., 2012) [Digital scan of original records in the National Archives, Washington, D.C.], subscription database, http://www.ancestry.com, accessed 29 January 2013.

1910 U.S. Federal Census (Population Schedule), Littleton, Colorado, ED 13, Sheet 3A, Dwelling 131, Family 132, Frank D. Lewis household, jpeg image (Online: The Generations Network, Inc., 2009) [Digital scan of original records in the National Archives, Washington, D.C.], subscription database, http://www.ancestry.com, accessed 29 January 2013.

1920 U.S. Federal Census (Population Schedule), Los Angeles Assembly District 64, Los Angeles, California, ED 219, Sheet 7, Dwelling 97, Family 214, Elgin Lessley household, jpeg image (Online: The Generations Network, Inc., 2009) [Digital scan of original records in the National Archives, Washington, D.C.], subscription database, http://www.ancestry.com, accessed 29 August 2010.

1930 U.S. Federal Census (Population Schedule), Los Angeles Assembly District 59, Los Angeles, California, ED 118, Sheet 1, Dwelling 3, Family 3, Elgin Lessley household, jpeg image (Online: The Generations Network, Inc., 2009) [Digital scan of original records in the National Archives, Washington, D.C.], subscription database, http://www.ancestry.com, accessed 29 August 2010.

1940 U.S. Federal Census (Population Schedule), Los Angeles Assembly District 59, Los Angeles, California, ED 60–190, Sheet 3B, Family 71, Elgin Lessly [sic] household, jpeg image (Online: FamilySearch Historical Collections, 2012) [Digital scan of original records in the National Archives, Washington, D.C.], https://www.familysearch.org, accessed 8 July 2012.

William McGann

Although William McGann worked as a member of Keaton's camera crew on only one film, 1923's *Three Ages*, he would go on to have a long and successful career as an assistant director, director and special effects director, mostly at Warner Brothers.

William Michael McGann was born on April 15, 1893, in Pittsburgh, Pennsylvania, the youngest child of Irish-born druggist Michael J. and Edna Jane Briggs McGann. They were also parents to Oliver (1879), Mary (1881), Constance (1887) and Edna (1889).

His biographical details are murky. Although some biographies insist that he attended the University of California–Berkeley, the school has no record of him.[1] What seems more certain is that he moved to Los Angeles in the early 1910s, around the time he was 20 years old. But then the details get shaky again. In 1922, he told *American Cinematographer* that he had become a cinematographer in 1913 after working as a still cameraman and a lab worker, but in 1913 he told the City Directory that he was an electrician with the Home Telephone Company.[2] In 1915, he was listed as a machinist.[3] In the same *AC* profile, he claimed to have been a volunteer aviator with the American Expeditionary Forces from 1917 to 1919, but his military records don't back him up. Clearly, McGann had quite an imagination.

Here are the facts as we know them: According to the City Directory, in 1917 he finally did become a cameraman, working for the William Fox Corporation[4] before registering for the draft. His draft registration information describes him as a tall, unmarried man with gray eyes, brown hair and no disabilities. Because he had no reason to get a deferment, McGann was drafted, serving in the Army from June to December 1918 at Camp Upton in New York.[5]

After he was discharged, he went back to Hollywood to work as a freelance cameraman. He shot two films for small production companies, *Hearts of Men* (Hiram Adams Productions) and *Man's Desire* (Lewis Stone Productions), then got his big break when he was hired by Douglas Fairbanks. He shot four major films for Fairbanks, including *The Mark of Zorro*. Around that time, he was invited to join the American Society of Cinematographers.[6] In 1922, he became a freelance cameraman, so when Keaton needed more people on his camera crew for his first feature a year later, McGann was available.

Three Ages was McGann's second-to-last project as a cameraman. He shot some one-reel *Hysterical History Comedies* with Bryan Foy (for whom he would work again in the 1930s as a director) for Universal in early 1924.[7] He went from there to becoming an assistant director at Warner Bros., helping directors like Millard Webb (*Her Marriage Vow*, 1924) and Roy del Ruth (*Footloose Widows*, 1926).

In 1929, he rose up the ladder when was promoted to direct canine star Rin-Tin-Tin's first all-talking film, *On the Border*,[8] after which Warner Bros. put him in charge of making Spanish-language versions of some of its films.[9]

He got to work with Keaton again in 1931 on an all-star fundraising movie for the National Vaudeville Association's tuberculosis hospital: In

The Stolen Jools (aka *The Slippery Pearls*), Norma Shearer's jewels are supposedly stolen and detective Eddie Kane must visit half of the players in Hollywood to track them down. Keaton played the leader of a Keystone Cops–like police squad. Laurel and Hardy, Joan Crawford, Barbara Stanwyck, Maurice Chevalier, Edward G. Robinson and the Little Rascals all made appearances.

Next Warner Bros./First National sent McGann to England to make nine quota quickies. After he returned to the States in 1934 and for the next six years, he directed 24 B pictures for the studio. The only one of note is a goofy film called *Sh! The Octopus* (1937), which became a punchline for attendees at Cinecon, a film buffs' convention, in 2002. In 1940 he went freelance as a director, working for RKO, Paramount, Republic, Universal and Warner Bros.

Four years later, he came back to Warner Bros., but this time as a special effects director. Finally he got the chance to work on major motion pictures, including *The Big Sleep* (1946), *The Treasure of the Sierra Madre* (1948) and *The Fountainhead* (1949), and he was nominated for an Oscar for his work on *A Stolen Life* (1946). He retired in 1953.[10]

McGann married three times: His first wife was Roberta C. Hall, whom he married on December 6, 1918.[11] By March of 1922, she took a trip to Honolulu without him.[12] There's no available record of their divorce. Next, he married Kathryn Louise Glaze, a typist in a law office, on June 8, 1929.[13] That marriage lasted 17 years, until they divorced in 1946, with a Mrs. Margaret Clinch Lumberg named as co-respondent.[14] He then married Mrs. Lumberg, but they separated in the late 1950s.[15] Out of all three marriages, there were no children.

William McGann died of a heart attack on November 15, 1977, aged 84.[16] He had been living at the Motion Picture Fund's retirement home in Woodland Hills. He is buried at the San Fernando Mission Cemetery.

Further Information

Actress/dancer Mae Madison's obituary in the *Daily Telegraph* says that she was married to McGann, but they were mistaken. Her first husband was writer Jack McGowan. The IMDB repeats the error.

Census Records

1900 U.S. Federal Census (Population Schedule), Wilkinsberg Ward 2, Allegheny, Pennsylvania, ED 529, Sheet 11, Dwelling 208, Family 251, M. J. McGann household, jpeg image (Online: The Generations Network, Inc., 2007) [Digital scan of original records in the National Archives, Washington, D.C.], subscription database, http://www.ancestry.com, accessed 14 April 2007.

1920 U.S. Federal Census (Population Schedule), Los Angeles Township, Los Angeles, California, ED 223, Sheet 5A, Dwelling 50, Family 174, William M. McGann household, jpeg image (Online: The Generations Network, Inc., 2007) [Digital scan of original records in the National Archives, Washington, D.C.], subscription database, http://www.ancestry.com, accessed 14 April 2007.

1930 U.S. Federal Census (Population Schedule), Los Angeles Assembly District 55, Los Angeles, California, ED 57, Sheet 15B, Dwelling 258, Family 363, William M. McGann household, jpeg image (Online: The Generations Network, Inc., 2007) [Digital scan of original records in the National Archives, Washington, D.C.], subscription database, http://www.ancestry.com, accessed 14 April 2007.

1940 U.S. Federal Census (Population Schedule), Los Angeles Assembly District 42, Los Angeles, California, ED 60–1321, Sheet 62A, Family 120, William M. McGann household, jpeg image (Online: FamilySearch Historical Collections, 2012) [Digital scan of original records in the National Archives, Washington, D.C.], https://www.familysearch.org, accessed 8 July 2012.

William Piltz

When William Piltz joined Keaton's crew for just one film, *The General*, he brought to the shoot more years of film experience than anyone else involved in the production.

William Jacob Piltz was born in Bayonne, New Jersey, on June 7, 1875. His parents were carpenter Albert and his wife, Bertha Taker Piltz, who had just immigrated to the United States from Germany that year. The Piltzes had three more sons, all considerably younger than William: Gussie (born 1885), Otto (born 1889), and Henry (born 1894).

The whole family was living in New York City in 1900 (William's occupation was listed as "conductor" without other specifics). By 1910, the now 35-year-old Piltz was back in Bayonne and employed as a printer in a film lab for Nestor Films, part of the thriving New Jersey film industry. When the company moved to Los Angeles in 1911, he did too.[1]

Piltz, who had been promoted within Nestor Films, first appeared in the *Los Angeles City Directory* in 1914, listing his occupation as cameraman.[2] But later that year, when the Static Club held its first dance, he was working for the New York Motion Picture Company (NYMPC).[3]

He became very active in the Static Club, conspiring with fellow Keaton cameraman Dev Jennings along with George W. Hill to shoot a film for the group's summer dance at the beach.[4] By January 1915, he got elected to the Static Club board of directors (along with future Keaton crew members Frank Williams and Dal Clawson), and in July he became the vice-president.[5] The club's magazine, *Static Flashes*, reported, "Mr. Piltz has proven an able official. He is ever ready and responsive in aid of meritorious photographic effects, a booster for the advancement of the club along the right lines, and a man whom it is a pleasure to know and call friend."[6]

In March of 1915, he left NYMPC and switched over to Henry Lehrman's L-KO Kompany,[7] where he worked with director Harry Edwards on comedy shorts that starred Billie Ritchie and Peggy Pearce. *Static Flashes* reported that Piltz "studies effects and details at all times, and in his own quiet and unassuming way goes after and creates results worth while. He is popular with his director, players and camera associates and a man of especial ability."[8] Additionally, "he is ever on 'the job,' be it climbing telephone poles or sitting atop a building. The Piltz brand of camera effects are notable and every effect clearly brought forth. It is this class of photography that adds to the popularity of L-KO comedies."[9]

At the time of the 1918 supplemental draft, he gave his profession as cinematographer "unemployed at present" because he was visiting his sick mother in Bayonne. (His mother recovered. In 1920 she was living in Bayonne with his brother Otto, who was also a cameraman. She last appeared in the 1930 census, an 80-year-old living with her youngest son Henry's family in Bayonne. Henry Piltz owned a film laboratory.) He was of medium height and build, blue-eyed, with brown hair.[10] Because he was married, he got a deferment.

His credits are hard to trace, possibly because credits on short films have not been thoroughly documented: he doesn't appear in the AFI feature film database, and the Internet Movie Database lists only *The General* and a short comedy for the Christie Company, *Sea Sirens* (1919) (Al Christie had also worked for Nestor). According to *Camera* magazine's "Pulse of the Studios," he worked for Christie Films from February through September of 1919, and then returned to L-KO and stayed until June 1920.[11]

In 1926, he joined the crew that traveled to Cottage Grove, Oregon, to make *The General*. There are no details about his work on the shoot.[12] From there, he became a salesman.[13]

On May 6, 1914, the 38-year-old Pilz married 19-year-old Fern LaVere Jackson, originally of Summit, Ohio, whose father was the co-owner of Jackson and Brown Rubber Goods in Los Angeles.[14] She would work as a splicer in a film laboratory.[15] Despite their age difference, the couple would stay together until his death.

Piltz died on November 2, 1944, at age 69,[16] of coronary thrombosis, one year after being diagnosed with atherosclerotic heart disease. *Variety* reported that it was from injuries suffered in an earlier hit-and-run car accident, but his death certificate does not confirm this. He was buried in

Hollywood Memorial Park Cemetery (now Hollywood Forever Cemetery). His wife then re-married and became a film cutter at Paramount Pictures. She died on September 11, 1969, following a heart attack.[17]

Census Records

1900 U.S. Federal Census (Population Schedule), Akron Ward 5, Summit, Ohio, ED 74, Sheet 15, Dwelling 312, Family 350, Walter Jackson household, jpeg image (Online: The Generations Network, Inc., 2011) [Digital scan of original records in the National Archives, Washington, D.C.], subscription database, http://www.ancestry.com, accessed 18 February 2012.

1900 U.S. Federal Census (Population Schedule), Manhattan, New York, New York, ED 821, Sheet 13, Dwelling 98, Family 252, Albert Piltz household, jpeg image (Online: The Generations Network, Inc., 2007) [Digital scan of original records in the National Archives, Washington, D.C.], subscription database, http://www.ancestry.com, accessed 28 September 2007.

1910 U.S. Federal Census (Population Schedule), Bayonne Ward 4, Hudson, New Jersey, ED 22, Sheet 12A, Dwelling 62, Family 216, John Nolan household, jpeg image (Online: The Generations Network, Inc., 2007) [Digital scan of original records in the National Archives, Washington, D.C.], subscription database, http://www.ancestry.com, accessed 3 August 2007.

1910 U.S. Federal Census (Population Schedule), Los Angeles Assembly District 70, Los Angeles, California, ED 0276, Sheet 7A, Dwelling 107, Family 157, Walter Jackson household, jpeg image (Online: The Generations Network, Inc., 2011) [Digital scan of original records in the National Archives, Washington, D.C.], subscription database, http://www.ancestry.com, accessed 17 February 2012.

1920 U.S. Federal Census (Population Schedule), Bayonne City, Hudson, New Jersey, ED 16, Sheet 10A, Dwelling 720, Family 242, Otto Piltz household, jpeg image (Online: The Generations Network, Inc., 2007) [Digital scan of original records in the National Archives, Washington, D.C.], subscription database, http://www.ancestry.com, accessed 28 September 2007.

1920 U.S. Federal Census (Population Schedule), Los Angeles Assembly District 63, Los Angeles, California, ED 162, Sheet 3B, Dwelling 662, Family 753, William Piltz household, jpeg image (Online: The Generations Network, Inc., 2007) [Digital scan of original records in the National Archives, Washington, D.C.], subscription database, http://www.ancestry.com, accessed 3 August 2007.

1930 U.S. Federal Census (Population Schedule), Bayonne City, Hudson, New Jersey, ED 0213, Sheet 7A, Dwelling 83, Family 150, Henry Piltz household, jpeg image (Online: The Generations Network, Inc., 2007) [Digital scan of original records in the National Archives, Washington, D.C.], subscription database, http://www.ancestry.com, accessed 28 September 2007.

1940 U.S. Federal Census (Population Schedule), Los Angeles Assembly District 57, Los Angeles, California, ED 60–125, Sheet 14A, Family 399, William Piltz household, jpeg image (Online: FamilySearch Historical Collections, 2012) [Digital scan of original records in the National Archives, Washington, D.C.], https://www.familysearch.org, accessed 8 July 2012.

Co-Directors

John Gillett: "What exactly would the co-director do?"

Keaton: "Co-direct with me, that's all. He would be out there looking through the camera, and I'd ask him what he thought. He would maybe say 'That scene looks a little slow'; and then I'd do it again and speed it up."
—*Sight and Sound* article "Keaton at Venice" by John Gillett and James Blue[1]

When Buster Keaton was making silent features as an independent filmmaker, most of his crew members stayed with him for several pictures—except for the co-directors. Each of them made just one film with him, then moved on. The reasons for this seem less mysterious when you look at when and why each was hired.

It was different when Keaton was making shorts. Eddie Cline, who learned his trade from Mack Sennett, co-directed all but two of them. Mal St. Clair, another Sennett refugee, worked on those two. They were both visual gag men, just like Keaton, and the directing job was less complicated than it would become once the films got longer and needed more plot and character to sustain them.

Cline stayed on to direct Keaton's first feature, *Three Ages*, then was tempted away with promises of directing dramatic films. At this point, Keaton could easily have taken over the directing himself. He later told Kevin Brownlow why he didn't: "You see, I'm the guy that made a picture called *The Playhouse* ... I played all the parts: written by Keaton, directed by Keaton, costumes by Keaton, and everybody on the cast list was Keaton.... Having kidded things like that, I hesitated to put my own name on as director and writer."[2]

So when it came time to do *Our Hospitality*, Keaton hired John Blystone. Blystone had been directing comedies since 1915 for Henry Lehrman, another former Sennett employee, as well as doing Tom Mix comedy–Westerns for Fox, so he should have fit in well with the Keaton company. Once the picture was completed, Blystone returned to Fox Films. Whether this was because he had been contracted only for one film, or because of conflict of some sort, either of style or with personalities, it's not known, and neither side was ever interviewed about why. This set the pattern for the Keaton features, with a co-director coming on board for one film and then leaving.

When it comes to *Sherlock Jr.* (1924), there's quite a lot of controversy over who co-directed it. While *Camera!* magazine reported in 1923 that Keaton was the sole director,[3] Keaton wrote in his autobiography that he wanted to help out his old friend and mentor Roscoe Arbuckle, so in early 1924 Keaton brought him in to direct the film. (Arbuckle had been banned from appearing on screen because of the scandal over his manslaughter trials following the death of Virginia Rappé.) Keaton wrote, "[T]he experiment was a failure. Roscoe was irritable, impatient and snapped at everyone in the company."[4] According to this version of the story, Keaton needed to let him go, but no one wanted to leave Arbuckle stranded. Keaton said that his business manager, Lou Anger, suggested asking Marion Davies to hire him for her next film, *The Red Mill*, and then Keaton finished *Sherlock* himself. Something about this doesn't add up, though, because that film didn't go into production until 18 months later. *Variety* first reported that *The Red Mill* would be Davies' next film in October 1925, with Marshall Neilan mentioned as a possible director.[5] By March 1926, *Variety* said that Neilan was off the picture because the preparation was taking too long, and Arbuckle was on.[6] They also reported that he'd be working under the pseudonym William Goodrich. Because the dates are so far apart, David Yallop argues that Arbuckle actually directed all of *Sherlock Jr.*[7] But Brownlow and Gill concluded that Arbuckle started it, but didn't finish, because he was busy directing two Al St. John comedies while Keaton did *Sherlock Jr.*[8] Unless some definitive evidence surfaces, we'll probably never know precisely who directed what in *Sherlock Jr.*

Keaton's next film, *The Navigator*, contained several dramatic scenes, so Keaton decided to employ someone who was comfortable directing drama. He hired Donald Crisp, who had worked with D.W. Griffith. Little did he know that Crisp wanted to be a comic director. Their teaming didn't work out well: Keaton let him go before the picture was finished, taking over direction himself.

Despite the fact that Keaton had more than proven he could direct, in 1924 Jack McDermott was hired to co-direct his next picture, *Seven*

Chances.[9] McDermott had acted in many Kalem comedy shorts, and he had directed some for Fox. He worked on the film for only two weeks: He and Keaton clashed over how to approach it, and then McDermott quit.[10] *Variety* reported that McDermott wanted to direct it as a straight farce, while Keaton insisted on physical comedy. McDermott told the star he was wasting money having him around, and they parted friends. Once again, Keaton finished the film by himself.

Next, screenwriter Lex Neal, a childhood friend of Keaton's, was hired to direct a film that never got made, *The Skyscraper*.[11] Its writer, playwright Robert Sherwood, had written himself into a corner and wasn't able to come up with an ending, so it was mutually agreed to abandon the project.[12] But Neal stayed on as assistant director for *Go West*. Neal started co-directing the following film, *Battling Butler*, but then he left to work for Fox Film Corporation and Keaton once again took over.[13]

Keaton's nominal co-director on *The General*, Clyde Bruckman, never disputed the fact that it was Keaton who really directed the film. He told Keaton biographer Rudi Blesh, "I was often ashamed to take the money, much less the credit."[14] Bruckman may have underestimated his own worth, but he was willing to admit that he was the one who brought the source material for the film, *The Great Locomotive Chase*, to his boss.

In part because of the train crash and partly because of several forest fires that delayed production, *The General* was an expensive film, so the front office wanted to spend less on the next one, *College*. Keaton's business manager, Harry Brand, insisted on hiring James Horne to co-direct. Horne was an efficient, cost-conscious former serial director with experience in comedy. Keaton wasn't happy about it, and later told author Kevin Brownlow, "I don't know why we had him, because I practically did *College*."[15]

Charles Riesner was different from Keaton's other co-directors. He actually brought Keaton the idea for *Steamboat Bill, Jr.*,[16] and Keaton liked it so much that he immediately bought it and hired Riesner to co-direct. Riesner brought lots of experience to the film, having worked for many years with Charlie Chaplin.

It was at this point that Keaton's producer (and brother-in-law) Joseph Schenck sold Keaton's contract to MGM, and he became part of the studio's assembly line method of filmmaking, which did not suit him well. In his autobiography *My Wonderful World of Slapstick*, Keaton titled the chapter about this time "The Worst Mistake of My Life." The choice of director was no longer his; in fact, he was no longer allowed to direct, or even co-direct, at all. Eventually, his entire crew was dispersed throughout the studio. But on the first MGM film, *The Cameraman*, he was lucky enough to be assigned another ex-vaudevillian, Edward Sedgwick. Despite the fact that the films progressively got worse, Sedgwick would work with him on all of his MGM features until they both left the studio in 1933.

Assistant directors were also an important part of the crew, but except for Sandy Roth (*Steamboat Bill, Jr.*) they weren't listed in the on-screen credits. *Camera!* magazine listed some; now they can be added to filmographies.

In all probability, once Keaton got into features, he never really needed a co-director. Perhaps Keaton just wanted them around as a sort of security blanket, or perhaps the business office foisted them on him, not trusting him to direct on his own. Whether it was Keaton himself or the front office, in every case, seasoned professionals were hired (all five feature co-directors started directing in the mid–1910s), and they probably didn't enjoy having their ideas questioned. Another possible reason for the co-directors' short tenure might be that, like someone with perfect pitch who can't understand tone deafness, Keaton couldn't grasp why other people didn't immediately recognize what was funny. He had that talent, and others couldn't duplicate it.

John Blystone

Like the rest of Keaton's co-directors, John Blystone (*Our Hospitality*) had a long career, working steadily in Hollywood for 24 years. He made the Fox Studio's first talking film, and he worked with many other comedians, including Alice Howell, Clyde Cook, Will Rogers and Laurel and Hardy.

John Gilman Blystone was born in Rice Lake, Wisconsin, on December 2, 1891. He was the second son of George H. and Francine Oliver Blystone, after George Oliver, born in 1890. The Blystones had two more boys, William Stanley in 1894 and Jasper Kepler in 1899. George H. Blystone worked in lumber camps and later as a furniture manufacturer.[1] The family moved to Eau Clair, Wisconsin, in the mid–1890s.

John Blystone moved to Los Angeles in 1911. Although he later told interviewers that he studied mechanical and electrical engineering at the University of Wisconsin at Madison, the school doesn't have a record of him.[2] In 1912, the City Directory listed his occupation as "electrician," but in 1936 he told the *Los Angeles Times* that he would take any odd job available in film.[3] In January 1914, his photo was included in the Universal Film

Company's ad in the Static Club's souvenir program for its first dance.[4] He was announced as a new director of Joker comedies for that studio in July 1914.[5] One of Universal's comedy units, Joker was a training ground for future stars Louise Fazenda, Max Asher, and Harry McCoy.[6] Blystone's first film credits were as an actor in films directed by Wallace Reid that same year for the Nestor Film Company, which distributed through Universal. One of them, *The Wheel of Life*, also featured another actor who became a director: Frank Borzage.

In 1915, Blystone was hired by the Lehrman-Knockout Kompany, which was founded by Mack Sennett veteran Henry Lehrman. Blystone directed and supervised over 20 comedy shorts for L-KO, most of them featuring Alice Howell. When she left the company in 1917, Blystone went with her to Century Film Corporation, where they continued to make shorts. Their first film there was *Balloonatics*, which has occasionally been confused with Keaton's film *The Balloonatic* (1923), and Blystone has sometimes been mistakenly credited on that short, although it was actually directed by Eddie Cline.[7]

On July 7, 1915, Blystone married Gwendolyn Davis, who also grew up in Eau Clair, Wisconsin; her family had moved to Los Angeles in the early 1910s. The *Los Angeles Times* society page was fulsome: "[I]t is the culmination of an old-time romance of school days. Miss Davis has always been considered one of the most beautiful girls of Hollywood and Los Angeles, fair to look upon, and her ladylike manner, sunny disposition and charming simplicity made her much sought after and beloved by all. Mr. Blystone, although a young man, has made a notable success in his business life and is quite popular in this city."[8] It was a noontime home wedding with yellow as the color scheme. The bride wore white taffeta and carried valley lilies, and the couple's honeymoon was a motor trip around Southern California. When they returned, they settled down in a bungalow on Fuller Avenue, and would have two daughters, Francine in 1918 and Betty in 1923, the same year Blystone directed *Our Hospitality*.

Blystone must have left L-KO amicably, because in December of 1918 Henry Lehrman hired him to work for the Fox Sunshine Comedies,[9] where Eddie Cline was also a director. Blystone directed shorts featuring Chester Conklin, Clyde Cook, Western star Tom Mix and Lupino Lane, whose acrobatic style was similar to Keaton's. Blystone stayed at Fox for the next 18 years with only two interruptions.

Our Hospitality was the first. Cline had left Keaton for the chance to make dramas for Sol Lesser, so the Keaton company was looking for a new co-director for Keaton's second feature. In May 1923, the *L.A. Times* reported,

"Blystone's appointment to the direction of the Keaton comedies was the result of long deliberation, according to Mr. [Joseph] Schenck. It was felt that the paramount consideration was to find a director able to bring out comic situations. This was one of the distinguishing features of the Clyde Cook comedies which Blystone directed, and also of his work with Tom Mix. The award of the contract to Blystone was made after careful analysis of the merits of half a dozen prominent comedy directors."[10] On paper, it looked like a good match; Blystone had nearly as many years of experience directing comedy as Cline had. But he did only the one film. In later interviews, neither Keaton nor Blystone ever discussed why he only made one film for Keaton, but when Kevin Brownlow asked Keaton about *Our Hospitality* in 1964, Keaton did compliment Blystone: "He was a good man, excellent ... Jack Blystone had some very good pictures under his belt. He was a good director."[11]

Blystone returned to Fox, signing a contract with the studio in July 1923.[12] He made several feature-length Tom Mix Westerns, as well as other films. The *New York Times* mentioned that he had a habit of acting along while scenes were being performed: "[M]aking no sounds, but with grimaces that are sometimes marvels of ferocity, he follows the actions and speeches of his players from his post beside the camera, silently urging them on by some mysterious telepathy."[13] The studio certainly thought well of him, because he directed *Mother Knows Best*, its first feature-length talkie. As the *L.A. Times* pointed out, "[T]he fact that Blystone was entrusted with its making is an indication of the esteem in which he is held by the studio officials."[14] Fox was the second studio (after Warner Bros.) to adopt sound for feature films, although it used the sound-on-film process, rather than Warner Bros.' sound-on-disk, and the paper called the film "a revelation."[15] Sound-on-film would soon become the industry standard, as it avoided some of the technical pitfalls inherent in trying to sync a separate disk with the film.

In 1934, a *New York Evening Post* writer who visited the *Change of Heart* set described Blystone as "the least temperamental man in the screen colony. Tall, low-voiced, quiet and usually slow of speech, nothing ever seems to disturb his serenity.... [I]t partly explains why film players are always eager to work on a Blystone picture."[16]

Blystone's two younger brothers had joined him in Hollywood. His youngest brother Jasper became an assistant director whose career lasted until 1951, working on more than 50 films, including some directed by John. Jasper even had a Keaton connection himself, working on the MGM film *The Jones Family in Hollywood* (1939), which was co-written by

Keaton and directed by Mal St. Clair. Stanley Blystone, a supporting actor with parts in at least 500 films and TV shows, worked until his death in 1956. Their older brother George came West in the early 1920s but he stayed out of the entertainment business, instead becoming a realtor and then a salesman at a brokerage firm.

For the most part, John Blystone stayed at Fox until 1936. His other notable films included *Charlie Chan's Chance* (1931) and three with Will Rogers: *So This Is London* (1930), *Too Busy to Work* (1932) and *The Country Chairman* (1935). His second time away from his home studio was in 1930 when Fox loaned him to Columbia for its remake of *Tol'able David* starring Richard Cromwell.[17] Remaining at one studio for such a long time was unusual enough for a director that in 1935 the *L.A. Times* commented on it: "[S]etting a new record of consistency John Blystone recently began shooting on his seventy-first production for the same studio, when he gave the signal to start cameras on Twentieth Century–Fox's *Gentle Julia*."[18] But the next year he allowed his contract to expire, telling the paper that he wanted "a choice of stories and a reasonable vacation period between pictures,"[19] which certainly suggests that he felt constrained and overworked at Fox.

His faith in his ability to find freelance work was justified: Blystone made seven pictures in the next two and a half years, during which time he worked for Universal, RKO, Samuel Goldwyn and Hal Roach. His Roach pictures are his best-known films other than *Our Hospitality*; he directed Laurel and Hardy's *Swiss Miss* and *Blockheads* (both 1938), and many Laurel and Hardy fans believe that *Blockheads* is the best of the team's later features.[20]

Now that he was doing well as a freelancer, and getting "a reasonable vacation period between pictures," Blystone used his vacation time well, traveling to Australia and Japan, as well as driving through the United States for six weeks.[21]

Suddenly, on August 6, 1938, John Blystone died of a heart attack at home,[22] on the same day as Warner Oland, the actor who played Charlie Chan, and whom Blystone had directed.[23] He was buried in the Valhalla Memorial Park in North Hollywood, California.

His widow Gwendolyn stayed active in charitable work, dying on November 27, 1978.[24] His older daughter Francine married William Irwin the year after Blystone's death,[25] and gave birth to a son named John Gilman in 1942.[26] Betty Blystone graduated from the Westlake School for Girls in 1940 and planned to attend Bennington College in Vermont.[27]

Census Records

1900 U.S. Federal Census (Population Schedule), Eau Claire Ward 6, Eau Claire, Wisconsin, ED 28, Sheet 9, Dwelling 182, Family 211, George Blystone household, jpeg image (Online: The Generations Network, Inc., 2007) [Digital scan of original records in the National Archives, Washington, D.C.], subscription database, http://www.ancestry.com, accessed 9 February 2007.

1910 U.S. Federal Census (Population Schedule), Eau Claire Ward 5, Eau Claire, Wisconsin, ED 53, Sheet 8B, Dwelling 161, Family 183, George H. Blystone household, jpeg image (Online: The Generations Network, Inc., 2007) [Digital scan of original records in the National Archives, Washington, D.C.], subscription database, http://www.ancestry.com, accessed 9 September 2007.

1910 U.S. Federal Census (Population Schedule), Eau Claire Ward 5, Eau Claire, Wisconsin, ED 53, Sheet 15B, Dwelling 318, Family 359, Clara B. Burdin household, jpeg image (Online: The Generations Network, Inc., 2007) [Digital scan of original records in the National Archives, Washington, D.C.], subscription database, http://www.ancestry.com, accessed 9 February 2007.

1920 U.S. Federal Census (Population Schedule), Los Angeles Assembly District 63, Los Angeles, California ED 166, Sheet 21B, Dwelling 475, Family 557, John G. Blystone household, jpeg image (Online: The Generations Network, Inc., 2007) [Digital scan of original records in the National Archives, Washington, D.C.], subscription database, http://www.ancestry.com, accessed 9 September 2007.

1930 U.S. Federal Census (Population Schedule), Beverly Hills, Los Angeles, California, ED 819, Sheet 4B, Dwelling 75, Family 75, John G. Blystone household, jpeg image (Online: The Generations Network, Inc., 2007) [Digital scan of original records in the National Archives, Washington, D.C.], subscription database, http://www.ancestry.com, accessed 9 September 2007.

1940 U.S. Federal Census (Population Schedule), Beverly Hills, Los Angeles, California, ED 19–39, Sheet 3A, Family 804, Gwendolyn Blystone household, jpeg image (Online: FamilySearch Historical Collections, 2012) [Digital scan of original records in the National Archives, Washington, D.C.], https://www.familysearch.org, accessed 14 July 2012.

Blystone, John Gilman. *World War I Draft Registration Cards, 1917–1918* (5 June 1918) (Online: The Generations Network, Inc., 2007) [Digital scan of original records in the National Archives, Washington, D.C.], subscription database, http://www.ancestry.com, accessed 28 May 2011.

Eddie Cline

Eddie Cline did pretty well for an ex–Keystone Cop, but rarely gets the respect he deserves. In his day, he was "regarded as one of the best comedy directors in the motion-picture industry" according to the *Los Angeles Times*.[1] But in a piece for *Film Dope*, Markku Salmi wrote, "Cline's vast non–Keaton output is, on the basis of a sampling which need go no further, pretty grim."[2] Although most of his more than 150 films aren't classics of world cinema, they were concise and full of the energy and simple joy he learned from his first film boss, Mack Sennett. As a director,

Cline got to indulge his love for cars, gadgets, practical jokes and sports, had a 30-year long marriage (a rare feat in Hollywood), survived in the entertainment industry for five decades, and even made a few pretty good movies.

Edward Francis Cline was born on November 4, 1891, in Kenosha, Wisconsin. His parents were railroad fireman Francis Cline and his wife, Mary Bailey Cline. A younger sister, Mary, was born in April 1896. The family moved to Los Angeles in 1905 or '06, at which time his father became a butcher.[3] Young Eddie attended Los Angeles High School, where he played football and baseball.[4] Already a smart aleck, he once showed up for a rugby game with lace ruffles sewn on his shorts.[5] According to his *Los Angeles Times* obituary, he was a good enough pitcher to be offered a pro baseball contract, but he turned it down,[6] making him yet another Keaton collaborator with a baseball connection. In high school, he was also involved with the Young Men's Institute theater group, directing stage effects and appearing in its production of *College Chums*.[7]

After Cline finished school in 1910, he tried his luck as a stage actor, and had some success; he was part of the cast of the musical farce *A Certain Party* on Broadway.[8] Mike Donlin, a former major league baseball player who later joined Keaton's studio team and appeared in *The General*, was one of the leads, so it's possible that Cline brought Donlin to Keaton, or vice versa. Despite his Broadway success, he still listed his profession as a clerk with the L.W. Blinn Lumber Company in the 1911 Los Angeles City Directory.[9]

In 1913, Cline had a different kind of success: He won what the *L.A. Times* called "a love marathon," when he got engaged to Minnie Elizabeth Matheis, 18, the "literally and figuratively engaging daughter of Mr. and Mrs. John Matheis,"[10] who had gotten engaged to Cline after three previous engagements in the past three months. But she was "so happy that nothing on the round earth could persuade her to for a moment consider adding another to her score." In addition to her multiple engagements, Matheis was a busy young lady, a member of the Alpha Phi Sorority and the president of the Matinee Musical Club. Apparently, the families approved of the match, because in 1915 both families moved to Duane Street—the Clines at 2212 and the Matheises at 2216.[11] This fourth engagement stuck: The couple got married on March 6, 1916.[12]

In a 1929 interview with the *L.A. Times*, Cline said he got his start in pictures as an extra in *Birth of a Nation*, and then was hired at the Sennett Studio as a handyman in 1914.[13] The handyman job was his big break, and his city directory listing became "photoplayer."[14] He also recalled meeting

Sennett for the first time: "I was in a garage pit underneath his Blitzen Benz [a race car]. I had been at the studio for weeks and had never seen the man. When I heard his voice above me I got so excited that I dropped all the works and just stared. He started roaring and wanted to know who I was."[15]

Cline's answer must have been pretty good, because he was soon promoted to being an assistant to Sennett directors. For the most part, this entailed sitting on the stage and writing down the action as the directors thought it up. But he also became kind of a jack of all trades, doing anything that needed to be done. In 1938, he wrote, "I distinctly recall one week when I played a juvenile lead opposite Mabel Normand, harried Charlie Chaplin, moved scenery and did errands for the boss."[16] He did all that for three dollars a day. He continued: "[T]here was something about the Keystone training which fired the imagination and fitted a man for more important work."

Among his many responsibilities was acting. What is most remembered from that time was his energetic robber-chasing as a Keystone Cop. Cline described a typical picture:

> Perhaps you remember the Kops emerging from their station. As they were running down the street, one of them would bump into a ladder, upsetting it. The camera would flash to a painter falling, a few buckets of paint with him. Both the painter and the paint would rain down upon the Kops and so, spattered, but not disheartened, they would continue their pursuit of the bad men.
>
> That one "barrier" was never quite enough. Disentangled from the paint pots, the Kops would then pile into an automobile, some 15 or 18 of them into a flivver that at best could hold but five. Then that car would be made to skid over wet pavements and finally crash into a wagon loaded with flour. This bit of inspired scripting over, the indefatigable Kops would have to dangle from ropes suspended from high buildings, with the robbers at the other end.[17]

In 1916, Cline worked on three films as an assistant director, and then he was promoted to director. His first films featured a pretty comedienne, Peggy Pearce. Titles included *Bubbles of Trouble* and *His Bread and Butter*. As critic James Agee observed, Sennett's studio "made two kinds of comedy: parody laced with slapstick, and plain slapstick."[18] Of the former, Cline made *East Lynne with Variations* and *His Busted Trust*; and of the latter, he made *A Bedroom Blunder* and *A Schoolhouse Scandal*. He directed many of the studio's stars, including Ben Turpin, Ford Sterling, Louise Fazenda and Mabel Normand.

In addition, he also made a number of Sennett's famous Bathing

Beauty films, and even claimed credit for coming up with the idea (he was one of many who claimed to have originated the Beauties). His version of the story is that in 1917, during World War I, U.S. Food Administrator Herbert Hoover asked the studios to make propaganda films to encourage people to eat underused foods. Cline was assigned to make a half-reeler (five or six minutes) about fish. One Saturday morning, he went to a fish market and shot yellowtail and barracuda from all conceivable angles. But the footage lacked excitement, so to jazz things up, he asked the actresses at the studio to put on their one-piece bathing suits. He packed them and some fish off to Playa del Rey and "photographed deceased barracudas in their fluttering hands."[19] To round things off, he shot the ladies, still in swimsuits, playing a game of baseball. When Sydney Chaplin saw the footage, he convinced Sennett to make it a series—the girls running around in bathing suits, without the fish. (Sennett gave his version in his autobiography. He said that in 1914 he realized that pretty young women often got their pictures in the paper, so he hired some to pose with his comics. It garnered the attention he wanted, so he decided to make movies with them.[20] However, Brent Walker points out that Sennett had been using bathing-suit–clad women in his films since 1911's *The Diving Girl*, made for Biograph.[21]) Cline's contributions to the series included *Those Athletic Girls* and *The Summer Girls*. Other comedies, like his *Hearts and Flowers*, also had bathing beauty interludes.

Eddie and Minnie Cline had a daughter named Patricia on September 5, 1918.[22] Less than a week later, on September 11, Minnie became sick with puerperal peritonitis, an infection caused by the rupture of a fallopian tube during labor, and she died on September 15.[23] The baby's name was changed in honor of her late mother, and she was called Minnie Elizabeth for a time; later she was called Betty. (Despite his loss, Eddie Cline must have made sure that his daughter kept in touch with her mother's family, because in 1943 her maternal step-grandmother filed an amended birth certificate for her, changing her name officially to Elizabeth Normand Cline.[24])

A year later, on June 2, 1919, Cline married Beatrice Cinci Ives Altmann, from Aberdeen, South Dakota.[25] Her brother Robert Ives went on to work as an assistant to Cline from 1923 to 1934. The couple had no children.

A few months after his second wedding, in October 1919, Cline and several other Sennett staffers[26] moved over to the Fox Sunshine studio. There he made films like *Training for Husbands* and *Ten Nights Without a Barroom*. By 1920, he had the comedy directing experience necessary for his next job: He was ready to help Buster Keaton direct and write his solo two-reelers.

In addition to his experience with comedy, Cline and Keaton had a lot in common. They both loved baseball, boxing and football. Cline was still a good ballplayer; his hitting skills were mentioned in newspaper stories about Keaton's studio baseball team.[27] Cline also enjoyed cars, posing with his brand-new Peerless Sedan Limousine for the *Los Angeles Times* in 1921.[28] Furthermore, he loved gadgets, which also made him a good fit with Keaton. The *Times* reported that he was noted for his radio "fishing" ability. Even though Hollywood was a poor reception district, "Eddie Cline with his combination Stromberg-Carlson receiver and Magnatron tubes has logged 72 stations."[29]

It's hard to understand exactly what being co-director to Buster Keaton actually meant. In the 1950s, Keaton writer Clyde Bruckman told biographer Rudi Blesh that most of the direction was Keaton's, and insisted that Cline would be happy to confirm it.[30] But Keaton generally used the word "we" In describing how his films were made. In 1922, he told the *Los Angeles Times* how *My Wife's Relations* evolved:

> The hazy idea of it was born when Eddie Cline and I saw a postman in the East, unable to read the inscription on a letter in a foreign settlement, compare it to the lettering on a signboard. That's where we got the idea, and little by little the thought was nourished and grew into a full-fledged comedy. We changed a bit here and a little there, added and subtracted and the final result was a comedy with laughs.[31]

In a 1959 *Coronet* magazine article called "The Biggest Laugh in Movie History," Keaton gave Cline credit for the conclusion of *Hard Luck*, which Keaton claimed was the biggest laugh he ever received: He dives through the bottom of an empty swimming pool, then comes back years later with a Chinese wife and children.[32]

Whatever his contributions as director might have been, one thing we can be certain of: Eddie Cline acted in several of Keaton's shorts, bringing that special Sennett energy to a variety of roles. He kept up his police credentials as a cop in *The Goat* and in *Neighbors*; he was also the monkey trainer in *The Playhouse*. As the hangman in *Convict 13*, he measured Keaton's neck for the noose. His truck gave Joe Roberts a solid whack in *The Scarecrow*; in *Daydreams*, he brought great feeling to the role of the angry director who chucks the incompetent chorus boy Keaton out of the theater. In *The Frozen North*, he was the theater janitor who wakes Keaton from his William S. Hart–induced dream. He "sold" the cart and horse to Keaton in *Cops*. He provided a shocking peek at his undies in *The Haunted House*, and he wouldn't take "Damfino" for an answer as the SOS receiver in *The Boat*.

While Keaton was vacationing in New York in October 1922, Cline was loaned by Keaton's producer and brother-in-law Joseph Schenck to producer Sol Lesser to direct a Jackie Coogan picture, *Circus Days*. After finishing that film, he returned to Keaton. While he was shooting *Three Ages*, he left Keaton permanently after Lesser offered him a contract to direct George M. Cohan's *The Meanest Man in the World*,[33] the story of a debt-collecting lawyer (Bert Lytell) who falls in love with a debtor (Blanche Sweet), then saves her from swindlers.

Cline was tempted by the promise of getting to "identify himself with making dramas and comedy-dramas of feature length," as *Moving Picture World* put it.[34] Despite his years as a comedy director, he had succumbed to the strange notion that dramatic films were better than comedies. In 1923, he was asked "[D]o you like to make dramatic features better than comedies?" and he answered "Naturally."[35] However, actor Raymond McKee in *Camera!* wasn't buying it: "Eddie Cline hereafter will confine his puttees and megaphone to serious pictures. Eddie is always handing someone a laugh. Go to it, Eddie!"[36]

He was appointed director general at Lesser's Principal Pictures Corporation. The company had gotten the rights to bestselling Western author Harold Bell Wright's first nine novels, and Cline directed one of them, *When a Man's a Man*. Then he set to work adapting Wright's biggest hit, *The Winning of Barbara Worth*, which was to be released by United Artists. The author travelled to Los Angeles and met with Cline for two weeks to lay out the scenario.[37] Marceline Day (who later co-starred in *The Cameraman*) was signed to play Barbara. But then Lesser sold the rights to Samuel Goldwyn for over $125,000.[38] Directed by Henry King and co-starring Ronald Colman and Vilma Banky, it was a huge hit, launching Gary Cooper's career. After this, Cline went back to making comedies. He didn't get to make another drama for seven years.

Although his career had its ups and downs, he didn't lack for work. For a while, he directed the famous child stars of the day: Jackie Coogan in *Peck's Bad Boy* and *Rag Man* and Baby Peggy in *Captain January*. He also directed Viola Dana in *Along Came Ruth*. Then in 1924 he returned to Sennett, where he made more two-reel comedies (though Sennett told the press that they were "five-reel features boiled down to two reels"[39]). In October of 1926, he signed a contract with Tom Mix to direct *Bronco Twister*,[40] but somehow the deal fell apart and Orville O. Dull got the job. In November of that year, Cline started work on comic Douglas MacLean's feature *Let It Rain*.[41]

Cline was well regarded as a comedy director. *Moving Picture World* wrote at the time that he "has made a niche of his own as a director of comedies by virtue of the many successful hits he has wielded a megaphone on. He understands comedy values and the logical spot for the injection of a 'gag' where business shows a tendency to drag."[42] He was even signed to make a film with the top box office draw of 1927, Colleen Moore, *I'll Tell the World*,[43] but the picture never got made.

Cline unsuccessfully kept trying to make dramas. On February 17, 1928, he signed a contract to make *The Boss of Little Arcady* with Charlie Murray.[44] It was to be a departure from comedy for both of them, but that picture also never got made, and the two made the comedy *Vamping Venus* instead.

The director's transition to sound was seamless. His first talkie was comedian Reginald Denny's *His Lucky Day* (Denny played Jeff Haywood in Keaton's *Parlor, Bedroom, and Bath*). Cline later told *American Cinematographer*, "I never worried about sound. I decided it was here to stay, so jumped in and tried to get the new order of things. Truthfully, I have found it no more difficult to direct in sound than in the silent days."[45]

Even though work kept him busy, he found time for other interests. He and his wife were quite social, turning up regularly in Grace Kingsley's good-natured gossip column "Hobbnobbing in Hollywood." And he still loved sports of all kinds. He became a stockholder in the Hollywood Stars baseball club, and he frequently attended games.[46] In addition, he was an avid golfer, playing in many celebrity tournaments.[47] According to the *L.A. Times*, he traveled to many away games with the USC football team, which later called him "a complete gridiron addict."[48] The paper also reported that he was "a lover of fast ponies" who at every opportunity "drives to Tia-Juana to watch the bangtails flash around the track."[49] On one trip south of the border he lost his entire stake and almost had to hock his spare tire just to get home. He was even spotted at a cricket match where "his wife and daughter declared they'd start getting Eddie in shape for the international matches next month."[50]

During the next decade he was even busier. Hal Hall in *American Cinematographer* wrote in 1930 that although Cline was a freelance director, "he worked 52 weeks out of last year and from present indications will work another 52 this year. Which is quite a record for any man in pictures."[51] He made more than 20 comedies, including five with the popular team of Wheeler and Woolsey. After returning briefly to Mack Sennett, he made some shorts with Andy Clyde.[52] Branching off into musical comedies, he directed Irene Dunne's screen debut *Leathernecking* (1930), for which he got to try new technology, two-strip Technicolor, for a hula dancing sequence. He also used this technology for the color short *Business Is Pleasure* with not-yet-star Betty Grable. Although he could direct musicals, Cline himself wasn't particularly musical. In fact, a 1925 article on the talents of Sennett's staff called him "a good listener."[53]

Finally, in 1930, he got another chance to make a drama: *The Widow from Chicago* was a crime melodrama starring Edward G. Robinson as a vice lord in the film just prior to the one that made him a star, *Little Caesar*. This success led to a greater variety of work for Cline. He made a Western, *The Dude Ranger*, in 1934, and then he re-teamed with producer Sol Lesser to remake their silent Western *When a Man's a Man*. In 1935, he got to make a straight drama about two men who join the newly formed Civilian Conservation Corps, *It's a Great Life*.

His directing style was energetic. Wheeler & Woolsey biographer Ed Watz wrote about his work in *Hook, Line, and Sinker*: "While Eddie Cline's directorial style was palpably featherweight at best, he was an able technician, emphasizing pace, timing and tempo during a period when stage-bound drawing room affairs became the rule of the day. Cline intercuts frequently from long shots to medium shots to close-ups; despite a talky script, the film bogs down only two or three times, a marked improvement over the faltering approach found in the team's earlier comedies."[54]

In addition, Cline was a good manager. Actor Victor Potel (of Keaton's *Doughboys*), while acting in *Along Came Ruth*, told the *Times* in 1924 that while punctuality was the rarest of studio virtues, Cline was its "consistent possessor."[55] In the 13 years Potel worked with Cline, Cline never delayed the morning shooting hour. *Moving Picture World* said of him: "[H]e is democratic and always has a moment for the person who asks him a question. He is liked and admired by the artists who work under his direction. There is never any friction on the 'sets' where he is directing. He believes in keeping his staff happy and many times during the filming of a dramatic episode he will turn the drama into a hearty laugh. Then, when it is retaken, it is what he sought—the dramatic situation as it should be."[56] Marjorie Lord, who acted in *High Flyers* (1937), said, "Eddie Cline had a great sense of comedy and there was always good humor bouncing between him, the cast, and the crew."[57]

Cline was aware that he wasn't in the pantheon of film greats. Hedda Hopper told this story: "In *Lady in a Jam*, director Greg La Cava kids Western pictures. But instead of using six-shooters, he has his toughies pull water pistols. Eddie Cline, the old Western director, said, 'There is no justice. If I pulled a so-and-so stunt like that, critics would nail me to the wall. But when La Cava does it, they'll call it art.' 'But,' countered Greg,

'I use a very thin stream of water from my pistols, with beautiful backlighting.'"[58]

Cline did have a few noticeable peculiarities. According to Jules White, director of Keaton's *Sidewalks of New York*, as well as most of Keaton's Columbia shorts plus many Three Stooges films, Cline had a tic that caused him "to blink like an owl."[59] He could also be absent-minded. White's brother Sam said that Cline's nickname was "ashes on the vest," because when he smoked, he'd forget to flick the ashes.[60] He had a persistent giggle. Actor Eddie Quillan said "[I]f you were an established star, like W.C. Fields or Bert Wheeler, Cline would become hysterical, laughing at whatever you were doing on camera, to encourage you. You'd think the man was having a fit, he'd act so uncontrollably daffy. It'd be an understatement to call Eddie Cline's behavior a royal pain in the neck, because in Cline's opinion everything you did was brilliantly funny, even if it wasn't."[61]

Because he got along well with people, he got re-hired, including for some of the films for which he's best remembered now. In 1932, he directed W.C. Fields in *Million Dollar Legs*, the story of a small, almost bankrupt country that decides to enter the Olympics. (Pauline Kael later called it "one of the silliest and funniest pictures ever made."[62]) Fields enjoyed working with him, so when he signed with Universal Studios in 1938, Cline was on the short list of directors Fields considered hiring, along with other former Keaton co-workers Mal St. Clair, Clyde Bruckman and Edward Sedgwick.[63] Cline was hired as a sort of second unit director for *You Can't Cheat an Honest Man*, working for ten days directing Fields while director George Marshall, who didn't get along with the star, worked on the rest of the film. His conflict with Fields didn't hurt Marshall's career: His next film was the classic comedy–Western *Destry Rides Again*.

Cline was then chosen to direct Fields' next film, *My Little Chickadee*, a Western co-starring Mae West. In a letter, Fields wrote: "I picked Mr. Cline because I thought him efficient, inexpensive and someone I could talk to and get a direct reply from."[64] However, Cline angered Fields by working behind his back with a screenwriter he didn't approve of. He was almost replaced by Eddie Sutherland, but Sutherland was already committed to another project.

At first, Cline tried to hold Fields to the script, then gave up. He learned that Fields usually tacked his ad libs onto the ends of their lines so they could be edited out, if necessary. This didn't solve another problem: Often the ad libs were so funny that the crew would laugh and spoil the take.

Many predicted that dealing with Fields and West, who had such distinct styles (and egos), would be difficult. The *Newsweek* review of the film said, "Hollywood observers tempered their admiration of a sure-fire box office entente with concern for Edward Cline, whose position as director was expected to develop into a job of refereeing."[65] But Fields' biographer James Curtis has said that the fights were minor. One bit of insight was provided by *L.A. Times* reporter Jimmie Fidler. He visited the set, reporting that "the scene called for a kiss and director Eddie Cline, after fumbling a moment with verbal instructions, took a shortcut. 'Look, Bill, kiss her like this,' and proceeded to demonstrate. W.C. watched for a moment and the stop sign he laughingly calls his nose began to glow with animation. He tapped Cline on the shoulder. 'If you don't mind Eddie,' he grumbled, 'I'll do my own rehearsing!'"[66]

Universal was happy with his work, finding him cooperative and reasonable in his demands.[67] The production went 14 days over schedule, but was $5,000 under its $630,000 budget. Shooting ended on January 5, 1940, and previews were three weeks later. The film went into general release on February 9, and the reviews weren't bad, although they weren't great, either. Edwin Schallert in the *Los Angeles Times* was typical: "[S]tory rather rambles along, never quite jelling [but] you are always waiting for the next wisecrack and there are plenty of amusing ones."[68] Despite the less-than-enthusiastic critical acclaim, the film was a hit, earning $2 million in gross receipts.

Work wasn't the only thing occupying Cline that year. His daughter Betty had married James Bain in Las Vegas on January 31.[69] Bain, who grew up in Los Angeles and attended Fairfax High and L.A. City College, was the manager of the Woodridge Golf Club in Chicago. Eventually they settled in Reseda, California, and had six children.[70] They retired to Evergreen, Colorado, in 1964 and she died in March 1965.[71]

Cline's *The Villain Still Pursued Her* was a return to the Sennett style of parody with slapstick, including a pie fight. It was based on an exceedingly popular 1844 Victorian melodrama called alternately *The Fallen Saved* and *The Drunkard*. Cline had a habit of remembering old friends, so he hired former Sennett stars for cameo roles. At the time, Keaton's career wasn't going well, so Cline hired him for the film as well.

Keaton played the protagonist's best friend who saves him from drink. It was one of his larger supporting roles. According to *L.A. Times* studio gossip columnist Philip Scheuer, it was a fun shoot. He reported, "[W]hen Buster Keaton, at the head of a riot squad, spotted Villain Alan Mowbray, he shouted, 'After him, men!' and dashed off in the opposite direction—

this last as a 'rib' for Cline—that worthy cheerfully called out 'Great!' Mr. Cline is the easygoing sort."[72] The contemporary reviews weren't great. *Variety* said it was "a missout from the entertainment standpoint."[73] But in 1993, Jim Kline in *The Complete Films of Buster Keaton* opined that the film "sustains its exaggerated style without becoming silly or resorting to low-brow antics."[74]

Cline went back to Fields for what many people thought was his best film ever. *The Bank Dick* was a difficult shoot, because Fields was drinking heavily and, at age 61, tired easily. Cline kept the shooting days short, and worked out gags by acting as Fields' stand-in. "I just try to imagine I'm Fields," Cline said.[75] Despite the problems, they made a movie the critics loved. No less than William Sarayon wrote in *Variety*, "The Modern Museum in New York might just as well take it right out of the first-run picture houses and show it to serious-minded people who study motion picture art without waiting for 20 years to go by first. It's just as funny now as it will be 20 years from now."[76] Unfortunately, *The Bank Dick* failed at the box office, and Fields was blamed for its failure because he didn't promote it.

Cline stuck with Fields through his last film as a star, *Never Give a Sucker an Even Break*. By then, Fields was quite ill and had to use cue cards. *Sucker* was also a commercial failure.[77]

In 1942, Cline became a cop for real. After months of training, he was sworn in as an auxiliary deputy sheriff, one of 403 assigned to help in emergencies during World War II.[78] The sheriff's department didn't publicize his earlier experience with the Keystone Cops when they announced his appointment.

Cline had a film career for as long as double-bills lasted. Between Fields films, he made several films for Universal, including two more throwbacks to the slapstick days, *Meet the Chump* and *Cracked Nuts* (the latter title was even a repeat of one of his earlier films). He directed more comedies with music, including *Moonlight and Cactus* and *Swingtime Johnny*, both with the Andrews Sisters. He supervised the comedy sequences in *Since You Went Away* with Claudette Colbert and Joseph Cotten.

In 1944, he returned to his stage roots. The comedy team Olsen and Johnson, whom he'd directed in *Crazy House* and *Ghost Catchers*, asked him to direct their new Broadway musical review *Laffing Room Only*. Lewis Nichols in the *New York Times* described it as "a series of variety tunes held together by a thin thread of machine-gun fire.... [I]t is big and loud, gaudy and not infrequently vulgar.... [S]ince this has been too quiet a town lately, it is good to have them back."[79] It was a hit, running for seven months with 232 performances.

According to actor Eddie Quillan, Cline began to pay too little attention to his movie directing job. While filming the 1944 musical comedy *Slightly Terrific*, after the action in a scene was done, there was a long pause and the assistant director finally yelled "cut." Said Quillan, "Cline—our director—was nowhere to be seen. Then I spotted him, off in the corner, on the phone, holding a racing form, placing a bet! After he hung up, he turned to a script girl and asked, 'How'd that last scene look to you?' Eddie Cline hadn't even bothered to watch it! Well, you can imagine—you can't hide that from the front office forever. He didn't last at Universal much longer."[80]

In 1947, Cline was back directing for the New York stage: *Heads or Tails* starring Werner Klemperer, later Colonel Klink of TV's *Hogan's Heroes*. This was not a success. *New York Times* critic Brooks Atkinson called it "a silly, haphazard comedy,"[81] but the review blamed the writers. It closed after 35 performances.

By the end of his film career, Cline was reduced to working for low-budget Monogram, making films based on George McManus' "Bringing Up Father" comic strip. (Coincidentally, this was the comic strip that William Randolph Hearst tried to sign the Three Keatons to film in the 1910s.)[82]

By 1949, television had come along, slowing the production of most B movies at Hollywood studios. Cline, like so many other show business veterans, found work in the new medium. He began by writing scripts for Hal Roach, who had converted his studio to only television production.[83] He was assistant director on the last five episodes of Olsen and Johnson's series *Fireball Fun-for-All*. He directed two pilots for Spike Jones, and in 1951 he worked with Keaton again on *The Buster Keaton Show*, for which they recreated many routines from their silent days.

Just as his old career was ending and his new one beginning, Cline's wife Beatrice died suddenly of a heart attack in their home on August 22, 1949.[84] She was 55 years old.

Cline finished out his career working for Spike Jones on his TV shows and stage revue. (Jones is now best remembered for his comic songs like "The Furher's Face" and "All I Want for Christmas Is My Two Front Teeth.") It wasn't a happy collaboration. According to Eddie Brandt, a writer on Jones' show, "He was the most talented of everybody. He'd remember old gags ... he would contribute, but he was a whipping post. Anything that would go wrong, Spike would take out on him. He would run and get sandwiches; he was just a coffee boy, the low man on the totem pole. But Spike had him around because he knew who Eddie Cline was. He was smart enough to have the best."[85] Brandt also said that Cline gave Jones gags that he would present as his own.

Cline outlived almost everyone else who worked with Keaton in the early days. So in April 1957, when Keaton was ambushed by Ralph Edwards for an episode of *This Is Your Life,* Cline was the sole representative of "that old crew who ate and slept comedy," as Keaton biographer Rudi Blesh put it.[86] (Donald Crisp was also on the show, but he only co-directed part of one film.) Cline told a story about Keaton's love of practical jokes: Virginia Fox was left stranded hanging on top of some moose antlers when Keaton called lunch.

During the last years of his life, Cline's drinking, which might have interfered with his directing abilities over the years, spun out of control. He died of a swollen liver caused by cirrhosis on May 22, 1961.[87] He was buried in the San Fernando Mission Cemetery.

Most of Cline's many films weren't innovative art. As Edwin Schallert wrote about his *Hook, Line, and Sinker,* "Those who want to laugh will gain lots of enjoyment. What matter if some of the jokes not only have whiskers but long gray beards? They sound just as amusing sometimes as they ever were."[88] Most directors don't get to be a Lubitsch, a Sturges or a Keaton. Nevertheless, Cline was a successful Hollywood director who made peppy, entertaining movies, treated his co-workers well, and had fun along the way. In a 1925 interview defending comedy, Mack Sennett said, "Without wishing to be sentimental—there is a world of satisfaction in being able to make people laugh and be happy."[89]

Cline himself wrote in 1938 for the *L.A. Times*: "A Keystone Kop was taught to take the bumps with a laugh. No matter how many gallons of paint deluged him, no matter how often he was knocked down and run over by automobiles, he came up smiling—it was his Destiny to win."[90]

Further Information

Wisconsin's Birth Registrar, his draft registration, and a 1934 boat passenger list give 4 November 1891 as his birthdate. His death certificate says 7 November 1892, and all previously published biographies use that date. He also used the later date in his film almanac and yearbook entries. Film historian Joan Myers came up with a plausible theory for the date discrepancy: in a time when people wrote their birthdate on forms less often, Cline may simply have forgotten the exact date.

Census Records

1900 U.S. Federal Census (Population Schedule), Kenosha City, Kenosha, Wisconsin, ED 3, Sheet 24B, Dwelling 444, Family 509, Francis E. Cline household, jpeg image (Online: The Generations Network, Inc., 2009) [Digital scan of original records in the National Archives, Washington, D.C.], subscription database, http://www.ancestry.com, accessed 9 May 2010.

1900 U.S. Federal Census (Population Schedule), Los Angeles Ward 7, Los Angeles, CA, ED 65, Sheet 4B, Dwelling 76, Family 109, John F. Matheis household, jpeg image (Online: The Generations Network, Inc., 2006) [Digital scan of original records in the National Archives, Washington, D.C.], subscription database, http://www.ancestry.com, accessed 2 March 2006.

1910 U.S. Federal Census (Population Schedule), Los Angeles Assembly District 71, Los Angeles, California, ED 154, Sheet 6A, Dwelling 158, Family 166, Frank E. Cline household, jpeg image (Online: The Generations Network, Inc., 2009) [Digital scan of original records in the National Archives, Washington, D.C.], subscription database, http://www.ancestry.com, accessed 24 November 2010.

1910 U.S. Federal Census (Population Schedule), Los Angeles Assembly District 72, Los Angeles, California, ED 196, Sheet 18B, Dwelling 308, Family 401, John F. Matheis household, jpeg image (Online: The Generations Network, Inc., 2009) [Digital scan of original records in the National Archives, Washington, D.C.], subscription database, http://www.ancestry.com, accessed 24 November 2010.

1920 U.S. Federal Census (Population Schedule), Los Angeles Assembly District 75, Los Angeles, California ED 466, Sheet 23A, Dwelling n/a, Family n/a, Edward F. Cline household, jpeg image (Online: The Generations Network, Inc., 2006) [Digital scan of original records in the National Archives, Washington, D.C.], subscription database, http://www.ancestry.com, accessed 4 February 2006.

1920 U.S. Federal Census (Population Schedule), Los Angeles Assembly District 75, Los Angeles, California ED 232, Sheet 15B, Dwelling 217, Family 446, Frances [sic] E. Cline household, jpeg image (Online: The Generations Network, Inc., 2006) [Digital scan of original records in the National Archives, Washington, D.C.], subscription database, http://www.ancestry.com, accessed 22 February 2006.

1920 U.S. Federal Census (Population Schedule), Los Angeles Assembly District 64, Los Angeles, California ED 9, Sheet 1B, Dwelling 23, Family 26, Mellville J. Matheis household, jpeg image (Online: The Generations Network, Inc., 2009) [Digital scan of original records in the National Archives, Washington, D.C.], subscription database, http://www.ancestry.com, accessed 28 November 2010.

1930 U.S. Federal Census (Population Schedule), Los Angeles Assembly District 57, Los Angeles, California, ED 130, Sheet 18B, Dwelling 401, Family 401, Edward F. Cline household, jpeg image (Online: The Generations Network, Inc., 2006) [Digital scan of original records in the National Archives, Washington, D.C.], subscription database, http://www.ancestry.com, accessed 4 February 2006.

1930 U.S. Federal Census (Population Schedule), Los Angeles Assembly District 55, Los Angeles, California, ED 9, Sheet 11A, Dwelling 222, Family 258, John F. Matheis household, jpeg image (Online: The Generations Network, Inc., 2006) [Digital scan of original records in the National Archives, Washington, D.C.], subscription database, http://www.ancestry.com, accessed 2 March 2006.

1940 U.S. Federal Census (Population Schedule), West Hollywood, Beverly Hills Judicial Township, Los Angeles, California, ED 19–62, Sheet 7B, Family 269, Edward Cline household, jpeg image (Online: FamilySearch Historical Collections, 2012) [Digital scan of original records in the National Archives, Washington, D.C.], https://www.familysearch.org, accessed 14 July 2012.

Cline, Edward Francis. *World War I Draft Registration Cards, 1917–1918* (5 June 1918) (Online: The Generations Network, Inc., 2009) [Digital scan of original records in the National Archives, Washington, D.C.], subscription database, http://www.ancestry.com, accessed 23 November 2010.

Cline, Edward Francis. *World War II Draft Registration Cards, 1942* (Online: FamilySearch Historical Collections, 2011) [Digital scan of original records in the National Archives, Washington, D.C.], https://www.familysearch.org, accessed 19 January 2012.

Donald Crisp

Donald Crisp lived a remarkable life, and the stories he told about it were exciting, fascinating, colorful ... and only occasionally true. Here are the tales he told. He said he was born in Aberfeldy, Perth, Scotland, in 1880, and alternately claimed that his father James Crisp was a cattle farmer, a country doctor or Royal Surgeon to Edward VII. Educated at Eton and Oxford, Crisp ran away at 16 (or was it 19?) to join the 10th Hussars and fight in the Boer War, where he suffered several wounds. There, so he claimed, he met a young journalist named Winston Churchill. Demobilized in 1902, he toured England as a theater actor and occasional opera singer (he told one writer that, as a child, he had been a member of the boy choir of St. Paul's Cathedral). Emigrating to the United States in 1906, Crisp found more work in the theater. The good money being paid by the Biograph Company soon attracted him, and his career in film was launched. During a career spanning more than 55 years, he once estimated that he worked on at least 450 films as an actor or director, including co-directing Keaton's *The Navigator* in 1924. But he also found time to be a British spy in Russia during World War I, and act as the gatekeeper for Bank of America's loans to Hollywood.

His real story was interesting enough, an all–American tale of reinvention and success. George William Crisp was actually born July 27, 1882, in St. Mary Stratford Le Bow (known as "Bow"), London, making him a Cockney, not a Scot.[1] He was the youngest son of James and Elizabeth Crisp. James was born in Redgrave, Suffolk, and he was employed as a farm laborer, a cow man–dairyman, worker at a chemical factory and as a general laborer. He was certainly not Royal Surgeon to the king. Elizabeth Christy Crisp, his mother, was born in Bow, London. In addition to George, the couple had seven other children, all older than George: Elizabeth in 1862, Emily in 1864, Ann in 1866, Eliza in 1869, James in 1871, John in 1873 and Mark in 1875.

George was the youngest by seven years. His family stayed at the same house for all of his youth, 3 Clay Hall Road. He was educated locally just as all of his brothers and sisters were (their profession was listed as "scholar" on the census when they were young). Despite what he told writers, Oxford University has no record of any students named George William or Donald Crisp.[2] In 1901, he was living with his parents in Bow, the last child still at home, where he worked as a carman (the driver of a vehicle to transport goods), not fighting with the Hussars in South Africa.

Parts of the stories he told are true. He did come to the United States in 1906, traveling from Liverpool aboard the S.S. *Carmania*, arriving in New York on July 26 with $70 in his pocket.[3] His stated destination was his sister Annie Donahue's place, at 116 63rd Street. He later told studio publicity departments that he came to have a look at what the earthquake and fire did to San Francisco, but lack of funds prevented him from going any further than New York City[4]; other times he told them he just came out of wanderlust.[5] But even a studio publicist concluded: "Probably the real reason for Crisp's coming to the United States was that here he'd find better opportunity to succeed in the career of his choice, the theater."[6]

He later said that the head of an American light opera company, John C. Fisher, was also on the boat and, after hearing Crisp sing in a shipboard concert, hired him to tour with them through Cuba and Mexico.[7] Although plausible, this can't be confirmed. In 1941, he told a publicist at 20th Century–Fox that on his return to New York from this supposed trip, he got his start in moving pictures by appearing in *The French Maid* (1907) for the American Mutoscope and Biograph Company.[8] This is also entirely possible because mutoscopes were made from 1895 to 1909, and he did continue to work for Biograph. If this part of his story is true, it's impossible to confirm, because so much has been lost—there aren't any records or extant films. He liked to tell writers about his salad days with John Barrymore. Here's a sample from a *New York Herald Tribune* article of 1942: "When Crisp found out about the mutoscopes, he decided to heck with his reputation, he would pick up some spare cash. Soon he convinced Barrymore that this was the true path to riches, and together the two would sneak off, daub their faces with cork and hair and scamper in front of the cameras."[9]

His first job for which there is a record was on the Broadway stage: He performed with George M. Cohan in Cohan's *The Yankee Prince*, which opened on Broadway on April 20, 1908.[10] Alongside the Four Cohans, he played a policeman and a waiter. The musical ran for 112 performances in New York, then toured the country. By November 1909, they were in Los Angeles.[11]

According to *Film Index International*, his first film was Biograph's *The Reckoning*, made in 1908 and directed by D.W. Griffith.[12] The earliest surviving film he appeared in was another by Griffith: *Through the Breakers* from 1909. The list of his fellow extras reads like a roster of the future of Hollywood: Mack Sennett, Henry Lehrman, Owen Moore and Robert Harron all appeared in a club scene with Crisp. As part of Griffith's stock company, he played everything from policemen to valets to Ulysses S. Grant in *Birth of a Nation*. His most memorable performance for Griffith was as Battling Burrows, the abusive father who murders his own daughter in *Broken Blossoms*.

Crisp had enough spare time between film assignments to appear on stage again in George M. Cohan's *The Little Millionaire*, which ran a respectable (for those days) 192 performances in 1911–12.[13] He said that Cohan and Sam Harris also hired him as a stage manager for the George M. Cohan Theater.[14] On January 1, 1912, he married another member of the *Millionaire* company, Helen Pease,[15] a 21-year-old former music teacher from Ypsilanti, Michigan. The marriage was a short one; she died the following year.[16]

In 1914, after moving with the Griffith company to Los Angeles, he began combining his acting career with film directing, making two-reel comedies and dramas, including several starring Dorothy Gish. In 1915, he acted in and was an assistant director on *Birth of a Nation*.[17] Then in 1916, he got a chance to direct his first feature, *Ramona*, based on the Helen Hunt Jackson novel set in early California. He directed one more feature for Clune Film Producing Company, *Eyes of the World*, in 1917, after which he was hired by Famous Players–Lasky Studio where he worked from 1917 to 1922. He made a wide variety of films there, including *The Clever Mrs. Carfax*, which starred the noted drag performer Julian Eltinge, who played both the male and female leads.

They really worked long hours. According to the *Moving Picture World*, one Sunday morning in 1914 he needed to shoot a mob scene for *His Lesson*. The extras had the day off, so he recruited everyone available: directors like W.C. Cabanne and Eddie Dillion, stars like the Gish sisters, Fay Tincher and Mae Marsh, and even cameraman Billy Bitzer, who had to be told several times not to look at the camera.[18] During the 18-day *Broken Blossoms* shoot, he was only able to act at night because he was directing during the day.[19]

Crisp remarried on December 15, 1917.[20] Hazel Marie Stark was an actress who had small parts in two films Crisp directed earlier that year, *A Roadside Impresario* and *The Cook of Canyon County*. For their honeymoon, the couple took a hunting trip in Crisp's Cadillac eight. The two had a rocky relationship. They separated and reconciled in 1919, but in

1920, he left her for good, moving back to London to work for Lasky British. When she filed for separate maintenance in 1921, she claimed cruelty (and one newspaper account made sure to remind readers that Crisp had played the brutal father in *Broken Blossoms*).[21] In May of 1923, she got a property settlement of $75,000.[22]

In Great Britain he made eight movies, including *The Bonnie Briar Bush* in 1921. He later told Read Kendall, a *Los Angeles Times* columnist, that he shot part of it in Aberfeldy, Scotland,[23] which he must have liked so much that he later claimed it as his birthplace. In 1920, however, he was still firmly English; he emphasized his nationality that year in an interview with *Moving Picture World*. He thought that only an Englishman could navigate the difficulties inherent in working there, like rainy weather and different sensibilities: "If I wanted to take a scene of the heroine alighting at the front door of a certain New York hotel, all I would have to do would be to hand the doorman a ten-spot. In England, the doorman would refer me to the desk clerk and the clerk to the manager and so on ad infinitum. None of them would want to take the responsibility of letting me shoot the scene."[24]

Before Lasky British went bankrupt in 1922, he directed its final film, *Tell Your Children*, with intertitles designed by an up-and-coming filmmaker, Alfred Hitchcock.

Crisp returned to Hollywood in May 1923 as a freelance director. Within two months, Sam E. Rork signed him to direct *Ponjola*, set in South Africa, and the publicity made much of his supposed Boer War experiences there.[25] After he finished that assignment, he went to work for Buster Keaton on *The Navigator*. (Keaton later mentioned to Kevin Brownlow that Crisp also worked on *Sherlock Jr.* toward the end of the shoot, including the day Keaton broke his neck.[26])

The experience didn't turn out the way either of them expected: Crisp wanted to become a comedy director, while Keaton had hired him to handle the dramatic scenes. When telling Christopher Bishop in 1958 about the film, Keaton said, "The one mistake we made there, and that was Donald Crisp—he was strictly from the D.W. Griffith school, a topnotch dramatic man—he [had] just made one of the best pictures for Paramount that year, called *The Goose Woman*. [Keaton was mistaken: Clarence Brown directed *The Goose Woman*.] But when he joined us, he turned into a gag man. He wasn't interested in the dramatic scenes; he was only interested in the comedy scenes with me. Well, that we didn't want."[27] A few years later, Keaton told Kevin Brownlow, "He came to work in the morning with the goddamnedest gags you ever heard in your life. Wild!

... We let him go before the underwater scene. That was a tedious job, and a lot of trouble to us. A director can't do anything with a scene like that; it's strictly between me and the cameraman and the technical man."[28] *Variety* reported at the time that Crisp and Keaton had a difference of opinion, and Keaton "decided to handle the megaphone himself."[29] Although Crisp's side of the story doesn't seem to have been recorded, he did leave one indelible mark on *The Navigator*: It's Crisp dressed as a sea captain in the frightening portrait that swings between the portals during Keaton's first terrifying night at sea.

After being fired by Keaton, Crisp again combined dramatic directing and acting in his next film, *Don Q., Son of Zorro* (1925) with Douglas Fairbanks. Then he signed a contract with Cecil B. DeMille and directed nine silent films for his company. He also acted occasionally in other studio's films, such as MGM's 1928 two-strip Technicolor *The Viking*. On February 14, 1930, he became an American citizen and officially changed his name to Donald.[30]

As an actor, his transition to sound seemed effortless. He appeared in the all-sound *The Return of Sherlock Holmes* in 1929 and never looked back. But his directing career came to an end after just one talkie, *The Runaway Bride*, in 1930. He later called it the most fortunate move of his life,[31] and gave three reasons why he gave up directing: star egos, the overabundance of studio heads' relatives who had to be hired, and the stress and strain of the job.[32]

He worked with his next wife on that final directing job. Jane Murfin wrote the screenplay, and they married two years later. She was a successful writer of both plays and films, so much so that the *New York Times* wedding article about them was titled "Jane Murfin Married."[33] She was born October 27, 1892, in Quincy, Michigan, to James Macklem and Henriette Livingston Macklem. After writing the Broadway hits *Lilac Time* and *Smilin' Through*, she came to Hollywood where she and her business partner, Lawrence Trimble, made films with his discovery, Strongheart the Dog.[34] Eventually she would write or co-write more than 60 screenplays, including *Leathernecking* (1930, directed by Eddie Cline), *What Price Hollywood?* (1932), *The Women* (1939) and *Pride and Prejudice* (1940). She even tried directing herself in 1924 for a film called *Flapper Wives*.

According to a *New York Times* article,[35] Crisp was "one of the busiest supporting actors" in the 1930s," appearing in a wide variety of roles, from Englishmen, Scotsmen and Frenchmen, to American Southerners. He played everything from a police inspector in Clara Bow's *Kick In* (1931) to Dr. Kenneth in *Wuthering Heights* (1939).

From what can be determined from newspapers and magazines, Crisp didn't start claiming he was Scottish until the late 1930s; earlier articles mentioned he was English. For instance, in 1916, he told *Moving Picture World* that he was born in London.[36] In the same magazine four years later he said his English origins would be the key to his success when he went to London to work at Lasky's British studio,[37] saying he thought his background would help him overcome difficulties an American director might have working there, including getting locations and understanding the class system. A 1924 *Los Angeles Times* list of directors from foreign countries included him with the English directors, not the Scottish.[38] His Paramount publicity materials said he was "an Englishman by birth" in 1930.[39] His 1932 wedding announcement called him an English actor.[40] Additionally, where his Scottish roots might be have been useful for publicity ballyhoo, they were never mentioned, as in the publicity for his appearance in the 1936 film *Mary of Scotland*.[41]

One early mention of Crisp's Scottish origins was in Hedda Hopper's column in March 1938. While praising his acting in the film *Jezebel*, she wrote, "[H]is Scotch heather got a bit into the Southern dialect, but that added zest to me."[42] He seems to have take up his new nationality with a vengeance; later that year, *Los Angeles Times* columnist E.V. Durling saw him socializing in the evening and reported, "Donald's a Scot and as the party nears its close insists on reciting such gems as 'Wee Laddie's First Soiree,' 'Kirsty Lindsay's Goose,' 'A Flae in the Lug,' 'Tibble and the Minister,' and 'The Goal Keeper's Ghost.'"[43]

In July 1939, he used his new persona when interviewed by Bosley Crowther of the *New York Times*. The piece, "Dollars and Sense," was all about how Crisp's Scottish roots made him terribly clever about money.[44] Crisp played the stereotype to the hilt, and Crowther highlighted his work on the Bank of America's loan committee, his modest accommodations in Chelsea instead of a swanky uptown hotel, and his old Scottish father's advice to save for a comfortable retirement.

Naturally, his studio publicity material also incorporated his new birthplace data, never failing to mention the tiny town of Aberfeldy in their tales of a small town boy made good. His 1947 Paramount file had him attending school there, and looking back upon the experience "with anything but happiness."[45] His 1957 MGM biography said that the family later moved to London, where he was educated.[46]

One possible reason for this total fabrication might have been to change his image as he grew older, in an attempt to get work. If so, it was a terrific success. After he proclaimed his Scottishness, he got lots of crusty yet warmhearted patriarchal roles, including the one that brought him an Academy Award: Gwilym Morgan, the Welsh father in 1941's *How Green Was My Valley*. He had similar roles in several Lassie movies throughout the 1940s, as well as in *National Velvet*.

Perhaps he just liked spinning stories (and seeing what he could get away with). He had already been lying about his military service to the press and publicity departments for years, beginning in 1914. He told Grace Kingsley of the *L.A. Times* that he was part of the 10th Hussars during the Boer War: "He went to Africa and fought all through the campaign, was wounded three times, and promoted to the rank of color sergeant for bravery. He carries several scars and wears a lot of medals."[47] By 1947, his stories had him rising to the rank of captain. He explained, "It wasn't a case of earning a promotion as much as it was outliving my comrades. Those Boers were mighty good shots."[48]

In 1947, he told a Paramount publicity scribe that he joined the British Army when World War I broke out and was transferred to the American forces when they became involved in the war. How he commuted between the trenches in France and the film lot in Hollywood was left unasked.[49]

Crisp also claimed to have spied on the Bolsheviks in Russia for British Intelligence right after World War I, flying in and out of Russia twice a week when he was making films for British Lasky.[50] The reporter didn't ask him how he managed to do that on top of his film responsibilities. In 1930 he told another Paramount writer this tale worthy of a Hollywood screenwriter:

> I remember 23 men were called into the office at one time. We were to engage in a great undertaking which was to save England from a certain foreign power. All Europe was a hotbed of intrigue and many governments were threatened with revolution. We received our instructions and then, realizing the immensity of our task, separated. I received valuable information in one place by trying to get guns and ammunition as props for a motion picture of the war I was going to film. But the enemy was extremely active. One day four of us were walking on a street in Berlin. Sudden gunfire startled us. I fell with a severe wound in my shoulder; my three companions were dead. Of the 23 men who started out on that mission, only seven were alive when our purpose was accomplished. Immediately after that, I was retired from the service with a silver collar-bone to replace the one which had been shot away.[51]

Crisp's military service was actually limited: He served in the United States Army Reserves during World War II, touring the country selling war bonds with Sergeant Gale Sondergaard.[52] But he made sure to wear his uniform when he picked up his Oscar.

He also liked to tell people that he worked for Bank of America, and this time there was a grain of truth. In 1929, the *Los Angeles Times* wrote, "A.P. Giannini asked a number of leaders in the motion picture industry to become advisory board members of the Hollywood branch of the Bank of Italy (forerunner to the Bank of America). These people not only lent the prestige of their names, but also gave advice and counsel.... In gold letters on the window of this bank are listed the names of the advisory board. Recognized leaders in the motion picture world, they are J.M. Schenck, chairman; Cecil B. DeMille, vice-chairman; Lou Anger, John E. McCormick, Donald Crisp, Samuel Goldwyn, Sid Grauman, Arthur King, M.C. Level, Charlie Murray, and Norma Talmadge."[53] For the next two decades, Crisp told writers that he worked for the bank in different capacities: as bank director,[54] as a member of the board of directors,[55] and on a loan advisory committee,[56] none of which can be independently confirmed. He isn't mentioned in books about the bank's history, but according to the bank's historian Gerald Nash, "a considerable share of the bank's profits came from its close involvement with the movie industry."[57] So although his stories are possible, given his track record, his involvement was probably less than he claimed. Perhaps acting is all about pretending to be what you're not, and Donald Crisp was a good actor.

Crisp and Murfin divorced in 1944. By all accounts it was an amicable split. She wrote her last produced screenplay, *Dragon Seed*, the year of their divorce, and then became a producer at MGM and did extensive work for charities, including the Motion Picture Relief Fund and the Community Chest.[58] Murfin died at home on August 10, 1955, from heart failure.[59] After her death, Crisp told Hedda Hopper, "We remained good friends to the end. She was the squarest shooter I've ever known."[60]

In 1942, Crisp estimated the number of films he'd appeared in at 135,[61] a number reasonably close to the 148 titles listed for him by 1942 on the Internet Movie Database. However, by 1956 he was telling the *Los Angeles Times* that he was about to make his 375th film[62] and by 1961 it jumped to 427.[63] (Between 1956 and 1961 he was actually in seven films.) The list maintained in his clipping file at the Margaret Herrick Library includes only 210 titles, although that's still a very respectable number. Because so many films are lost, especially the early silent films, it may never be possible to know exactly how many he appeared in.

Undoubtedly to Keaton's great surprise, Crisp turned up for Keaton's episode of *This Is Your Life* in 1957, telling stories about the risks Keaton took in his films, in particular, the house front falling around him in *Steamboat Bill, Jr.* and the day he was almost lost underwater while filming

The Navigator, despite the fact that Crisp wasn't present at either incident.

Crisp continued to act until 1963. His final role was playing a grandfather in *Spencer's Mountain*.

Following a series of strokes in 1972, he moved into a room lined with books and memorabilia at the Motion Picture and Television County Home and Hospital. His final interview, with Al Bine in 1973, found him "courtly, articulate and relevant."[64] He was still going to see new movies and hoping to return to acting.

Donald Crisp died on May 25, 1974, aged 93. The immediate cause was a heart attack, complicated by renal failure and his earlier strokes. He was buried at Forest Lawn in Glendale.[65]

Despite Crisp's decades of telling tall tales, his truthful grand-nephew, John Rayment, stated everything correctly on his death certificate: age, birthplace, parents' names and their birthplaces.[66] It was all there, waiting for the right researcher to come along.

That researcher, Lorna Mitchell, arrived in 1996. That year, a group of Aberfeldy film buffs wanted to honor their native son with a plaque. They asked a librarian in nearby Perth to look into his background.[67] Mitchell ordered a copy of Crisp's death certificate. The discrepancies between it and Crisp's stories led her to continue looking, and she found his birth certificate at Tower Hamlet's library in London. She also discovered that he lied about his war record and schooling. She concluded, "It seems to have been the done thing at the time for people in Hollywood to invent things to make them seem more interesting."[68] Nevertheless, she told a *Scottish Daily Record* reporter in 2001 that "it is nice to think that he chose Aberfeldy, even if there is no actual connection."

To crib from another film by John Ford, who directed Crisp to his Academy Award, does it really matter who shot Liberty Valance? Ford seemed to think so, but he also knew that once the legend was printed, it wasn't going to change. And despite Lorna Mitchell's research into the truth about Crisp's life, the lies Crisp told writers are still in almost everything written about him.

Census Records

1871 England Census, St. Mary Stratford Le Bow, London, England, Page 26, Schedule Number 143, James Crisp household, jpeg image (Online: The Generations Network, Inc., 2007) [Digital scan of original records in the National Archives of the United Kingdom, Kew, Surry, England], subscription database, http://www.ancestry.com, accessed 16 February 2007.

1881 England Census, St. Mary Stratford Bow, London, England, Page 1, Schedule

Number 3, James Crisp household, jpeg image (Online: The Generations Network, Inc., 2007) [Digital scan of original records in the National Archives of the United Kingdom, Kew, Surry, England], subscription database, http://www.ancestry.com, accessed 16 February 2007.

1891 England Census, St. Mary Stratford Bow, London, England, Page 51, Schedule Number 343, James Crisp household, jpeg image (Online: The Generations Network, Inc., 2007) [Digital scan of original records in the National Archives of the United Kingdom, Kew, Surry, England], subscription database, http://www.ancestry.com, accessed 16 February 2007.

1900 U.S. Federal Census (Population Schedule), Ypsilanti Ward 1, Washtenaw, Michigan, ED 110, Sheet 10A, Dwelling 236, Family 269, Frederick Pease household, jpeg image (Online: The Generations Network, Inc., 2010) [Digital scan of original records in the National Archives, Washington, D.C.], subscription database, http://www.ancestry.com, accessed 22 March 2010.

1901 England Census, St. Mary Stratford Bow, London, England, Page 12, Schedule Number 83, James Crisp household, jpeg image (Online: The Generations Network, Inc., 2007) [Digital scan of original records in the National Archives of the United Kingdom, Kew, Surry, England], subscription database, http://www.ancestry.com, accessed 16 February 2007.

1910 U.S. Federal Census (Population Schedule), Detroit Ward 1, Wayne, Michigan, ED 6, Sheet 22B, Dwelling 139, Family 404, Helen Pease household, jpeg image (Online: The Generations Network, Inc., 2010) [Digital scan of original records in the National Archives, Washington, D.C.], subscription database, http://www.ancestry.com, accessed 22 March 2010.

1910 U.S. Federal Census (Population Schedule), Manhattan Ward 16, New York, New York, ED 845, Sheet 9B, Dwelling 66, Family 166, Donald G. Crisp household, jpeg image (Online: The Generations Network, Inc., 2006) [Digital scan of original records in the National Archives, Washington, D.C.], subscription database, http://www.ancestry.com, accessed 14 October 2006.

1920 U.S. Federal Census (Population Schedule), Los Angeles Assembly District 63, Los Angeles, California ED 163, Sheet 7B, Dwelling 163, Family 200, Donald Crisp household, jpeg image (Online: The Generations Network, Inc., 2006) [Digital scan of original records in the National Archives, Washington, D.C.], subscription database, http://www.ancestry.com, accessed 14 October 2006.

1930 U.S. Federal Census (Population Schedule), Los Angeles Assembly District 56, Los Angeles, California, ED 73, Sheet 25A, Dwelling 401, Family 465, Donald Crisp household, jpeg image (Online: The Generations Network, Inc., 2006) [Digital scan of original records in the National Archives, Washington, D.C.], subscription database, http://www.ancestry.com, accessed 14 October 2006.

1940 U.S. Federal Census (Population Schedule), Los Angeles Assembly District 57, Los Angeles, California, ED 60–115, Sheet 6B, Family 1853, Donald Crisp household, jpeg image (Online: FamilySearch Historical Collections, 2012) [Digital scan of original records in the National Archives, Washington, D.C.], https://www.familysearch.org, accessed 14 July 2012.

James Horne

If you were to take Buster Keaton's word for it, James Horne wasn't much of a director. Perhaps for what Keaton needed in a co-director, that was true, but it's far from the whole story.

Kevin Brownlow, who interviewed Buster for his influential book on silent film, *The Parade's Gone By*, reported on Keaton's unflattering reaction to Horne: "Keaton said that *he* did most of the directing. 'James Horne was absolutely useless to me,' he said uncharitably. 'Harry Brand, my business manager, got me to use him. He hadn't done many pictures, and no important ones. Incidentals, quickies. I don't know why we had him, because I practically did *College*.'"[1]

Uncharitable, indeed. While it's understandable why Horne's efficient style might have grated on Keaton (and some of Keaton's annoyance might have been caused by Brand foisting Horne on him), film professor Richard Koszarski called Horne "one of the most important early American serial directors."[2] Horne might not have been a great artist, and he clearly didn't work well with Keaton, but he provided hundreds of hours of entertainment, so he deserves a better epitaph than Keaton's description of him as "useless."

James Wesley Horne was born on December 14, 1881, in San Francisco, California. His father was Charles Wesley Horne and his mother was Edith Woodthorpe Horne, who was part of a theatrical family. Edith's sister Georgia was best known for being the youngest Ophelia to play opposite the greatest American Hamlet of the day, Edwin Booth,[3] and her niece, Georgie Cooper Stevens, ran a traveling stock company with her husband.[4] Charles Horne died when his son was two years old,[5] and then Edith Horne married a newspaper reporter, Alfred T. Dobson.

At age 13, Horne began his acting career as a member of the Belasco-Mayer stock company at the Alcazar Theater in San Francisco, which was part of David Belascos's theatrical empire (Belasco was the most successful theatrical producer of his time).[6] For the next decade or more, he toured the country as an actor with different companies. On September 1, 1909, when he was 27, Horne was a minor member of the opening night cast of the musical romance *The Love Cure* at the New Amsterdam Theater on Broadway; the show ran 78 performances.[7] Between shows he was backstage, employed as a stage and box office manager.[8] He worked as a hotel clerk and tried selling real estate for a bit, too. At the time of the 1900 census, his occupation was listed as "treasurer," and he was living with his parents in San Francisco. By the 1910 census, he had married and was now divorced, living in a boarding house in Oakland, California, and was the treasurer of a theatrical company. Nothing is known about his first wife.

Finally, in 1912, when he was around 30, he got his first film job, as a scenario writer with the Kalem Company,[9] and was sent to the company's Glendale, California, studio. He also performed in front of the camera

Filming *College* (1927). From left to right: unknown, director James Horne, director of photography Dev Jennings, second cameraman Bert Haines, Buster Keaton, unknown script supervisor. (*From the collections of the Margaret Herrick Library, Academy of Motion Picture Arts and Sciences.*)

occasionally, in films like *Cheyenne Massacre* and *On the Brink of Ruin*. After a year with Kalem, he was allowed to direct, and that soon became his career. Before long, he was making serials including *Stingaree* (1915), about a dashing bandit in the Australian outback, and *The Girl Detective* (1915).

That detective was played, in later episodes, by the woman he soon married. Cleo Ridgely was born Freda Cleo Helwig on May 12, 1893, in New York City. Both of her parents died when she was young, so she and her two sisters lived with different family members. She later said she decided to become an actress when she saw her cousin, Victor Moore, work as a comedian on stage.[10] She began at New York's Hippodrome Theater, and then went into film. She worked for Kalem, Lubin and Rex Studios.[11] In 1910, she married Richard Ridgely, a director at Edison.[12] Cleo became famous for a publicity stunt sponsored by *Motion Picture Story Magazine*: She and her then husband rode on horseback across the United

States, stopping along the way to make personal appearances in which she recited poetry and answered questions about her trip and the movie industry.[13] The trip, which began in 1912, took 18 months. In 1914, she went back to work for Kalem, and then separated from Ridgely in March 1915 and divorced him in 1916.[14]

Cleo Ridgely played the Girl Detective for six months, after which she was hired by the Lasky Company.[15] There she made several films with Wallace Reid. Pearl Gaddis of *Motion Picture Classic* described her at the time as a pink and white and gold bon-bon: "[H]er hair is frankly golden, with lots of light and curls, and her eyes are blue ... a warm, sunny blue, frank and smiling as a child."[16] In 1916 she and Horne married, and on March 28, 1917, she gave birth to twins, June and James Jr., following which she retired temporarily from acting. In 1922, she appeared in four films, including a melodrama, *The Forgotten Law*, directed by her husband. Then she retired again, although she occasionally took small parts over the years.

Horne did not fit the stereotype of a "typical," imposing Hollywood director. His draft registration said he was of average height and slender build. When he caught a huge fish in 1919, *Moving Picture World* announced "105 Pounds of Director Lands 125 Pounds of Tuna."[17] The fish reportedly broke all fishing records at Catalina Island, and it took him two hours and 35 minutes to land it. Also unusual for a Hollywood director, he was modest. In 1916, he wrote: "I aim to get the personalities of my players on the screen rather than my own."[18]

Horne continued to make serials for Kalem until 1917, when he left to become a freelance director, directing more serials, including *Bulls Eye* (Universal, 1917, 18 episodes), *Hands Up* (Astra Films, 1918, 15 episodes), and *The Third Eye* (Universal, 1920, 18 episodes). Denver Harmon, later an electrician for Keaton, worked on the latter. In 1920, Buster's good friend Lew Cody gave Horne a chance to direct his first feature, *Occasionally Yours*. Cody starred as a commitment-fearing playboy who loved women, but was frightened of spending a lifetime with just one. Over the next five years, Horne directed 18 features, including several comedies with Douglas Maclean and Richard Talmadge.

After spending a year making comedy shorts for Hal Roach, he went back to being a freelance feature director in 1926.[19] He occasionally crossed paths with Keaton friends and colleagues; for example, his films included a Viola Dana comedy, *Kosher Kitty Kelly*, and *The Cruise of the Jasper B*, featured Snitz Edwards as the villain. With this track record, and possibly because of Horne's connections with Keaton friends Lew Cody and Viola

Dana or his professional association with Snitz Edwards, Keaton's new business manager Harry Brand hired him to direct *College*.

Keaton wasn't pleased with the choice, as he told Kevin Brownlow. Their styles didn't mesh. Horne wrote an article for *Photoplay* magazine in 1916, and he described how he made films: "I believe in system—which is another word for efficiency—in active photography. I have my work laid out from day to day. I have found that everyone works better under a bit of speed pressure than when taking one's time.... Amazing as it may seem, my cameraman, Howard Oswald, has not had a retake in two years."[20] His philosophy was a sensible one for a serial director, under pressure to get each weekly installment done. His ability to work fast and cheap was exactly what Harry Brand thought was needed for Keaton's first film after *The General*, which had turned out to be expensive.

But Keaton worked completely differently. He described his methods to George Pratt in 1958:

> We didn't shoot by no schedule at all. We didn't know when we started whether we was going to have the camera up five weeks or ten weeks. And it didn't make a difference. We owned our own camera. We're not paying rent on anything.... [W]e may lay out a routine in a nice set that we've built for this and we start out in this thing and we find out we're not getting any place. The material is not working out the way we thought it would ... we could feel it. Not only looking at our own rushes, we could feel it also. Now, in a broom closet or something like that, we're liable to find a very good routine. So we shift right then and there.[21]

With Horne's insistence on scheduling, organization and no retakes, and Keaton's more relaxed approach, *College* must have been an unhappy experience for both parties.

Following *College*, Horne made two features starring Jobyna Ralston (Harold Lloyd's frequent co-star), and then he went back to the Roach Studios. He directed many two-reelers featuring Charley Chase, Laurel and Hardy, and Harry Langdon. He even made a brief return to acting in 1931, playing the villainous head of the Riff-Raff tribe in Laurel and Hardy's *Beau Hunks*. In 1932 he moved to Universal, where he made more shorts, including some co-written by his first cousin once removed, former cameraman and soon-to-be major director George Stevens (*The More the Merrier*, *Shane* and *Giant*). Three years later, he again returned to Roach, where he made more Laurel and Hardy shorts, including their last, *Thicker Than Water* (1935), and then directed three of their best features: *Bonnie Scotland* (1935), *The Bohemian Girl* (1936), and *Way Out West* (1937).

After making one more comedy feature, *All Over Town* with Olsen and Johnson in 1937, he went back to his roots: serials. He made 12 serials of 15 episodes each for Columbia, including *Terry and the Pirates* (1940) and *The Iron Claw* (1941). According to *Classic Images* film writer Robert Edwards, his later serials "are marked by the same slapstick sensibility as his comedies, with results so campy they verge on the surreal. They are highly regarded today by fans of the genre."[22]

In May of 1942, James Horne suffered a stroke.[23] A month later, he was hospitalized with a mild cerebral hemorrhage, and then he had a second stroke on June 29, which caused his death at age 60.[24] He was buried at Forest Lawn, Glendale.

Cleo Ridgely Horne survived him by many years, and continued to play small parts in films. She died at home on August 18, 1962, from a coronary occlusion.[25] She was buried next to her husband.

Their twins also tried acting. James Horne, Jr. appeared in about two dozen films, including *Gunga Din* (1939),[26] before serving as a combat photographer in World War II. Then, in the 1950s, he moved to New York and became a top advertising model. His first wife was Ann Fredericks, an aspiring actress whose birth name was Gladys Ann Jelensky,[27] and his second was Francesca Marlowe, the international director of the Barbizon School of Modeling who wrote *Male Modeling: An Inside Look*. He died on December 29, 2008, at age 91, of cancer. June Horne took a few small parts before marrying actor-director Jackie Cooper on December 11, 1944.[28] They had a son, John Anthony Cooper, in 1946, but the couple divorced in 1949.[29] In 1953, she re-married and moved to Florida.[30] She died in Los Angeles, on September 17, 1993.[31]

Further Information

Some sources mistakenly say that actress Victoria Horne was his daughter. However, her parents were Ignatz and Mary Hornstein of New York City, no relation to James Horne.

Census Records

1870 U.S. Federal Census (Population Schedule), San Francisco Ward 10, San Francisco, California, Sheet 2, Dwelling 17, Family 18, James Horne household, jpeg image (Online: The Generations Network, Inc., 2011) [Digital scan of original records in the National Archives, Washington, D.C.], subscription database, http://www.ancestry.com, accessed 4 June 2011.

1880 U.S. Federal Census (Population Schedule), San Francisco, San Francisco, California, ED 213, Sheet 22, Dwelling 151, Family 201, John W. Woodthorpe household, jpeg image (Online: The Generations Network, Inc., 2011) [Digital scan of original records in the National Archives, Washington, D.C.], subscription database, http://www.ancestry.com, accessed 4 June 2011.

1900 U.S. Federal Census (Population Schedule), Manhattan, New York, ED 614, Sheet 1, Dwelling 1, Family 1, Jacob Hirzel household, jpeg image (Online: The

Generations Network, Inc., 2011) [Digital scan of original records in the National Archives, Washington, D.C.], subscription database, http://www.ancestry.com, accessed 25 July 2011.

1900 U.S. Federal Census (Population Schedule), San Francisco Assembly District 43, San Francisco, California, ED 261, Sheet 1, Dwelling 3, Family 3, Alfred T. Dobson household, jpeg image (Online: The Generations Network, Inc., 2006) [Digital scan of original records in the National Archives, Washington, D.C.], subscription database, http://www.ancestry.com, accessed 14 October 2006.

1910 U.S. Federal Census (Population Schedule), Scranton, Lackawanna, Pennsylvania, ED 0088, Sheet 4A, Dwelling 57, Family 69, Cleon Schultz household, jpeg image (Online: The Generations Network, Inc., 2011) [Digital scan of original records in the National Archives, Washington, D.C.], subscription database, http://www.ancestry.com, accessed 25 July 2011.

1910 U.S. Federal Census (Population Schedule), Oakland Ward 7, Alameda, California, ED 150, Sheet 16A, Dwelling 252, Family 308, Lottie A. Weir household, jpeg image (Online: The Generations Network, Inc., 2006) [Digital scan of original records in the National Archives, Washington, D.C.], subscription database, http://www.ancestry.com, accessed 13 September 2006.

1920 U.S. Federal Census (Population Schedule), Burbank Township, Los Angeles, California, ED 17, Sheet 3B, Dwelling 83, Family 84, James W. Horne household, jpeg image (Online: The Generations Network, Inc., 2007) [Digital scan of original records in the National Archives, Washington, D.C.], subscription database, http://www.ancestry.com, accessed 8 August 2007.

1930 U.S. Federal Census (Population Schedule), Glendale Township, Los Angeles, California, ED 964, Sheet 6, Dwelling 137, Family 138, James W. Horne household, jpeg image (Online: The Generations Network, Inc., 2006) [Digital scan of original records in the National Archives, Washington, D.C.], subscription database, http://www.ancestry.com, accessed 14 October 2006.

1940 U.S. Federal Census (Population Schedule), Glendale Township, Los Angeles, California, ED 19–192, Sheet 10A, Family 207, James W. Horne household, jpeg image (Online: FamilySearch Historical Collections, 2012) [Digital scan of original records in the National Archives, Washington, D.C.], https://www.familysearch.org, accessed 14 July 2012.

Horne, James Wesley. *World War I Draft Registration Cards, 1917–1918* (16 September 1918) (Online: The Generations Network, Inc., 2006) [Digital scan of original records in the National Archives, Washington, D.C.], subscription database, http://www.ancestry.com, accessed 14 October 2006.

Horne, James Wesley. *World War II Draft Registration Cards, 1942* (Online: FamilySearch Historical Collections, 2011) [Digital scan of original records in the National Archives, Washington, D.C.], https://www.familysearch.org, accessed 19 January 2012.

Charles Riesner

Although he co-directed just one Keaton film, *Steamboat Bill, Jr.*, Charles Riesner was a busy guy. He didn't just produce, write and direct films, he also acted in and directed theater, started various businesses, and wrote songs and books. He was the only co-director to bring his own project to Keaton instead of being hired to direct one that was already planned. As his son wrote, "My old man was a hustler—always on the move."[1]

Charles Francis Riesner was born on March 14, 1887, in Minneapolis, Minnesota. His father, Johannes N.F. Riesner, had been a poet and a comedian in his native Hungary, but after the family moved to the United States in the mid–1880s he changed his name to John and earned his living as a machinist in a garage.[2] His mother, the former Anna Costello, had been a singer.[3] Riesner, the eldest boy, had four sisters and two brothers: Lena (1879), Anna (1889), George (1890), Rudolph (1894), Hattie (1898) and Frances (1902).

He began his show business career in 1899, when he was 12, selling sheet music to the audience at the Bijou Theater in Minneapolis.[4] Next he worked as a stagehand before becoming a prizefighter—he gave exhibitions of fancy bag punching in the Twin Cities[5]—which became his first vaudeville act. He married another vaudevillian, Henrietta Gores, who performed in a roller-skating act, on June 5, 1908.[6] After their marriage, the couple toured the country.

By 1910, the rest of the Riesner family had moved to San Francisco, where his father found work as a café manager. In the meantime, Charles and his wife became musical comics, writing and performing in a skit about stage life called "It's Only a Show," which they toured on the Orpheum circuit. The *Salt Lake Tribune* called them "light-footed, fun-making singers … Riesner portrays the inexperienced actor. He also 'shows some steps' which must be seen to be appreciated."[7] The *San Antonio Light* called it "the laughing and applause hit of the show."[8] Both the act and the marriage split up in 1915.

Later that year he was hired for his first "legitimate" show, the touring company of Irving Berlin's *Stop! Look! Listen!*,[9] in which he played Abel Conner, a press agent. Also in the cast was a 20-year-old dancer, Miriam Hope, whom he married on October 30, 1917.[10] Her real name was Miriam Hegarty, and before she joined the touring company she lived in Brooklyn with her mother Clara and two older sisters, Clara and Regina. Her father John had been a lithographer and an artist and was no longer living with the family.

Riesner made his film debut in 1916, playing small parts in Keystone/Triangle shorts, including *His First False Step* with Chester Conklin and *His Lying Heart* with Ford Sterling, and he also worked in the writing department. According to authors Kalton Lahue and Terry Brewer in *Kops and Custards*, "Riesner soon became the fair-haired boy in the script department. He would spend his free time in the five-and-ten-cent stores looking for gag ideas, asking himself what could be done with the various items he found. Once he had a gag worked out, it was filed in a special cabinet under its proper heading—as kitchen gag, garage gag, lawn gag, party gag, etc. The list went on for pages, and Chuck guarded his file with extreme caution against forays by other writers anxious to make an impression on Sennett."[11]

Although Riesner was in the movies, he didn't quit vaudeville. When he registered for the draft in 1917, his employer was listed as the Western Vaudeville Circuit and he had no fixed residence.[12] He didn't serve in the Army, although he did tour the country on a recruiting drive. During that trip, he co-wrote the hit song "Goodbye Broadway, Hello France" with Benny Davis and Billy Bakette.[13] He also co-wrote other songs that weren't nearly as popular, including "My Irish America Rose" with Bryan Foy and "Pick a Four Leaf Clover (and Send It Over to Me)" with Abe Olman.[14] Around the same time, he toured vaudeville with heavyweight fighter Jack Dempsey; Riesner told jokes and dancers performed in the first act, and Dempsey took on all comers in the second.

In 1918, Riesner was back in the movies, hired as an assistant director for several of Charlie Chaplin's best mid-career films for First National, including *A Dog's Life* and *Pay Day*. He also acted in them, usually playing the villain, and he was proud of being an effective bad guy. His best-remembered "heavy" role was as the bully in *The Kid*. He later told the *L.A. Times* that he gauged his ability by the number of letters he didn't receive: "If a villain is liked and gets fan letters and requests for photographs he is slipping in public esteem. Heavies are supposed to be very unpopular if their work is good. It would break my heart if I received a fan letter."[15]

At the same time, Darryl F. Zanuck was unhappily employed, very briefly, as a writer by Chaplin, and he painted an unflattering portrait of the boss: "We would sit around working up gags among ourselves. Riesner's job was to invent gags but not reveal them to Chaplin. He would place all the props, [and] then let Chaplin 'discover' the gag. We'd sit in the background, holding our breath, waiting for him to fall on it. If you made a suggestion—you're dead! He would always find the gag and damn near on every occasion he would bawl the hell out of us for not discovering it."[16] Zanuck only stayed for two weeks.

Chaplin worked slowly, so Riesner had plenty of time off between pictures to work on other projects. In 1919, he even co-wrote a bathing girl scenario with Bryan Foy for a Chaplin imitator, Billy West.[17] He also directed comedy shorts for Century Film, the Vitagraph Company of America and Universal Studios from 1920 to 1923.[18] Several starred Brownie the Dog.

In 1918, he and his wife had a son, Dean Franklin, who soon acquired the nickname Dinky. Riesner told the *L.A. Times* how he encouraged his son's artistic tendencies in utero: "[B]elieving the mother to wield the greatest prenatal influence, I set about to induce a mental condition that would cause my wife to exert a subconscious influence over Dinky before birth.... At night I would compose songs and write plays. These I would send to my wife for correction. Many times I would purposely make mistakes so she could detect them."[19] Miriam Riesner's opinion was not recorded. Dean would be an only child.

In 1923, little Dean landed a part in Chaplin's *The Pilgrim*. He later told the story in the documentary *Unknown Chaplin*: "They needed a kid and they said, 'Who has a kid?' They needed a brat."[20] Chaplin helped him overcome his initial reluctance to slap Uncle Charlie by telling him he enjoyed being hit, and Dean played the part with gusto. With this success, his father decided to form Dinky Dean Productions with Lew Lipton (who later wrote for Keaton) as the manager.[21] They planned to produce four films per year for four years[22] but actually made only one comedy, *A Prince of a King* (aka *Gigi*). Dinky's mother put an end to his career on screen so he could have a more normal childhood.[23]

Riesner went back to work at Chaplin's studio as the assistant director for the *Gold Rush* scenes shot in Los Angeles. Then he was hired by Warner Bros. to direct Chaplin's half-brother Syd Chaplin's films like *Oh What a Nurse!* and *The Better 'Ole*. In 1927, Syd stopped making films at that studio, so Riesner became a freelance director.[24]

Riesner pitched to Keaton the opening for *Steamboat Bill, Jr.* in which the rugged steamboat captain meets his beret-wearing, ukulele-toting Eastern son for the first time. Keaton wrote "[T]his was as much as Chuck Riesner needed to tell me about the story for me to buy it."[25] Keaton also hired him to co-direct.

Riesner later wrote about a conflict on the set between himself and the producer (probably Harry Brand): He insisted that Keaton's new work clothes needed to be perfectly tailored, "an outfit befitting a captain's son, as swanky as anything that ever graced the bridge of the *Queen Mary*."[26] The producer worried that it wasn't comical enough because it wasn't eccentric or exaggerated. However, since they would have lost half a day's shooting if they waited for a comedy uniform to be made, they shot it with what they had. Riesner said, "When the picture was completed and playing to packed theaters, I won my argument." He pointed out that the comedy was in the contrast between the neat uniform and the roughneck father and weather-beaten boat.

Dean Riesner told one story from the film's making in the documentary *A Hard Act to Follow*, about the famous scene in which the two-ton front of a building crashed down around Keaton, a second-story window being the only thing that saved him from certain doom: "If Buster were six inches out of position, it would have driven him into the ground like a little tent peg. My father, who was a very religious man—he had a lot of different religions—but at this time he was a Christian Scientist. He had a practitioner with him, and they were praying all day, and he couldn't bear to see it."[27] Keaton told his biographer Rudi Blesh that Riesner stayed in his tent while they were filming that scene.[28] The younger Riesner called it "one of the most spectacular stunts ever done."

Riesner shot two different endings for the film. Blesh gave Keaton's side of the argument:

> Director Reisner [sic] had the same brilliant idea that, sooner or later, seized every expert. "Buster," he said, "I want you smiling as you swim into the camera with the minister."
> "Oh no you don't," said Buster.
> Riesner would not give up. "It's a natural gag," he maintained.
> "All right," Buster finally said. "But we'll shoot it both ways, then preview with the smile."
> The audience took offense. It was worse than Cal Coolidge smiling and no more believable. A groan of disappointment rose in the theatre.
> "Even the ash can groaned when we dumped it there," says Buster of the offending scene.[29]

Nevertheless, when Brownlow asked him how he rated Riesner as a comedy director, Keaton said, "He was a good one."[30] After *Steamboat Bill, Jr.*, Keaton's contract was bought by MGM, and he lost control over his stories and co-director.

Riesner directed two more pictures as a freelance director, *Fools for Luck* with W.C. Fields at Paramount and *Noisy Neighbors* for Paul Bern Productions. Then he was hired by MGM in 1928. One of his earliest films there was *The Hollywood Revue of 1929*, and one its high points was Keaton's Princess Rajah dance number. It was based on a routine Keaton had done while in the Army in World War I, but originated on film with Arbuckle in *The Cook*, the final film Keaton made with Arbuckle before leaving for his stint in the Army.

In 1931, Riesner and his wife bought a mansion in Laguna Beach. Because a murder-suicide had taken place at the home (former Broadway musical comedy star Adele Ritchie shot and killed a social rival, Doris Murray Palmer, then shot herself[31]), they paid only $7,500—$5,000 less than its appraised value.[32] They remodeled it into a showplace[33] and joined the artistic community there, taking part in groups like the Beloved Vagabonds and the Laguna Community Players.[34] Riesner enjoyed giving speeches; at the Community Presbyterian Church, he spoke on "Laguna Beach—Where Nature's God Hath Wrought."[35] People tried to convince him to run for sheriff, but he refused.[36]

In 1931, although still in the movie business, he opened a sporting goods store[37] on Wilshire Boulevard in Los Angeles, and his signature was over the entrance. His brother-in-law Ernie Mason managed it for him, and his brother George was the sales manager.[38] It wasn't the best time to start a business, with the Depression at its height, and the store appears to have been in business for only about a year.

A man of varied talents, he also wrote the children's book *Little Inch High People*, which was published in 1938.[39] The *L.A. Times* reported that Disney and MGM negotiated for the rights, but no film ever got made. In addition, he contributed a chapter, "Getting People to Laugh is Serious Business," for Ira Price's *A Hundred Million Movie-Goers Must Be Right*.[40] In it, he tried to explain how to make comedy funny, and succeeded about as well as anybody else has. In 1941, he told gossip columnist and former actress Hedda Hopper that he was writing an autobiography to be called either *Between Salaries* or *Short Thoughts from a Long, Long Memory*, but nothing came of it.[41]

He stayed at MGM until 1935, directing stars Marie Dressler, Polly Moran, Jackie Cooper, Guy Kibbee et al. Then he spent eight months in England, where he made *Everybody Dance* for Gaumont British.[42] After his return, he continued as a freelancer, making films at Paramount and Republic. In 1941 he returned to MGM, where his films included *The Big Store* with the Marx Brothers and *Lost in a Harem* with Abbott and Costello. After that, he went to work for Bryan Foy at Eagle-Lion Films as a producer-director for a few years.[43] Riesner would direct one more film as a freelancer, *The Traveling Saleslady*. In 1950 he had a heart attack and decided to retire, although he continued to work in film promotion, co-founding a company called Hollywood Starmakers.[44]

Miriam Riesner died on March 1, 1947, following a heart attack at home.[45] Riesner married twice more, to Emille Russell (an old friend from Minneapolis)[46] and Irene Ganzer Jeub.[47] He died on September 24, 1962, also from a heart attack.[48]

His son Dean became a successful screenwriter, beginning his career under contract to Warner Bros. in 1939.[49] The younger Riesner was best known for his work with Clint Eastwood; he wrote *Play Misty for Me* and *Dirty Harry* (he was responsible for contributing one of Eastwood's most famous lines: "Do you feel lucky? Well, do you, punk?"), but he wrote a variety of scripts from *The Helen Morgan Story* (1957) to *Starman* (1984). His television work included episodes of *The Outer Limits* and *Rawhide* as well as the mini-series *Rich Man, Poor Man*. He later became a script doctor on projects such as *The Godfather III* and *Blue Thunder*. In 1953, he accompanied his then-wife Maila Nurmi to a costume ball, where she wore a dress inspired by Morticia of Charles Addams' cartoons. She won the costume contest, and when an ABC television executive asked her to host a horror film show, Riesner gave her a stage name: Vampira. After they divorced, he married Marie Moorehouse (who, as a baby in 1920, had appeared in a movie, *The Old Nest*). He died on August 30, 2002.[50]

Further Information

In some articles and even film credits his name was spelled Reisner, but when he signed his draft registrations, he wrote Riesner.

Census Records

1900 U.S. Federal Census (Population Schedule), Brooklyn Ward 28, Kings County, New York, ED 521, Sheet 4, Dwelling 45, Family 90, John Heggerty household, jpeg image (Online: The Generations Network, Inc., 2011) [Digital scan of original records in the National Archives, Washington, D.C.], subscription database, http://www.ancestry.com, accessed 2 September 2011.

1900 U.S. Federal Census (Population Schedule), Minneapolis Ward 3, Hennepin County, Minnesota, ED 52, Sheet 7, Dwelling 241, Family 338, John Riesner household, jpeg image (Online: The Generations Network, Inc., 2006) [Digital scan of original records in the National Archives, Washington, D.C.], subscription database, http://www.ancestry.com, accessed 14 October 2006.

1910 U.S. Federal Census (Population Schedule), Brooklyn Ward 28, Kings County, New York, ED 0889, Sheet 8A, Dwelling 87, Family 199, Clara J. Hegarty household, jpeg image (Online: The Generations Network, Inc., 2007) [Digital scan of original records in the National Archives, Washington, D.C.], subscription database, http://www.ancestry.com, accessed 9 May 2007.

1910 U.S. Federal Census (Population Schedule), San Francisco Assembly District 33, San Francisco, California, ED 72, Sheet 9A, Dwelling 200, Family 200, John Riesner household, jpeg image (Online: The Generations Network, Inc., 2006) [Digital scan of original records in the National Archives, Washington, D.C.], subscription database, http://www.ancestry.com, accessed 14 October 2006.

1920 U.S. Federal Census (Population Schedule), Los Angeles Assembly District 63, Los Angeles, California ED 167, Sheet 12A, Dwelling 5, Family 15, Charles F. Riesner household, jpeg image (Online: The Generations Network, Inc., 2006) [Digital scan of original records in the National Archives, Washington, D.C.], subscription database, http://www.ancestry.com, accessed 14 October 2006.

1930 U.S. Federal Census (Population Schedule), Beverly Hills, Los Angeles, California, ED 825, Sheet 16A, Dwelling 366, Family 427, Charles F. Riesner household, jpeg image (Online: The Generations Network, Inc., 2006) [Digital scan of original records in the National Archives, Washington, D.C.], subscription database, http://www.ancestry.com, accessed 14 October 2006.

1940 U.S. Federal Census (Population Schedule), Los Angeles Assembly District 57, Los Angeles, California, ED 60–137, Sheet 3B, Family 96, Charles Riesner household, jpeg image (Online: FamilySearch Historical Collections, 2012) [Digital scan of original records in the National Archives, Washington, D.C.], https://www.familysearch.org, accessed 14 July 2012.

1940 U.S. Federal Census (Population Schedule), Laguna Beach, Orange, California, ED 30–50D, Sheet 61B, Family 545, Miriam Riesner household, jpeg image (Online: FamilySearch Historical Collections, 2012) [Digital scan of original records in the National Archives, Washington, D.C.], https://www.familysearch.org, accessed 14 July 2012.

Malcolm St. Clair

> St. Clair's silent films ... fizzed and his sound films fizzled. It was as simple and as tragic as that.
> —Andrew Sarris[1]

Mal St. Clair is the only Keaton co-director to get much respect from film critics and historians. In 1927 and 1928, he was named one of the top ten directors in a national poll of film writers, along with King Vidor, Erich von Stroheim and Victor Sjöström.[2] William Everson called him the American Lubitsch, with the same joy, charm, and elegance.[3] He even made it into film critic Andrew Sarris' influential book *American Cinema: Directors and Directions 1929–1968*. He was the only member of Keaton's crew to have a biography written about him, *Malcolm St. Clair: His Films, 1915–1948*, published in 1996.

His time with Keaton helped make him the director he was. Although he made only two shorts with Keaton, *The Goat* and *The Blacksmith*, his biographer Ruth Anne Dwyer suggests that being part of the Keaton circle "proved to be a most important inspiration to the future work of St. Clair. Literally, St. Clair's work can be divided into 'pre' Keaton and 'post' Keaton, so profound an effect had Buster."[4]

But like Keaton, he didn't act like a self-important genius. "Found! The Most Modest Man of Movies" was the *Los Angeles Times*' title for a 1929 interview with him.[5] Dwyer summed up her impressions from the many interviews she did: "St. Clair had the wonderful ability to laugh at himself, and did so frequently, a quality which charmed his many friends. Literally everyone to whom I spoke thought he was wonderful, full of life, and radiated energy. More than one person reported that working with him was exhilarating, that the atmosphere on his sets was always great fun, marked with high good humor."[6] This could almost be describing Keaton. Like Keaton's films, St. Clair's films suffered with the coming of sound.

Malcolm Oswald St. Clair was born on May 17, 1897, in Los Angeles, California. He had two older brothers, Aubrey (born 1890) and Bernard (born 1894), as well as a younger brother, Eric (born 1902). Their parents Norman and Ann Elizabeth (née Fleetwood) were from England, and Norman was a famous architect and artist. He died of tuberculosis when St. Clair was only 14.[7]

His father had wanted him to become an architect (older brother Aubrey did so), but Mal wanted to work for a newspaper.[8] After he graduated from high school, he went to work for the *Los Angeles Express*.[9] He started as an office boy, about which he said, "There isn't any lower form of life than being a newspaper office boy. It was terrible."[10] Sports editor Harry Carr let him draw caricatures for the sports pages. One of the other cartoonists, Lige Conley (aka Lige Crommie), went to work as one of Mack Sennett's Keystone Cops, and he introduced St. Clair to Sennett as a gag writer in August of 1915.[11] Sennett quickly figured out that he wasn't a very good gag writer, but his impressive height (6'3") and lanky figure would make him a fine Cop, and so for the next seven months, he fought crime onscreen. (See the Eddie Cline entry for a description of the Cops.)

In 1916, he got promoted to the regular acting company where his first part was as a butler in *His Last Laugh*. He made several comedy shorts, and the *Los Angeles Times* called him "one of the best comedians on the Triangle-Keystone lot."[12] The paper printed this story:

> When St. Clair first went to work for Triangle-Keystone, which was his initial attempt in pictures, he was so sure that he wouldn't make good that he had some cards printed which read: "Malcolm St. Clair, formerly with the Triangle-Keystone Company." The popular funster has never had an opportunity to use them thus far, and chances are very good that he never will. He has made good in spite of himself.

He went back to gag writing in 1917 while acting in *Lost: A Cook*; he made so many suggestions that the director, F. Richard Jones, stormed off of the set to complain to Sennett. Sennett looked at St. Clair's sketches and switched him to the scenario department,[13] where he worked for 18 months, with a brief interruption in April and May of 1918 when he appeared in two Hal Roach comedies.

Despite being the right age, St. Clair never served in World War I, later telling an interviewer that the Army rejected him because he was 40 pounds underweight.[14] (Adolphe Menjou once said that St. Clair was "as thin as Theda Bara's nightgown."[15]) But his draft registration tells a different story, stating that he was supporting a dependent (probably his mother), so he wasn't called up.[16] As Allene Talmey wrote about him in 1927 for a book of celebrity profiles, "he is a glorious faker. Most of his stories, starting conservatively from true events, tack to fiction.... All this talent for invention makes him an impossible witness, but a fine director."[17]

St. Clair's next step was to become a co-director in 1919. Collaborating with William H. Watson, Bert Roach and Erle C. Kenton, he made two films with Teddy the Dog and one with Ben Turpin. Then he was ready to go solo.

His solo directing career at Sennett lasted from 1919 to 1921, but it was rocky; as he put it, "I was hired and fired, two fires to every hire."[18] During the "hired" times, he made several two-reelers, including *Don't Weaken*, about a nouveau riche family, and *Bright Eyes*, which had no intertitles in the second reel and such sophisticated gags that it got him fired for good. During the "fired" times, he made comedy shorts at other studios, including Rainbow, Reelcraft, Fox, FBO and, of course, Keaton.

St. Clair was introduced to Keaton by Virginia Fox, the former Sennett Bathing Beauty who co-starred in many of Buster's shorts.[19] She knew that Keaton was looking for a new co-director, and she told him that St. Clair was talented and available. He got the job. To thank her, St. Clair and his fiancée Cordelia Andrews treated her to an evening at the Coconut Grove. Because Fox didn't have a boyfriend at the time, St. Clair brought along a friend of his: Darryl Zanuck, whom Fox would marry in 1924.

As Grace Kingsley of the *Los Angeles Times* wrote, "the shade of the Ambassador Coconut Grove is responsible for a lot of engagements these days."[20] Another one was St. Clair's; mutual friends had introduced him to Andrews there. Cordelia Gould Andrews was a society girl originally from Vermont, but her family spent part of the year in Pasadena. Her father's occupation on the census was "own income" and her mother was from an old New England family. Cordelia married St. Clair in early July 1921.

There's no record of why Keaton wanted another director. According to the announcement in the trade paper *Motion Picture World*, "St. Clair will alternate with Eddie Cline in sharing directorial honors with the 'frozen-faced' laugh maker. The trio will collaborate in the preparing of stories."[21] Plainly there were no hard feelings, because Cline acted as a cop in St. Clair's first film for Keaton *The Goat*. St. Clair also had a role himself, appearing as Dead Shot Dan, the criminal for whom Keaton is mistaken.

St. Clair and Cline had history together: In addition to both of them surviving working for Sennett, St. Clair had appeared in one of Cline's earliest films as a director, *His Bread and Butter*, in 1916. While at Keystone, he had learned how to construct gags and how to keep the action moving. Despite the press beforehand, St. Clair made only two films with Keaton, very different from each other. Author Jim Kline called *The Goat* "one of his most thoroughly enjoyable short masterpieces"[22] and *The Blacksmith* "his least inspired short film."[23] In a way, it's surprising that *The Blacksmith* was the latter film, because it's a throwback to the sort of disjointed films Keaton made earlier with Arbuckle.

Despite the fact that he only made two films for Keaton, working with Buster changed the way St. Clair thought about comedy. Before, his films were a collection of fast gags loosely connected to a slight plot. After, they were structured around a central problem as in *The Goat*, in which Keaton must prove he isn't a murderer.[24] Even if they were funny, he began to cut out extraneous gags, and he also started making films about average people, not comic exaggerations. The pacing of his films changed as well, building from simple gags to more complex ones. But there remained one major difference between the two filmmakers: St. Clair's female characters were more than props. They had ambitions and adventures of their own, where many of Keaton's female characters were simple plot devices.

Between making *The Goat* and *The Blacksmith*, St. Clair and Zanuck developed for the Film Booking Office (FBO) studio a two-reel serial about boxing, *The Leather Pushers*. Starring a newcomer, Reginald Denny, it wasn't a cliffhanger serial like *The Perils of Pauline*; instead, it was similar to modern television sitcoms with the same characters and situations appearing in each episode, but with each story being self-contained. Universal soon took over the project, and Universal head Carl Laemmle fired them after they asked for a raise. To add insult to injury, Laemmle's son's dog bit Zanuck on the way out.[25] St. Clair later said that this was the inspiration for their Rin-Tin-Tin scripts, so it turned out not to be a total loss.

After he left Sennett's revolving door for good, St. Clair moved on to Robertson-Cole Pictures, where he made six shorts with Carter and Flora Parker DeHaven. These were polite family comedies about a well-off young married couple. Then he and FBO took another chance on a boxing serial, *Fighting Blood*. According to *Variety*, this serial was so popular that its installments were billed above the feature film.[26] FBO signed him up for another serial that was due to begin shooting in six weeks.

Warner Bros. hired St. Clair to spend the waiting time shooting his first feature, *George Washington, Jr.*, based on a popular George M. Cohan musical comedy. Then he and Zanuck went back to FBO to shoot seven episodes of *The Telephone Girl*, which concerned Gladys Murgatroyd, a telephone operator at a New York hotel. Zanuck wrote the scenarios. Dwyer described them: "Gladys meets her adversities and life's difficulties with determination and wit, and inevitably solves problems with a clever ploy."[27] Assistant director Pandro Berman said it was the best job he ever had, even with low salaries and an 18-hour work day.[28] (Berman went on to head FBO after it became RKO, and produced, among other films, the Fred Astaire–Ginger Rogers musicals.)

The box office results for *George Washington, Jr.* were good enough for Warner Bros. to give St. Clair a two-picture contract. Canine star Rin-Tin-Tin was also under contract to Warners. St. Clair had seen his first film and thought it was terrible, but Rinty was terrific. He and Zanuck got an appointment with the studio heads, brothers Harry and Jack Warner, and pitched their ideas, with St. Clair going down on all fours to act out the dog's part.[29] They got approval that very day, a Friday, and were in the studio the following Monday shooting *Find Your Man*. Rinty saved his lumberjack master from drowning, freezing, attacks by polar bears and wolves, ambushes, and forest fires—all in 70 minutes. The film made money, so the three—St. Clair, Zanuck and the dog—were re-teamed for *The Lighthouse by the Sea*, a melodrama about a blind lighthouse keeper; rum-runners intend to beat him but he is saved by his beautiful daughter and Rinty. When it also did well, St. Clair was allowed to make a crime-romance called *On Thin Ice*. Unfortunately, the studio hated it and fired him.[30]

Next he made a society comedy called *After Business Hours* for Columbia, then a Poverty Row–level studio. The film got good notices and inspired Paramount to hire him to make more of the same. During the next four years at Paramount, St. Clair would do the best work of his career.

"Pictures of light love and lighter laughter, sparkling with charm and fresh imagination, and blessed with a surcease of bunk and blah" is how *Photoplay* summed up his work in 1926.[31] Paramount gave him access to film stars, much more generous budgets, and the freedom to select material, cast, costumes, sets and technical staff. He used this freedom to make films in which "real life could never look so good," as his biographer said.[32] Added to that was his notion "that there is a new type of sex abroad today. Sex with a sense of humor."[33]

His first film there was *Are Parents People?* starring Adolphe Menjou and Florence Vidor as a couple on the verge of divorce. Their daughter (Betty Bronson) reunites them by flirting disgracefully with men and giving them something to worry about together. Film historian William K. Everson was a fan, writing that it "managed to be charming, wistful, and even joyous while dealing with the serious subject of divorce.... We are almost a reel into the film before the first subtitle appears, yet the film has told us all we need to know about the relationship between the married couple and why it was deteriorating, and told us via images and editing. Later on, the decisions of the teen-aged daughter are conveyed by close-ups of her shoulders straightening or her ankles crossing, uncrossing, and setting themselves determinedly as the decision is made.... When, after a wholly innocent night together, teen-aged daughter and prospective boyfriend are interrogated by the worried parents, the situation, the question, and the response are carried without either a title or a close-up—merely daughter and boyfriend successively shaking their heads vigorously in response to an anxious parental inquiry."[34] This kind of non-verbal storytelling wouldn't be possible once talkies came in, and even less so once Hollywood's Production Code began to be enforced in 1934.

St. Clair made 12 more films at Paramount. *The Grand Duchess and the Waiter* is often considered his best. Florence Vidor played an impoverished duchess living beyond her means at a hotel, while Menjou played a rich man who disguises himself as a waiter to meet her. The scenarist, Pierre Collins, called it "seven reels of seduction between two charming persons."[35] It was listed in *Film Daily's* Honor Roll for 1926, topping *Battleship Potemkin*, *Lady Windermere's Fan* and *Tramp, Tramp, Tramp*.[36]

But St. Clair didn't limit himself to stories about the rich. Some critics preferred *The Show Off*, because it's an unsentimental comedy about ambitious working-class people. Ford Sterling played the title role, a man whose continuous boasting gets him into trouble. Louise Brooks was the girl next door; she and St. Clair made two more films together.

Brooks was partly responsible for the low regard that St. Clair's films later fell into. In her many late-in-life interviews with film historians, she said things like, "I felt that Mal was a terrible director, although I thought he was a charming man, a lovely man. In those days, anyone could become a director ... Mal came from the mugging school of Sennett and he did everything by making faces."[37] Both Brooks' biographer Barry Paris and Dwyer theorize that she was still angry that St. Clair didn't give her the part of Dorothy in *Gentlemen Prefer Blondes* (1928). In St. Clair's defense, author Anita Loos saw Brooks' screen test and said, "Louise, if I ever write a part for a cigar store Indian, you will get it."[38] However, to put Brooks' criticism of St. Clair in context, she had terrible things to say about all of her directors except for G.W. Pabst. James Cruze was "the strangest man I ever met"[39]; Howard Hawks was "nice and unobtrusive ... he didn't do anything at all,"[40] and Eddie Sutherland "didn't know anything about directing, acting, cutting, or camera angles."[41] The fact that she had once been married to Sutherland might explain her comments about him. She did have a lot of good things to say about Buster Keaton.

Then sound came and spoiled the party. St. Clair avoided making a sound film for as long as he could. Paramount loaned him to Harold Lloyd to replace the ill Ted Wilde on the silent version of *Welcome Danger*, but he didn't stick around for the sound re-shoots. (Another Keaton alum, Clyde Bruckman, directed them.) Around that time, St. Clair did an interview with the *L.A. Times* and is quoted as saying, "I am wondering how much of their fire and spontaneity of players like Clara Bow will lose, when they are compelled to slow up and speak lines. A great deal, I am inclined to believe."[42] He also made the silent version of *The Canary Murder Case* but left the sound version to Frank Tuttle. Dwyer thinks that he hated dealing with sound because it interfered with telling a story visually.[43] The microphones forced the actors to stay in one spot, and they couldn't improvise. In addition, he couldn't talk to them during the scene, he could no longer edit his films himself; and in comedy, timing and editing is everything. *Films in Review* later quoted him as saying, "It is as important to have a picture move as it is to have it talk ... I do not think the practice of putting dialogue before all else is wise or effective."[44]

Finally in September of 1929, he bit the bullet and made a sound film for RKO: *Side Street*, a gangster melodrama with Owen, Tom and Matt Moore as brothers—a policeman, a surgeon and a bootlegger. The *New York Times* thought it was "highly entertaining" and "thoroughly realistic," despite some overdone brogue dialogue.[45]

After five more talkies for four different studios, St. Clair and his wife took an 18-month European vacation. Grace Kingsley reported that "while abroad, St. Clair did not altogether idle his time away. He made hay while the sun shone while in Nice by collaborating with Rex Ingram and Benavente, noted Spanish playwright, on the writing of an original story for the screen."[46] He returned to Hollywood in 1931.[47] His comedies *Olsen's Night Out* and *Goldie Gets Along* got good reviews, but despite that he left the business again and went to Mexico to paint pictures for two and a half years.[48] It wasn't just sound technology that soured him on Los Angeles; his marriage also ended in 1934. The *L.A. Times* said "it came as no surprise."[49] Cordelia St. Clair stayed in Los Angeles. She died on June 12, 1981.[50]

When he came back in late 1935, old friend Darryl Zanuck, now the head of 20th Century–Fox, gave him a job in the studio's B-picture unit. His work there included the Jones Family films, a series about the adventures of a likable middle-aged couple and their three children. Buster Keaton co-wrote the scripts of *The Jones Family in Hollywood* and *Quick Millions.*

St. Clair again reunited with Keaton when he directed the two silent sequences of *Hollywood Cavalcade* in 1939. In the first Keaton "invents" custard pie–throwing and in the second, he takes the female lead (Alice Faye) for a wild motorcycle ride, recycling gags from his silent films (particularly *Sherlock Jr.*)—but instead of doing them for real, he and Faye were filmed in front of a rear-projection scene. Jim Kline wrote that "none of the recreated gags match the effectiveness of the originals" but "one of the joys of *Hollywood Cavalcade* is seeing Buster in glorious Technicolor"[51]—it was Keaton's first color film.

St. Clair remarried on February 6, 1937.[52] The bride was Margaret Murray Holt, who came from a rich family; her father invented the sliding service ladder for stores, patented in 1893.[53] (Roscoe Arbuckle had made good use of one in Keaton's first film, *The Butcher Boy*.) It was her second marriage, too. They lived in Pasadena.

After the last Jones family movie in 1940, Zanuck fired St. Clair and he went to third-rate Republic to make the first Higgins Family film, which started another successful series. He was then hired by RKO to make *The Bashful Bachelor* with the radio comedy team of Lum and Abner. It was successful enough to get Zanuck to rehire him.

St. Clair's work during that stint at 20th Century–Fox included four Laurel and Hardy pictures. Laurel and Hardy biographer Simon Louvish wrote, "Both Stan and Babe got on with him very well, and were delighted to work, after so much disappointment, with a craftsman who appeared to be on their wavelength. The result was *Jitterbugs*, probably the best, among a bad bunch, of the post–Hal Roach features."[54] However, Louvish said that another one of St. Clair's efforts, *The Big Noise*, "has long been considered by the fans as the worst Laurel and Hardy film ever."[55] St. Clair stayed at Fox until 1948, when the B-film unit was phased out.

St. Clair and Keaton crossed paths again when he was set to direct some of Keaton's local Los Angeles television shows, but he was diagnosed with colon cancer in 1950,[56] and died two years later, on June 1, 1952, at age 54. He was cremated and buried at the Mountain View Mausoleum in Altadena, California. Two of his brothers survived him: Aubrey was an architect in Laguna Beach and Eric, after a try at film acting, became a painter in San Juan Capistrano.[57] Margaret St. Clair lived on for many years. She died in October 1988.[58]

Census Records

1900 U.S. Federal Census (Population Schedule), Los Angeles Ward 1, Los Angeles, California, ED 6, Sheet 17, Dwelling 491, Family 491, Norman St. Clair household, jpeg image (Online: The Generations Network, Inc., 2011) [Digital scan of original records in the National Archives, Washington, D.C.], subscription database, http://www.ancestry.com, accessed 18 June 2011.

1900 U.S. Federal Census (Population Schedule), Newbury Town, Orange, Vermont, ED 144, Sheet 4, Dwelling 82, Family 89, George Andrews household, jpeg image (Online: The Generations Network, Inc., 2010) [Digital scan of original records in the National Archives, Washington, D.C.], subscription database, http://www.ancestry.com, accessed 10 April 2010.

1910 U.S. Federal Census (Population Schedule), Pasadena Township, Los Angeles, California, ED 297, Sheet 8A, Dwelling 162, Family 212, George Andrews household, jpeg image (Online: The Generations Network, Inc., 2010) [Digital scan of original records in the National Archives, Washington, D.C.], subscription database, http://www.ancestry.com, accessed 10 April 2010.

1910 U.S. Federal Census (Population Schedule), Pasadena Township, Los Angeles, California, ED 300, Sheet 12B, Dwelling 359, Family 376, Norman St Clair household, jpeg image (Online: The Generations Network, Inc., 2006) [Digital scan of original records in the National Archives, Washington, D.C.], subscription database, http://www.ancestry.com, accessed 13 August 2006.

1920 U.S. Federal Census (Population Schedule), Los Angeles Assembly District 63, Los Angeles, California ED 162, Sheet 3A, Dwelling 646, Family 73, Ann St. Clair household, jpeg image (Online: The Generations Network, Inc., 2006) [Digital scan of original records in the National Archives, Washington, D.C.], subscription database, http://www.ancestry.com, accessed 13 August 2006.

1920 U.S. Federal Census (Population Schedule), Newton Ward 3, Middlesex, Massachusetts, ED 368, Sheet 5A, Dwelling 91, Family 93, George Andrews household, jpeg image (Online: The Generations Network, Inc., 2010) [Digital scan of original records in the National Archives, Washington, D.C.], subscription database, http://www.ancestry.com, accessed 10 April 2010.

1930 U.S. Federal Census (Population Schedule), Pasadena Township, Los Angeles, California, ED 1267, Sheet 5A, Dwelling 130, Family 137, Aubrey St. Clair household, jpeg image (Online: The Generations Network, Inc., 2011) [Digital scan of original records in the National Archives, Washington, D.C.], subscription database, http://www.ancestry.com, accessed 19 June 2011.

1940 U.S. Federal Census (Population Schedule), Los Angeles Assembly District 59, Los Angeles, California, ED 60–190, Sheet 12B, Family 366, Malcolm St. Clair household, jpeg image (Online: FamilySearch Historical Collections, 2012) [Digital scan of original records in the National Archives, Washington, D.C.], https://www.familysearch.org, accessed 14 July 2012.

Edward Sedgwick

Like Buster Keaton, Edward Sedgwick was a child of vaudeville; his family toured as the Five Sedgwicks. But this wasn't Sedgwick's only parallel to Keaton: Like Buster's theatrical career, his also began at the age of three. Then, after success in film (which included directing all of Keaton's MGM features), his career slowed down, but had a rebirth with the advent of television.

Edward Martin Sedgwick was born on November 7, 1891, in Galveston, Texas, the oldest of three siblings. His parents, Edward and Josephine (Fenie) Walker Sedgwick, both originally from Louisiana, also had two daughters, Josephine (Josie), born in 1894, and Eileen, born in 1898. Edward Sr. was a longshoreman,[1] but around 1903 he decided to start the family in the traveling entertainment industry.[2] A hurricane on September 8, 1900, completely destroyed most of Galveston, and there was less work on the docks. Edward Jr. later told people that the family worked in circuses, road shows, dramatic stock companies and minstrel shows.[3] But even before that, he already had some theatrical experience; he claimed later that his first stage appearance was at age three in the play *The Celebrated Case*, staged in Galveston.[4]

By 1909, the Five Sedgwicks advertised themselves as "repertoire vaudeville artists" performing skits with titles like "The Artist's Mistake," "The White Squaw" and "Going to the Ball."[5] By 1910 they had put together their own troupe, the Sedgwick Vaudeville Company, playing in Galveston, where a local newspaper review said, "[T]he bill was one of general excellence and the efforts of the Sedgwick family and Mr. Lee Edmunds provoked much laughter."[6] The show opened with a farce called "The Two Senators" featuring Edmunds as an Irish senator and young Sedgwick as a German senator, with Mrs. Sedgwick as an Irish landlady. His sister Josie was "exceptionally good in her conception of a French maid," and youngest sister Eileen was described as a "hit" as the hotel bellboy. Following the skit, a lightning cartoonist drew caricatures while Eileen (in blackface) sang "Shaky Eyes." The show concluded with another skit, "Fun in a Dissecting Room," "a mirth-provoking farce filled with ridiculous situations ... Edmunds is seen as a superstitious darky, who, in order to earn 75 cents, consents to visit a graveyard at midnight and deliver a corpse to the dissecting room of a surgeon." Clearly, with all that blackface, the show was of its time.

Sedgwick later told reporters that he'd been a football star at the University of Texas, where he studied engineering[7]; another article mentioned his fame as a catcher for the baseball team at the same school.[8] It's far more likely that a brief biography from 1914 was instead correct in stating that he attended St. Mary's University in Galveston and the Peacock Military Academy in San Antonio, not the University of Texas.[9] Director King Vidor, another boy from Galveston, attended the latter in 1908.[10]

Given his size, it's believable that Sedgwick might have been a football player. When he registered for the draft in June 1917, he was classified as "tall" and he weighed 304 pounds.[11] He gave that as grounds why he shouldn't be drafted. But he had another reason to keep him out of the Army: He had married Rose Adams, an actress, on October 26, 1912, when they were both 21.[12] They had one daughter, Mary, on December 4, 1919.[13] Men with dependents weren't drafted into the American Army at that time.

Like many in show business, he probably embellished his autobiographical details: He later told a writer from *Moving Picture World* that in addition to working in vaudeville, he was a Mexican border correspondent for the Associated Press.[14]

In 1914, Sedgwick got his start in films with the Lubin Company, as documented by an announcement in *Moving Picture World*: "Ed. Sedgwick, a very well-known actor, in both vaudeville and musical comedy, has deserted the stage, and is at the present time with the Lubin Company under Romaine Fielding, whose company is in winter studios at Galveston, Texas. Mr. Sedgwick's family is also with him, including his two sisters, Eileen and Josie."[15]

The family must have liked working in the movies, because in 1915 all of the Sedgwicks moved to Los Angeles, just then becoming the hub for the movie industry. Sedgwick and his sisters soon found acting work at Universal, where Edward appeared in more than 21 comedy shorts including *Hired, Tired and Fired* and *When Slim Was Home Cured*, often with Eileen. Josie was in several short Westerns.

His sisters continued to act in films—Josie went on to star in dramas at Triangle and Ince, and then she appeared in many Westerns for Universal. She stopped making films in 1926, except for one talkie in 1932.[16] Eileen became a Universal serial star, appearing in 12 of them including *The Lure of the Circus* (1918) and *Terror Trail* (1921) before retiring from film in 1929 when she married Clarence Hutson, a real estate broker and later on an executive at 20th Century–Fox.[17]

In the meantime, however, Edward became a screenwriter. He was hired by Fox Studio in 1917, where he wrote dramas like *The Yankee Way* and a 15-part serial, *Bride 13*. For a while, he, his wife and daughter lived on 51st Street in New York City. For the 1920 census, he was still listing his occupation as writer of picture plays, but that soon changed. Later that same year, Fox gave him the chance to direct a 20-part serial he co-wrote, *Fantomas*. The studio must have been satisfied with his work, because they let him continue directing. By 1921, he was back in Los Angeles,[18] still employed by Fox, directing six comedy–Westerns with Tom Mix between 1921 and 1922.

By then an experienced Western director, he went back to Universal Pictures in 1922,[19] where he was paired with Hoot Gibson. During the next three years, they made more than 20 films together.[20] In addition, Sedgwick made two melodramas, *The Flaming Hour* and *The First Degree*.

After he shot the chase sequence (without credit) for Universal's blockbuster *The Phantom of the Opera*,[21] the studio moved him up to its larger-budget "Jewel" films. In 1925 and 1926, he made five of them, ranging from *Two Fisted Jones* with Jack Hoxie and Keaton co-star Katherine McGuire, to *Lorraine of the Lions*. The latter was a curious adventure movie about a four-year-old who could control all of the animals in her father's circus. Universal promoted it as "a tangle of adventure over two continents, a desert island, and the sailing routes of the Pacific Ocean."[22] His supervisor at Universal (and *Lorraine* screenwriter), Isadore Bernstein, told the *Los Angeles Times*, "Sedgwick's greatest point is his ability to blend pathos with humor, to go from sob stuff to the ridiculous or reverse, in any atmosphere or type of story."[23]

In his spare time, he co-wrote the song "You Told Me to Go" with popular orchestra leader Abe Lyman and Henry Cohen.

Also in 1925, Universal announced ambitious plans for a film based on an upcoming novel by Sedgwick, *Pony Express*. Cast with "stars of the first magnitude," it was a story of the conquest of the West, in which "spectacular battles, including a reproduction of Custer's last fight, based on the famous painting, will be merged with other thrilling spectacles."[24] *Variety* reported in July that his production was in a race with one by James Cruze to finish first. The project was never completed, and neither the novel nor the film ever appeared. Cruze's *Pony Express* was released in September 1925.

In April 1926, Sedgwick signed a contract with MGM.[25] He was to remain there for seven years, making all kinds of films—but, interestingly, given his previous experience, no Westerns.

His first movie was a farce, *Tin Hats*. He went on to direct three films with William Haines: a baseball movie, *Slide, Kelly, Slide* (in which Keaton crew member and baseball player Ernie Orsatti appeared), a golf film, *Spring Fever*, and a story about cadet life, *West Point*. Marquis Busby of the *Los Angeles Times* wrote of the latter, "It shows a fine knowledge of comedy points."[26] This would be useful in his next assignment.

In January 1928 the *L.A. Times*' Grace Kingsley announced it this way: "Buster Keaton, starting his new contract with the Metro-Goldwyn Mayer studios, naturally wanted the best comedy director he could obtain. So Irving G. Thalberg assigned Edward Sedgwick to direct the frozen-faced comedian in his first picture."[27] They went on to work together on nine films.

Given their similar backgrounds as child performers in vaudeville, the two had a lot in common. The *L.A. Times* said in February that they had met before, when Keaton was seven years old and one of the Three Keatons and Sedgwick was 12 and one of the Five Sedgwicks.[28] They got along so well that when Keaton rented a bungalow near MGM for a dressing room, he let Sedgwick use the other half as an office.[29]

Their collaboration started out with a great film, *The Cameraman*; in fact, it's considered by many to be Keaton's last great film. When author Rudi Blesh interviewed Keaton in the 1950s for his biography of Keaton that would come out after Keaton's death in 1966, Buster described their first day of working together: "I walked on without a care in the world. Automatically started to work as I have all my life. Started feeling around for bits of business and material." Keaton decided that he wanted to do a bit with a drunk, a fat lady and a kid. Accustomed to his staff finding whatever he needed quickly, he was annoyed to learn that at MGM, "you had to requisition a toothpick in triplicate." Eventually the actors were found. Keaton continued, "I wait for him to tell me what to do. For a half hour it goes on. 'Do this! No, do that! Shoot this over. Fat lady, *must* you stand in front of Mr. Keaton?' Finally Sedgwick says, 'Buster, line these goddam people up and get this _____ shot over with.' 'Me?' I ask. 'You,' he says. That's when we became friends, Sedgwick and I, and I began to call him Junior."[30]

There was still room for improvisation, as demonstrated by this story about how the production manager (and former bit-part player) Edward Brophy was drafted into acting: Keaton reminisced, "They went on location to the beach, and then it was discovered that the company needed a man to play with Keaton in the bathhouse scene. 'You do it,' said Sedgwick. 'I ain't no actor,' answered 'Broph.' 'If you don't,' said Sedgwick, 'you'll have a fine time explaining how come we went on location and didn't get any scenes.' 'In that case,' said Brophy, 'I'm an acrobat if you say so!'"[31] Keaton explained in his autobiography that Sedgwick wanted to play the part himself, but he turned him down because "the audience would expect a man of his size to throw me out of the bathhouse if irritated. What I wanted was a fellow about my size who looked like a grouch but not the sort who dares start a fight."[32] Keaton knew exactly what he was doing. The two men trying to change into bathing suits in a tiny dressing room runs for four minutes and is one of the funniest scenes in the film. Brophy went on to become a full-time actor in 1934, playing many comic parts, including the voice of Timothy Q. Mouse in *Dumbo* (1941).

After the success of *The Cameraman*, Keaton begged MGM for his own independent unit, but the studio refused.[33] His films became less and less funny, and even Sedgwick couldn't stop the slide in quality. The changes in comedies with the coming of sound, Keaton's personal troubles, and the difficulties of working within a large and bureaucratic studio all contributed to the decline of Keaton's films. Sedgwick was a good company man, not a maverick filmmaker. In 1927 he had boasted to *Moving Picture World* that during his six years with Fox, four with Universal, and a year and a half with MGM, "he has not missed a single week's pay."[34]

In 1933, right after making *What! No Beer?*, Sedgwick left MGM at the same time as Keaton. He became a freelance director, working for most of the major studios throughout the decade: Universal, Paramount, Roach, RKO, Columbia and even MGM again. *Horseplay*, Sedgwick's next picture after *Beer*, was co-written by Keaton writer Jean Havez's widow Ebba, whom he would soon marry. (After Jean died in 1925, she had stayed in Keaton's social circle, attending events like Constance Talmadge's wedding in 1929.[35]) In August 1933, Rose Sedgwick went to Reno to sue for divorce.[36] Edward Sedgwick and Ebba Ahl Havez were married on September 3, 1933, at the Church of St. Paul, followed by a reception with more than 200 guests at Sedgwick's mother's house.[37]

After making five comedies with Joe E. Brown in the late 1930s, Sedgwick's career slowed down. He made one film with Laurel and Hardy, *Air Raid Wardens*, in 1943. In his biography of the team, Simon Louvish, wrote, "Eddie Sedgwick should have been an ideal partner for Stan in this attempt to regain their passions of old. But there is no passion in *Air Raid Wardens*. An air of ineptitude and fatigue hangs over it all."[38] He worked on only two more films: *A Southern Yankee* in 1948 (a remake of Keaton's *The General*, with Keaton working as a gag writer) and *Ma and Pa Kettle Back on the Farm* in 1951.

In 1946, *L.A. Times* writer Philip Scheuer found Keaton again sharing an office with Sedgwick on the MGM lot. They called it the Boars' Nest.[39]

In between helping to write and stage gags, Keaton invented contraptions and did needlework. He explained that for the previous Christmas, he "set out to make my missus a half-dozen towels as a surprise—as a kid around the theater, you get in the habit of handling a needle and thread—and before I knew it, I'd done 30 for our friends." During the interview, people constantly stuck their heads in the window to say hello. Although this was a low point in both of their careers, the Nest seemed like a cheerful place.

Sedgwick's career might have been finished if it were not for a remark he had made to an actress in 1937. He told the story to writer Walter Ames: "'I saw this beautiful dame walking around the lot. She was one of the Goldwyn Girls. I'd seen her tell a story and watch her facial expressions change. She'd illustrate it with everything she had.' ... Sedgwick told how he finally got up the nerve to talk to her and said, 'Young lady, if you play your cards right, you can be the greatest comedienne in show business.' He said she gave him a withering look like he was a wicked old man. That only convinced him he was right."[40] She later said, "I figured he was one of the guys who came around measuring the starlets for tights."[41]

A few years later, Lucille Ball met him again and realized he knew what he was talking about.[42] (Sedgwick's story probably isn't completely accurate, because by 1937 Ball was no longer a Goldwyn Girl and was playing featured roles in films like *Stage Door*.) She was happy to take his and Keaton's advice on comedy when she made films like *Easy to Wed* (1946) and *The Fuller Brush Girl* (1950). In later years, although she mentioned Sedgwick and was obviously close to him, she credited Buster with training her.

Edward and Ebba Sedgwick became her surrogate parents, according to Ball biographer Kathleen Brady.[43] He gave her away in her church wedding to Desi Arnaz, and he was her children's godfather.[44] They hired him when they formed their television production company, Desilu, where he helped them develop projects.

Edward Sedgwick died suddenly of a heart attack at home on May 7, 1953. He was buried at Holy Cross Cemetery in Culver City.[45] He was one of the first eight honorees to receive stars on the Hollywood Walk of Fame in 1958. His star is located at 6801 Hollywood Boulevard, in front of the Hollywood and Highland shopping complex.[46] Ebba Sedgwick died on June 18, 1982, from a stroke. She was also buried in Holy Cross Cemetery.[47]

Census Records

1900 U.S. Federal Census (Population Schedule), Galveston Ward 5, Galveston, Texas, ED 123, Sheet 4A, Dwelling 57, Family 79, Edward Sedwick [sic] household, jpeg image (Online: The Generations Network, Inc., 2011) [Digital scan of original records in the National Archives, Washington, D.C.], subscription database, http://www.ancestry.com, accessed 12 September 2011.

1910 U.S. Federal Census (Population Schedule), Manhattan Ward 16, New York, New York, ED 0857, Sheet 4B, Dwelling 21, Family 55, Thyre Ahl household, jpeg image (Online: The Generations Network, Inc., 2007) [Digital scan of original records in the National Archives, Washington, D.C.], subscription database, http://www.ancestry.com, accessed 4 August 2007.

1920 U.S. Federal Census (Population Schedule), Manhattan Assembly District 10, New York, New York, ED 798, Sheet 5B, Dwelling 29, Family 113, Edward Sedgwick household, jpeg image (Online: The Generations Network, Inc., 2006) [Digital scan of original records in the National Archives, Washington, D.C.], subscription database, http://www.ancestry.com, accessed 11 September 2006.

1930 U.S. Federal Census (Population Schedule), Los Angeles Assembly District 55, Los Angeles, California, ED 69, Sheet 15A, Dwelling 348, Family 459, Edward M. Sedgwick household, jpeg image (Online: The Generations Network, Inc., 2006) [Digital scan of original records in the National Archives, Washington, D.C.], subscription database, http://www.ancestry.com, accessed 11 September 2006.

1940 U.S. Federal Census (Population Schedule), Beverly Hills, Los Angeles, California, ED 19–40, Sheet 8A, Family 140, Edward Sedgwick household, jpeg image (Online: FamilySearch Historical Collections, 2012) [Digital scan of original records in the National Archives, Washington, D.C.], https://www.familysearch.org, accessed 14 July 2012.

Assistant Directors

Although all of Keaton's films almost certainly had assistant directors, only Sandy Roth on *Steamboat Bill, Jr.* received onscreen credit. The names of five early ADs did appear in the "Pulse of the Studios" charts in *Camera!* magazine: Al Gilmore, Al Werker, John "Chick" Collins, Mr. Rose, and Walter Reed.[1] Unfortunately, *Camera!* stopped printing the "Pulse" chart in February 1924.

Assistant directing was a tough job. *Motion Picture Classic* ran an article in 1926 entitled "Pity the Assistant Director!," which described their duties:

> The assistant director bears most of the responsibility in making a picture—yet he receives poor pay and no credit. His job consists of handling most of the details of the company—he helps choose the cast, arranges for costumes, orders the sets, studios, the script, handles mob scenes, takes care of the extras' troubles and that's only the half of it.... He arrives at the studio at 7:30 a.m., sometimes earlier, to begin rounding up his work for the day. Perhaps two members of the cast have sent word they are ill—if they are extras, the assistant gets in touch with the casting director and suggests two suitable ones to take their place. It is necessary that he be familiar with the extras and also with their wardrobes. If the missing ones

happen to be important members of the cast, the assistant plans to shoot scenes in which they are not needed. Then he makes out his reports—in most cases he keeps typewritten records of everyone employed on the set and every scene taken. He puts in a busy day and about 6 p.m. returns home, where he is usually deluged with phone calls pertaining to his job.[2]

Here are a few of the busy men who did this for Keaton's films.

AL GILMORE

Camera! first reported in September 1920 that Lou Anger, Keaton's business manager, was the assistant director. But in late October an "Al Filmore" got the credit.[3] It's probable that this was a typo; no Filmores could be found, but an Al Gilmore did work for Keaton for a few years.

Unfortunately, not much information is available about him. Keaton mentions Gilmore in his autobiography, but says he was the unit's physical trainer, who treated his injuries during *One Week*.[4] That might have been one of his many A.D. duties, or the studio could have told *Camera!* that the trainer was the A.D. He was listed as a person who "materially aided" on *Seven Chances* in a syndicated article, but the article didn't specify how.[5] Finally, he turned up as the purchasing agent for the studio from 1926 to 1928, according to *Film Daily Year Book* and the city directory.[6] That would have been when the company was working on *The General* and *Steamboat Bill, Jr.* After that, he disappeared both from Keaton credit lists and from other sources.

AL WERKER

Al Werker was Keaton's assistant director in 1922. He went on to a long career as a director.

Alfred Louis Werker was born in Deadwood, South Dakota, on December 2, 1895, or 1896 (the 1900, 1920 and 1930 censuses and his 1922 passport application say 1895, but both of his draft registrations and death certificate say 1896). His parents split up when he was young; his father Louis moved to Colorado and his mother Frances stayed in South Dakota and married a man named Charlie Dingee.

Werker went to school in San Diego, California. His first film credits were as assistant director for two Westerns made for Triangle Studio in 1917, *Firefly of Tough Luck* and *The Regenerates*. He was back in San Diego when he registered for the draft in 1917, working as a theatrical advance agent for a company called Wark Producing.[7] A tall, slender man with gray eyes and brown hair, he was single at the time, so he got drafted.[8]

When he finished his service, he moved to Los Angeles and went to work for Mary Pickford's studio,[9] where he was the property man-assistant director on seven of her films, from *The Hoodlum* in 1919 through *Little Lord Fauntleroy* in 1921. After he left Pickford in May 1921, he became Lou Anger's assistant at the Keaton studio's business office. A year later, he transferred back to the filmmaking side and became Eddie Cline's assistant director.[10]

Werker left Keaton's crew after the final short, *The Love Nest*, when he applied for a passport, on October 24, 1922, and sailed to Europe on November 9 of that year.[11] He planned quite a tour, spending a year traveling from the British Isles to "Czech-Slovakia," returning to the U.S. on November 6.[12] That same year, he married Frances Allen, from Brooklyn, New York, in 1923. In 1931, they had a son, Alfred L. Werker, Jr.

Back in the States, he went back to working as an assistant director, this time on Western star Fred Thomson's films at Robertson-Cole Pictures, and he followed the star when he went to Monogram Pictures and Paramount Pictures. By 1925, he had become a co-director on *Riding the Wind* (1925), and continued with *The Tough Guy* (1926), *Pioneer Scout* (1928) and *Kit Carson* (1928). Thomson died of tetanus after completing *Carson*.

After Thomson's untimely death, Werker moved up to the director's job when Fox Studios signed him in May of 1929.[13] He stayed at Fox for 13 years, becoming a solid studio director, working on everything from *Chasing Through Europe* with Harry Brand to *The Adventures of Sherlock Holmes*. His last film at Fox was *A-Haunting We Will Go* (1942) with Laurel and Hardy.

After that, he became a freelance director, working at RKO Pictures, Columbia Pictures, Universal Studios and Eagle-Lion Films with Bryan Foy and former Keaton co-director Charles Riesner. In 1949, he was nominated for a Directors Guild award. His last film was *The Young Don't Cry* in 1957 with Sal Mineo.

He retired to Laguna Beach, California. On July 28, 1975, he died at home of heart failure.[14] His wife Frances died of cardiac arrest seven years later, on December 11, 1982.[15]

Census Records

1900 U.S. Federal Census (Population Schedule), Borough of Brooklyn, New York City, NY, ED 102, Sheet 2, Dwelling 90, Family 138, William Allen household, jpeg image (Online: The Generations Network, Inc., 2008) [Digital scan of original records in the National Archives, Washington, D.C.], subscription database, http://www.ancestry.com, accessed 9 May 2008.

1900 U.S. Federal Census (Population Schedule), Lead City, Lawrence, South Dakota, ED 28, Sheet 7, Dwelling 142, Family 156, Charlie Dingee household, jpeg image (Online: The Generations Network, Inc., 2008) [Digital scan of original records in the National Archives, Washington, D.C.], subscription database, http://www.ancestry.com, accessed 9 May 2008.

1920 U.S. Federal Census (Population Schedule), Los Angeles Assembly District 63, Los Angeles, California ED 157, Sheet 11A, Dwelling 137, Family 2149, Alfred L. Werker household, jpeg image (Online: The Generations Network, Inc., 2008) [Digital scan of original records in the National Archives, Washington, D.C.], subscription database, http://www.ancestry.com, accessed 9 May 2008.

1920 U.S. Federal Census (Population Schedule), Los Angeles Assembly District 63, Los Angeles, California ED 168, Sheet 10B, Dwelling 218, Family 231, Alfred L. Werker household, jpeg image (Online: The Generations Network, Inc., 2008) [Digital scan of original records in the National Archives, Washington, D.C.], subscription database, http://www.ancestry.com, accessed 9 May 2008.

1930 U.S. Federal Census (Population Schedule), Los Angeles Assembly District 55, Los Angeles, California, ED 70, Sheet 1A, Dwelling 10, Family 10, Alfred L. Werker household, jpeg image (Online: The Generations Network, Inc., 2008) [Digital scan of original records in the National Archives, Washington, D.C.], subscription database, http://www.ancestry.com, accessed 9 May 2008.

JOHN L. "CHICK" COLLINS

"Chick" Collins (sometimes spelled "Chic") became better known as a stuntman and actor, but *Camera!* says that early in his career he was the A.D. on *Three Ages*.

John L. Collins was born in Steuben, New York, on December 3, 1898. His parents were Michael and Catherine Magel Collins. His father was a train switchman. Not much information is available about his early career. He was first mentioned in *Variety* in 1919: "'Chick' Collins, fresh from the wars, is at Branton as casting director."[16] *Three Ages* appears to be the first Keaton film he worked on.[17] In addition to *Camera!*'s credit, his name is seen onscreen on the in-joke football team line-up list. He also worked on *Our Hospitality* as a stunt man; Keaton told Rudi Blesh that Collins had begged to do the dangerous scene in the river rapids for him.[18]

He went on to have a long career as a stuntman, actor and stand-in. Most of his work was uncredited, but the *AFI Catalog* listed 42 films he worked on between 1932 and 1952. Highlights included stunts in the 1931 *Dr. Jekyll and Mr. Hyde* and in *King Kong*. His most visible part was probably Capital, the tramp Joel McCrea meets on the train in *Sullivan's Travels*. His final film was *Singin' in the Rain* in 1952.

He died on November 25, 1981, of lung cancer,[19] and was buried at Holy Cross Cemetery, Culver City, California.

Census Records

1900 U.S. Federal Census (Population Schedule), Hornellsville Ward 5, Steuben, New York, ED 92, Sheet 20, Dwelling 473, Family 500, Michael Collins household, jpeg image (Online: The Generations Network, Inc., 2010) [Digital scan of original records in the National Archives, Washington, D.C.], subscription database, http://www.ancestry.com, accessed 5 August 2010.

1930 U.S. Federal Census (Population Schedule), Los Angeles Assembly District 55, Los Angeles, California, ED 19, Sheet 8A, Dwelling 307, Family 308, John L. Collins household, jpeg image (Online: The Generations Network, Inc., 2010) [Digital scan of original records in the National Archives, Washington, D.C.], subscription database, http://www.ancestry.com, accessed 5 August 2010.

1940 U.S. Federal Census (Population Schedule), Los Angeles Assembly District 56, Los Angeles, California, ED 60–94, Sheet 4A, Family 104, John L. Collins household, jpeg image (Online: FamilySearch Historical Collections, 2012) [Digital scan of original records in the National Archives, Washington, D.C.], https://www.familysearch.org, accessed 22 July 2012.

Mr. Rose

The assistant director of *Our Hospitality* is a man of mystery. Not even his first name has been recorded in Keaton baseball team line-ups, assistant director lists in film yearbooks or film databases. *Camera!* often made spelling errors in its "Pulse of the Studio," so perhaps this was one of them.[20] He might have been Harry Roselotte. The *Cottage Grove Sentinel* mentioned that he was the set decorator on *The General*, and everybody called him "Rosie."[21] However, no other information about Roselotte is available either.

Walter Reed

Walter Reed assisted on *Sherlock Jr.* and had worked with Roscoe Arbuckle on stage and at Keystone. (Proponents of the Arbuckle-directed-*Sherlock-Jr.* theory could use this as evidence. For what its worth, *Camera!* listed Keaton as the director from the beginning.)

Walter Chapman Reed was born in Montana on June 7, 1873. Nothing is known about his early life. Eventually he became a vaudevillian and a musical comedy actor. In 1908, the *Los Angeles Herald* described him as an "eccentric Irish comedian,"[22] and apparently he told jokes in between songs and dances.

In early 1909, Reed appeared in a series of musicals modeled on the British Drury Lane pantomimes at the Auditorium Theater in Los Angeles. The company included another up-and-coming comic, Roscoe Arbuckle. Reed played one of the ugly stepsisters in *Cinderella*, in which Arbuckle played a baron.[23] The two played robbers in *Little Red Riding Hood*; the *Los Angeles Herald* said they "jingle their bells throughout their foolery and are just about foolish enough to be really diverting."[24] Two weeks later they had "ample opportunity to display their talents" in *Ali Baba and the Forty Thieves*.[25] They finished the season with *Babes in the Woods* and a musical version of *Uncle Tom's Cabin*, with Arbuckle playing Uncle Tom.

Reed and Arbuckle formed a stock company along with Reed's wife Florence and Arbuckle's wife, Minta Durfee. The Reed-Arbuckle Company spent June through October of 1909 in Bisbee, Arizona, a prosperous town of 20,000 at the time, and then they toured other mining towns in the state.[26] Playwright-actor Claude Kelly and leading lady Madeline Rowe joined them.

There were several shows in the company's repertoire. One was a blackface show called *Way Down South*. The *Bisbee Daily Review* called it "fun, fast, and furious."[27] It included "coon" songs, a hoe-down, a steamship race, lots of slapstick, and a touching rendition of "My Old Kentucky Home" sung by Madeline Rowe that received several encores. It played to two packed houses. *On Broadway* also drew full houses, and "the audience was kept in a continuous state of laughter and applause by the lively comedy."[28] Reed played an Irish shoemaker and Arbuckle a German tailor, but the reviewer didn't bother to mention the plot. *King Slodo* was a burlesque of a popular opera, *King Dodo*. Reed and Arbuckle disguised themselves as women to invade a harem. They were caught and condemned to death, but they managed to escape, keeping the audience "in roars of laughter."[29] *Woman Hater* featured Arbuckle as an impecunious college student, Reed as his crusty uncle, and Durfee as the landlady's fascinating daughter.[30] But their best play, according to *Daily Review* writer Lee Hamilton, was *The Man from Boston*.[31] Reed played the man of the title, a tutor named Oliver Sullivan. Arbuckle was the "dyspeptic, dogmatic, and irritable" Colonel Saunders. Again, plot description was ignored in favor of praise for the musical numbers. Hamilton thought it could be as great a success as any musical comedy touring, with "crisp and uproarious dialect, screaming situations and climaxes that left nothing to be desired."

By April 1910, Arbuckle and Durfee had left the company and returned to Los Angeles, leaving Reed to tour with the re-named Walter (Finnegan) Reed Musical Comedy Company. He often played an Irish character named Finnegan in one-act plays he wrote himself, such as *Ten Bar Rooms in One Night, Finnegan at Coney Island* and *Swat the Fly*.[32] About the latter, Reed told the Bisbee newspaper that it "portrays the dangers of flies and is based on government study for extermination by a high official.... In an extemporaneous speech he informs the audience of the dangers and instructs the servant (Finnegan) what to do to assist him."[33] He told the reporter he was pleased with the reception Bisbee had given them.

Reed was hired by Mack Sennett as a scenario writer for Keystone in 1915,[34] although he occasionally acted, playing Arbuckle's father in *Miss Fatty's Seaside Lovers*. Soon he moved up to being an assistant director on *Crooked to the End, Village Vampire* and *Oily Scoundrel*. Florence Reed also appeared in some Keystone films, including *Gypsy Joe*.

Reed became a director when he went to Fox Film Corporation in 1916. His work there included *Aerial Joyride* with comic Raymond Griffith. In 1918 he took out an ad in *Camera!*: "Creator, Director, Scenarioist [sic], and Player WALTER REED For the silent as well as the spoken theatricals."[35] In March of that year, he joined Arbuckle's scenario staff.[36] When he registered for the draft on September 6, 1918, he was acting at the Republic Theater in Los Angeles. His draft registration card describes him as a short man of medium build, with blue eyes and auburn hair.[37] His age and marital status kept him out of the Army. He and his wife told the 1920 census enumerator they were both theatrical actors.

In November 1923, he became the assistant director of *Sherlock Jr.* according to *Camera!*[38] He also played the pawnbroker who loans the villain four dollars for Joe Keaton's stolen watch.

His path crossed with Arbuckle's several more times. In the Arbuckle-directed *Curses* (1925), he played Bartine Burkett's father, and he co-wrote two shorts for Educational with him in 1931, *Ex-Plumber* and *Marriage Rows*.

By 1940, he was a widower, unable to work (the census didn't specify why), living in Perris, California. On May 29, 1943, he died at the Motion Picture Relief Home in Calabasas, California, at the age of 69, following a stroke.[39] He was buried at the Holy Cross Cemetery.

Census Records

1910 U.S. Federal Census (Population Schedule), Bisbee City Ward 1, Arizona, ED 0005, Sheet 38A, Dwelling 429, Family 428, John B. Anderson household, jpeg image (Online: The Generations Network, Inc., 2010) [Digital scan of original records in the National Archives, Washington, D.C.], subscription database, http://www.ancestry.com, accessed 9 April 2011.

1910 U.S. Federal Census (Population Schedule), Bisbee City Ward 1, Arizona, ED

0005, Sheet 17A, Dwelling 31, Elizabeth James household, jpeg image (Online: The Generations Network, Inc., 2010) [Digital scan of original records in the National Archives, Washington, D.C.], subscription database, http://www.ancestry.com, accessed 9 April 2011.

1910 U.S. Federal Census (Population Schedule), Los Angeles Assembly District 75, Los Angeles, California, ED 0081, Sheet 12B, Dwelling 267, Family 282, Charles W. Durfee household, jpeg image (Online: The Generations Network, Inc., 2010) [Digital scan of original records in the National Archives, Washington, D.C.], subscription database, http://www.ancestry.com, accessed 9 April 2011.

1920 U.S. Federal Census (Population Schedule), Belvidere Township, Los Angeles, California ED 10, Sheet 13A, Dwelling 125, Family 127, Walter Reed household, jpeg image (Online: The Generations Network, Inc., 2010) [Digital scan of original records in the National Archives, Washington, D.C.], subscription database, http://www.ancestry.com, accessed 3 August 2010.

1940 U.S. Federal Census (Population Schedule), Perris, Riverside, California, ED 33–33, Sheet 4A, Family 70, Walter C. Reed household, jpeg image (Online: FamilySearch Historical Collections, 2012) [Digital scan of original records in the National Archives, Washington, D.C.], https://www.familysearch.org, accessed 22 July 2012.

SANDY ROTH

Unlike the rest of Keaton's assistant directors, Sandy Roth actually got an onscreen credit for *Steamboat Bill, Jr.* Prior to *Steamboat Bill*, he had already worked with the director, Charles Riesner, on five earlier films, so he probably got hired as part of his team.

Roth was born Sanford Lewton Rothenberg in San Francisco, California, on January 8, 1887. (He later shaved four years off of his age; even his death certificate says 1891.) His father, Louis Rothenberg, a wholesale liquor merchant, was originally from Germany, and his mother's parents were also German, but Sarah Wolf Rothenberg was born in England. His sister Madeline was born in 1892. As a young man, Sanford worked as a clerk in his father's business.

By the time he made his vaudeville debut in April 1910, he had shortened his name to Roth.[40] His act, which included an imitation of the famous Scottish comic Harry Lauder, made a hit with the audience. By August, he had expanded to Italian and other Scottish impersonations.[41] In 1916, the *Los Angeles Times* described his act: "[S]tories, too, are the forte of Sandy Roth, who interprets some of the most famous short prose and poetic pieces of the day in character."[42]

Around the same time, he started playing bit parts in films, appearing in several of Harold Lloyd's Lonesome Luke and "glass" character films. When he registered for the draft on June 5, 1917, he was listed as an actor at Fox Studios.[43]

During World War I, he served in the Naval Reserve at Mare Island Naval Training Camp (near San Francisco) as a storekeeper on active duty from December 14, 1917, to January 10, 1919, but he wasn't officially discharged until September 30, 1921.[44] His description in his military records says that he was 5'4½", with brown eyes, dark brown hair, and a ruddy complexion. In addition to his storekeeper duties, he was also in charge of amusements. During his time at Mare Island, he talked D.W. Griffith's film distributor into screening *Hearts of the World* for free at the training camp, which raised $442 for the chaplain's fund.

When he got out, Roth went back to vaudeville, joining the George White Company in San Jose.[45] The 1920 census found him working as an assistant manager in a theater and living with his parents in San Francisco.

In 1922, he moved to Los Angeles and became a gag man for Al St. John.[46] Next he went to work for Warner Bros. Studios; his first recorded assistant directing credit was for *Broadway After Dark*, a 1924 drama directed by Monta Bell, starring Adolphe Menjou and Norma Shearer. His second film, *The Man on the Box*, was his first collaboration with Charles Riesner; it was the first of five films they made with Syd Chaplin. Roth also worked on films with directors Roy del Ruth, Lloyd Bacon and Henry Lehrman.

In 1927, when Keaton hired Charles Riesner to direct *Steamboat Bill, Jr.*, Roth came along; they both left Warner Bros. to work on it. It was a difficult shoot on location in Sacramento, but Roth took time to serve as a judge with Carl Harbaugh at the "Miss Yolo" beauty contest. The winner, Faye Baker, got to visit the set and had her picture taken with Keaton.[47]

Roth next worked with Del Lord at the Mack Sennett Studio, making three shorts in the *Taxi Driver* series.[48] Then he returned to Riesner (and Keaton, briefly): He was one of three assistant directors on *The Hollywood Revue of 1929*. Roth stayed at MGM for the rest of his career, working with Riesner on 11 more pictures, including several starring Marie Dressler and Polly Moran. He also assisted Frank Borzage, Jacques Tourneur, George B. Seitz, and Harry Beaumont.

Although he was primarily an assistant director, he continued to act. The *Los Angeles Times* reported in 1931 that "he has been assistant to Charles Brabin, but Brabin, deciding that he had talent for acting, took him out of the assistant position and gave him a role in *The City Sentinel* [the title was later changed to *The Beast of the City*]. Sandy met with an accident during the filming of a scene in which he injured one of his legs badly. However, he was courageous and has been working, though going about on crutches when not actually in a scene."[49] He didn't let the accident stop him from playing roles in *Hell's Highway* (1932) and *Midnight Mary* (1933), but he kept his day job.

His path again crossed Keaton's when he worked on the Marx Brothers' *At the Circus*—Keaton wrote gags for the film. Jimmie Fidler, *L.A. Times* Hollywood columnist, wrote about that shoot: "[T]o give you a rough idea of an assistant director's life, Mr. Roth likes to display one day's order requiring him to have on the set: ten black and white horses, ten elephants, a monkey symphony, a giraffe, two rabbits and two pigeons, a week-old lamb—and a radio tenor."[50] Roth also assisted on the Marxes' *Go West* and *The Big Store*.

Sandy Roth died of a heart attack on November 4, 1943, at the age of 56.[51] He was buried at Forest Lawn Cemetery in Glendale, California. His wife, Jean, survived him.

Census Records

1900 U.S. Federal Census (Population Schedule), San Francisco, California, ED 230, Sheet 5, Dwelling 87, Family 96, Louis B. Rothenberg household, jpeg image (Online: The Generations Network, Inc., 2006) [Digital scan of original records in the National Archives, Washington, D.C.], subscription database, http://www.ancestry.com, accessed 14 October 2006.

1910 U.S. Federal Census (Population Schedule), San Francisco Assembly District 40, San Francisco, California, ED 257, Sheet 1B, Dwelling 13, Family 25, Louis R. Rothenberg household, jpeg image (Online: The Generations Network, Inc., 2006) [Digital scan of original records in the National Archives, Washington, D.C.], subscription database, http://www.ancestry.com, accessed 14 October 2006.

1920 U.S. Federal Census (Population Schedule), San Francisco Assembly District 31, San Francisco, California ED 153, Sheet 11A, Dwelling 9, Family 3, Louis Rothenberg household, jpeg image (Online: The Generations Network, Inc., 2010) [Digital scan of original records in the National Archives, Washington, D.C.], subscription database, http://www.ancestry.com, accessed 16 April 2011.

1940 U.S. Federal Census (Population Schedule), Los Angeles Assembly District 59, Los Angeles, California, ED 60–193, Sheet 1A, Family 7, Sanford L. Rothenberg household, jpeg image (Online: FamilySearch Historical Collections, 2012) [Digital scan of original records in the National Archives, Washington, D.C.], https://www.familysearch.org, accessed 22 July 2012.

Writers

According to Buster Keaton, two distinct kinds of writers worked for him: gag men ... and useless so-and-sos from New York. The gag men stuck around and the others departed after a picture or two. In his autobiography *My Wonderful World of Slapstick* (1960) he wrote:

> One reason I never took extravagant praise seriously was because neither I, my director, not my gag men were writers in any literary sense. The writers most often on my staff were Clyde Bruckman, Joe Mitchell, and Jean Havez. They never wrote anything but gags, vaudeville sketches, and songs. I don't think any of them ever had his name on a book, a short story, or even an article in a fan magazine, entitled "How to Write Gags for the Movies." They were not word guys, at all. They didn't have to be. The only words we had to write were for the title and subtitles. The fewer subtitles we used the better it was for the picture.... From time to time we brought famous and talented writers from New York. I do not recall a single one of these novelists, magazine writers, and Broadway playwrights who was able to write the sort of material we needed.[1]

He was a little inaccurate about the gag men's literary output, but his point remains: Writing for movies is different from other kinds of writing, and the skills aren't necessarily transferable.

The gag men started working with him on the shorts. Jean Havez, who had been a songwriter and Sennett scenarist, was first. He collaborated with Roscoe Arbuckle, and then stayed with Keaton when Arbuckle went into features in 1920. Lex Neal, an old vaudeville friend from Muskegon, probably wrote some gags for him as early as 1921, and went on to co-write a couple of Keaton features. Joseph Mitchell, a former actor, and Clyde Bruckman, an ex-sportswriter, joined the company in mid–1921.

When one writer worked out, sometimes Keaton (very sensibly) tried to get another one like him. In the fall of 1922, he tried to hire Bugs Baer, who had been Bruckman's co-worker at the *Los Angeles Examiner*. However, Baer hadn't told his employers at the Hearst Company that he was quitting, and they demanded his return.[2] Tommy Gray, who was a sort of Havez Jr., did work with them for a few months in early 1922.

Havez, Bruckman and Mitchell stayed with Keaton when he went into features, and they co-wrote *Three Ages, Our Hospitality, Sherlock Jr., The Navigator* and *Seven Chances*. At that time, not much was documented about the behind-the-scenes filmmaking process. The *Los Angeles Times* ran one article about writing *The Navigator*, which is detailed in the Bruckman entry. One other small glimpse appeared in *Camera!*, called "Like Their Music." *Camera* reported that a radio had been installed in the scenario room, and they enjoyed a concert when the writers "feel the need for a respite from the grind of work.... The making of comedy is a severe nerve-strain. In the discussion over the working out of various situations, differences of opinion rose, and time and again Buster played peacemaker by 'giving them the air' with his radio."[3]

The team broke up temporarily in late 1924 when Keaton closed his studio for two months while he went on vacation, and he loaned them out to other studios.[4] The change became permanent when Jean Havez died of a heart attack on February 12, 1925.

At this point, Keaton started hiring other writers. The first was Robert Sherwood from New York. He wrote a story about a boy and a girl stuck in a half-finished skyscraper; unfortunately, he couldn't think of a way to get them down so he didn't finish the story and the film didn't get made.[5] Sherwood went on to win three Pulitzer Prizes for plays, to co-write the films *Rebecca and Foreign Correspondent* for Alfred Hitchcock, and to win a screenwriting Oscar for *The Best Years of Our Lives*.

It's hard to say who actually wrote the films after *Seven Chances* because, as Keaton later said to film historian Kevin Brownlow, "Well, we had to put somebody's name up that wrote 'em."[6] So the name in the credits may not actually be the person responsible for writing the film.

After the Sherwood script for *The Skyscraper* fell through, Keaton hired Raymond Cannon, a Los Angeles–based magazine editor and actor who had written comedies for Douglas McLean. He signed a contract with the studio and co-wrote *Go West*, after which the Keaton company loaned him to Universal and he never returned.

So Keaton's studio sent to New York for more writers. To adapt the stage play *Battling Buttler*, three vaudeville sketch writers—Al Boasberg, Paul Gerald Smith and Charles Smith—were hired. Lex Neal started out on the film as the co-director, but he left to work for Fox Studio. After *Butler*, the three New Yorkers stayed to co-write *The General*, joined by Clyde Bruckman. Paul Gerald Smith left in the middle.

After *The General* made less money than anticipated, Keaton's management hired experienced Hollywood comedy writers Carl Harbaugh and Bryan Foy to try to make a more commercial film, *College*. Harbaugh also got the writer's credit for *Steamboat Bill, Jr.* However, this is the film that Brownlow mentioned when Keaton said they had to put somebody's name up, so it's the one writer credit that is most suspect.

It was at this point that Keaton moved over to Metro-Goldwyn-Mayer. The first draft of *The Cameraman* was written by Byron Morgan, a writer under contract to MGM. A former *Saturday Evening Post* author whose stories about auto racing impressed Famous Players–Lasky, Morgan was originally hired to write screenplays for Wallace Reid, such as *What's Your Hurry* (1920) and *Too Much Speed* (1921). He worked for Fox Film Corporation, Universal Studios, and Robertson-Cole Pictures before going to MGM in 1928.[7] He was announced in *Variety* and the *Los Angeles Times* as the writer of *Snapshots* (an early title for *The Cameraman*) in early 1928,[8] but by March, *Variety* reported that Keaton wasn't satisfied with it and had sent it back to Morgan for revision: "Keaton claims there was not enough comedy angles to the story."[9] Ultimately, Morgan didn't get screen credit, which suggests his version didn't contribute much to the final film. The script was given to Lew Lipton, who had previously worked with the director Edward Sedgwick, and Keaton's stalwart gag man Clyde Bruckman.

On all of his films, Keaton certainly contributed to the writing, as he did the directing, but he liked to work collaboratively, bouncing ideas off of other writers. Even though Bruckman believed he was there mostly as a left fielder, all of the writers were an important part of why Keaton's films are so funny.

Al Boasberg

Al Boasberg was called "America's greatest natural gag man."[1] Not only did he contribute gags to *Battling Butler* and *The General*, he wrote hundreds of vaudeville routines and additions to film dialogue and radio acts. Boasberg was also the man who wrote the stateroom scene in the Marx Brothers' *A Night at the Opera*.

Albert Issac Boasberg was born in Buffalo, New York, on December 5, 1892.[2] His parents were Herman and Harriet Freedman Boasberg, and he had two sisters, Florence and Phyllis, and a brother, Nathan. Harriet Boasberg died when Al was 11. According to his biographer Ben Schwartz, at that point Boasberg's family life dissolved and he was left a lonely, isolated boy.[3]

Boasberg later liked to joke about his childhood. In 1926, he told an interviewer that he got his education "in a Dokes poolroom. Having completed a post graduate course he became a tire salesman and had lots of fun watching the wheels go round."[4]

Herman Boasberg was a jeweler, and by 1910 he owned a jewelry store with his son-in-law, Samuel Cohen (Florence's husband). Nathan and Al both worked for them as salesmen. According to *Variety*, "from the difficulties the family had with their customers Al managed to get plenty of laughs. It was all in fun to him and throughout his life he clowned about the Boasberg customers who did not come through with the coin, as promised, for the 'ice' they were proudly wearing."[5] His *New Yorker* profile quoted the first gag he tried out on an actor: "Did you hear about the excitement at the hotel?" he asked. Pause. "A paperhanger hung a border." Long pause. "But it was only a rumor."[6] The actor was impressed and told him he should sell his work. His father wanted him to stick with the family trade, but Boasberg found it dull.[7]

On July 21, 1916, Al married Hilda Levy in Niagara Falls.[8] Four years younger than her husband, she was from North Tonowanda, a town not far from Buffalo.[9] She worked as a canvasser (which, at that time, meant travelling salesperson, not political campaigner). By the 1917 draft, the couple had moved to Rochester where he worked for the Herber Motor Car Company.[10] The 1920 census found them living with the Levy family in Manhattan by which time Boasberg was working as a tire salesman. The marriage ended in 1922, when she left to study art in Italy.[11]

There are a few different versions of the story of Boasberg's start in show business. According to Arthur Ungar in *Variety*, Boasberg began by forming a comedy act and performing in amateur night shows. That didn't go well. Next he decided to try to get a job in film publicity, so he put a sign extolling Paramount Pictures' films on his car, drove to their office in Albany, New York, and presented himself as being ready for a job. He got it.[12] *Moving Picture World* also wrote that he worked for Paramount as a field exploitation man in 1921.[13] The next year, he was hired by Robertson-Cole Pictures to do similar work for them.(Robertson-Cole soon changed its name to Film Booking Offices of America. It later became RKO.) In his spare time, Boasberg wrote gags and sketches for burlesque and vaudeville performers.[14]

Schwartz says Boasberg spent all of his free time watching vaudeville.

His friends encouraged him to try selling gags, so he went to Phil Baker backstage and sold him three pages of jokes for $100. In Baker's act he played a smug comic whose accordion act got heckled by a stooge planted in the audience. Boasberg's material brought him rave reviews and a part in Irving Berlin's 1923 *Music Box Revue*.[15] Baker returned the favor by introducing him to his former partner, a violin comic named Jack Benny. Boasberg wrote an act for Benny that established the character Benny would play for the rest of his career. Schwartz summed up his talent: "Boasberg took their semi-successful acts and zeroed in on what was truly unique about them."[16]

His gags must have been pretty good, because in late 1925 he was one of the New York writers hired by Buster Keaton.[17] Boasberg moved to Hollywood and went to work on *Battling Butler*.

As Schwartz wrote, with four writers it's hard to definitely cite anything in the film as Boasberg's. However, he thinks that an exchange between Keaton and the boxer's girlfriend is his. The young woman is looking at her broken shoe, and Keaton asks, "How's your heel?" She looks at her boyfriend and says, "Oh, he's all right."[18] Boasberg also had a small part in the film, as the bandleader at the wedding.

He stayed with Keaton for his next film, *The General*, traveling with the company to the location in Cottage Grove, Oregon. According to a brief biography in the town's newspaper, "he appears too serious for a gag man. One wouldn't laugh at him and one never would suspect that he spends most of his time thinking of how to make others laugh."[19]

Boasberg even wrote a story for the paper himself, about the old-timers' reunion among some of the actors in the film. He could still write good publicity: "As Tom Nawn remarked, 'Who'd thunk that all we old renegades could come together in this delightful little place?' What would the old Enrich House steps say? [He probably meant Ehric House, a New York City boarding house that catered to vaudevillians.]—What would the Dowlin Bar think and what would the old White Rats headquarters or the Comedy Club have to say—if her favorite scamps were reported so far away?"[20]

Variety reported that he was cast in "an important part" but it would not "permit Boasberg to neglect his 'gagging' as he must come through with at least five or six ideas a day."[21] However, Boasberg doesn't seem to appear in the final film, although he might have been in a portion that was later cut. According to Keaton fan Tracy Doyle, that scene featured Snitz Edwards and offered a longer explanation of how Keaton learned of the Northern Army's plans.[22]

In late July, the *Cottage Grove Sentinel* reported that sparks from one of the train engines ignited a massive forest fire that Keaton and all 600 members of his crew helped fight.[23] By the time the story got to Hollywood, the fire was caused by a small one Boasberg and Keaton set to keep warm early in the morning (which makes no sense, because the area was suffering from a record heat wave that summer).[24] The story was still getting reprinted as fact as late as 1971, in Max Wilk's *The Wit and Wisdom of Hollywood*.[25]

In August, after *The General* was finished, Boasberg resigned. *Variety* reported that Boasberg "asked Keaton to be relieved and the result was that Keaton gave him a bonus for his services and held an open invitation for him to return at any time,"[26] although three decades later Keaton wrote in his autobiography: "[W]hen talkies came in Al Boasberg became the best-paid gag writer in Hollywood, a walking marvel of verbal firecrackers and yak-getting wows. But he had been a terrible flop when he tried to do sight gags for us. So were a hundred other writers we imported from New York. It is possible, of course, that we kept sending for the wrong ones."[27]

Boasberg went back to work for Robertson-Cole-FBO-RKO, this time as a title writer and gag man.[28] He worked on the films *Her Father Said No* and *California or Bust*. Sometimes the studio loaned him out to First National, which was how he came to write the titles for Eddie Cline's *Ladies' Night in a Turkish Bath*.

Although he seems to have had steady work in the movies, Boasberg also kept writing for vaudeville performers. In 1927, *Moving Picture World* said that "at present he owns twenty-one vaudeville acts, which brings in an income not to be sneezed at."[29] One of his sketches from 1926 launched the career of Burns and Allen. It was called "Lamb Chops." Here's a sample:

> **George:** Do you like to love?
> **Gracie:** No.
> **George:** Well, then do you like to kiss?
> **Gracie:** No.
> **George:** Well, what do you like?
> **Gracie:** Lamb chops.
> **George:** How many lamb chops can you eat?
> **Gracie:** Four.
> **George:** You mean, a little girl like you can eat four lamb chops alone?
> **Gracie:** No, silly, not alone. But with potatoes I could....[30]

His personal life was also busy. Right after he finished working on *The General*, Boasberg traveled to Chicago and married Rosadel Stadecker. The *L.A. Times* called her a "Chicago society girl"; they met during one of his trips there.[31] Only five months later they separated, with Boasberg declaring that "we were very much in love and we parted on the best of terms. However, my uncertain hours and the frequent demands made upon me for extra work and location trips could not coincide with our idea of marriage. We decided it would be better to be divorced."[32]

This short-lived relationship didn't sour him on marriage, however. Only four months after that, he married Roslyn Goldberg, a 25-year-old woman from Minneapolis. They honeymooned on the Great Lakes and stopped in Buffalo to visit his childhood home.[33] This time, the marriage stuck; they stayed together until he died.

With so much experience in writing verbal gags for vaudeville sketches, the coming of sound didn't cause Boasberg any problems. MGM hired him in 1928, primarily as a dialogue writer.[34] In fact, he worked on two of Keaton's talkies (*Free and Easy* and *Doughboys*) as well as some films directed by Keaton alumni, like *Everything's Rosie* (Clyde Bruckman), *The Stolen Jools* (William McGann), which included Keaton in the cast, and *Cracked Nuts* (Eddie Cline). Because gag writers were seldom credited, it would be nearly impossible to create a complete list of everything he worked on. The most unusual film he contributed to was Tod Browning's *Freaks*, the circus melodrama that had the distinction of being the longest-banned film in the United Kingdom. According to Ungar, when another writer's name would appear on the screen, he would laugh and say, "So I'm Hollywood's ghost writer, so what?" But it bothered him more than he would admit.[35]

At the same time, he helped to launch another vaudeville comic, Bob Hope. A success in the Midwestern circuit, Hope's jokes didn't work in New York. Boasberg wrote a four-act showcase, *Antics*, for Hope's 1930–31 tour, which Schwartz called "the culmination of both their vaudeville careers."[36] Here's a sample exchange with his two audience plants:

> **Plant 1:** How do you like it?
> **Plant 2:** It sounds just as bad over here.
> **Hope:** Just a minute. Don't you boys know you can be arrested for annoying an audience?
> **Both plants:** You should know.[37]

Boasberg had unusual working methods. Groucho's son Arthur Marx wrote, "Boasberg was what was known as a character. He was a large, heavy-jowled man—well over six feet tall and weighing about three hundred pounds—and he had an affinity for bathtubs and bathrooms. He did about 80 percent of his writing in the bathtub, immersed in hot water up to his neck. He kept a dictaphone by the tub, and another one next to the toilet."[38]

When Jack Benny got a chance to be a guest on Ed Sullivan's radio show in 1932, he immediately called Boasberg for material. Their opener was: "Hello folks. This is Jack Benny talking. There will now be a slight pause while you say 'who cares?'" The appearance went over so well that Benny was hired to host *The Canada Dry Show*, and he hired Boasberg to write for him.[39] Boasberg opened his own independent radio production company in New York, for which he hoped to write, cast and produce programs.[40] It didn't work out and he soon went back to Hollywood.

Next he tried directing films. After directing three shorts for RKO in 1929 and 1930, he got the chance to direct a feature in 1933. *Myrt and Marge* was a backstage musical comedy. Bryan Foy produced, and it featured an early appearance by the Three Stooges. Ungar said that it "was the only chore Al ever wanted to forget."[41] However, Joel and Ethan Coen like it well enough: It's the movie George Clooney and Tim Blake-Nelson watch while they discuss the perfidy of women (and learn that John Turturo didn't turn into a toad) in *Oh Brother, Where Art Thou?*

Boasberg returned to RKO and wrote and directed comedy shorts starring Leon Errol. Leonard Maltin wrote, "[W]hile most of these films were uncinematic, to say the least, they all had one asset—great dialog."[42]

In 1935, Boasberg was back at MGM, working with Irving Thalberg's newest hires, the Marx Brothers, on *A Night at the Opera*. He re-wrote the script and toured with them as they tested the material. Once again, it's hard to know exactly which jokes were Boasberg's, but Arthur Marx told the story behind one particular scene. Boasberg hated to be hurried, and producer Thalberg was nagging him. So one day he called him and said he had the material ready and he'd leave it in his office, but he was going home. Thalberg and the three Marx Brothers hurried over, but there was no script on the desk, or in the drawers or filing cabinets. Then Groucho Marx looked up. Boasberg had torn the script into one-line pieces, and tacked it to the ceiling. It took them five hours to piece it together, but Groucho felt it was worth it, because it was the first draft of the stateroom scene.[43] Despite that, Boasberg didn't get his name in the credits, and the lack of credit bothered him.

When *Opera* was a big hit, Thalberg hired Boasberg and two junior writers to write the Brothers' next film, *A Day at the Races*. Boasberg was to receive the primary credit for it. But he wanted the credit to read "Original Story and Screenplay by Robert Pirosh and George Seaton. Comedy scenes and Construction by Al Boasberg." MGM responded by moving his name down to third place following the other writers. When he threatened to sue, MGM took his name off the film completely. He swore never to work in movies again.[44]

Meanwhile, Boasberg had gone back to work for Jack Benny's radio show in 1936. On June 16, 1937, he signed a new contract with Benny, who agreed to pay him $1,500 a week to look over the show's scripts.[45] That night, at 1:30 a.m., Al Boasberg died at home following a heart attack.[46] He was buried in the family plot at Forest Lawn Cemetery in Buffalo.

Respectful obituaries appeared in newspapers throughout the country. Many papers ran the United Press article as a front-page story. However, one headline that was almost worthy of Boasberg's pen was on the front of the *Van Nuys News*: "Death Denies Author Pleasure of a Valley Home: Al Boasberg Planning to Move to Van Nuys, Stricken Thursday."[47] Even better, they might not have been kidding.

Although many today don't know his name, even if they know his work, Al Boasberg hasn't been forgotten in his hometown. The Al Boasberg Award is given annually "for excellence in comedy" at the Buffalo International Film Festival.[48]

Census Records

1900 U.S. Federal Census (Population Schedule), Buffalo Ward 24, Erie, New York, ED 202, Sheet 2, Dwelling 32, Family 37, Herman Boasberg household, jpeg image (Online: The Generations Network, Inc., 2007) [Digital scan of original records in the National Archives, Washington, D.C.], subscription database, http://www.ancestry.com, accessed 27 March 2007.

1910 U.S. Federal Census (Population Schedule), Milwaukee Ward 3, Milwaukee, Wisconsin, ED 83, Sheet 15B, Dwelling 282, Family 286, Barnard Goldberg household, jpeg image (Online: The Generations Network, Inc., 2007) [Digital scan of original records in the National Archives, Washington, D.C.], subscription database, http://www.ancestry.com, accessed 27 March 2007.

1910 U.S. Federal Census (Population Schedule), Buffalo Ward 21, Erie, New York, ED 204, Sheet 4A, Dwelling 80, Family 65, Samuel H. Cohen household, jpeg image (Online: The Generations Network, Inc., 2007) [Digital scan of original records in the National Archives, Washington, D.C.], subscription database, http://www.ancestry.com, accessed 16 March 2007.

1920 U.S. Federal Census (Population Schedule), Manhattan Assembly District 20, New York, New York, ED 1388, Sheet 14A, Dwelling 58, Family 888, Louis Levy household, jpeg image (Online: The Generations Network, Inc., 2007) [Digital scan of original records in the National Archives, Washington, D.C.], subscription database, http://www.ancestry.com, accessed 27 March 2007.

1930 U.S. Federal Census (Population Schedule), Los Angeles Assembly District 58, Los Angeles, California, ED 194, Sheet 45A, Dwelling 70, Family 341, Al Boasberg household, jpeg image (Online: The Generations Network, Inc., 2007) [Digital scan of original records in the National Archives, Washington, D.C.], subscription database, http://www.ancestry.com, accessed 27 March 2007.

Clyde Bruckman

One of the saddest stories you come across in most Keaton biographies is what happened to one of his gag men, Clyde Bruckman. Despondent over his career, he killed himself in 1955. But the man Leonard Maltin called "one of the all-time great comedy writers" shouldn't be remembered for how he died; he should be remembered for how he lived and worked.[1]

An only child, Clyde Adolf Bruckman was born on June 30, 1894, in San Bernardino, California.[2] His parents were Rudolph and Bertha Smith Bruckman. His father was a bartender in 1900, but by the time of the census ten years later he'd become the owner of his own liquor store.

Two years later, in 1912, Rudolph Bruckman committed suicide. According to newspaper reports, he'd been seriously injured 18 months earlier in a car accident that killed his wife's younger brother, Frank Smith.[3] He had complained that if his head didn't get better, he'd be in an asylum. In spring 1912, he and his wife and son took "an extended eastern trip, hoping the change would benefit him, but without avail."[4] At the end of October, he began to put his house in order and signed a deal to sell his business, claiming he planned to move to the beach to improve his health. But on November 7, he "closed up the last of his business affairs at the Farmers' Exchange National Bank, went to his private office and wrote a farewell to his wife and family ... walked through his liquor store and greeted the attendant heartily, and, stepping out the rear door to the alley, fired the two shots that ended his life." He shot himself through the heart and died instantly.[5] At the inquest, the coroner said that the evidence showed without a doubt that he was not in his right mind, and the jury ruled suicide.[6] His sudden death must have been a shock, not only for the family he left behind, but for the customers in his store and for other friends—hundreds of people attended his funeral.[7]

A couple of years later, 19-year-old Clyde Bruckman moved to Los Angeles and found a job as a sportswriter for the *Los Angeles Times*. His byline first appeared on April 4, 1914, on a recurring column, "Foul Tips," a compilation of the day's baseball news. Two days later he wrote an article, "Peculiarities of Batters," that shows he was already an observant reporter and pretty good writer. He argued that "a ball player without peculiarities is as scarce as a prizefighter without an alibi," and he supported that theory with ten succinct examples from the Coast League ("Boles has a selected spot on the field where he crouches on his knees with his bat between his legs when on deck. Walt puts several acres of dirt on his hands, removing the same by wiping it off on his uniform."[8] As a sportswriter, he mostly focused on baseball, and did a series of biographical sketches of local players.

The next year, he left the *Times* and moved over to the *Los Angeles Examiner*, but rarely had a byline, so it's impossible to tell which articles were written by him. After a few years, he wrote bylined longer articles. Even today, his prose is still funny. For example, before the 1918 season, he wrote:

> In certain quarters this spring there has been a great deal of moaning about the general weakness and deficiencies of the Vernon baseball club. The moaning at times has taken on the tune of a mournful wail, rising like a dirge to the somber skies. The self-appointed mourners picked the Tigers to finish seventh in a six-club league and so on. Yesterday we went out to look over this funeral gathering, half expecting to see prominent undertakers and embalmers hovering around the bench, like vultures seeking carrion prey. We expected to see pallbearers in abundance and to hear players humming "Hearts and Flowers" and to see them in uniforms of black, but it was not so. The Terrible Tigers do not look like a corpse, collective or otherwise. Instead they look like a ball club that is very much alive and headed for points higher than last place.[9]

He predicted accurately; the Tigers finished the season in first place of the Pacific Coast League. The Vernon Tigers were owned by Keaton's mentor, Roscoe Arbuckle.

On July 29, 1916, Bruckman married Lola Margaret Hamblin in Los Angeles.[10] He was 22 and she was 21. Born in Kansas City, Missouri, on July 2, 1895, to blacksmith Simon and Mary Hamblin, she had four brothers and, at the time of her marriage, worked as a telephone operator.

Bruckman also began to write baseball stories for *The Saturday Evening Post*. *Camera!* called him a protégé of Charles Van Loan, a former *Examiner* writer who'd become famous for his short stories.[11] The *Post*, which sold more than two million copies per issue, was a general interest weekly magazine primarily known for publishing entertaining fiction by still remembered (in the 2000s) authors like Edith Wharton, Ring Lardner, H.G. Wells and P.G. Wodehouse, as well as those who were popular in their day, like Fannie Hurst and Mary Roberts Rinehart.

His *Post* story "Reverse English," which appeared in the October 21, 1916, issue, describes the circumstances that convinced pitcher Filbert "Bugs" Brennan to settle down and lead the Moguls to win the World Series. Third baseman Steve describes Bugs as a young pitcher just up from the minors who "looked like he might have something in his head besides the lining," but "his big fault lay in his restlessness. His mind would travel from here to China and back while you winked your eye."[12] During the pre-season, "the kid made a circus out of a training camp grind, furnishing everything but the tent."[13] But his manager "knew Bugs was a great young pitcher in the making if someone didn't kill him before he got made."[14]

By August, Bruckman says, his pitching was still unreliable: "Bugs was the rankest in-and-outer you ever saw. One day the batters couldn't do nothing but stand there and guess when the ball went past, and the next time he pitched they'd all but cripple our infielders."[15] The team's season was equally hit-and-miss, and by the last game they were fighting the Portland Ducks for third place in a six-team league. The night before that game, Bugs went out drinking with some con men. He turned up back at the hotel at two a.m., minus his money, watch and diamond pin. At the ballpark, after a rough first inning, Bugs pitched brilliantly, "getting better every inning like they tell about in the books."[16] The Moguls won, and the team's pride was saved.

That night a man came to visit Bugs, to tell him what had become of his money and valuables. It seems that Brennan had made a bet on the game the night before—on the Ducks. Bugs paused, thought, then said, "When a fellow can pour somethin' down his throat that will make him bet against himself, it's time to get on the water wagon, an' stick on. That's me!"[17] So the next season, that was how Bugs gained discipline and was able to surprise the rest of the league, taking the Series from a stronger club. He even pitched a shutout in the final game. Even though Steve said it wasn't meant to be a moral lesson, he thought, "Any man can change his signs!"[18]

One story in a prestigious national magazine wasn't enough to convince Bruckman to quit his day job at the paper, but he kept trying and he sold a second story to the *Post*. "Joe Gum" (May 5, 1917) told the story of a talented and arrogant shortstop. "His batting was all it could be. He stood up to the plate swell; took a clean snappy swing at the ball; and, as far as we could see, he didn't have a weakness.... He had a couple of bad points: He liked Joe Gum too well and was too fresh. The combination was awful!"[19] His teammate called him "the president of the hate-me society."[20] When Joe put the club on a 14-game winning streak, he got even worse: "He started telling us about out boots and giving us suggestions on how to play our positions. That was the brick that broke the hodcarrier's back."[21] To top it off, he beat everyone at poker. After a fistfight left his opponent knocked out cold, the rest of the team decided to just wait for Joe's luck to change.

That day came when they discovered Joe's weakness: He couldn't hit slow pitches that were low and inside. The team they were playing against found out quickly and Joe was left "mauling the air."[22] His fielding fell apart, too. He got so bad that the first baseman said, "Only the natural fear of the electric chair kept me from killing him outright."[23] The Mixers slid to third place in the league and they finally got a replacement shortstop. Joe went to the Redskins, the worst team in the other league: "They'd finished last in the National League so many years the place has been awarded to them as a homestead."[24] The manager was overjoyed that Joe would never gum up another game for them.

After he left, the team settled down and easily clinched the pennant. However, Joe wasn't finished with them: He led his broken-down team to the World Series, where they beat the Mixers in four games. To add insult to injury, in the final game he hit the longest home run ever, on a low, slow inside pitch. It gave the already unwell manager a relapse.

That was Bruckman's only other published *Post* story, which started running far fewer stories about baseball. Instead, non-fiction about the wartime misery in Europe and stories about American troops filled the pages. So Bruckman pursued other opportunities.

When he registered for the draft in 1917, the recording official wrote that he was a tall, stout man with blue eyes and brown hair. Because he was married, he didn't have to serve.

Something led him to the movie industry, and he started working in film in early February of 1919. The comedy team of Eddie Lyons and Lee Moran hired him to write intertitles for their shorts at Universal Studio.[25] According to film historian Hans J. Wollstein, former vaudevillians Lyons and Moran were "the first successful screen-comedy team.... [They] created a polite, white-collar comedy style far removed from the often vulgar slapstick so popular at certain other studios at the time."[26] They were one of Universal's biggest box office successes, but the team parted company in 1920. *Film Reference* credits Bruckman with the story for their *Three in a Closet*.[27]

It's easy to see how he got hired with his talent for writing clever sentences, ones that would work well on title cards. A few sentences from his baseball story "Reverse English" could easily have translated to the screen:

> Our fielders stole base hits like they were all descendants of Jesse James.[28]
> The Seal coaches stood on the lines and told Bugs a great deal about his life, his ancestors and where his next stop would be.[29]
> The whole club flew into more pieces than there are in a watch.[30]

A pretty good pitcher himself, Bruckman joined other writers as a member of the Scribes amateur team. When they played against another amateur team, the Boobs, the *L.A. Times* reported that Bruckman "was a bear, striking out nineteen Boobs, and if there had been any more of them present he would have served them the same way."[31]

Although the census taker in 1920 described him as a newspaper reporter, by this time Bruckman had secured a second movie industry job at Warner Bros. studio, writing for comedian Monty Banks. Banks had filled in for Buster Keaton with the Arbuckle company while Buster was in the Army; he appeared in *The Sheriff*, *Camping Out*, and *Love*.[32] Bruckman wrote eight shorts for Banks, including *His Naughty Night* in 1920 and *Where Is My Wife?* in 1921.

He continued working for the *Examiner* until April 5, 1921, when his last article was published; it was about the first day of the baseball season, and titled "The Open Season for Grandmothers' Funerals Starts Today."[33] Ten days later, *Variety* reported that he was hired to write comedies for the Special Pictures Corporation,[34] a company that employed stars like Ford Sterling. It soon went out of business.

Then in mid–1921, Bruckman ran into the first baseman from the Scribes team, Harry Brand. Brand had also left the newspaper business to become Buster Keaton's publicity man, and he suggested that Bruckman come work for Keaton. Following a lunch meeting, Bruckman, with his obvious comedic writing background and love of baseball, was hired.[35]

Although he wasn't initially listed in the credits, Bruckman began writing gags for Keaton's shorts along with Jean Havez and Joseph Mitchell. According to Keaton biographer Rudi Blesh, Buster remembered Bruckman's complaints about having to find sedentary gags that Keaton could do after he broke his ankle during an on-set accident filming the first version of *The Electric House*.[36]

Writing for Keaton changed a lot when the company graduated into feature films. Keaton told film historian Kevin Brownlow that, "especially after we stopped making wild two-reelers and got into feature-length pictures, our scenario boys had to be story-conscious because we couldn't tell any far-fetched stories.... An audience wanted to believe any story we told them."[37]

Bruckman worked with Keaton on some of Buster's greatest films: *Three Ages*, *Our Hospitality*, *Sherlock Jr.*, *The Navigator* and *Seven Chances*. Later he was nostalgic for these days:

> We were one big happy family. And that's something you don't know until—and if—you've been in one. In such a situation, gags are never a

problem. You feel good. Your mind's at ease, and working. I was at Buster's house, or he at mine four or five nights a week—playing cards, horsing around, dodging the issue. Then, at midnight, to the kitchen, sit on the sink, eat hamburgers and work on gags until three in the morning. And how we'd work![38]

In May of 1924, the *Los Angeles Times* described the gestation of *The Navigator*. Keaton said to Bruckman, Havez, and Mitchell: "There's the boat. Now write me a comedy."

> [So] all three inspected the *Buford* from the lowest deck to the top of the main mast. Everything from the anchor to the smokestack was considered for its possible comedy values.... For two whole days, the gag men shot possibilities at each other and Buster while they built up the story. A stenographer sat hard by taking down the suggestions.... At the end of a week of this sort of thing, the stenographer had more than 400 pages of single-spaced gag ideas. These ideas were whipped into story form by Buster and his henchmen in several more days of work.[39]

While he worked with Keaton, Bruckman also moonlighted, writing gags for former professional wrestler-turned-comic Bull Montana in 1922

Buster Keaton's creative team on *Three Ages* (1923), from left to right: Joseph Mitchell, Clyde Bruckman, Keaton, Jean Havez, Eddie Cline. (*From the collections of the Margaret Herrick Library, Academy of Motion Picture Arts and Sciences.*)

and '23, for the shorts *A Punctured Prince* and *Glad Rags*, and he also wrote the story for Montana's *Rob 'Em Good* as well as the intertitles for the Viola Dana-Tom Moore feature *Rouged Lips*, the story of a poor orphan who meets a rich boy.

Keaton's Bruckman-Mitchell-Havez team was temporarily broken up in December 1924 when Keaton took a vacation[40]; the breakup became permanent in February after Havez died unexpectedly. In his stead, Keaton hired other writers, and Bruckman became a freelancer. Clearly, Keaton and Bruckman parted on good terms, because they continued to work together, off and on, for the rest of Bruckman's life.

His first project was to co-write with Bryan Foy the two-reeler *Bashful Jim* for Mack Sennett, directed by Keaton co-director Eddie Cline. The two-reel comedy starred Ralph Graves and Alice Day, the sister of Marceline, who would go on to become the leading lady in Keaton's *The Cameraman*. His next project, in 1925, was another short for Sennett, *Remember When*, starring Harry Langdon. Then it was back to Monty Banks, writing the story for the feature *Keep Smiling*, and also contributing gags to Harold Lloyd's *For Heaven's Sake*. Possibly he also did some work on Keaton's *Battling Butler* the following year—the *Kokomo Daily Tribune* reported that he was on its writing staff.[41]

When Bruckman ran across a great story, William Pittenger's memoir *The Great Locomotive Chase*, he brought it to Buster. It told the history of the Civil War Andrews Raid, an attempt by 22 Union Army members to steal a train and drive it North, destroying an important Confederate supply line as they went. With some changes, it became Keaton's greatest film, *The General*. On May 9, 1926, Keaton's cast and crew, including Clyde and Lola Bruckman, arrived in Cottage Grove, Oregon, where most of the film was shot.[42] According to the *Cottage Grove Sentinel*'s brief biography of Bruckman, he was the assistant director, but by the time the film came out at the end of the year, Keaton insisted that Bruckman receive a co-directing credit.[43]

That credit launched Bruckman's directing career. His first solo directing job took him back to Monty Banks, for his feature *Horse Shoes*. Banks played a milquetoast lawyer who solves a mystery and wins his employer's daughter (Jean Arthur, who had played a tiny role in Keaton's *Seven Chances*). According to *Moving Picture World*, "in recognition of his splendid work," the producers hired him to direct Banks' next film, *A Perfect Gentleman*.[44] This was Banks' last American film; he moved to England and continued his film career there.

Bruckman then took some time off from directing to write gags for

The Cameraman. Keaton mentioned in his autobiography that he was on the job for the bathhouse scene in Venice, California.[45]

At this point, Hal Roach signed him to a long-term contract. As film historian Joe Adamson observed, "one of Bruckman's skills was his ability to adapt to the comic persona with whom he was working,"[46] and he went to work with a comedy team very different from Keaton, Lloyd or Banks: Laurel and Hardy. He would direct some of their best silent shorts, including *The Battle of the Century* in 1927 and *Leave 'Em Laughing* in 1928.

Then he returned to Harold Lloyd, co-writing *Welcome Danger* as a silent film. When Lloyd decided to remake it as a sound film, Bruckman took over the direction from another Keaton alumnus, Mal St. Clair. According to the *L.A. Times,* at a preview, Lloyd found "that in almost every instance gags were funnier in sound than in silent form.... [I]t is safe to say that fully 40 percent has been added to the laugh value of the picture by the addition of sound and dialog."[47]

Bruckman's next directorial job for Lloyd, *Feet First*, took the company to Honolulu to shoot some scenes, after which he made a comedy with Robert Woolsey (without his partner Bert Wheeler), *Everything's Rosie.*

On October 4, 1931, Lola Bruckman was taken to the hospital for an emergency operation to remove an intestinal obstruction. She died four days later, just 36 years old.[48]

Perhaps because of the sudden death of his wife, Bruckman started drinking heavily. According to Harold Lloyd, during the production of his next film *Movie Crazy* "he had a little difficulty with the bottle and we practically had to wash him out and I had to carry on."[49] Most biographies agree that this was the beginning of the end of his career.

Nevertheless, he continued to work. He directed a few more shorts for Mack Sennett, including W.C. Fields' *A Fatal Glass of Beer*, judged by Leonard Maltin to be "undoubtedly the wildest, and at the same time the subtlest, of his four for Sennett."[50] He not only directed for Sennett, he also co-wrote scripts such as *Uncle Jake* and *Roadhouse Queen.* Over at Fox, he directed a Lew Ayres feature, *Spring Tonic*, in 1935. His final directing job, again for Fields, was to become one of Fields' most famous films: *The Man on the Flying Trapeze.* However, according to comedy historians Ted Okuda and Edward Watz, the *Hollywood Reporter* wrote that Fields and actor-screenwriter Sam Hardy had to take over the picture's direction for two days due to Bruckman's "absenteeism" (read: alcoholism). Thanks to this article in a major trade paper, Bruckman's difficulties with alcohol and his unreliability on the job affected his ability to get work as a director; in fact, he never got another directing job.[51]

Instead he went back to comedy writing for Keaton, working on seven of his ten shorts for Columbia, including the first (and considered by many the best), *The Pest from the West*, which Leonard Maltin called "one of Keaton's funniest films."[52] Maltin also praised *Nothing but Pleasure*: "a funny and beautifully constructed comedy."[53] Many of the gags were recycled from Keaton and Bruckman's silent films, but they were still funny.

In 1938, Harold Lloyd hired him to help write gags for his second-to-last feature, *Professor Beware*. Bruckman also co-wrote ten films for Universal in the early 1940s, including several musicals, such as *Swingtime Johnny* directed by Eddie Cline, and *South of Dixie*.

Of the films he wrote during this time period, the ones shown most often now are shorts he wrote for the Three Stooges. In 1935, he had directed the Stooges in *Horse's Collars*, and in the following years, he wrote more than 30 of their shorts, including some considered among their best: *Three Little Beers, Half-Shot Shooters, Three Sappy People*, and *You Nazty Spy!*[54] In an article for *The Three Stooges Journal*, Brent Seguine called Bruckman's *Cash and Carry* one of the Stooges all-time best, with "one 'nyuk' after another." He particularly liked the dialogue, for instance, "I didn't know they put money in cans. *They don't.* Sure. See. Canned coin."[55]

Some time during the 1930s, Bruckman married a second time. Gladys Marie Prevost was born on October 3, 1903, in Oklahoma, where her father Joseph worked as a coal miner. Joseph and his wife Jeanne were French immigrants. In the 1910s, the family moved to Santa Ana, California, and her father became the foreman of a lumberyard. In 1926, she was working as a saleslady and living with her parents.[56]

Beginning in 1935, when the bottom fell out of his career, Bruckman tried to cut back on expenses, even trying—desperately—to sell his home, which was advertised for sale in January: "A steal. 4 bedrooms, 3 baths, library, game room, 2 servants rooms."[57] But it didn't sell. Ads for it ran periodically until April 7, 1941. The final ad read "Want reasonable offer or accept some trade for 717 N. Elm Dr."[58] He must have found a buyer, because on April 27 and 28, the Bruckmans had a sale of some of their furnishings. The ad said: "House sold. Must vacate." Items included carpets, books, a bedroom suite and 11 John Decker paintings of stage personages,[59] probably now worth a small fortune. He and his wife moved to a house in West Los Angeles, and eventually ended up in an apartment at 934 Sixth Street in Santa Monica.

According to Joe Adamson, Bruckman's best writing during the 1940s was uncredited. He contributed to Abbott and Costello's 1944 feature *In Society*, considered one of the team's best.[60]

In 1945, his work for Universal brought him trouble. All comic writers recycled old routines, but Harold Lloyd felt that one particular reuse rose to the level of wholesale copyright infringement.[61] He sued Universal for $1.7 million, alleging that his former employees Bruckman and Warren Wilson had misappropriated sequences from *The Freshman*, *Movie Crazy* and *Welcome Danger* for *She Gets Her Man*, *Her Lucky Night*, and *So's Your Uncle*.

By the time the case went to trial in September, the damages requested had gone down to $400,000.[62] Lloyd testified that the magician's coat scene in *Movie Crazy* was "one of the three or four funniest scenes I've ever played. It's what we call the 'little gold nugget' we're always looking for. It really made the picture." Bruckman and Universal's lawyer questioned him about the origin of some of the other gags in the film; "specifically referred to were a William Fox picture made in 1927 and an MGM film featuring Buster Keaton." Lloyd denied seeing one of the sequences and called the other "a bewhiskered idea long relied upon for laughs."

The judge awarded Lloyd $60,000 for the *Movie Crazy* sequences used in *So's Your Uncle*.[63] Universal appealed, but the Ninth Circuit Court upheld the judgment.[64] Universal decided to settle out of court for the rest; the *L.A. Times* reported that the check was for more than $100,000.[65] Lloyd's lawyer told the *New York Times* that it was the largest amount ever paid in an American copyright infringement action, exceeding $117,000.[66] Lloyd also brought a similar suit against Columbia, Bruckman and co-writer Felix Adler, alleging plagiarism of *The Freshman* and *Movie Crazy* in the Three Stooges shorts *Three Wise Saps* and *Loco Boy Makes Good*.[67] Columbia also settled out of court for undisclosed amounts.[68] These cases didn't help Bruckman's career.

From that point forward, he was unable to find work in features. According to Okuda and Watz, he was let go from the Columbia shorts unit because his alcoholism got worse; however, he got story credit on films that were remakes of his earlier work.[69] His final script for the Stooges was *Goof on the Roof* in 1953.[70]

When television came along, Bruckman found work. Again returning to Keaton, he wrote for Buster's local Los Angeles TV show in 1950, as well as on several episodes of Abbott and Costello's show in 1953 and '54. But his career was going badly. In 1954, Columbia had started plundering old footage for new Three Stooges shorts, so there wasn't much work for a writer. Jules White, the head of Columbia's short subjects department, said that late in the year Bruckman visited, needing "a job very desperately. He came to me and said, 'Please, give me a picture to do.' I didn't have any to do."[71]

Like his father, Clyde Bruckman committed suicide. According to the *Los Angeles Times*, at about 4:15 p.m. on January 4, 1955, he parked his car and walked into a restaurant at 20th Street and Wilshire Blvd. in Santa Monica.[72] He went into the men's room and shot himself in the head with a .45 automatic he'd borrowed from Buster Keaton, leaving a typewritten note that said he had no money to pay for a funeral.[73] He was buried at the Fairhaven Memorial Park in Santa Ana, California.[74]

Gladys Bruckman moved back to Anaheim, close to her family. She was living with her nephew in Modesto, California, when she died on June 9, 1983, aged 79, of peritonitis that was a consequence of diverticulitis. She was also buried at Fairhaven.[75]

Bruckman did a lot to form modern-day ideas about how Keaton worked. He was the only crew member Rudi Blesh quoted extensively in his biography *Keaton*,[76] and Bruckman insisted consistently that everything to do with Keaton's films came directly from Keaton:

> You seldom saw his name in the story credits. But I can tell you—and so could Jean Havez if he were alive—that those wonderful stories were ninety percent Buster's. I was often ashamed to take the money, much less the credit. I would say so, Bus would say, "Stick, I need a left fielder," and laugh. But he never left you in left field. We were all overpaid from the strict creative point of view. Most of the direction was his, as Eddie Cline would tell you.... Comedian, gag man, writer, director—then add technical innovator. Camerawork. Look at his pictures to see beautiful shots, wide pans and long shots, unexpected close-ups, and angles that were all new when he thought them up.[77]

He probably shortchanged his own contributions; just because it didn't feel like work, doesn't mean that it wasn't. But Keaton never underestimated how valuable Bruckman had been to him. He told Kevin Brownlow that Bruckman and Havez were the two best writers he ever had.[78]

Further Information

One difficulty in researching Bruckman is that an *X-Files* TV show episode was called "Clyde Bruckman's Final Repose." In homage to Keaton's crew, writer Darin Morgan named his characters Bruckman, Eddie Cline, and Jean Havez, but the plot about the murder of several psychics had nothing to do with them. He won an Emmy for his script and caused lots of false drops for Bruckman researchers.

Census Records

1880 U.S. Federal Census (Population Schedule), Denmark, Oxford, Maine, ED 122, Sheet 101, Dwelling 100, Family 100, Edward M. Smith household, jpeg image (Online: The Generations Network, Inc., 2009) [Digital scan of original records in the National Archives, Washington, D.C.], subscription database, http://www.ancestry.com, accessed 31 October 2009.

1900 U.S. Federal Census (Population Schedule), San Bernardino Ward 3, San Bernardino, California, ED 226, Sheet 7, Dwelling 46, Family 52, Rudolph A. Bruckman household, jpeg image (Online: The Generations Network, Inc., 2007) [Digital scan of original records in the National Archives, Washington, D.C.], subscription database, http://www.ancestry.com, accessed 2 April 2007.

1910 U.S. Federal Census (Population Schedule), San Bernardino Ward 2, San Bernardino, California, Los Angeles, California, ED 118, Sheet 5A, Dwelling 113, Family 129, Rudolph Bruckman household, jpeg image (Online: The Generations Network, Inc., 2007) [Digital scan of original records in the National Archives, Washington, D.C.], subscription database, http://www.ancestry.com, accessed 2 April 2007.

1910 U.S. Federal Census (Population Schedule), St. Joseph Ward 6, Buchanan, Missouri, ED 81, Sheet 45B, Dwelling 344, Family 352, Simon L. Hamblin household, jpeg image (Online: The Generations Network, Inc., 2009) [Digital scan of original records in the National Archives, Washington, D.C.], subscription database, http://www.ancestry.com, accessed 31 October 2009.

1910 U.S. Federal Census (Population Schedule), Coalgate Ward 3, Coal, Oklahoma, ED 75, Sheet 10B, Dwelling 305, Family 306, Joe Prevost household, jpeg image (Online: The Generations Network, Inc., 2009) [Digital scan of original records in the National Archives, Washington, D.C.], subscription database, http://www.ancestry.com, accessed 28 December 2009.

1920 U.S. Federal Census (Population Schedule), Los Angeles Assembly District 73, Los Angeles, California, ED 401, 12 January 1920, Sheet 11A, Dwelling 9, Family 11, Clyde A. Bruckman household, jpeg image (Online: The Generations Network, Inc., 2007) [Digital scan of original records in the National Archives, Washington, D.C.], subscription database, http://www.ancestry.com, accessed 2 April 2007.

1920 U.S. Federal Census (Population Schedule), Santa Ana Township, Orange, California, ED 81, Sheet 6B, Dwelling 139, Family 172, Joe Prevost household, jpeg image (Online: The Generations Network, Inc., 2009) [Digital scan of original records in the National Archives, Washington, D.C.], subscription database, http://www.ancestry.com, accessed 28 December 2009.

1930 U.S. Federal Census (Population Schedule), Beverly Hills, Los Angeles, California, ED 820, Sheet 9B, Dwelling 178, Family 179, Clyde Bruckman household, jpeg image (Online: The Generations Network, Inc., 2007) [Digital scan of original records in the National Archives, Washington, D.C.], subscription database, http://www.ancestry.com, accessed 30 March 2007. Bruckman, Clyde Adolf. *World War I Draft Registration Cards, 1917–1918* (5 June 1918) (Online: The Generations Network, Inc., 2007) [Digital scan of original records in the National Archives, Washington, D.C.], subscription database, http://www.ancestry.com, accessed 27 March 2007.

Bruckman, Clyde Adolf. *World War II Draft Registration Cards, 1942* (Online: FamilySearch Historical Collections, 2011) [Digital scan of original records in the National Archives, Washington, D.C.], https://www.familysearch.org, accessed 19 January 2012.

Raymond Cannon

Writing the scenario for *Go West* was only a small part of Raymond Cannon's long and eventful life. After a rollercoaster Hollywood career, he had a great second act as a sport-fishing expert, spending most of his time off of the Baja California coast.

Ulises Tildman Cannon was the fifth and youngest son of a farmer and part-time Baptist preacher. He was born September 1, 1892, on a farm near Sharp's Chapel and Long Hollow in Union County, Tennessee; his parents were Newton Cannon and Sarah Lincoln Bolinger.

Different sources tell different tales about what he did before he went into film. The 1910 census found him living alone and working as a salesman at a soda fountain in Knoxville, Tennessee. According to his biographer Gene Kira, he attended a Baptist divinity school to please his mother, but got expelled,[1] so he moved West, singing in vaudeville and working as a reporter in Dallas and Fort Worth. He also told Kira that he spent ten days in a Chihuahua jail for being a correspondent during the Mexican Revolution.[2] The story he told in his 1934 *Motion Picture Almanac* entry was slightly different. Although he mentioned the Baptist seminary, he also said he attended a military academy in Sweetwater, Tennessee, followed by touring with Roy Watson's dramatic stock company through the South and Southwest.[3]

However he got there, he was in Los Angeles by the early 1910s with a new name, Raymond.[4] His first acting job was in 1912 at the Bentley Grand Theater in Long Beach,[5] around the same time that he found work in films, first with Thomas Ince's company.[6] In 1913, he was part of the cast of *The Adventures of Kathlyn*, the first cliffhanger serial, for the Selig Polyscope Company.[7]

By 1916, several members of his family had joined him in California. According to the Register of Voters, he shared a house with his brothers Manuel (a steward) and Thornburg (a bricklayer), as well as their mother. All except Raymond were registered Republicans; he declared himself a Socialist.[8]

When he registered for the draft in 1917, Raymond was still working at Selig.[9] His draft registration form says that he was tall with brown eyes and brown hair, and was totally deaf in one ear. It was enough to keep him out of the Army.

On April 6, 1918, the first issue of *Camera! The Digest of the Motion Picture Industry* came out. Elmer M. Robbins published it every Saturday, and it featured news, reviews and gossip, as well as information on who was hiring. Similar to *Variety*, it covered only the film business. Its office was three doors down the street from the Photoplayer's Equity Association.[10] Just one month after it began publishing, it ran this paragraph: "Raymond Cannon is working with Griffith, when he is not boosting for the Equity and also for *Camera!* Cannon has said and done some very nice things for us, and we like the son of a gun."[11] By June, Cannon had become the magazine's business manager,[12] although he continued to work as an actor, and listed himself in the Casting Column as a juvenile.[13] He attempted to cut back on his magazine responsibilities in December 1919.[14] His publisher, Robbins, died on March 2, 1920,[15] and Cannon bought the magazine in June 1921[16] and sold it a year later, appearing as publisher for the last time on May 13, 1922.[17] The magazine merged with *Film Tribute* on January 5, 1924,[18] and ceased publication on February 16, 1924.

The 1920 census found him living alone in a boarding house on Hollywood Boulevard, just three blocks from the *Camera!* offices.

As *Camera!* said, he did act for D.W. Griffith, appearing in several Dorothy Gish films, and he played Sporty Malone with Lillian Gish in *True Heart Susie* (1919). When Griffith moved to Mamaroneck, New York, in 1920, Cannon stayed in Los Angeles and became a freelancer, working with Douglas MacLean at Thomas Ince Studios in *Chickens* (1921) and future Keaton co-star Marion Mack at Robertson-Cole Pictures in *Mary of the Movies* (1923).

On February 9, 1920, he married Fanchon Royer.[19] She was born in Des Moines, Iowa, on January 21, 1902. She moved to Hollywood in 1918 and found work as an extra at Famous Players–Lasky Corporation.[20] Although she tried to find more work as an actress—in her ad in *Camera!* she called herself "a versatile ingénue"[21]—that career didn't take off, so she went to work for *Camera!* as its Society Editor; she first appeared on the masthead on January 24, 1920, but within a week, she was the assistant editor.[22] By September, she had become the editor.[23] Her goodbye editorial appeared on May 20, 1922, although she continued to occasionally contribute articles.[24] From there, she became a writers' and actors' agent, forming a company with actress Martha Mattox.[25] A versatile woman, she also worked as a publicist.[26] The birth of three children—Royer (1922), Elwood (1926), and Sandra (1930)—didn't seem to slow her down.

In the meantime, Cannon tried to break into directing in 1923 at Fine Arts Studios, but his initial film was never completed.[27] According to "Pulse of the Studios" in *Camera!*, it was an untitled farce written by Royer, and Cecil Holland was the star. It was listed in the publication only for one week.[28]

In 1924, Cannon left acting for good and started writing screenplays. His earliest sales were to comic Douglas MacLean: *Going Up, The Yankee Counsel, Never Say Die* and *Introduce Me*.[29] The last title got pretty good reviews; the *New York Times* said it "evoked hilarious laughter"[30] and the *Los Angeles Times* wrote, "*Introduce Me* couldn't very well help being anything but a very funny comedy."[31] His next scenario was a drama for someone else he'd acted with, Marion Mack.[32] Called *The Carnival Girl*, it was the film she made just before leaving for Oregon to make *The General* with Buster Keaton.

Keaton's regular writing team broke up when Jean Havez died in February of 1925, so Keaton hired Cannon at that point. After work started on *Brown Eyes* (later called *Go West*) in May 1925, the announcement in the *Los Angeles Times* said, "[F]or this picture, and for subsequent Keaton comedies, the Schenck organization has signed Raymond Cannon, veteran comedy director, writer and actor, to collaborate with Keaton and Lex Neal, his director, in the preparation of all of his stories.... [He] is considered one of the best 'gag' men in pictures."[33] But Cannon stayed with Keaton for just the one film. In September, the *L.A. Times* reported that Cannon was to be loaned out to Universal Studios.[34] In later interviews, neither side discussed what happened to cause Cannon to leave Keaton.

Cannon then worked on four comedies at Universal, including *Taxi, Taxi* with Edward Everett Horton, which the *L.A. Times* called "an amusing little picture that is remarkably well done."[35] In 1927 he moved to Metropolitan Pictures where he wrote *The Rejuvenation of Aunt Mary*.[36] Later that year he was signed to write *Ladies Must Dance* for Fox Film Corporation, but the film was never made.[37]

Despite this, the careers of Cannon and Royer must have been prospering because in 1926 they began building a house in the Burbank hills. Inspired by a Swiss village house, it was to be "upon a hilltop in the midst of an eight-acre estate much of which will be devoted to the outdoor amusements.... [A] large swimming pool and tennis courts will be augmented by an old Swiss smokehouse for informal gathering."[38] By October 1927, the house was finished, and *L.A. Times* gossip columnist Grace Kingsley described it as "a picturesque chalet sort of a house perched on a lovely hill and silhouetted against the distant purple mountains."[39]

The couple decided to try production again in 1928, and this time they were more successful. The film was called *Life's Like That* and it starred Wade Boteler and Grant Withers.[40] The plot was described as "conventional family man indulges in an affair; complications lead to his becoming mayor of the city," according to *Film Index International*.[41] Cannon wrote and directed it; Royer produced. This venture led to Cannon getting a one-year contract as a director at Fox Film Corporation.[42] He made four films there: *Red Wine, Joy Street, Imagine My Embarrassment,* and *Why Leave Home?*

Then, in 1931, Cannon and Royer divorced.[43] Royer went on to produce many more films; she was famous as the only woman producer in Hollywood in the 1930s.[44] A year after her divorce from Cannon, she married actor Jack Gallagher and the couple had two children, Fanchon and Jaquelyn. They divorced in 1936.[45] Later she became a book author, writing primarily about Mexican and Catholic history. She died on December 13, 1981, in Puebla, Mexico.[46]

Cannon spent the next decade as a freelance director and writer at smaller studios like Monogram Pictures and Grand National Pictures, although he also had a one-year contract at Universal Studios. There in 1934 he met Carla Laemmle when he directed her in a comedy short.[47] They became a couple and stayed together until his death. She and Cannon never married; she told her biographer Rick Atkins that at first, money was scarce and her mother was alone, and later it just wasn't a priority.[48]

Rebekah Isabelle Laemmle was born in Chicago on October 20, 1909. She changed her name to Carla after her family joined her father's brother Carl in Universal City, California. Uncle Carl was the head of Universal Studios, and he signed her to a contract as an actress and a dancer. She danced in several musicals, including *The Broadway Melody* (1929) and *The King of Jazz* (1930), but the part she is most remembered for was as a stagecoach passenger in Tod Browning's *Dracula* (1931)—she spoke the film's first lines. In the 1940s, she became a freelance dancer, working at MGM, Warner Bros., and RKO.[49]

Cannon took an interest in China and Eastern philosophy. He helped form a Chinese culture club[50] and became the public relations director for China City, a new Chinatown in Los Angeles.[51] He also publicized and staged theatrical events, including one he wrote, "Her Majesty the Prince" in 1936.[52] Carla Laemmle starred.

Cannon made one last try at a movie career, writing and directing *Samurai* in 1945 for Cavalcade Pictures. Then, as he told Kira, "my doctor told me to give up that goddamn movie business and go fishing."[53] He did, but the cure wasn't instantaneous; in 1949, he almost died of a bleeding ulcer. Friends held a benefit to raise money for ulcer surgery, and after several months of recovery, he went back to fishing. He wrote that he became "a vagabond of the sea—a way of life that has given me many rewarding and fun crammed years."[54] To support himself, he started writing about it. His first book, *How to Fish the Pacific Coast*, was published in 1953. That same year, he started writing a fishing column for *Western Outdoor News* that he continued to write for the next 24 years. Carla Laemmle was his typist, illustrator, researcher and editor. He spent the next 12 years researching the waters off of Baja California, which he called "being sentenced to Paradise."[55] His book *The Sea of Cortez* was published in 1965 and according to Laemmle, "it became an instant and highly acclaimed best seller."[56]

He died on June 7, 1977, due to complications from the treatment he was getting for lung cancer.[57] His ashes were scattered in the Sea of Cortez.[58]

Carla Laemmle kept busy until the end of her life, occasionally acting and contributing commentaries to DVDs. In 2009, she celebrated her 100th birthday by co-writing a book, *Growing Up with Monsters: My Times at Universal Studios in Rhymes*. She died on June 12, 2014, in Los Angeles.

Census Records

1900 U.S. Federal Census (Population Schedule), Frisco Township, Canadian, Oklahoma, ED 19, Sheet 5, Dwelling 86, Family 87, Newton Cannon household, jpeg image (Online: The Generations Network, Inc., 2011) [Digital scan of original records in the National Archives, Washington, D.C.], subscription database, http://www.ancestry.com, accessed 28 November 2011.

1910 U.S. Federal Census (Population Schedule), Knoxville Ward 1, Knox, Tennessee, ED 86, Sheet 13B, Dwelling 148, Family 347, Ulysses T. Cannon household, jpeg image (Online: The Generations Network, Inc., 2009) [Digital scan of original records in the National Archives, Washington, D.C.], subscription database, http://www.ancestry.com, accessed 19 September 2009.

1910 U.S. Federal Census (Population Schedule), Minneapolis Ward 8, Hennepin, Minnesota, ED 0136, Sheet 7A, Dwelling 123, Family 136, Harriet Havens household, jpeg image (Online: The Generations Network, Inc., 2007) [Digital scan of original records in the National Archives, Washington, D.C.], subscription database, http://www.ancestry.com, accessed 2 April 2007.

1920 U.S. Federal Census (Population Schedule), Los Angeles Assembly District 63, Los Angeles, California, ED 152, Sheet 16A, Dwelling 147, Family 162, Cora M. Hyans household, jpeg image (Online: The Generations Network, Inc., 2007) [Digital scan of original records in the National Archives, Washington, D.C.], subscription database, http://www.ancestry.com, accessed 2 April 2007.

1930 U.S. Federal Census (Population Schedule), Los Angeles Township, Los Angeles, California, ED 1595, Sheet 1B, Dwelling 410, Family 462, Raymond Cannon household, jpeg image (Online: The Generations Network, Inc., 2007) [Digital scan of original records in the National Archives, Washington, D.C.], subscription database, http://www.ancestry.com, accessed 2 April 2007.

1940 U.S. Federal Census (Population Schedule), Los Angeles Assembly District 56, Los Angeles, California, ED 60–97, Sheet 12B, Family 396, Carrie Belle Laemmle household, jpeg image (Online: FamilySearch Historical Collections, 2012) [Digital scan of original records in the National Archives, Washington, D.C.], https://www.familysearch.org, accessed 28 July 2012.

Bryan Foy

Bryan Foy co-wrote *College*, produced over 200 films, pioneered sound films, headed Warner Bros. Pictures' low-budget film unit and ran his own production company for years. Nevertheless, the headline on his *Los Angeles Times* obituary was "One of 'Little Foys' Succumbs."[1]

His father was Eddie Foy (born Edwin Fitzgerald), a successful Broadway and vaudeville star. His mother was Madeline Morando Foy, a former dancer born in Torino, Italy, and Foy's third wife. They had eleven children, but only seven lived. Bryan Robert Foy was the eldest, born on December 8, 1896, in Chicago, Illinois. He was followed by Charles (1898), Richard (1901), Mary (1902), Madeline Jr. (1904), Eddie Jr. (1905), and Irving (1910).

In August 1912, Eddie Foy debuted a new act with his family.[2] The Seven Little Foys were a great success. Madeline Jr. later described the act: "We'd all come out in a line, and my father would bring out a little suitcase in which was my brother Irving, who was two years old. Then we'd sing a medley; each one would step down and sing a song. Then Eddie, Charlie, and Mary would dance. We used to do a march at the finish of the act. Old-fashioned and corny, I guess, but it was cute."[3] When asked what he did in the act, Bryan Foy said, "Well, I was the tallest."[4] After her family finished performing, Mrs. Foy would come out and take a bow, too. (The 1955 Bob Hope movie was wrong: Eddie Foy wasn't forced to bring his kids into the act because his wife had died.)

In 1915 the family was hired by Mack Sennett to make films for Keystone.[5] According to Sennett expert Brent Walker, it went badly: "[F]rom day one, Foy ... asserted his ego and objected to just about every activity director Dell Henderson initiated into the film.... Sennett ultimately sent Foy and his seven offspring packing."[6] Edwin Frazee took over direction and they managed to finish one short, *A Favorite Fool*, before the Foys left.[7] It didn't discourage Bryan Foy from working in film; in fact, Sennett later hired him as a writer.

But first he tried something that wasn't part of show business: He enlisted in the Navy.[8] On May 29, 1918, he signed up for a four-year hitch in the Naval Reserve. His military records say that he was five feet, nine inches tall, with hazel eyes, brown hair, and a sallow complexion. He was ordered into active service on July 30, 1918. However, he developed an untreatable tic; the doctor wrote, "[P]atient is nervous and easily excitable at which times condition is aggravated and seriously interferes with his duties." So Seaman Second Class Foy got an honorable medical discharge on January 28, 1919. It seems they forgot to pay him, so in 1936 they sent him a check for $116. According to a 1938 newspaper profile, he still had the twitch and the nervousness twenty years later.[9]

His mother had died on June 14, 1918, of bronchial pneumonia.[10] Foy rejoined his family in New Rochelle, New York, but he stayed out of the act, which changed its name to Eddie Foy and the Younger Foys.[11] They broke up in 1924, when Eddie Foy remarried and retired.

Bryan Foy tried songwriting next. He had previously co-written music for his father's act.[12] He collaborated with another future Keaton crew member, Charles Riesner, on "My Irish American Rose."[13] His biggest hit was "Mr. Gallagher & Mr. Shean," which stage comics Ed Gallagher and Al Shean built their vaudeville act around.[14] The *Los Angeles Times* said that it "was one of the last songs to make a fortune before radio began to cut into royalties."[15] Unfortunately, Foy didn't get any of them and in 1922 he sued for some and lost.[16] The song was later recorded by Bing Crosby with Paul Whitehead's Orchestra.

In 1920 he married Vivian, who was born in Russia.[17] Grace Kingsley said she was "very lovely."[18] They adopted a daughter, Mary Jane, in 1929.[19]

He briefly tried to leave show business again and went to work as a stockbroker, but that only lasted for three months.[20] He started writing with Charles Riesner again, but they changed from songs to films. They co-wrote a bathing girl scenario that was to star Chaplin imitator Billy West for the Rothacker Film Company.[21] No finished film with that description exists now; either it was never made or it has been lost. Foy later told *Moving Picture World* that his first film work was a two-reel comedy called *Dog Days*.[22] No film with that title appears in film indexes, but Riesner was working on a series of films starring Brownie the Dog for Universal Studio in 1920 and 1921 so it was probably one of them.

In March 1922 Foy was hired by Fox Studios in Los Angeles to write comedy scenarios.[23] The studio promoted him to director only a year later. He directed a Sunshine Comedy short, *Somebody Lied* with future star Jean Arthur.[24] The following year he moved to Universal Studios.[25] There his independent company made a series of one-reel comedies called *Hysterical History*.[26] His subjects ranged from Benjamin Franklin to Antony and Cleopatra.

He returned to gag writing in 1925, working with Eddie Cline and Clyde Bruckman on *Bashful Jim*, a Mack Sennett production. Next he went to work for Keaton and co-wrote *College* with Carl Harbaugh.[27] In later interviews, Keaton disparaged both Harbaugh and director James Horne, but he never mentioned Foy.

In 1927 he signed a long-term writer's contract with Warner Bros. Studio.[28] He co-wrote *The Fortune Hunter*, a Syd Chaplin film that was directed by Riesner.[29] It was the beginning of Foy's long career at that studio.

Next he was put in charge of their Vitaphone productions. Both he and the productions moved to the Brooklyn studio in October 1928.[30] Vitaphone was the studio's process to accompany film with sound, which was recorded on separate disks, then synched to the film. Foy supervised four hundred shorts that featured vaudeville singers, dancers, and comics.[31] One of them, *Chips Off the Old Block*, featured his brothers and sisters. He also assisted the director Alan Crosland on the first talkie, *The Jazz Singer*.[32] And with only Jack Warner's knowledge, he turned *The Lights of New York* from a two-reeler into the first all-talking feature film.[33] It wasn't great cinema, but it made lots of money and helped accelerate the change from silent film to sound.

He and the Vitaphone Variety Company were back in Hollywood in June 1930.[34] The following year he started his own production company.[35] Among the Bryan Foy Productions were Al Boasberg's *Myrt and Marge*, a nudist colony movie (*Elysia, Valley of the Nude*) and Masquers Club shorts, which starred many Keystone veterans. Film historian Leonard Maltin said, "[F]amiliar faces and far-out humor were the order of the day in the Masquers Comedies. They tried very hard to go off the beaten track. Often they succeeded and sometimes they did not. But the ingenuity that went into them always shines through."[36]

In 1935 he went back to work for Warner Bros., where he was put in charge of low-budget films. Over the next six years, he supervised over 125 movies. *Variety* said, "The pix Foy supervised made up in energy and entertainment pizzazz what they lacked in polish and sophistication."[37] His films had titles like *Jail Break*, *Smart Blonde*, *Wine, Women, and Horses*, *White Bondage*, and *Sh! The Octopus.* Historian Richard Maltby described his method: "[A]ccording to legend, Bryan Foy kept a large pile of scripts permanently on his desk. A completed film's script would go to the bottom of the pile, and after it had worked its way up to the top, it would be remade with a different cast, setting, period, or alteration of other details."[38]

Warner Bros. decided to make fewer, more expensive films when World War II started, so in 1941 Foy went to 20th Century–Fox.[39] He stayed for five years; his films included *Berlin Correspondent* and *Guadalcanal Diary*.

He had become sick of being called "King of the B's," he said in an interview with the *New York Times* in 1945. "He prefers to call the films he makes 'little pictures,' which is his way of differentiating between the million or so he spends on them and the two million plus that goes into the production of a super A picture."[40] Foy said, "When a picture makes money despite a panning from the critics, then it must have something." However, he did admit that when he was at Warner Bros., he didn't bother to buy stories—he just re-wrote films the studio had made earlier. "Why, I remade *Tiger Shark* at least five times," he said. But he'd since reformed, and was currently buying fresh material.

In 1946, he went back to work with Charles Riesner, becoming the vice-president in charge of production at Eagle-Lion Films. According to what he told the *Los Angeles Times*, he got busy right away: "Eight weeks ago I walked in here and took over. I found we had no studio to speak of, no stories, no actors. Since then we have equipped eight full stages, built new cutting rooms and enlarged our offices. We have bought 17 story properties ... acquired 25 acres in the valley for exterior sets, signed such players as Sylvia Sidney and Franchot Tone."[41] He became an independent producer at Eagle Lion in 1948, and left in 1949.[42]

Vivian Foy died on December 4, 1949, of colon cancer. She was 53 years old.[43]

Bryan Foy kept working. He signed a three-year deal with Warner Bros. to produce. His work included the studio's first 3-D film, *House of Wax*, with Vincent Price. Next he spent four years at Columbia, then he went back to independent production. Fittingly, his final film was for Warner Bros. in 1963: *PT 109*, a biopic about John F. Kennedy's wartime service. He stayed active in the Screen Producers Guild and tried to put together deals, but they didn't work out.[44] According to a friend, "he spent most of his time at the race track."[45]

He died on April 20, 1977, following a heart attack, at age 82. He'd suffered from heart disease for over ten years.[46] Despite the *L.A. Times* obituary headline writer, Foy had become much more than a Little Foy. While he might not have liked *Variety*'s obituary headline "Rajah of 'B' Pics," it was accurate.[47] He was interred at the Calvary Mausoleum in East Los Angeles with his wife, not in the family plot in New York where the rest of his brothers and sisters were eventually buried.[48]

Census Records

1900 U.S. Federal Census (Population Schedule), Manhattan, New York, New York, ED 534, Sheet 7, Dwelling 36, Family 128, Edwin Foy household, jpeg image (Online: The Generations Network, Inc., 2007) [Digital scan of original records in

the National Archives, Washington, D.C.], subscription database, http://www.ancestry.com, accessed 14 April 2007.
1920 U.S. Federal Census (Population Schedule), New Rochelle Ward 2, Westchester, New York, ED 121, Sheet 2B, Dwelling 44, Family 45, Edwin Foy household, jpeg image (Online: The Generations Network, Inc., 2007) [Digital scan of original records in the National Archives, Washington, D.C.], subscription database, http://www.ancestry.com, accessed 14 April 2007.
1930 U.S. Federal Census (Population Schedule), New Rochelle Ward 2, Westchester, New York, ED 258, Sheet 13A, Dwelling 187, Family 312, William Kennedy household, jpeg image (Online: The Generations Network, Inc., 2007) [Digital scan of original records in the National Archives, Washington, D.C.], subscription database, http://www.ancestry.com, accessed 14 April 2007.
1930 U.S. Federal Census (Population Schedule), Los Angeles Assembly District 55, Los Angeles, California, ED 1966, Sheet 10B, Dwelling 257, Family 256, Bryan Foy household, jpeg image (Online: The Generations Network, Inc., 2011) [Digital scan of original records in the National Archives, Washington, D.C.], subscription database, http://www.ancestry.com, accessed 15 December 2011.
1940 U.S. Federal Census (Population Schedule), West Los Angeles, Los Angeles, California, ED 60–219, Sheet 3B, Family 47, Bryan Foy household, jpeg image (Online: FamilySearch Historical Collections, 2012) [Digital scan of original records in the National Archives, Washington, D.C.], https://www.familysearch.org, accessed 28 July 2012.
Foy, Bryan Robert. *World War II Draft Registration Cards, 1942* (Online: FamilySearch Historical Collections, 2011) [Digital scan of original records in the National Archives, Washington, D.C.], https://www.familysearch.org, accessed 19 January 2012.

Tommy Gray

Tommy Gray's name doesn't appear in the writing credits for any of Keaton's films. However, there's evidence that he worked on some of the shorts, and maybe even part of *Three Ages*.

Thomas Joseph Gray was born on March 22, 1888, in Manhattan. When he was seven, his father James died. His mother Mary was widowed with two more children, Daniel, who was five, and Mary, a newborn. She went out to "day work," probably as a cleaner. She married Francis Wenzel, a wholesale produce merchant, and the family moved from West 39th Street to West 46th Street. Later they moved one more block north to West 47th Street.

In 1910, the census enumerator was told that Gray was a newspaper reporter. He worked for *Variety*. However, he was also writing songs. He told a reporter that he'd started writing while he traveled between firms when he was a salesman working for a ladies' cloak and suit manufacturer.[1] Fred Fischer, a music publisher, liked them and gave him a job. One of his biggest hits, "Any Little Girl, That's a Nice Little Girl, Is the Right Little Girl for Me" was published that year.

He was a successful lyricist, writing material for vaudeville performers Bert Williams, Trixie Friganza, and Mae West. For the latter, his compositions added to her naughty persona. They included "Isn't She a Brazen Thing" and "It's an Awfully Easy Way to Make a Living." According to biographer Emily Wortis Leider, West failed to pay him in full for his services, and he sued her for $169. *Variety* covered the suit and she quickly realized that stiffing one of their writers was a bad idea. She paid up.[2]

He also wrote sketches, monologues, and talking acts for vaudeville performers. His 1912 ad for *Variety*'s year-end issue said that he'd written "successful Gray-matter" for over 300 acts.[3]

On May 31, 1913, he started writing a weekly humor column for *Variety*, "Tommy's Tattles." It was a series of quips about stage, screen, and anything else that he found amusing. Items from his first included:

> Newspaper headline reads "Do Moving Pictures Hurt Children?" They do if their parents are in vaudeville.
>
> Met a song writer yesterday who wasn't in business for himself. Something must be wrong somewhere.
>
> Man in Waterbury was dead for two weeks and nobody knew it. Anything can happen in Waterbury.[4]

In addition, he worked on such Broadway musicals as *The Red Canary*, *Ned Wayburn's Town Topics* and *His Little Widows*. He wrote the book and lyrics for the 1915 Lou Anger-Sophye Barnard revue *Safety First*. Like Jean Havez, he was a charter member of the American Society of Composers, Authors and Publishers (ASCAP) when it formed in 1914.

He occasionally tried acting. In 1911 he wrote himself a vaudeville act, but *Variety* didn't report on its reception.[5] He tried again in 1915, and *Variety* critic "Wynn" wrote, "Tommy has a great line of comedy for his vaudeville turn, throwing a comedy bit in between each of his six numbers."[6] He sang songs like "Fido Is a Hot Dog Now" and "I'm to Be Shot at Sunrise," and he had a trained clam that did simple sums in his fourteen-minute act. While he still needed "to become a little better acquainted with his surroundings up on the rostrum," it was "safe to register him as a sure thing for the big time." Despite the encouragement, seven days later *Variety* reported, "One week of New York vaudeville satisfied Tommy Gray, the author-near-actor. Several people told Tommy he may be the best actor in the world, but then he would still be a better author, and Tommy has listened to common sense."[7]

He first tried writing for movies in 1917, contributing stories and scenarios to Klever Komedies, a small production company based in New York. They made shorts starring Victor Moore as a hapless bumbler. (Moore went on to a long stage and screen career, and was best remembered for playing Vice-President Throttlebottom in *Of Thee I Sing*.[8]) Gray worked on eighteen of them.

When he registered for the draft that year on June 5, he was a 29-year-old single man of medium build, with gray eyes, red hair, and no disabilities.[9] His profession was author, which nicely covers all of his activities. He wasn't inducted, but in July 1918 he applied for a passport to travel to England and France to entertain the troops with the America's Over There Theater League under the YMCA. The League sent small units to military bases and they performed vaudeville acts and one-act sketches.[10] After the armistice, a revue he wrote called *The League of Notions* was produced at the Oxford Theater in London.[11]

By January 8, 1920, he had returned to his family in New York. His brother had become a commercial salesman and his sister was a private stenographer. He quickly went back to work, co-writing *Jim's Girl*, a comedy melodrama that the *Los Angeles Times* critic found diverting,[12] as well as Mae West's new eighteen-minute act.[13] A short biography said, "Tommy makes a living furnishing wise cracks to comedians, monologue artists, and musical comedies. He has written several plays, but he finds it more profitable to spread his talents over a dozen or so productions."[14]

In January–February 1921, he took a cruise to the Caribbean; his passport said he was traveling for his health.[15] He arrived in Los Angeles on December 11, 1921, to "join the scenario staff of the Buster Keaton Comedy Company," according to *Variety*.[16] Keaton was working on *Cops* at that time. They reported that Gray couldn't "decide whether to accept a continuous contract to write or divide his time between Hollywood and Broadway," but by March he had decided to divide his time: His "Tommy's Tattles" byline in *Variety* was no longer "Los Angeles" but "New York."[17]

His trip did affect his column. Some of his observations on California included:

> People who were born in California are never at a loss to know what to talk about. They just all keep talking about California.[18]
>
> There is one thing the picture producers agree on, they are all making "Bigger and Better Pictures."[19]
>
> Will Hays has issued orders to the mothers of all female screen stars, telling them not to have any more than 6,000 pictures taken in any one week depicting scenes of "home life."[20]

But only one line had anything to do with his co-workers:

> If song titles are going to become popular for the movies, why not the following? "Everybody Works but Father." A picture with a great message. Full of home scenes. See dear old father suffering pain, wounded by his own yeast explosion.[21]

He could have been inspired by the yeast misbehavior in *My Wife's Relations* (in addition to the Jean Havez song) and it's possible that he did some work on that film. It came out two months after he left.

He returned to Los Angeles in early 1923, and he was listed as part of Keaton's "largest scenario department of any individual star" in January 1923.[22] He was announced as part of the team that was to work on *Three Ages*, but his name doesn't appear in the film's credits. However, he is on the football team list in the modern part of the story.

In March, Universal Studios announced that he was joining their staff.[23] There aren't any records of his work there, but one article said that he "wrote and supervised all of their comedies."[24] This could have been an exaggeration, because that article was also announcing that he was resigning to go work for Harold Lloyd.

His writing for Lloyd is the film work he is best remembered for. He wrote the titles for three of Lloyd's films: *Hot Water*, *Girl Shy*, and *The Freshman*. From the latter, his work included the title card "A large football stadium with a college attached," one of the most accurate descriptions of an American university ever.[25]

In June 1924 he caught pneumonia. According to *Variety*, he was "never strong physically, the fever ravaged him."[26] His sister Mollie was on vacation visiting him, and she took him back to New York. He kept writing; his last "Tommy's Tattles" appeared on November 5. His final comment was, "When someone makes one phonograph record they are immediately billed as 'The Famous Phonograph Artist'; when they appear in one film, they are 'Motion Picture Stars'; but when you play in vaudeville you have to be able to do something."[27]

He died at home on November 30. The papers reported that it was due to a bronchial aliment.[28] He was only 36 years old. He was buried at the Calvary Cemetery in New York.

Census Records

1900 U.S. Federal Census (Population Schedule), Manhattan Borough, New York City, New York, ED 302, Sheet 16, Dwelling 49, Family 392, Mary Gray household, jpeg image (Online: The Generations Network, Inc., 2010) [Digital scan of original records in the National Archives, Washington, D.C.], subscription database, http://www.ancestry.com, accessed 7 January 2010.

1910 U.S. Federal Census (Population Schedule), Manhattan Ward 22, New York City, New York, ED 1342, Sheet 7B, Dwelling 26, Family 170, Francis Wenzel household, jpeg image (Online: The Generations Network, Inc., 2010) [Digital scan of original records in the National Archives, Washington, D.C.], subscription database, http://www.ancestry.com, accessed 7 January 2010.

1920 U.S. Federal Census (Population Schedule), Manhattan Assembly District 5, New York City, New York, ED 423, Sheet 14A, Dwelling 36, Family 368, Francis Wenzel household, jpeg image (Online: The Generations Network, Inc., 2010) [Digital scan of original records in the National Archives, Washington, D.C.], subscription database, http://www.ancestry.com, accessed 7 January 2010.

Carl Harbaugh

If you only knew of Carl Harbaugh from Buster Keaton's remarks, you wouldn't think very highly of him. In 1964 Kevin Brownlow asked, "What did Carl Harbaugh write then when he wrote your scenarios?" Keaton replied, "He didn't write nothing. He was one of the most useless men I ever had on the scenario department. He wasn't a good gag man; he wasn't a good title writer; he wasn't a good story constructionist."[1] However, Mack Sennett and Hal Roach disagreed; Harbaugh wrote many comedies for them.

Carl Lee Harbaugh was born on November 10, 1886, in Washington, D.C. His parents were Lewis and Maria Louise Spraul Harbaugh. His father was a clerk, and his mother ran a theatrical boarding house. Her guests included Maurice Barrymore (John, Lionel, and Ethel's father), George M. Cohan, and Enrico Caruso.[2]

That must have influenced her son, who began his career in entertainment as an actor. He was first mentioned in the *New York Times* in 1908, as part of the cast of a comedy called *Ticey*.[3] In 1911 he toured with dramatic actress Catherine Calvert and Company in *The Signal*, a one-act play about the Black Hand extortion racket; he played a comic relief German music teacher.[4] The next year he played a Chinese man in the first act and a detective disguised as a steward through the rest of *The Greyhound*, which had 108 performances on Broadway.[5] In 1913 he was in the touring cast of David Belasco's *Ready Money*.[6] (Belasco ran many companies that toured the United States and was the most successful theatrical producer of his time.) Harbaugh returned to Broadway in *The Bludgeon* in 1914. Of the latter, the *New York Times* said he "played a drunken cad of a lover of the unpleasant wife most excellently."[7] Like many other theatrical actors, he worked in films too, such as *What the Milk Did* in 1912 for Universal Studios and *The Bomb Boy* in 1914 for Pathé Frères Company. He married Frances Lawson Bouis and they had a daughter, Harriett, on February 24, 1916.

In 1915, he co-wrote his first screenplay with Raoul Walsh. *Regeneration* was the story of a small-time gang leader who was reformed after he met and fell in love with a social worker. The backgrounds were shot on location in the Bowery. Harbaugh also co-starred in it as the district attorney. It was the first feature-length gangster movie. Walsh went on to a long and successful directing career.

Regeneration was made for William Fox's studio in Fort Lee, New Jersey, and Harbaugh stayed with Fox as an actor, writer and director until 1919. He got lots of variety, doing everything from co-starring with Theda Bara in *Carmen* in 1915 to directing and adapting *The Scarlet Letter* in 1917. Next he tried starting his own production company, Carl Harbaugh Productions, but they made only one film in 1919, *The Other Man's Wife*. It has the distinction of being comic George Jessel's film debut. He spent 1920 directing shorts for a small company, Oliver Films. Then he moved to Los Angeles and went back to directing features at Fox for a year. Except for one short, *Fowl Play* in 1929, that was the end of his directing career.

Frances Harbaugh had moved back to her parents' house in Baltimore by the time of the 1920 census, taking their daughter with her. She died on January 12, 1922, in a sledding accident. According to the *Baltimore Sun*, she was coasting down a hill near her home and she ran into a telegraph pole and fractured her skull.[8] She died before firemen could get to her. She was 29 years old. Her husband had been visiting and had just left for Hollywood three days before the accident.

Harbaugh next went to work with Raoul Walsh at Goldwyn Studios. They spent two months in Tahiti shooting *Lost and Found on a South Sea Island*; Harbaugh played the heavy, Waki. Back in Los Angeles, he got a job with actress Mae Murray's company, Tiffany Productions. He acted in *Jazzmania* (1923) and wrote *Mademoiselle Midnight* (1924) for them.

In 1925 he went to work as a writer for Hal Roach. He made several two-reelers directed by Stan Laurel just before he (Laurel) teamed up with Oliver Hardy. He also wrote two shorts co-directed by James Horne: *Wife Tamers* and *Don Key (Son of Burro)*. In August 1925 he collaborated on Mary Pickford's *Sparrows*.[9] Next he was hired by Mack Sennett and he wrote more two-reelers including *The Flirty Four-Flushers* directed by Eddie Cline. Then he was hired to write for Keaton. Horne joined Keaton's crew at the same time.

Harbaugh was an experienced comedy writer, and they wanted a commercial film. His name was on the credits of *College* (along with Bryan Foy) and he acted in it as the crew coach. Harbaugh's style clashed with Keaton's as badly as Horne's did. According to film historian Randy Skretvedt, Harbaugh's "justification for outlandish and improbable gags was, 'The prop got there because the goddamned prop man *put* it there!' Character motivation and logical plot development were not things that kept Mr. Harbaugh up late at night."[10] These were things that Keaton did worry about, and he kept working (or stayed on the baseball field) until he figured them out.

Harbaugh also received the story writing credit for *Steamboat Bill, Jr.* even though the director, Charles Riesner, brought the story to Keaton. What he actually did hasn't been recorded; in fact, his contributions are what inspired Keaton's remarks to Kevin Brownlow in this chapter's first paragraph. However, he was definitely on location with the crew in Sacramento: He helped assistant director Sandy Roth judge the Miss Yolo beauty contest.[11]

Harbaugh went back to writing for Sennett in 1927 and stayed until 1930, making more two-reelers. The 1930 census found him living in Hollywood with his mother and daughter. The census worker was told that he was a short story writer. He didn't get many film writing credits that decade: one short for Educational (*Ship a Hooey!* in 1932), one Our Gang feature for Roach (*General Spanky* in 1936) and a feature for the short-lived General Productions (*Three Legionnaires* in 1937).

In 1937 he started getting bit parts in films at Paramount, often for his old friend Raoul Walsh. When Walsh moved to Warner Bros. in 1939, Harbaugh followed. When he registered for the 1942 "old man's draft" he said he was unemployed, but he gave Walsh's name as "someone who will always know your address."[12] Throughout the 1940s and '50s, he had uncredited roles in most of Walsh's films including *High Sierra* (1941) and *White Heat* (1949).

Carl Harbaugh died on February 26, 1960, at the Motion Picture Hospital following a heart attack. He had suffered from heart disease for five years. He was buried at Forest Lawn, Hollywood.[13]

Census Records

1910 U.S. Federal Census (Population Schedule), Election District 3, Baltimore, Maryland, ED 9, Sheet 3A, Dwelling 27, Family 42, Clarence Bouis household, jpeg image (Online: The Generations Network, Inc., 2009) [Digital scan of original records in the National Archives, Washington, D.C.], subscription database, http://www.ancestry.com, accessed 29 September 2009.

1920 U.S. Federal Census (Population Schedule), Baltimore Ward 27, Baltimore,

Maryland, ED 456, Sheet 5B, Dwelling 92, Family 105, Clarence I. Bouis household, jpeg image (Online: The Generations Network, Inc., 2009) [Digital scan of original records in the National Archives, Washington, D.C.], subscription database, http://www.ancestry.com, accessed 29 September 2009.

1930 U.S. Federal Census (Population Schedule), Los Angeles Assembly District 55, Los Angeles, California, ED 64, Sheet 17A, Dwelling 151, Family 534, Carl L. Harbaugh household, jpeg image (Online: The Generations Network, Inc., 2007) [Digital scan of original records in the National Archives, Washington, D.C.], subscription database, http://www.ancestry.com, accessed 14 April 2007.

1940 U.S. Federal Census (Population Schedule), Los Angeles Assembly District 42, Los Angeles, California, ED 60–1306, Sheet 12B, Family 304, Carl Harbaugh household, jpeg image (Online: FamilySearch Historical Collections, 2012) [Digital scan of original records in the National Archives, Washington, D.C.], https://www.familysearch.org, accessed 28 July 2012.

Harbaugh, Carl Lee. *World War I Draft Registration Cards, 1917–1918* (5 June 1917) (Online: The Generations Network, Inc., 2011) [Digital scan of original records in the National Archives, Washington, D.C.], subscription database, http://www.ancestry.com, accessed 10 December 2011.

Jean Havez

Jean Havez was a success before he went into films. He wrote vaudeville skits, musical plays and over 100 popular songs, including Keaton's father Joe's favorite, "Everybody Works but Father." He didn't do too badly in Hollywood, writing gags for Roscoe Arbuckle and Harold Lloyd as well as Keaton. He, along with Clyde Bruckman, was one of Keaton's favorite gag writers.[1]

Jean Constant Havez was born in Baltimore on December 24, 1872. His father Jean, who was born in France, was a steward at the Merchant's Club. His mother Alice, a native Marylander, was a hairdresser. He had an older brother, Herbert (born in 1865), and an older sister, Alice (born in 1867).

He had more formal education than most members of Keaton's crew. After six years at Public School Number 9, he attended the German Private School for two years and Maupin's University School for two years. From age 15 to 17 he went to Baltimore City College, where he received a diploma. Then he spent two years studying chemistry at Johns Hopkins. On his college application he wrote, "I wish to pursue the study of Chemistry not that I ever expect to make my living by it, but simply to cultivate a branch of science that I have always had the greatest interest in." His grades ranged from "passed" to "very good," but he didn't finish his degree.[2]

Havez was a reporter for the *Evening News* before he went into show business, according to H.L. Mencken.[3] He became an advertising man and representative for Lew Dockstader's Minstrels,[4] one of the most famous minstrel troops at the turn of the century (Al Jolson was a member). Then he started writing skits and songs for them, including "Never Bank on a Travelling Man," "When You Ain't Got No Money Then You Needn't Come Around," the aforementioned "Father" and its follow-up, "Uncle Quit Work Too." The Minstrels toured the United States and had three shows on Broadway from 1904 to 1907. He also wrote the book and most of the songs for their 1908 show *Bull Durham*.

Havez didn't desert his hometown; Mencken wrote: "Whenever he returned to Baltimore from Broadway for a visit to the home folks, there was a party that would last for days." He described him as "a fellow of huge bulk, powerful thirst, and notable amiability."[5] On one trip home, he managed the "High Balls" baseball team in their joke-filled defeat of the "Rum Dumbs." His brother Herbert kept score.[6] Plainly Jean was preparing for his future role as umpire for the Keaton ball games.

He left Dockstader and started freelancing. In 1910 he formed a partnership with Leo Donnelly to write monologues, duologues, sketches, songs and parodies for performers, in addition to press work and publicity.[7] (Donnelly had co-written Lou Anger's German soldier sketch with Joe Mitchell. He later became a stage and film actor.) They opened an office in the Long Acre Building in New York City. They co-wrote an article for *The Green Book Album* in 1912 that set out their philosophy of comedy writing and served as an advertisement for their services. "The Fun Factory" states "fun—that is, stage fun—is manufactured just as surely as are locomotives and vacuum cleaners."[8] They wrote solely for the audience and were indifferent if the performer (or their worthy spouse) thought it was funny, noting that what seems least funny when read is usually most funny to an audience. They pointed out that writers must know the comedian's limitations, personalities, and possibilities. For example, a sketch they wrote for Al Jolson and Stella Mayhew had lines like "A vacuum is a place where the Pope lives"[9] and "Remember the tattooed man? When the fire broke out he ran up and down the hall without any clothes on. Everybody stopped and paid a nickel to see the moving pictures."[10] Havez and Donnelly admitted that wasn't funny itself, but Jolson and Mayhew knew how to put it over. The firm's motto was "Don't tell us how good you are. Let us find out for ourselves."[11] This could sum up Keaton's approach to comedy too.

Havez also worked with singer Bert Williams; they co-wrote Williams' numbers for the *Ziegfeld Follies* of 1911 and 1914. One of their biggest hits was "Darktown Poker Club." In 1912, Havez wrote the book and lyrics for his own original musical *The Girl from Brighton*. The *New York Times* review was a bit snarky: "With the aid of a large and lively company, the writer and composer succeeded in giving the audience what it seemed to like."[12]

He was a charter member of the American Society of Composers, Authors and Publishers (ASCAP) when it formed on February 13, 1914.[13] The group's purpose is to make sure that composers are paid for the performance of their work and their rights are protected.

Havez moved to Los Angeles in 1915 and went to work for Mack Sennett at Keystone. Who wrote which film is lost; even Brent Walker in his through Keystone filmography couldn't identify the scenario writers for most of the films of that time.[14] He identified three shorts Havez worked on: *Dizzy Heights and Daring Hearts* (1915), a Chester Conklin film co-written with Clarence Badger; *Better Late Than Never* (1916), directed by Eddie Cline (Havez got an assistant director credit); and *A Dash of Courage* (1916), directed by Charlie Chase. The *Variety* reviewer "Jolo." thought he saw Havez in a bit part in the latter.[15]

He was briefly married to an up-and-coming young singer, Cecil Cunningham, in 1915.[16] She was 26 and he was 42. She had trained to be an opera singer, and even appeared as Phyllis in a revival of Gilbert and Sullivan's *Iolanthe* on Broadway in 1913. She went on to perform in musical comedies and as a vaudeville headliner, often singing Havez's songs. In October of 1915, she ended her Orpheum tour in Los Angeles, "exchanging the spotlight for firelight," intending to give up show business.[17] By August 1917 Havez filed a suit for separation. They aired their mutual grievances in the newspapers: He charged that she had dumped him after she'd become a success and bragged about her earnings,[18] and she said that he was lazy and she'd been supporting him for years.[19] The divorce was finalized in 1918.[20] Cunningham later quit singing and went on to be a movie character actress when talkies came. Her two most famous roles were as an ex-trapeze artist insulted by W.C. Fields in *If I Had a Million* (1932) and as Irene Dunne's Aunt Patsy in *The Awful Truth* (1937).

Havez moved between in New York and Los Angeles periodically. He co-wrote *Oh Doctor!* with Roscoe Arbuckle and Joseph Roach in mid–1917. Buster Keaton played the spoiled son of Arbuckle the doctor; this seems to be the first film he and Havez worked on together.

Havez was three months too young to avoid having to register for the draft in September 1918.[21] The registrar said he was tall and stout, with brown hair. He was still in New York and his present occupation was "dramatic author." He had already married a second time; his second wife was Ebba Ahl. She was born on July 31, 1894, in Sweden to Edward and Thyra Kruger Schon Ahl. Her father was Swedish and her mother was Danish. She immigrated to the United States in 1896,[22] performed in musical comedies and toured vaudeville under the name Doris Vernon. When she appeared in *My Home Town Girl* in Elyria, Ohio, the local paper called her "a scream in the role of a Swedish scrub woman."[23] In December 1917 Havez wrote a special comic repertoire for her and her harpist, Isabel White. Havez and Ahl got married on May 1, 1918, in Jersey City, and she retired.[24]

Havez continued to write songs and musical comedies. He collaborated with Irving Berlin on "Dream on Little Soldier Boy" for *Yip, Yip, Yaphank*, a musical review put on at Camp Upton in 1918. He wrote (with Elmer Harris) a musical farce for Trixie Friganza, *Poor Mamma*, and in November 1919 when it played at the Mason Operahouse [sic] in Los Angeles, Arbuckle's whole staff, their wives and friends came out to see it.[25] Grace Kingsley in the *L.A. Times* called it "a gigantic jag of joy"[26] and recounted its "nice little plotlet": A middle-aged widow with five children goes to New York on a fling and marries a young man. They go to her home, and she tries to hide that she has children. It ends with those children gathered around as she sings a tearjerker, "Mother." Friganza was famous for her avoirdupois, and Havez gave her a special number, "There's lots more fun in putting it on than there is in taking it off," which she accompanied with a dance based on thinning exercises. The show played to a packed house. He returned to the Mason in 1920, writing the book for *The Satires of 1920*. The ballroom dance team Fanchon and Marco starred; the plot involved a Texas oil magnate who tries to produce a Hollywood movie.[27]

In March 1919 Havez signed a contract with Joseph Schenck and was back in Los Angeles and Arbuckle's scenario department.[28] He co-wrote, with Arbuckle, his last three collaborations with Keaton: *Back Stage, The Hayseed* and *The Garage*.

Arbuckle started making features, and Havez stayed with Keaton. His name didn't appear in the credits for the shorts, but *Moving Picture World* says that Keaton hired him in May 1920.[29] Havez also had a bit part in *The Goat*, playing the policeman caught carefully cleaning his gun when Keaton was trying to escape an angry Joe Roberts. Biographer Rudi Blesh said that Havez was with the group struggling to find sedentary gags after Keaton broke his ankle. Reportedly Havez said, "If we can't have falls and chases, what's left?"[30] They came up with *The Playhouse*, one of Keaton's best shorts.

Havez also wrote for other comedians. He joined Harold Lloyd's staff in June 1921[31] and co-wrote Lloyd's first four features: *A Sailor-Made Man, Grandma's Boy, Dr. Jack* and *Safety Last!* According to *Camera!* magazine, he was signed to write for the Hallroom Boys in late 1922.[32] He also teamed up with Lex Neal to write 1924's *Racing Luck,* comedian Monty Banks' first feature.

After so much work, Havez and his wife travelled to Europe on a vacation. His passport application said they planned to go to France, Italy, Belgium, Germany, Norway, Egypt, Spain, and the British Isles.[33] They arrived back in New York on August 29, 1922.[34] He returned to Los Angeles to co-write Keaton's features. He worked on *Three Ages, Our Hospitality, Sherlock Jr., The Navigator,* and *Seven Chances.*

Both Rudi Blesh and *Variety* said that Havez came up with the plot for *Our Hospitality.*[35] The *Variety* review said, "Jean Havez has built up a comedy masterpiece about as serious a subject as a feud."[36] Their reviewer, "Con.," really admired the film: "It marks a step forward in the production of picture comedies and may be the beginning of the end of the comedy picture without a plot or story that degenerates into a series of 'gags.' *Our Hospitality* classes as one of the best screen comedies … and will set a new fashion in picture comedy conception."

According to Blesh, Havez also came up with the plot for *The Navigator.* The writers were sitting, absorbing the idea that Keaton had just rented an ocean liner, and Havez said, "I've got it. I want a rich boy and a rich girl who never had to lift a finger…. I put these two beautiful spoiled brats—the two most helpless people in the world—adrift on a ship, all alone. A dead ship. No lights, no steam."[37] The writers just had to figure out how to get them on the boat and set it adrift.

Havez had a small part in *Seven Chances,* meeting Snitz Edwards by an elevator. After they finished that film, the studio closed for two months and Havez was loaned to John W. Considine to write for Peter the Great, a dog star.[38]

It's possible that he helped with some of the early work on *Go West.* Keaton told Blesh that at a rainy-day story conference they were discussing the problem of finding the right leading lady. Keaton decided to hire a nice Jersey cow, but Havez said, "I deeply misdoubt you can train a cow even as good as an actress."[39] Keaton proved him wrong, but he wasn't there to see the results: Jean Havez died at home on February 12, 1925, of acute pulmonary edema, which is a complication of heart failure.[40] He was buried at the Hollywood Memorial Park Cemetery.

Ebba Havez stayed in Los Angeles and became a screenwriter herself. She married Edward Sedgwick in 1933; her story continues in that entry.

Census Records

1870 U.S. Federal Census (Population Schedule), Baltimore Ward 11, Baltimore, Maryland, Sheet 15B, Dwelling 852, Family 990, John [sic] C. Havez household, jpeg image (Online: The Generations Network, Inc., 2007) [Digital scan of original records in the National Archives, Washington, D.C.], subscription database, http://www.ancestry.com, accessed 15 May 2007.

1880 U.S. Federal Census (Population Schedule), Baltimore Ward 11, Baltimore, Maryland, ED 96, Sheet 10B, Dwelling 79, Family 92, J.C. Havez household, jpeg image (Online: The Generations Network, Inc., 2007) [Digital scan of original records in the National Archives, Washington, D.C.], subscription database, http://www.ancestry.com, accessed 15 May 2007.

1900 U.S. Federal Census (Population Schedule), Baltimore Ward 15, Baltimore, Maryland, ED 199, Sheet 6, Dwelling 71, Family 88, Alice Havez household, jpeg image (Online: The Generations Network, Inc., 2011) [Digital scan of original records in the National Archives, Washington, D.C.], subscription database, http://www.ancestry.com, accessed 31 October 2011.

1910 U.S. Federal Census (Population Schedule), Manhattan Ward 16, New York, New York, ED 0857, Sheet 4B, Dwelling 21, Family 55, Thyre [sic] Ahl household, jpeg image (Online: The Generations Network, Inc., 2011) [Digital scan of original records in the National Archives, Washington, D.C.], subscription database, http://www.ancestry.com, accessed 31 October 2011.

Lew Lipton

Lew Lipton wrote the stories for Keaton's last two silent films, *The Cameraman* and *Spite Marriage*. He also worked with him after they both left MGM.

Lipton was born Herman Lipshitz on February 23, 1892, in Chicago, Illinois. He was the third child of Issac and Esther Lipshitz. His father moved to the United States from Russia in 1886 and his mother joined him in 1887. Issac was a presser at a store. Herman had an older sister, Fannie, an older brother, Julius, and two younger sisters, Florence and Annette.

By 1900 the family had moved to Manhattan. Ten years later, they had moved north from Cherry Street to East 98th Street. Herman worked as a diamond setter. In his 1934 *Motion Picture Almanac* biography he wrote that he attended the Art Institute of Chicago,[1] but the school's records department can't confirm this because their files from that time were damaged.[2] In the same biography he said that he was a commercial artist and newspaperman in Chicago and New York before he went into the film business, but this also can't be independently confirmed. No World War I draft registration or 1920 census record for him is available. He experimented with different names, possibly to avoid anti–Semitism. In 1920 he called himself Lewis Lipsky in *Variety*[3] and in 1921 he appeared in the Los Angeles City directory as Lew Lipton.[4]

He married Ruth Colman in 1915. She was also a Chicago native, born on January 6, 1895. In a 1937 interview he told the story of how they met: "He was driving a crazy-looking foreign-made racer which he had purchased second hand. A handsome young lady saw it, laughed at it, accepted an invitation to ride in it. She became Mrs. Lipton. 'I figured then and I still think now that was the limit of good luck a man could expect from a racing car,' said Lew, 'so I gave them up.'"[5] They had two children: Channing, born in 1916, and Anita, born in 1918.

If his *Motion Picture Almanac* entry is correct, he started in the film business at Famous Players–Lasky as a title illustrator in 1917. Next he worked for comedian Carter De Haven as a title writer. Then he went to Universal Studios. His first credit in the *AFI Catalog* is as title artist for Tod Browning's *Outside the Law* in 1920. In 1922 *Camera!* announced that he was forming a company to produce a series of comedies[6] but no information about finished films is available. Five months later they listed him as the assistant director on a Jackie Coogan film directed by Eddie Cline, *Circus Days*.[7] By August 1923 he was the production manager for Dinky Dean Productions, a company headed by Charles Riesner.[8] It disbanded after one film, and Lipton went to work for MGM.

He was mainly known as a gag man or comedy constructionist during his four years at MGM. He was assigned to direct *Baby Mine* in 1927, but after cast changes and budget problems a more experienced director, Robert Z. Leonard, took it over.[9] Lipton was in charge of comedy productions for the studio when Keaton arrived, and he worked on the story of *The Cameraman*.[10] He also wrote gags for the film; Keaton mentioned in his autobiography that Lipton helped with the bathhouse scene.[11] He received the story credit for *Spite Marriage* as well.

Lipton became a freelance writer in 1929. He wrote the story for *A Man from Wyoming* for Paramount and *The Cohens and the Kellys in Africa* for Universal. Like all film writers, he contributed to projects that were never finished, like Howard Hughes' proposed comedy that was to use outtakes from *Hell's Angels* in 1930.[12]

In 1931 he signed a two-year contract with RKO to supervise their short comedies. Among his productions were the *Traveling Man* series; two of the earliest were written and directed by Roscoe Arbuckle: *That's*

My Line and *Beach Pajamas*. He also wrote feature screenplays for them, including *Sweepstakes* and *Suicide Fleet*. Meanwhile, his wife Ruth had become the director of the Beverly Hills Community Players; she also wrote plays for them.[13]

After Lipton's contract ended, he was hired by an independent company, Kennedy Productions. They were trying to start a film industry in St. Petersburg, Florida, and Aubrey Kennedy signed Buster Keaton to a two-year, six-picture contract (he had just left MGM).[14] At the beginning there was nothing but optimism, according to an Associated Press story: "Lipton says he is enthusiastic about the opportunity for pictures here.... 'The other day I saw a pack of dreamy-eyed, ear-drooping bloodhounds," he said, "and at once it came to me that this would be the ideal place to make *Uncle Tom's Cabin*. I saw that it could be made here mostly out of doors with perfectly natural sets that would cost a fortune in Hollywood. So I think we will have Keaton do *Uncle Tom's Cabin*."[15] Another story said it was to be a burlesque of that melodrama.[16] However, at some point they decided on a different project called *The Fisherman*.[17] Keaton tells what happened in his autobiography:

> I arrived in Florida in the spring of 1933, just when the hot weather was beginning to drive the tourists home. I had a story that seemed sound, and in no time we were ready to start shooting. But the weather made that impossible ... it was not enough to put ice on top of the camera to keep the emulsion from melting off the film. We also had to keep cold air blowers going all of the time on both sides of the camera.... Yet we might have managed somehow if it hadn't been for the insects. They really finished us.[18]

At the time, Lipton told the *St. Petersburg Times* that Keaton was leaving because Kennedy had misrepresented the studio facilities.[19] The company was dissolved and the backers paid everyone off. A few months later, the Internal Revenue Service confiscated the studio property for taxes.[20] Lipton went back to freelancing in Hollywood, selling stories and screenplays to various studios. He also sold work that never got made; one that got reported in the *New York Times* was a story called "Show Business" which Paramount bought and assigned to Fannie Hurst to adapt.[21]

Between screenplays, he wrote a 1937 book called *Ideas*. Columnist Jack Stinnett said, "It makes, perhaps, the strangest reading that has come between covers for some time, for the book is just what the title implies: ideas for movies, a round dozen of them, written in a jerky, telegraphic style that races through slots with seven league boots. Dialogue is suggested. Characterization is hinted. Settings merely sketched. *Ideas* is exactly what Hollywood ordered."[22]

His final film writing credit was in 1942 for *Wedded Blitz*, a Leon Errol short comedy. Errol was a popular vaudevillian tuned film comic who made many short farces involving marriage.

While Lipton had career ups and downs, his wife Ruth wisely started a career of her own: She sold real estate in the expensive Beverly Hills, Brentwood, and Bel-Air neighborhoods. She was so successful that she founded an agency in 1942.[23] She started out with a partner, Margaret Logan, but later it became the Ruth Lipton Agency. The *L.A. Times* real estate section was full of their ads for the next four decades.

Meanwhile, their daughter Anita tried an acting career. She changed her name to Nora Perry and signed a two-year contract with MGM. She had some small roles, but in 1942 she became the executive secretary for her mother's real estate firm. In 1946 she married Thomas Warner, Jr.[24]; he was the heir to an automobile parts manufacturing fortune and it was his fourth marriage. They were estranged two years later and their divorce became final in 1950.[25]

Lipton's son had his share of problems. An aspiring songwriter, Channing Lipton was arrested in 1942 for trying to extort $250,000 from Louis B. Mayer. He wanted revenge because he thought that Mayer had blacklisted his father, preventing him from finding writing work.[26] Channing was eventually acquitted on one count of attempted extortion, and the jury failed to reach a verdict on a second count.[27] He enlisted in the Army in 1944. When he was discharged in 1946, he changed his name to Rex Lipton and became a film and sound editor at Universal Studios.

Lew Lipton moved to New York and tried writing plays for Broadway. He and co-writer Ralph Murphy came close with one inspired by a story by Buster Keaton. *Lambs Will Gamble* tells the story of Ed Cummings, the owner of a Palm Springs gambling club[28] that caters to the Hollywood elite and other rich people. One wet Saturday night, a motley assortment of them gets stranded at the club due to a flood. The group includes an obnoxious Mayer-like film producer,[29] a leading man, an up-and-coming starlet, a gossip columnist and his blond bombshell escort, a tobacco heiress and her current husband (an impecunious count, naturally), a Supreme Court judge and his stuffy wife, a few extra bluebloods, and the sheriff who came to shut the place down. Then the producer is murdered and the leading man gets blamed. Luckily the judge is there so they can have a trial. The doorman confesses, then escapes. The play ends with the customers being rescued by water airplane.

In 1946 this yarn was bought by Broadway producers Helen Bonfils and George Sommes. They hoped to cast Keaton, but he didn't join them.[30]

It had a pre–New York tour, starting in New Haven on April 25 and continuing to Philadelphia. It was scheduled to open on Broadway on May 16,[31] but it never did. The reviews from Philadelphia were brutal. Samuel L. Singer of the *Inquirer* wrote, "It is a tasteless concoction—the humor is on a low level, sometimes falling painfully flat."[32] Edwin H. Schloss of the *Record* called it "one of the most witless shambles of the season."[33] It also had tough competition; the list of successful premieres that season included *Life with Father, Oklahoma, Harvey, I Remember Mama, Carousel, Born Yesterday,* and *The Glass Menagerie.*[34]

Lew Lipton died on December 27, 1961, in New York City. He was buried at Forest Lawn Cemetery in Glendale, California. Ruth Lipton continued working at her real estate office until she had a stroke at age 82. She died three months later, on August 29, 1977.[35] She was buried next to her husband in Glendale.[36] Their daughter Nora Warner took over the business.[37] Their son Rex Lipton died in 1987 of complications from bladder cancer.[38]

Census Records

1900 U.S. Federal Census (Population Schedule), Manhattan, New York, New York, ED 73, Sheet 21, Dwelling 26, Family 335, Issac Lipshitz household, jpeg image (Online: The Generations Network, Inc., 2007) [Digital scan of original records in the National Archives, Washington, D.C.], subscription database, http://www.ancestry.com, accessed 9 May 2007.

1910 U.S. Federal Census (Population Schedule), Manhattan Ward 12, New York, New York, ED 393, Sheet 4A, Dwelling 4, Family 65, Israel [*sic*] Lipshitz household, jpeg image (Online: The Generations Network, Inc., 2007) [Digital scan of original records in the National Archives, Washington, D.C.], subscription database, http://www.ancestry.com, accessed 22 May 2007.

1930 U.S. Federal Census (Population Schedule), Chicago Ward 7, Cook, Illinois, ED 269, Sheet 10B, Dwelling 17, Family 216, Julius Lipp household, jpeg image (Online: The Generations Network, Inc., 2007) [Digital scan of original records in the National Archives, Washington, D.C.], subscription database, http://www.ancestry.com, accessed 9 May 2007.

1930 U.S. Federal Census (Population Schedule), Los Angeles Assembly District 56, Los Angeles, California, ED 75, Sheet 17A, Dwelling 201, Family 201, Lew Lipton household, jpeg image (Online: The Generations Network, Inc., 2007) [Digital scan of original records in the National Archives, Washington, D.C.], subscription database, http://www.ancestry.com, accessed 14 April 2007.

1940 U.S. Federal Census (Population Schedule), Los Angeles Assembly District 57, Los Angeles, California, ED 60–141, Sheet 8A, Family 187, Fannie J. Lipton household, jpeg image (Online: FamilySearch Historical Collections, 2012) [Digital scan of original records in the National Archives, Washington, D.C.], https://www.familysearch.org, accessed 28 July 2012.

Lipton, Lew. *World War II Draft Registration Cards, 1942* (Online: The Generations Network, Inc., 2011) [Digital scan of original records in the National Archives, Washington, D.C.], subscription database, http://www.ancestry.com, accessed 16 October 2011.

Joseph Mitchell

Joseph A. Mitchell had the misfortune to share a name with the author of *Joe Gould's Secret* and *Up in the Old Hotel*, as well as thousands of other Joe Mitchells. This makes him difficult to research. He was the most elusive of the main members of Keaton's crew.

Joseph Albert Mitchell was born in Pittsburgh, Pennsylvania, on May 22, 1866. His father came from France and his mother, Margaret Nicoli Mitchell, from Germany. He had one younger brother, Peter.

He began in show business as a stage actor. Finding a complete list of his credits seems impossible, but there are some notices in newspapers that were probably him. In 1891 he played two parts in John J. McNally's farce *Boys and Girls*: Professor Theo Soff and Bill Bolter. According to the *New York Times*, the play "revolves around the predicaments of a man who has been left an income of $50,000 on condition that he spend it, and on his failing to do so it is to go to friends and relatives. The fun arises out of the effort of the friends and relatives to prevent him from complying with the condition."[1] The show was "filled with many songs, grotesque dances, and lively choruses." The company toured the United States. The *Boston Daily Globe* singled him out: "Mr. Joseph Mitchell rendered valuable aid with genuine comedy work."[2] The *Salt Lake City Daily Tribune* even called the play "the funniest piece seen on the theater stage this season."[3]

During the 1893–94 season he appeared in *The Stowaway*, "a melodrama replete with stirring scenes and situations" according to the Globe.[4] The reviewer reported that Mitchell, by his clever impersonations, won his fair share of applause. He played Dicky Dials, the stowaway of the title. The hero is lured to a yacht by the villain, and Dicky saves him from a watery grave by popping up through a hatchway at a critical moment.

Mitchell was also listed in the casts of *Kit, the Arkansas Traveler* (New York City, 1885, and Piqua, Ohio, 1886), *Bells of Haslemere* (Boston, 1889), and *The Smart Set* (Boston, 1900).[5] In 1905–06 he was in the cast of a musical comedy, *The Funny Mr. Dooley* (which was co-written by Charles H. Smith, a writer on *The General*).[6] Mitchell and the lead actor Paul Quinn spun off the Dooley character into a vaudeville act. *Variety* reviewer "Rush." saw it at Pastor's Theater in New York City in 1907 and described the nineteen-minute act:

> A first-rate novelty talking act is *Mr. Dooley and the Land Agent*. Paul Quinn is a clever Irish comedian with a homegrown brogue and a makeup

that fixes the type without any offensive grotesqueries. The talk runs along entertainingly and to a good percentage of laughs. Joe Mitchell handles the "straight" part adequately. He is the land shark, holding out glowing inducements to the unsophisticated investor in "Lemon City" properties. The Irishman "falls for" a purchase, helped along by a picture of a flourishing city painted on the drop. They exit to look over the ground. A dark stage for half a minute gives an opportunity to change drops and when the lights go up "Lemon City" is shown. The "flourishing metropolis" is a desolate swamp with signboards to designate the locutions of the various busy thoroughfares. There is more bright talk and the closing lines verge on the serious. The sketch, light as is the plot, is amusingly interesting and should meet a cordial reception.[7]

Quinn and Mitchell toured with variations on their *Lemon City* sketch for over a decade. The 1915 version was called *The Phony Bluff Gold Mine*. The *Evening Public Ledger* in Philadelphia said it was the funniest act on the bill; it "pans out well with many nuggets of wit, all of which are the 15-carat variety. The act is in no way tarnished with old material, and is polished in a way which reflects much credit on the author, Joe Mitchell."[8] The act broke up in 1918.[9]

When he wasn't on the road, Mitchell lived with his brother Peter's family in Philadelphia and at Zeisse's Hotel in that city. He also wrote for other performers; he was the co-writer (with Leo Donnelly) of Lou Anger's German Soldier sketch in 1909.[10] Anger may have introduced him to Keaton a few years later.

Mitchell came to Los Angeles in 1920. When Keaton first appeared in *Camera!* magazine's "Pulse of the Studios" column in September of that year, Mitchell was listed with Jean Havez as a writer.[11] In 1921 he and Lex Neal were hired by the CBC Film Sales Company to write for the Hallroom Boys,[12] a comedy series featuring Sid Smith and Jimmy Adams that was based on a popular comic strip. Harry Cohn was the production supervisor (he was the first C of CBC); a few years later, the company became Columbia Pictures.

But Mitchell hadn't left Keaton; six weeks later, *Camera!* announced "Joe Mitchell, actor and author, has been placed in charge of the scenario department at the Buster Keaton studios."[13] He worked with Keaton on the shorts and the features through *Seven Chances* in 1925. He was loaned to Mack Sennett when the studio closed for two months in late 1924. But after Havez's death in February 1925 he didn't return to Keaton.[14]

Now a freelance writer, Mitchell wrote the stories for *A Regular Fellow* (1925), a Raymond Griffith film for Famous Players–Lasky, *The Love Thrill* (1927) for Universal and *Ragtime* (1927) for James Ormont Productions.

That seems to have been the end of his show business career. He was then in his early '60s, so it's possible that he retired. He still gave "writer—motion pictures" as his profession to the census taker in 1930. In 1940, he told them he was a freelance writer and that he'd worked thirty hours in the previous week. He lived next door to his brother's widow Mary, his nephew Leo and niece Margaret. He never married.

Mitchell died on April 21, 1950, of pneumonia, at age 83. He had also suffered from chronic myocarditis and Alzheimer's. He was buried at the Holy Cross Cemetery in Los Angeles.[15]

Census Records

1910 U.S. Federal Census (Population Schedule), Philadelphia Ward 46, Philadelphia, Pennsylvania, ED 1177, Sheet 6B, Dwelling 301, Family 144, Peter P. Mitchell household, jpeg image (Online: The Generations Network, Inc., 2008) [Digital scan of original records in the National Archives, Washington, D.C.], subscription database, http://www.ancestry.com, accessed 1 November 2008.

1920 U.S. Federal Census (Population Schedule), Philadelphia Ward 46, Philadelphia, Pennsylvania, ED 1761, Sheet 2B, Dwelling 53, Family 58, Peter P. Mitchell household, jpeg image (Online: The Generations Network, Inc., 2008) [Digital scan of original records in the National Archives, Washington, D.C.], subscription database, http://www.ancestry.com, accessed 1 November 2008.

1930 U.S. Federal Census (Population Schedule), Los Angeles Assembly District 55, Los Angeles, California, ED 47, Sheet 3A, Dwelling 77, Family 89, Joseph A. Mitchell household, jpeg image (Online: The Generations Network, Inc., 2007) [Digital scan of original records in the National Archives, Washington, D.C.], subscription database, http://www.ancestry.com, accessed 27 March 2007.

1930 U.S. Federal Census (Population Schedule), Los Angeles Assembly District 55, Los Angeles, California, ED 47, Sheet 3A, Dwelling 74, Family 86, Mary H. Mitchell household, jpeg image (Online: The Generations Network, Inc., 2007) [Digital scan of original records in the National Archives, Washington, D.C.], subscription database, http://www.ancestry.com, accessed 27 March 2007.

1940 U.S. Federal Census (Population Schedule), Los Angeles Assembly District 59, Los Angeles, California, ED 60–149, Sheet 3B, Family 55, Joseph A. Mitchell household, jpeg image (Online: FamilySearch Historical Collections, 2012) [Digital scan of original records in the National Archives, Washington, D.C.], https://www.familysearch.org, accessed 28 July 2012.

Lex Neal

Lex Neal was an old friend of Keaton's from summer vacations in Michigan. He worked on *Go West* and *Battling Butler*.

Robert Alexander Neal was born on March 10, 1894, in Chester, South Carolina. His parents were grocery merchant William H. and Nancy Stokes Neal, and he had an older sister, Willie.

Lex Neal became a stage performer when he was fairly young. His name first appeared in *Variety* in 1909 when he was touring the vaudeville circuit with Edward Jolly and Winifred Wild. According to their advertisement, "We are positively America's greatest singing comedy piano act."[1] At first they passed him off as an English nobleman, "a cousin of the Rt. Hon. Earl of Loudet."[2] They performed a sketch called "P.T. Barnum, Jr." When they played Yonkers, New York, in February 1910, *Variety*'s reviewer thought that the 30-minute sketch was "an exceptionally taking comedy piano act staged with good taste."[3] Lex Neal was "a very bright boy." His rendition of "I'm Just an American Kid" followed by a short dance brought "ringing applause." Jolly played ragtime piano and told stories about his experiences in southern Tennessee, then Wild and Neal sang a duet, "I'd Go to the End of the World with You."

The April 1910 census caught him lodging in Spokane, Washington. He lied to the census enumerator about his age—he was 16, but he said 18. His widowed mother was living with her married daughter in Columbia, South Carolina, at that time. The Jolly-Wild tour continued; in May 1910 they were in Salt Lake City where the local paper said, "[A]ll three are good musicians and all three likewise seem to have taken a post-graduate course in comedy, for they have been universally successful in pleasing."[4]

By 1914 Neal was touring on his own. The *Los Angeles Times* noted his appearance at the Empress Theater: "Lex Neal, the Beau Brummel entertainer, has a good line of patter and music."[5] His act went over well in Utah, too; the *Ogden Standard* said, "[H]e is a finished song and dance artist and has some other ideas that make a big hit."[6]

He became friends with Buster Keaton when they both spent their summers in Muskegon, Michigan. The two co-founded a sandlot baseball team, which began Keaton's love of the sport.[7] Keaton wrote in his autobiography that Neal introduced him to whiskey and a hangover one day, and Keaton didn't drink again until he was a soldier.[8] In 1915, Neal wrote a drinking song to celebrate the town:

> M-U-S-K-E-G-O-N
> Muskegon, Michigan
> That's the place for me.
> I always want to be
> Where everyone is on the level,
> And if you like, can raise the devil.
> Down at the clubhouse we'll meet again,
> And all sing this refrain—
> M-U-S-K-E-G-O-N!
> Muskegon, Michigan[9]

In 1915 Neal teamed up with Lew Earl, a founder of the Actors' Colony in Muskegon, for a song and comedy act.[10] By 1917 that partnership had ended and Neal was employed at a New York City theater located at Broadway and 46th Street. His draft registration card says he was a short, slender, brown-eyed, black-haired single young man.[11] He served from May 28, 1918, to February 6, 1919, primarily at a medical depot–base hospital. He was demobilized at Camp Hancock, Georgia, and left with the rank of corporal.[12]

After his discharge, he went right back to New York. When the 1920 census was taken, he was a married theatrical performer living in Brooklyn, but there was no Mrs. Neal listed. It could have been a census taker's error or a very short marriage. When the 1930 census was taken, he told them he'd never been married.

In 1920 he also toured with actress Billie Stewart in a sketch called "Vamping the Vamp." The *San Antonio Evening News* said, "[T]heir set represents the interior of a movie studio, which gives them the opportunity for some classy stepping, singing, and cross talk and a bit of satire."[13]

By March 1921 he'd moved on to the real thing. *Variety* reported that he was writing for Keaton, but while they took a break, he went to work with a comedy team called the Hallroom Boys.[14] Then he wrote comedy shorts for the short-lived Wilnat Films.[15] Things happened quickly in Hollywood; by 1922 *Motion Picture World* was calling him the "well-known comedy scenarist" when he was hired by Warner Bros. Pictures.[16] In August of that year he "joined the William Beaudine forces in a position which might be termed scenario aide, gag man, utility pinch hitter or whatnot" according to *Camera!*[17] He wrote three features: *Daring Youth*, *Boy of Mine* and *A Self-Made Failure*. However, he didn't abandon the Keaton group: He was on the football team list in *Three Ages* and he collaborated with Keaton's gag man Jean Havez on *Racing Luck*, a Monty Banks movie.[18] Then he officially went back to work with Keaton.

Neal was hired to direct a film that never got made: In May 1925 the *L.A. Times* announced, "The story is tentatively titled *The Skyscraper*, and is built along new comedy lines. Robert Sherwood, dramatic critic and authority, wrote the original."[19] Keaton mentioned what happened in his autobiography. In the story, he and a girl were stuck on top of a half-finished skyscraper. "There was only one thing wrong with Sherwood's story. He couldn't think of a believable way to get us down from the top of the building.... After all of that build-up the audience would expect me to rescue the girl. Sherwood went home without delivering the finish."[20]

Neal stayed on for Keaton's next two films, *Go West* and *Battling Butler*. Keaton said in his autobiography, "He worked out fine with us as a combination gag man, story constructionist, and title writer."[21] Filmographies list him as the assistant director on *Go West*.[22] He also started out as the co-director of *Battling Butler* but when he left to direct comedy shorts for Fox Film Corporation, Keaton finished it.[23] He did get a writing credit for it, along with Al Boasberg, Paul Gerald Smith, and Charles Smith.[24] After only four years in town, the *Los Angeles Times* labeled Neal "a veteran Hollywood comedy director."[25]

The shorts he directed for Fox included *A Flaming Affair* and *A Polar Baron*. But a contract with Harold Lloyd in August 1926 lured him back to writing.[26] He worked for Lloyd for six years, collaborating on *The Kid Brother, Speedy, Welcome Danger, Feet First,* and *Movie Crazy*. He wasn't the only Keaton alumni working for Lloyd; *Welcome Danger* was directed by Mal St. Clair and Clyde Bruckman, and *Feet First* and part of *Movie Crazy* were done by Bruckman.

Keaton told a story about a practical joke played on Neal. Lex was thrilled to buy his first house, and could talk about nothing but his plans for improving it. One day he drove home and couldn't find the house. He drove up and down the street so many times that he was worried the residents would call the police. He went to Keaton's house and spent the night. The next morning, he called the bank that held his mortgage and got the address. They drove over. Keaton wrote, "It was easy to see why Lex had been unable to identify it. Someone had planted bushes and trees about ten feet tall all over the front yard.... By then poor Lex was so rattled that he could not quite believe it was his house until he unlocked the door and saw his own furniture."[27] The perpetrator was Johnny Gray, another one of Lloyd's gag men. When Neal confronted him, Gray said, "That's the thanks I get from *you*. You are as ungrateful as all of my poor relatives put together. I spend a small fortune improving your property. And all I get for it is abuse."

Neal's engagement to Yvonne Howell, a Sennett Bathing Beauty (and comedian Alice Howell's daughter), was announced in February 1928, but they didn't get married.[28] She later married George Stevens, the director. Neal married Eleanor Horne on April 7, 1931.[29] He was 37 and she was 29. It was her second marriage.

In 1932, when *Movie Crazy* didn't do well at the box office, Lloyd decided to change his screen persona—and hire new writers. Paramount Pictures soon added Neal as a gag man. He worked uncredited on a wide variety of movies there, from *King of the Jungle* to W.C. Fields' *The Old*

Fashioned Way.[30] In 1933 he joined the writing staff at Universal Studios.[31] In the late 1930s he moved to Warner Bros., then Dixie National Pictures in 1940.

He died in a diabetic coma on July 4, 1940, aged 46. He had been diagnosed with the disease four years earlier. He was buried in the Los Angeles Veteran's Cemetery in Westwood, California.[32]

Census Records

1900 U.S. Federal Census (Population Schedule), Chester Township, Chester, South Carolina, ED 7, Sheet 25, Dwelling 504, Family 522, William Neal household, jpeg image (Online: The Generations Network, Inc., 2007) [Digital scan of original records in the National Archives, Washington, D.C.], subscription database, http://www.ancestry.com, accessed 22 May 2007.

1910 U.S. Federal Census (Population Schedule), Columbia Ward 1, Richland, South Carolina, ED 79, Sheets 2B-3A, Dwelling 29, Family 35, Thomas Hanna household, jpeg image (Online: The Generations Network, Inc., 2007) [Digital scan of original records in the National Archives, Washington, D.C.], subscription database, http://www.ancestry.com, accessed 22 May 2007.

1910 U.S. Federal Census (Population Schedule), Spokane Ward 2, Spokane, Washington, ED 164, Sheet 3A, Dwelling 7, Family 49, Walter B. Mitchell household, jpeg image (Online: The Generations Network, Inc., 2007) [Digital scan of original records in the National Archives, Washington, D.C.], subscription database, http://www.ancestry.com, accessed 9 February 2007.

1920 U.S. Federal Census (Population Schedule), Brooklyn Assembly District 22, Kings, New York, ED 1405, Supplemental Sheet, H.K. Clark household, jpeg image (Online: The Generations Network, Inc., 2006) [Digital scan of original records in the National Archives, Washington, D.C.], subscription database, http://www.ancestry.com, accessed 14 October 2006.

1930 U.S. Federal Census (Population Schedule), Los Angeles Assembly District 55, Los Angeles, California, ED 1962, Sheet 11A, Dwelling 159, Family 215, Lex Neal household, jpeg image (Online: The Generations Network, Inc., 2007) [Digital scan of original records in the National Archives, Washington, D.C.], subscription database, http://www.ancestry.com, accessed 22 May 2007.

Charles Smith

Charles Smith co-wrote *Battling Butler* and *The General*, and he played Annabelle Lee's father in the latter. Before he was a screenwriter he was part of a successful vaudeville act, Smith and Campbell. He went on to play a small part in a notorious Hollywood mystery.

Charles Henry Smith was born on July 12, 1866, in Germany. He immigrated to the United States in 1869 and became a naturalized citizen in 1894. When he was twenty, he went into vaudeville with a partner, Jack Campbell.[1] They started with a blackface song and dance act. After several years, they stopped using makeup and introduced a rapid-fire conversation act with Campbell as the comedian and Smith as the straight man. Theatrical manager Robert Grau credited them with being the first; he said, "Their style, methods, and material have suffered more from pirating than any other in existence."[2] The *New York Times* gave a sample:

> Campbell: You are, without a doubt, the best night-owl I ever saw.
> Smith: What became of you last night?
> Campbell: You shouldn't have quit me so quick.
> Smith: Why not?
> Campbell: After I left you, I found a gold watch.
> Smith: Gee whiz, that was good.
> Campbell: No, that was bad.
> Smith: Why?
> Campbell: The man who owned it came along and I had to give it right back to him.
> Smith: That was bad.
> Campbell: No, that was good.
> Smith: How's that?
> Campbell: He gave me $10 for finding it.
> Smith: That was good.
> Campbell: No, that was bad.
> Smith: Why?
> Campbell: I blew in the ten.
> Smith: That was bad.
> Campbell: No, that was good.
> Smith: Why so?
> Campbell: I got drunk on it.
> Smith: That was good.
> Campbell: No, that was bad.
> Smith: Why?
> Campbell: I was arrested for disorderly conduct.
> Smith: That was bad.
> Campbell: No, that was good.
> Smith: Why?
> Campbell: My wife paid my fine.
> Smith: That was good.
> Campbell: No, that was bad.
> Smith: How's that?
> Campbell: I owe her ten dollars.
> Smith: That is bad.
> Campbell: No, that's good.
> Smith: Why?
> Campbell: I'll never pay her.
> Smith: That's good.
> Campbell: That's great.[3]

The reviews ranged from "occasionally they are actually funny"[4] to (at the same venue, one week later) "Smith and Campbell do a talking act that is full of ginger and almost entirely new. They rattle off snap shots of repartee in a rollicking way and keep the house in a roar of merriment."[5] They also acted in musicals such as *Gay Coney Island*.[6] They separated for a few years; Campbell toured with *A Trip to Chinatown* and *The Stranger in New York*[7] while Smith co-wrote *The Funny Mr. Dooley*[8] and helped to manage the production company.[9] (Another Keaton writer, Joe Mitchell, was part of the cast.)

During his travels, Smith ran into a young Buster Keaton and signed his autograph album.[10]

Smith married Beatrice Lapla in 1890. They had four children: Edith (1892), Beatrice (1893), Sidney (1896) and Frances (1903). The marriage ended in the early 1900s. Beatrice married Henry Seebeck, a real estate man, and they moved to Queens. Smith married another vaudevillian, Lillian Ashley, in 1907.

In 1909, *Variety* caught Smith and Campbell's seventeen-minute act. "Dash." described it:

> The pair are on one of those pleasure fishing trips in which Campbell can see no pleasure whatever and his discomforture at sleeping in the open, cooking his own meals and washing the dishes gives rise to one of the brightest lines of conversational matter that has been heard in some time.... It would never do to overlook a medley of old-time popular airs that takes you back about twenty years and as Smith says, "It goes as good now as it did then." Smith and Campbell have again put one across, waist high.[11]

They broke up the act in 1911. Smith became the general director of Roland West's theatrical company[12]; West was another former vaudeville actor who became a writer-producer.[13] (He also worked for Joseph Schenck, directing Norma Talmadge in *De Luxe Annie* in 1918.) West wrote a play about a man who invents an invisibility ray, *The Unknown Purple*, which Smith co-directed.[14] It was a big hit of the 1918–1919 season on Broadway, with 273 performances. Smith also wrote the playlet "Our Boys," an 18-minute sketch about a native-born father and a German-American father whose sons were both courageously fighting in World War I.[15] Additionally, he co-wrote two feature films with West in 1921, *The Silver Lining* and *Nobody*.

In 1925, Smith was hired to co-write *Battling Butler* along with stage veterans Al Boasberg, Paul Gerald Smith, and Lex Neal.

Smith stayed to co-write Keaton's next film, *The General*. He also appeared in the film as Annabelle Lee's father. In an article for the *Cottage Grove Sentinel*, Boasberg wrote that Smith was part of the group of old-timers renewing their friendships "made years ago when show business was 'one long laugh between the hunger and the hardships.' ... [A] merry crew, these youngsters, and a source of plenty of wholesome fun. But don't wisecrack about age unless you get a good running start."[16] (At the time, Smith had just turned 60.) The rest of the group included Joe Keaton, Mike Donlin, Tom Nawn, James Bryant, and Ed Foster. Boasberg helpfully pointed out that their combined age was 335 years; unlike with current filmmakers, age discrimination didn't happen with Buster Keaton.

Smith went on to co-write more films, including Viola Dana's *Naughty Nanette* in 1927 and three for Universal Studios in 1929, *Girl on the Barge*, *Clear the Decks*, and *Port of Dreams*. According to the *AFI Catalog*, his final credit was as a production manager on *The Bat Whispers* (1930), which was directed by Roland West. This was West's last film as a director. West next started a café with his girlfriend (and Keaton co-star in *Speak Easily*) Thelma Todd. They hired Smith to be the secretary-treasurer.

That's how Charles Smith happened to be sleeping in the apartment over the garage where Thelma Todd died on December 16, 1935.[17] He said that he didn't hear anything, and a sound test done by detectives on December 22 backed him up. From his bedroom, "they heard nothing when the car started and idled and only a faint sound when the engine was raced."[18] His wife Lillian was out of town.[19] Smith went to the grand jury on December 23, then he disappeared from the *L.A. Times'* news stories.[20] Todd's death was ruled as accidental carbon monoxide poisoning, but rumors persist that it was suicide or murder.

Smith and his wife continued to live in that apartment; he died there on July 11, 1942, of chronic myocardial degradation due to atherosclerosis, just one day before his 76th birthday. He was cremated.[21]

Census Records

1900 U.S. Federal Census (Population Schedule), Manhattan, New York, New York, ED 961, Sheet 3, Dwelling 29, Family 59, Charles Smith household, jpeg image (Online: The Generations Network, Inc., 2010) [Digital scan of original records in the National Archives, Washington, D.C.], subscription database, http://www.ancestry.com, accessed 25 April 2010.

1910 U.S. Federal Census (Population Schedule), Queens Ward 1, Queens, New York, ED 1160, Sheet 19A, Dwelling 227, Family 336, Henry Seebeck household, jpeg image (Online: The Generations Network, Inc., 2010) [Digital scan of original records in the National Archives, Washington, D.C.], subscription database, http://www.ancestry.com, accessed 25 April 2010.

1920 U.S. Federal Census (Population Schedule), Manhattan Assembly District 11, New York, New York, ED 824, Sheet 15B, Dwelling 12, Family 434, Charles H. Smith household, jpeg image (Online: The Generations Network, Inc., 2010) [Dig-

ital scan of original records in the National Archives, Washington, D.C.], subscription database, http://www.ancestry.com, accessed 16 May 2010.
1930 U.S. Federal Census (Population Schedule), Los Angeles Assembly District 57, Los Angeles, California, ED 109, Sheet 1A, Dwelling 3, Family 3, Charles H. Smith household, jpeg image (Online: The Generations Network, Inc., 2007) [Digital scan of original records in the National Archives, Washington, D.C.], subscription database, http://www.ancestry.com, accessed 16 May 2007.

Paul Gerald Smith

Paul Gerald Smith co-wrote *Battling Butler* for Keaton in 1926. But that was only a small part of his long writing career.

Paul Smith was born September 14, 1894, in Omaha, Nebraska. He later wrote, "The Paul and the Smith are on the level, but the Gerald is merely for identification purposes."[1] His parents were Carlton and Eva McDonagh Smith. He had one older sister, Dorothy. His father was a columnist for the *Chicago Chronicle*.[2]

Paul got his start in show business in Chicago when he was 13, according to his grandson.[3] His baseball team needed uniforms, so they put on a vaudeville show and made enough money to buy the uniforms.

He wrote one-act plays for a church club run by the Paulist Fathers while he clerked for a real estate agency and occasionally sold news and poetry to the *Chicago Tribune*. This led to a job reviewing movies for *Screen Options*, a trade publication.[4] In a short autobiography, he also mentioned working as a mail clerk at the Illinois Steel Company and a stint on a ranch in Nebraska.[5]

He joined the Marines during World War I, arriving in France just as the fighting was ending. So he organized a show, *The Sixth Marine Revue*, and they toured the Rhine Occupation Area. He later said that the act ("which for some unforeseen cause was successful"[6]) made him decide to devote himself to writing for the stage.

He returned to Chicago and married his high school sweetheart, Mary Alice Lundgren, on October 22, 1919.[7] They were both 25. At the time of the 1920 census, they were living with her family in Chicago and he was the owner of an advertising agency. His grandson wrote that he was working as a reporter for the *City Press* while he wrote scenarios for films, plays and special material for vaudeville acts.[8]

They decided to move to New York City. He wrote comedy sketches and song lyrics, and within three years he owned, controlled, or produced over eighty-five acts.[9] In 1922 Irving Berlin and Sam Harris hired him to write sketches for their *Music Box Revue*; it ran for 330 performances.[10] So he decided to write his own full-length review, *Keep Kool*. It had a successful run in 1924, and it led to more work on *Ziegfeld Follies* of 1924 and 1925 and the *Greenwich Village Follies*.

Keaton's business manager Lou Anger hired vaudeville veterans to help adapt the stage play *Battling Buttler*, among them Lex Neal, Al Boasberg, Charles Smith, and Paul Gerald Smith.[11] A publicity piece for the film said that the latter three formed a club called "The Three-Must-Get-Gag-Men"; if any one of them failed to come up with his daily share of gags, he had to pay a fine.[12]

Smith was part of the crew that traveled to Cottage Grove, Oregon, to work on *The General*, but he and Keaton came "to a parting of the ways" there, according to *Variety*, and he drove back to New York City.[13] The magazine didn't give any details about the rift. It's unusual because Keaton was known for avoiding arguments.

Smith returned to Broadway and wrote the book for successful revues such as Texas Guinan's *Padlocks of 1927* and *Earl Carroll's Vanities of 1928* as well as the musical comedies *Heads Up* and his most famous work, *Funny Face*. The latter starred Adele and Fred Astaire and had music and lyrics by George and Ira Gershwin; it ran for 244 performances.[14]

In 1929, he moved to Los Angeles for good. In the following twenty years, he co-wrote over 50 features including *Sidewalks of New York* starring Keaton, *Welcome Danger* and *Feet First* for Harold Lloyd, and six films directed by Eddie Cline, mostly "B" musicals like *Moonlight and Cactus*. A freelancer, he wrote for Universal, Fox, Paramount, RKO, Warner Bros. and Hal Roach. He also contributed songs to some of the films he wrote. For example, he wrote the hilariously lousy lyrics for the songs "composed" by Broderick Crawford in the 1940 movie *I Can't Give You Anything but Love*. He wrote a column called "Smithereens" for the weekly entertainment magazine *Rob Wagner's Script* from 1931 to 1940.[15] In addition, he wrote a radio series called *Gateway to Hollywood* for station KHJ in Los Angeles. During World War II he wrote sketches for USO entertainers.

He and his wife had four children: Paul Gerald II, Mary, Jean, and Carl.

According to his grandson, he continued to write, but tastes in entertainment changed in the 1950s and his work stopped selling. He and Mary Alice retired to San Diego. He died at the Naval Hospital there on April 4, 1968, following a heart attack. He was buried at the Holy Cross Cemetery in San Diego.[16] Mary Alice died on October 2, 1969, of meningitis and pneumonia, her resistance lowered by a year-long bout with generalized lymphosarcoma. She was also buried at Holy Cross.[17]

Census Records

1900 U.S. Federal Census (Population Schedule), Chicago Ward 26, Cook County, Illinois, ED 813, Sheet 19A, Dwelling 194, Family 352, Marvin McDonagh household, jpeg image (Online: The Generations Network, Inc., 2011) [Digital scan of original records in the National Archives, Washington, D.C.], subscription database, http://www.ancestry.com, accessed 20 December 2011.

1920 U.S. Federal Census (Population Schedule), Chicago Ward 25, Cook County, Illinois, ED 1476, Sheet 8A, Dwelling 105, Family 199, Andrew Lundgren household, jpeg image (Online: The Generations Network, Inc., 2007) [Digital scan of original records in the National Archives, Washington, D.C.], subscription database, http://www.ancestry.com, accessed 16 April 2007.

1930 U.S. Federal Census (Population Schedule), Beverly Hills, Los Angeles, California, ED 8, Sheet 18A, Dwelling 406, Family 479, Paul G. Smith household, jpeg image (Online: The Generations Network, Inc., 2007) [Digital scan of original records in the National Archives, Washington, D.C.], subscription database, http://www.ancestry.com, accessed 16 April 2007.

1940 U.S. Federal Census (Population Schedule), Los Angeles Assembly District 57, Los Angeles, California, ED 60–143, Sheet 15B, Family 429, Paul G. Smith household, jpeg image (Online: FamilySearch Historical Collections, 2012) [Digital scan of original records in the National Archives, Washington, D.C.], https://www.familysearch.org, accessed 28 July 2012.

Smith, Paul Gerald. *World War I Draft Registration Cards, 1917–1918* (5 June 1917) (Online: The Generations Network, Inc., 2011) [Digital scan of original records in the National Archives, Washington, D.C.], subscription database, http://www.ancestry.com, accessed 20 December 2011.

Smith, Paul Gerald. *World War II Draft Registration Cards, 1942* (Online: FamilySearch Historical Collections, 2011) [Digital scan of original records in the National Archives, Washington, D.C.], https://www.familysearch.org, accessed 19 January 2012.

The Rest of the Crew

It takes a large crew to make a film. In addition to the directors, writers and cameramen noted in other entries, Keaton also had teams of people in other departments.

Fred Gabourie was Keaton's most important collaborator, his right-hand man. He was the technical director, which included set design, construction, props management and location scouting. Bert Jackson assisted Gabourie with props and locations.

Every film must have had a costume supervisor, but information is available on only two: Walter Israel and Clare West.

Keaton was in charge of editing his films, but he did have an assistant, Sherman Kell; a former railroad conductor for the Illinois Central Railroad helped edit *The General*.

The studio's business office contributed to Keaton's films, too—sometimes, simply by not bothering him too much. Lou Anger, the manager, was there at the very beginning of Keaton's film career; he introduced Roscoe Arbuckle to Keaton. Harry Brand, the publicist, wrote the first rough draft of how we see Keaton today, as a comic and mechanical genius. Joseph Schenck, the producer, isn't in this book: there is simply too much material. A whole book needs to be written about him. Fortunately, Denise Morse and Joe Yranski are working on his biography.

Because of the *Cottage Grove Sentinel*'s reporting, the longest crew list we have is for *The General*. However, not very much information is available about most of them. For example, *The General* is the only film credit known for people like Harry Barnes, the casting director, and Jack Little, the explosives expert. Because there is almost no information on them, they won't be covered here. However, the only woman on the crew, script supervisor Chrystine Francis, did leave enough of a record for a short entry.

Many people from Keaton's crew aren't in this book, but Ernie Orsatti got an entry. As a props assistant, he wasn't crucial to Keaton's development as a filmmaker, but on *Our Hospitality* he did help pull Keaton out of the river. Because he went on to have an important professional baseball career, he's included here.

Lou Anger

Buster Keaton's business manager really did go from rags to riches. Lou Anger was born into a poor immigrant family and he became a studio executive. The cliché could come true sometimes.

Louis Anger was born on February 12, 1878, in Philadelphia, Pennsylvania. His father, Hermann Anger, had immigrated to the United States on June 1, 1854, from Prussia when he was 27 years old. His mother Lena came from Bavaria (Germany wasn't unified until 1871). They lived in New York City and Tennessee before settling in Philadelphia. Hermann worked as a peddler. Louis was the youngest of six children; his siblings were Adeline (born 1857), Samuel (1860), David (1863), Emanuel (1867) and Jacob (1874).

Anger started out in show business in burlesque. He teamed with vaudevillian Henry Dixon in a "Dutch" comedy act, which meant they played broad stereotypes of German characters (Dutch is a corruption of Deutsch).[1] In 1908 Anger struck out on his own (Dixon became a burlesque producer) with a monologue called *The German Soldier*. It was written by Leo Donnelly and Joe Mitchell[2]; the latter later joined Keaton's writing staff. *Variety* reviewed the 15-minute monologue: "Anger is a clever dialectician and delivers his stories to make the points count.... Soldier life in the Government's employ and history of famous battles are used as the base of his stories with a plentiful supply of tangle talk.... The Camden audience was convulsed."[3] His act must have been pretty good, because it was still going strong in 1914 when the *Los Angeles Times* called his monologue "excellent fooling, well worth listening to three or four times, and Lou enters into his part so perfectly that he almost exhales beer and sauerkraut."[4]

Anger appeared in stage musicals, too. His first role was in *The Gay Hussars* in 1910; he played Wallerstein, a barber-lieutenant. The *New York Telegraph* said, "Judging by the applause he receives at every performance, he has arrived."[5] There he met fellow performer Sophye Barnard. They married just a few weeks later, on June 22, in Chicago.[6] Sophye Isaacs was born on February 23, 1886, to Leon and Sarah Barnard Isaacs. Her family also came from Philadelphia. She sang in Broadway musicals, including *The Red Widow*, which ran from November 6, 1911, to February 24, 1912, and *The Man with Three Wives* in 1913.[7] She made her first vaudeville appearance at Keith and Proctor's in New York on March 25, 1912.[8] According to the *Los Angeles Times* in 1914, "the nightingale of the week is Sophye Barnard, who, however, is not billed as a nightingale but 'the girl with the thrushing voice'—whatever that may mean. Miss Barnard wears a stunning gown in black and silver, accented, part of the time, by a violet spot-light. She has a fine, well-trained voice, and sings with enthusiasm."[9]

In 1913 Anger was third on the bill (after Gaby Deslys and Al Jolson) in *The Honeymoon Express* at the Winter Garden on Broadway. Fanny Brice was also in the cast. Anger played Gardonne, a hotelkeeper. It was a hit, running for 156 performances.[10]

In 1914, with the beginning of World War I, he changed his solo act. The title became *The Neutral Soldier* and he described what would happen after the war: The leaders will have all of the glory while the soldier who did the fighting will be chopping down a tree to make a wooden leg.[11] (When Anger died right after World War II, his *New York* and *Los Angeles Times* obituaries revised the name of his act to *The Old Soldier*.)

Barnard and Anger toured together often. In 1913, before the war, they even went to England and sailed home on the RMS *Lusitania*, fated to be sunk by German U-Boats.[12] In 1915 they played in a revue called *Safety First*.[13] The book and lyrics were by Tommy Gray (another future Keaton gag man) who managed to combine a plot involving a phony movie-producing company, a burlesque battlefield scene for Anger's soldier character, several interruptions by a kicking chorus line, and plenty of songs for Barnard. Philadelphia's *Evening Public Ledger* reported that the audience "enjoyed the act immensely, despite the heat, and demanded a number of bows."[14] Later, an *L.A. Times* writer said that when Anger toured without her, he missed her so much "that he wept himself out of his comedy stunt."[15]

By 1916 his soldier act had run its course. At age 38, Anger moved to the business side of entertainment when Joseph Schenck hired him as a manager.[16] Schenck was born in Rybinsk, Russia, on December 25, 1878, so he was a few months younger than Anger.[17] His family moved to New York City in 1892. He and his brother Nicholas built a pharmacy business, then used some of the profits to buy amusement parks. Marcus Lowe bought one of them in 1907, and the brothers became partners in Lowe's Consolidated Enterprises (which eventually became MGM). After Schenck married Norma Talmadge in October 1916, he started a film production company of his own and Anger went to work for him.

There's no record of all of Anger's job responsibilities, but he did negotiate with talent. For example, Anger was the one who talked to Roscoe Arbuckle, offering a tempting deal to leave Mack Sennett that included creative control and a salary of $1,000 per week.[18]

Then on March 19, 1917, Anger was walking to work and he ran into an old friend.[19] Buster Keaton was wandering around the Upper East Side of New York City, nervous about his new solo career in live musical comedy. Anger invited him to come along to Schenck Studios. Keaton hesitated, because he thought that films were secondhand and derivative—a painting versus the real scene. But Anger talked him into coming. Anger introduced him to Arbuckle, Arbuckle introduced him to filmmaking, and Keaton changed his mind about movies. He went onto the payroll at $40 per week.

In September 1917, Schenck decided to move Arbuckle's company to California and Anger came along.[20] According to a 1919 *Los Angeles Herald* article, he was Arbuckle's business manager and confidant; at the studio, "you will hear Lou Anger pattering around overhead with bills and discounts and other things and wondering if such and so comes F.O.B., C.O.D., or C.O.N., the latter meaning 'Cash on the Nail.'"[21] He also dispensed business advice. When Keaton, Al St. John, and Arbuckle wanted to buy a gravel pit in 1918, Anger asked them some useful questions like, "Do you know anything about gravel pits?"[22] When they said no, he advised them to put their money into movies, the one business they did know about. This would have been excellent advice, except the next year oil was discovered on the property. Keaton was still a little put out by not becoming a multi-millionaire when he wrote about it in his autobiography in 1960.

In May 1919 Arbuckle bought the Vernon Tigers, a triple–A league baseball team, and Anger managed them, too.[23] His brother-in-law Byron Houck had been part of the team since the previous February[24]; it seems likely that Anger introduced him to film work. Houck went on to work with Keaton's camera crew until 1926.

Sophye Barnard made her last appearance on Broadway in the cast of *Cheer Up*, a musical review, at the Hippodrome.[25] In it, she introduced "Poor Butterfly," the song she was most remembered for.[26] In late 1917, the *Los Angeles Times* reported, "She is happy to leave the East and settle down in a bungalow in Long Beach." She briefly tried a film career; *Theatre Magazine* said that she was signed by Balboa Studio, but there were no finished films.[27] After she retired from acting, she performed occasionally at benefit concerts and parties.

When Arbuckle started making features, Schenck gave Keaton his own production company. Anger became Keaton's business manager. He was also the assistant director for a few weeks, according to *Camera!*[28] Keaton always got along with him, probably because, as Blesh noted, "Lou Anger let the actors and technicians alone."[29]

Anger also had a good sense of humor, as shown in a November 1923 *L.A. Times* article entitled "Keaton's Bill for Expenses Rouses Anger." Keaton and cameraman Elgin Lessley had gone to Sonora, California, to shoot a scene in the snow for *Sherlock Jr.* "Lou Anger, general manager of the Keaton studio, nearly collapsed when Buster and the cameraman put in a joint expense account of $7.84. "Save it, Buster," advised Anger, "and show it to von Stroheim and Mr. DeMille."[30]

One day in March 1917, Anger had introduced Keaton to Natalie Talmadge. The sister of Norma and Constance Talmadge, she was working as a script girl at her brother-in-law's studio. Their courtship was on and off again for four years, but in 1921 Keaton asked her to marry him.[31] Lou and Sophye Anger were among the few people Keaton told, and they went along with him on the train to New York for the wedding.

In 1923, Anger tried his hand at producing. He formed Lou Anger Productions in February and he produced three short Clyde Cook comedies.[32] Cook was an Australian comic who had made several shorts with John Blystone at Fox Films. *Variety* speculated that Anger did it to give Arbuckle a chance to direct, but frequent Chaplin co-worker Albert Austin got the job.[33] One of the shorts, *The Misfit*, co-starred Keaton's great foil Joe Roberts.

Anger remained Keaton's manager until August 1926. After *The General*, Schenck decided to promote him, and publicist Harry Brand took over. Keaton told Rudi Blesh that this was the beginning of his career troubles: "It all started with Schenck taking Lou Anger from me. He wanted him to go around the country finding new theater locations for United Artists."[34] Schenck had bought the controlling interest in UA in February 1923 and became the head of the studio.[35]

After a break in 1928 when he tried the real estate business,[36] Anger stayed with United Artists for the rest of his career. He became the vice-president of the theater chain.[37] He continued working in real estate, too, representing Schenck's interests in projects such as the Roosevelt Hotel, the United Artists theater at Broadway and Wilshire, and the Talmadge Apartment House (he and his wife lived there).[38] In the late 1930s he managed and owned the Agua Caliente racetrack in Tijuana for a year. Before the sale, *L.A. Times* columnist E.V. Durling wrote, "Greater love of horse racing than this has no man. Lou's friends are trying to persuade him to forget the idea and take up something more peaceful, like tiger taming."[39]

Lou Anger died of dermatomyositis on May 21, 1946.[40] He had suffered from the disease for six months. Dermatomyositis is one of a group of muscle diseases known as the inflammatory myopathies, which are characterized by chronic muscle inflammation accompanied by muscle weakness.[41] Dermatomyositis' main symptom is a skin rash that precedes or accompanies progressive muscle weakness. His obituaries reported the wrong cause of death; *Variety* said pneumonia, the *Los Angeles* and *New York Times* said heart attack.[42] He was buried in Forest Lawn, Glendale.

His will left his entire estate, valued at $200,000, to his wife.[43] She continued to be active in charitable and civic groups like the Southland Assistance League.[44] She died of pulmonary edema after ten years of rheumatic heart disease on December 16, 1965, in San Diego, California.[45] She was cremated.

If you read much film history, you might begin to believe that Anger's story was ordinary—a few years' struggle, then vast wealth. Most early Hollywood executives were first or second generation immigrant Jewish-Americans from poor families just like him. However, his siblings' stories were the norm. His sister Adeline married Abraham Bendon, a sugar maker. Brother Samuel was a peddler like his father, though in the 1900 census he called himself a "dealer in merchandise." David became a sign painter for a grocery company. Emanuel was also a sign painter for a while, then he went to work in an insurance office. Jacob went to work as an automotive machinist in Detroit. One nephew, David's son Harry, toured in vaudeville as a comic, then became the manager of the Capitol Theater in Los Angeles.[46] Lou Anger had rare luck and talent.

Census Records

1880 U.S. Federal Census (Population Schedule), Philadelphia, Philadelphia County, Pennsylvania, ED 62, Sheet 13, Dwelling 116, Family 193, Hermann Anger household, jpeg image (Online: The Generations Network, Inc., 2007) [Digital scan of original records in the National Archives, Washington, D.C.], subscription database, http://www.ancestry.com, accessed 27 March 2007.

1900 U.S. Federal Census (Population Schedule), Philadelphia Ward 2, Philadelphia County, Pennsylvania, ED 55, Sheet 4, Dwelling 63, Family 68, David Anger household, jpeg image (Online: The Generations Network, Inc., 2007) [Digital scan of original records in the National Archives, Washington, D.C.], subscription database, http://www.ancestry.com, accessed 14 December 2007.

1900 U.S. Federal Census (Population Schedule), Philadelphia Ward 20, Philadelphia County, Pennsylvania, ED 436, Sheet 6, Dwelling 109, Family 116, L.E. Issacs household, jpeg image (Online: The Generations Network, Inc., 2010) [Digital scan of original records in the National Archives, Washington, D.C.], subscription database, http://www.ancestry.com, accessed 2 April 2010.

1900 U.S. Federal Census (Population Schedule), Camden Ward 5, Camden, New Jersey, ED 31, Sheet 8, Dwelling 130, Family 152, Samuel Anger household, jpeg image (Online: The Generations Network, Inc., 2007) [Digital scan of original records in the National Archives, Washington, D.C.], subscription database, http://www.ancestry.com, accessed 14 December 2007.

1910 U.S. Federal Census (Population Schedule), Philadelphia Ward 38, Philadelphia County, Pennsylvania, ED 956, Sheet 13A, Dwelling 488, Family 488, David Anger household, jpeg image (Online: The Generations Network, Inc., 2007) [Digital scan of original records in the National Archives, Washington, D.C.], subscription database, http://www.ancestry.com, accessed 14 December 2007.

1910 U.S. Federal Census (Population Schedule), Newark Ward 16, Essex, New Jersey, ED 143, Sheet 11B, Dwelling 115, Family 263, Emanuel Anger household, jpeg image (Online: The Generations Network, Inc., 2007) [Digital scan of original records in the National Archives, Washington, D.C.], subscription database, http://www.ancestry.com, accessed 14 December 2007. 1920 U.S. Federal Census (Population Schedule), Philadelphia Ward 38, Philadelphia County, Pennsylvania, ED 1364, Sheet 10B, Dwelling 223, Family 257, David Anger household, jpeg image (Online: The Generations Network, Inc., 2007) [Digital scan of original records in the National Archives, Washington, D.C.], subscription database, http://www.ancestry.com, accessed 14 December 2007.

1920 U.S. Federal Census (Population Schedule), Detroit Ward 2, Wayne, Michigan, ED 60, Sheet 11A, Dwelling 67, Family 76, Jacob Anger household, jpeg image (Online: The Generations Network, Inc., 2007) [Digital scan of original records in the National Archives, Washington, D.C.], subscription database, http://www.ancestry.com, accessed 9 May 2007.

1930 U.S. Federal Census (Population Schedule), Los Angeles Assembly District 55, Los Angeles, California, ED 161, Sheet 6A, Dwelling 258, Family 236, Lew [sic] Anger household, jpeg image (Online: The Generations Network, Inc., 2007) [Digital scan of original records in the National Archives, Washington, D.C.], subscription database, http://www.ancestry.com, accessed 27 March 2007.

1940 U.S. Federal Census (Population Schedule), Los Angeles Assembly District 58, Los Angeles, California, ED 60–308, Sheet 7B, Family 229, Lou Anger household, jpeg image (Online: FamilySearch Historical Collections, 2012) [Digital scan of original records in the National Archives, Washington, D.C.], https://www.familysearch.org, accessed 21 July 2012.

Anger, Louis. *World War I Draft Registration Cards, 1917–1918* (12 September 1918) (Online: The Generations Network, Inc., 2007) [Digital scan of original records in the National Archives, Washington, D.C.], subscription database, http://www.ancestry.com, accessed 14 December 2007.

Anger, Louis. *World War II Draft Registration Cards, 1942* (Online: FamilySearch Historical Collections, 2011) [Digital scan of original records in the National Archives, Washington, D.C.], https://www.familysearch.org, accessed 19 January 2012.

Harry Brand

Harry Brand was a great publicist. He made sure that the world knew not only about Keaton's films, but also about his mechanical ingenuity and love of sports, and he wrote the first draft of Keaton history. After that, he went on to a long and successful career at 20th Century–Fox. "The secret to Brand's success was his personality. He was known for his camaraderie and his ability to get along with everybody," according to film historian Pam Munter.[1]

Harry Robert Brand was born in New York City on October 16, 1896. His parents Louis and Celia Berry Brand, Jewish immigrants from Austria, already had two sons, Jacob (born in 1890) and Herman (born 1894). Following Harry's birth, they had one more son, Edward, born in 1904. Louis Brand was a tailor.

By 1900, the family had moved to Los Angeles. Two years later, Harry broke his leg and it was set improperly,[2] which left him with a limp for the rest of his life. The diagnosis on his draft registration was "ankylosis of left knee."[3] (Ankylosis means that the bones were fused inside a joint.) He went to Los Angeles High School, where he edited the school paper and was the treasurer of the debate team,[4] and then briefly attended the University of Southern California, intending to become a lawyer. He never completed his studies.[5]

His first job was as a reporter for the *Los Angeles Tribune*, which later became the *Evening Express*.[6] Despite his leg problems, he joined the Los Angeles Athletic Club where he played handball.[7] It was a great place for a young man to make business connections.

When he registered for the draft in 1917, he was still a reporter for the *Tribune-Express*.[8] His draft registration described him as a short man of medium build, with green eyes and black hair. Not surprisingly, his left knee problems kept him out of the Army.

Brand soon became a sports reporter.[9] He was the third baseman on a team of baseball writers who played against Baron Long's team on September 8, 1919. Long was a nightclub owner, and his team was considered "a little worse than the scribes."[10]

By the next year, Brand had a new profession: He had become Al St. John's press agent at Joseph Schenck's office.[11] The 1920 census found him living with his retired father, mother, and two of his brothers, and working at his new profession, although he still had time to keep up useful political connections. In 1921, he filled in as the secretary to Los Angeles Mayor

Meredith Pinxton "Pinkie" Snyder,[12] a Democrat. At the time Brand was registered as a Republican, so perhaps he really did get along with everybody.[13] Snyder didn't get re-elected and left office in July.

After this, Brand returned to doing publicity for Joseph Schenck's studios full-time, now promoting Keaton, whom he kept in the papers in all sort of creative ways. When actor Joe Roberts found a two-headed scorpion on location in Chatsworth, *Camera!* ran a full report.[14] Brand got six paragraphs in the same journal on the family discussion of what Joseph Keaton, Jr.'s first word was ("papa," "mama," and "goo" were among the choices).[15] Like Keaton, Brand loved baseball, and Keaton's baseball team frequently turned up in the sports pages of the *Los Angeles Times.* Keaton's September 1922 trip to New York even appeared there, because the writer was certain he'd delay his return until after seeing the World Series.[16] Examples of Brand's work can be found throughout this book. For instance, some of the best promotions include his clever "Inventions to Revolutionize Cinema Making" in this book's Gordon Jennings entry and his tribute to Keaton's thrift when he went on location for *Sherlock Jr.* in the Lessley entry. All of this helped Keaton maintain a public persona as an ingenious, sports-loving, regular guy. In addition, the story about Keaton's childhood autograph book mentioned in the Charles Smith entry reminded people of what a showbiz veteran Keaton was.

But his slickest achievement from this time was a story about Schenck's wife:

> The other day Tony Gaudio, major domo of the Norma Talmadge photographic force, was talking on the United lot with Myer Epstein, a United Studio lieutenant. Up the studio street came a stunning young girl, slender, graceful and radiant.
> "Some good looker," opined Epstein, a connoisseur on feminine allurements.
> "Gosh, she looks an awful like Norma Talmadge," said Tony.
> "Say, doesn't she, though. Must be some girl that's coming out to ask if they need a double for Norma. I heard I heard there was a girl in town that looked just like her."
> The object of all this speculation drew alongside. She turned upon them a smile that intensified her radiance. The two men gasped. Was she flirting with them! Then she spoke,
> "Hello boys!"
> Gaudio and Epstein gasped again. It was Norma Talmadge herself![17]

Busy as he was, Brand still found time to help found and become the president of the Western Associated Motion Picture Advertisers Society in 1922. WAMPAS was best known for sponsoring the annual WAMPAS Baby Star campaign that honored 13 young actresses that the publicists thought were on the verge of stardom. Alumni included future Keaton co-stars Kathryn McGuire and Marceline Day as well as Clara Bow, Joan Crawford, and Ginger Rogers.

In 1925, Brand briefly moved to New York City to be the publicity director for United Artists (Schenck had become the president of the company in 1923), but he was back in Los Angeles by early October.[18]

Schenck's next assignment for him was less successful. Keaton's business manager, Lou Anger, had moved to overseeing real estate for United Artists, so Keaton chose Brand to replace him.[19] However, after *The General* cost more than expected, Schenck became much more concerned about expenses, and Brand took his worries to heart. As Keaton told his biographer Rudi Blesh, "Once he was in the job he suddenly turned serious. He was grim. He was watching the dailies—how much is spent on this, how much is spent on that? He worries, he frets, he begins losing sleep. He felt he had to do something, like a guy that has to tear down a car that's running perfectly."[20] Keaton had another objection: Brand's name was added to the credits of *College* as supervisor. It was done with Schenck's permission, but without Keaton's knowledge. But Keaton decided not to fight having Brand listed as the supervisor.[21]

Brand's contribution to *Steamboat Bill, Jr.* was substantial. Keaton was originally going to have a flood at the film's climax, but Brand objected—he was worried about insulting real victims of the recent Great Mississippi Flood. He ordered it to be replaced with a cyclone. This was an expensive change (Keaton estimated that it cost $40,000) and it delayed the film's release, but the wind-based gags were spectacular.[22] Ultimately though, Brand was wrong: During the film's run, the Okeechobee hurricane struck Florida, killing over 4,000 people and leaving over 500,000 homeless, yet nobody took the film as an insult to them.

When Schenck sold Keaton's contract to MGM in late 1927, Brand moved to the Fox Film Corporation. He spent seven months traveling and supervising the location shooting for *Chasing Through Europe* (1929), a film about the adventures of a news cameraman.[23] He also wrote screenplays for the comedies *Plastered in Paris* (1928) and *Masked Emotions* (1929). Frederica Sagor Maas co-wrote *The Farmers Daughter* with him in 1928, and wrote in her autobiography, "The nicest part of the assignment was working with two witty and entertaining young gag men—Harry Brand and Henry Johnson.... The story was the old well-tried vaudeville skit of the city slicker (played by Arthur Stone) who goes after the farmer's daughter (played by Marjorie Beebe), intent on making her, with lots of tumbling in the hay. It was so bad, so corny, it was nauseating.... All that

Harry Brand, Henry Johnson, and I could do was spoof it up all we could. We became hysterical at the gags we concocted—gags, of course, that never went into the script."[24]

Brand returned to publicity in late 1929. The *Los Angeles Times* reported that Sid Grauman and "demon publicity scribbler" Brand had only one press pass between them at a golf event, so they cut it in half—and got away with it.[25]

All agreed that he was fun to be around. Maas wrote, "He was a good raconteur, once he got out of his shell. Harry was a shy man, perhaps because of his lameness, of which he was extremely self-conscious."[26] But things were different around the boys at the studio. Screenwriter Kyle Crichton remembered, "The atmosphere on the Fox lot in those days was marvelously wacky. There was one vice-president whose duties were strictly confined to handling bets. Nobody seemed to do any work, but pictures kept getting made.... Ringmaster for this bedlam was Harry Brand, the wonderful little fellow who headed the publicity department and inserted a provocative nudge if the excitement seemed to be dying down."[27]

In November 1931, Brand had an emergency appendectomy, which was mainly notable because he had to miss the Notre Dame–USC football game the next Saturday, for which he had 50-yard line seats. The sportswriter for the *L.A. Times* said that Brand would have rather lost a leg.[28]

When Schenck and Darryl Zanuck formed 20th Century Pictures in 1932, Brand joined the company as the head of publicity. Film historian Tino Balio gave a useful description of what the job entailed:

> The publicity department of a major studio was organized like the city room of a newspaper. Publicity directors ... functioned as editors who assigned stories and reviewed finished copy before it was released. They also personally handled front-office news concerning such matters as the hiring and firing of key studio personnel, the acquiring of important properties, and the financial affairs of the company. A suicide, a messy divorce or a scandal turned their job into public relations with the goal of protecting the image of the studio or salvaging the reputation of a star.[29]

Brand married Sybil Susan Morris Leavy on June 30, 1933, in Las Vegas.[30] She was born May 8, 1899 (or maybe 1903—she gave different birth years at different times), in Chicago, Illinois. Her parents were Abraham and Hattie Morris. The family moved to Los Angeles when she was two, and her father became a successful stockbroker.[31] Prior to her marriage to Brand, she had been married to Gabriel Leavy[32] and they had a son, George, whom Brand later adopted. She was tireless in raising money for charities. (Her husband said that Bob Hope once lamented, "There's no disease left for me to sponsor. Sybil Brand has taken them all."[33]) A civic leader, she served on the Public Welfare Commission for 18 years and the Institutional Inspections Commission, which was re-named the Sybil Brand Commission in honor of her 90th birthday.[34] The Los Angeles County jail for women was also named for her, after she campaigned for the bond measure to build it.

In 1935, 20th Century merged with Fox Film Corporation and Brand became the publicity director for the new company, where he stayed until he retired in 1962. Along the way, he ran the publicity campaigns for everyone from Shirley Temple, Ronald Colman, Alice Faye, Jack Oakie, Betty Grable and Henry Fonda to Marilyn Monroe. His most publicized remark concerned Marilyn: When she married Joe DiMaggio, he said, "We're not losing a star. We're gaining an outfielder."[35] Keaton's son James Talmadge worked for him as the head of the stills section.

Brand scored some pretty good publicity for himself on occasion. Bennett Cerf wrote in his newspaper column: "Harry Brand, super-publicist of 20th Century–Fox, ran smack into an open door one day and acquired a black eye as a result. Completely undismayed, he had his picture taken and mailed it to a glamour girl who recently had a row with the studio and walked out, signing with a rival unit. Across the bottom of the picture he wrote, 'Nobody can call you dirty names while I'm around.'"[36]

His brothers also stayed in Los Angeles. Herman (Heine) worked at the Biltmore Hotel, Jack was a liquor distributor, and Edward became a municipal court judge.[37] Brand's stepson George became a film music editor, working on *The Godfather Part II*, *Dune* and *Gorky Park.*

After Brand semi-retired, he still kept an office at the studio, cutting back his work week to only four days, when he served as a consultant.[38] He also assisted his wife with her philanthropic and civic work. She said, "He's always there, helping out any way he can (with props from the studio, films for premieres, and a great sense of humor when it comes to taking phone messages by the fist-full)."[39] The couple was so busy that they needed 19 phones on three separate phone lines at home.[40]

Harry Brand died on February 22, 1989, aged 92.[41] He had a heart attack after a bout of pneumonia, following thirty years of chronic obstructive pulmonary disease. He was cremated and his ashes were scattered in the Pacific Ocean. His stepson George died two months later of cancer and respiratory failure.[42]

Sybil Brand died on February 17, 2004,[43] following a heart attack. She was either 101 or 104 years old. She was also cremated, and her ashes joined her husband's.

Further Information

Marion Meade in *Buster Keaton: Cut to the Chase* claimed that he went to jail over a phony film company, the Harry Brand Advanced Motion Picture Company, but this is incorrect. The Brandt AMPC was a fraudulent film company that operated in 1912, when Brand was still in high school. ("Brandt Advanced Motion Picture Company." *Variety*, 27 September 1912, 30.)

Census Records

1900 U.S. Federal Census (Population Schedule), Los Angeles Ward 4, Los Angeles, California, ED 35, Sheet 6, Dwelling 64, Family 70, Louis Brand household, jpeg image (Online: The Generations Network, Inc., 2007) [Digital scan of original records in the National Archives, Washington, D.C.], subscription database, http://www.ancestry.com, accessed 2 April 2007.

1910 U.S. Federal Census (Population Schedule), Los Angeles Assembly District 73, Los Angeles, California, ED 191, Sheet 10B, Dwelling 218, Family 218, Lewis [sic] Brand household, jpeg image (Online: The Generations Network, Inc., 2010) [Digital scan of original records in the National Archives, Washington, D.C.], subscription database, http://www.ancestry.com, accessed 15 January 2001.

1920 U.S. Federal Census (Population Schedule), Los Angeles Assembly District 75, Los Angeles, California ED 458, Sheet 10A, Dwelling 326, Family 228, Louis Brand household, jpeg image (Online: The Generations Network, Inc., 2007) [Digital scan of original records in the National Archives, Washington, D.C.], subscription database, http://www.ancestry.com, accessed 30 March 2007.

1920 U.S. Federal Census (Population Schedule), Los Angeles Assembly District 63, Los Angeles, California ED 184, Sheet 8B, Dwelling 77, Family 77, Abe Morris household, jpeg image (Online: The Generations Network, Inc., 2010) [Digital scan of original records in the National Archives, Washington, D.C.], subscription database, http://www.ancestry.com, accessed 15 January 2011.

1930 U.S. Federal Census (Population Schedule), Los Angeles Assembly District 57, Los Angeles, California, ED 109, Sheet 20B, Dwelling 242, Family 243, Harry Brand household, jpeg image (Online: The Generations Network, Inc., 2007) [Digital scan of original records in the National Archives, Washington, D.C.], subscription database, http://www.ancestry.com, accessed 30 March 2007.

1930 U.S. Federal Census (Population Schedule), Los Angeles Assembly District 57, Los Angeles, California, ED 97, Sheet 4A, Dwelling 51, Family 51, Abriel [sic] Leavy household, jpeg image (Online: The Generations Network, Inc., 2009) [Digital scan of original records in the National Archives, Washington, D.C.], subscription database, http://www.ancestry.com, accessed 26 August 2009.

1940 U.S. Federal Census (Population Schedule), Beverly Hills, Los Angeles, California, ED 19–39, Sheet 61A, Family 108, Harry Brand household, jpeg image (Online: FamilySearch Historical Collections, 2012) [Digital scan of original records in the National Archives, Washington, D.C.], https://www.familysearch.org, accessed 21 July 2012.

Chrystine Francis

As the script supervisor, Chrystine Francis was the only woman on the crew of *The General*.

Chrystine Francis Malstrom was born on March 27, 1903, in Tacoma, Washington, to Gustave and Harriet Schreyer Malstrom. Her father was a newspaper linotype operator.[1] Malstrom joined two older siblings, Alvin (born in 1900) and Gustava (1901).

She graduated from Stadium High School in Tacoma[2] and in late 1920 or early 1921 she moved to Los Angeles, an aspiring actress with secretarial skills.[3] She had some success with acting: In 1922, she was in a touring company with the play *Abie's Irish Rose*. She played the lead, Rosemary Murphy, an Irish-Catholic girl who marries Abie Levy, a Jewish boy, to the consternation of both of their families.[4] In 1924 she appeared in *Pony Express*, a comedy short produced by Lou Anger that stared Clyde Cook. In 1925, she played an attractive housemaid who makes a wife jealous in the Cameo Comedy short *Be Careful, Dearie*.[5] She was also busy on the Hollywood social scene; starting in 1925, the *Los Angeles Times'* "Society of Cinemaland" and other gossip columns regularly reported on her attendance at luncheons and parties, often along with her friend Doris Deane Arbuckle, Roscoe's second wife.[6]

The Arbuckle connection may have been how she heard about the job of script supervisor (then called script girl) on *The General*. She arrived in Cottage Grove on May 9, 1926, along with the first group of crew members, including Keaton, Fred Gabourie, Bert Jackson, and Clyde Bruckman.[7] There's no record of her exact duties on *The General*, but according to a 1929 guide to film jobs, *Hands of Hollywood*, the script girl "takes care of the script, or copy of the continuity, for the director. She checks off each scene as it is taken and numbers and describes added scenes. She also makes notations such as kind of hat, coat, etc., a player was wearing; wet clothes after a plunge; torn clothes, scars, black eyes, scratches, etc., after a fight; because scenes are not always taken in their exact script order.... The script girl must write notes of camera entrances and exits, i.e., whether they were from right or left, and notes of the position of important movable props for scene matching."[8]

The *Cottage Grove Sentinel* reported that during the entertainment at the farewell dance, after several piano numbers, Joe Keaton's song and dance, and a Shakespearean reading, Francis performed a Charleston, and "each number was heartily encored."[9]

After *The General* she continued doing secretarial work in Los Angeles, including typing for stunt pilot turned author Dick Grace. He told the story of how they met in his autobiography: One day she and the cast of *Abie's Irish Rose* visited the set of a jungle action film that Grace was working on.[10] He asked Francis to dinner and offered to take her on a flight.

Later he asked if she'd "like to be his co-pilot for life" and she said she would.[11] They announced their intention to marry in February 1930,[12] but didn't wed until June 10, 1938.[13] There's a discrepancy about their wedding date. Grace's autobiography said it happened seven years earlier, a few months before he wrote the story for *Lost Squadron* (1932), which she typed up. He described a small ceremony in front of a few friends, followed by a large reception with many fliers and stunt performers.[14] The *Los Angeles Times* reported on a large wedding with over 100 aviation enthusiasts in attendance, which could have been the reception Grace mentions, but it took place on June 10, 1938. Both the autobiography and the newspaper agreed on the name of the official who performed the ceremony, Judge Guerin. It seems like he shifted the date because was reluctant to mention that she had worked as his secretary.[15]

Richard Virgil Grace was an aviator who had crashed airplanes for many films, most spectacularly in 1927's *Wings* (he broke his neck in that stunt). He was born January 10, 1898, in Morris, Minnesota. He learned to fly in the Naval Air Service during World War I.[16] After the war he became a barnstorming flier who did wing-walking and plane-changing in mid-air.[17] He came to Hollywood in 1920 and did airplane stunts in Tom Mix's *Sky High* (1922). He continued to work with Mix on *Eyes of the Forrest* (1923) in addition to other films like *Lilac Time* (1928). He wrote three autobiographies and the stories for the aforementioned *Lost Squadron* and also *Devil's Squadron* (1936). He dedicated his final autobiography *Visibility Unlimited* to Francis using his nickname for her, "Rabbitface."[18] He taught her how to fly a plane and said she was "a five-foot, hundred pounds of good solid steady nerve."[19] He wrote that he loved her because she was always calm and never begged him to quit flying or "wished" that he did something else,[20] yet he could tell how worried she was by her tight grip on her twisted handkerchief before he did a stunt.[21]

Chrystine Grace died on February 12, 1952, in New York.[22] Dick Grace died thirteen years later, on June 25, 1965, in Los Angeles.[23]

Further Information

Francis' name was often misspelled "Christine" in newspapers, but on the census and in her husband's autobiographies it was "Chrystine."

Census Records

1920 U.S. Federal Census (Population Schedule), Tacoma, Pierce, Washington, ED 355, Sheet 6B, Dwelling 130, Family 133, Gustave Malstrom household, jpeg image (Online: The Generations Network, Inc., 2013) [Digital scan of original records in the National Archives, Washington, D.C.], subscription database, http://www.ancestry.com, accessed 2 November 2013.

Malstrom. *Washington Birth Index, 1905–1995* (27 March 1903) (Online: The Generations Network, Inc., 2012) [Digital scan of original records in the Washington State Archives, Olympia, Washington], subscription database, http://www.ancestry.com, accessed 2 November 2013.

Fred Gabourie

Fred Gabourie had the most interesting job in the world: He solved problems for Buster Keaton. His official title was "technical director," but his responsibilities included set design, construction, props management, location scouting ... and seemingly anything else that came up. Keaton called him "a whiz at his job."[1]

Gabourie was born on September 19, 1879, in Tweed, a small village in Eastern Ontario, Canada, near the Bay of Quinte.[2] He was the youngest of Frederick and Frances Lenora Meareau Gabourie's seven children, and they were members of the Iroquois tribe of the Seneca Nation. According to Gabourie's son, Judge Fred W. Gabourie, his grandfather worked in a grain mill.[3] He said that his father and grandfather rarely talked about the past, except to say that times were hard in Canada so the whole family moved to Michigan. Fred Gabourie's formal schooling ended in the fifth grade.

On April 21, 1898, the Spanish-American War began, and on May 19, at the age of 19, Gabourie left his parents' home in Detroit to enlist.[4] He served as a private with the 33rd regiment of the Michigan Volunteer Infantry as a hostler, tending to the horses. His Army record says he was 5'8", with brown eyes and black hair. The 33rd was mustered on May 20 and left eight days later for Camp Alger in Falls Church, Maryland.[5] They soon went to Tampa, Florida, and from there to Cuba. They fought in one battle, an attack at Aguadores, which was planned to divert attention from the main battle at San Juan Hill. Three men from the regiment were killed or died from wounds, but disease was the greatest danger; yellow fever broke out and 50 men died. The 33rd returned to Detroit on September 2, and Gabourie was furloughed from September 5 to November 3.[6] He finally mustered out on November 9, 1898.

Perhaps his Army experience gave him a taste for travel, because he became a stage carpenter, constructing sets for stage shows and vaudeville.[7] One Broadway show he worked on, *Everywoman* (billed as "a modern morality play in five canticles"), toured widely.[8] The show opened February 9, 1911, in New York City where the *New York Times* critic called it "a three-hour exposition of various platitudinous statements about life, and without any essential originality in the form of driving the lesson home."[9] The lesson: Life upon the wicked stage ain't nothing for a girl. Nevertheless, the critic found positive things to say about the sets; the play "was staged with a considerable amount of lavishness and good taste." Judge Gabourie later said that his father met Keaton in New York during his years in the theater.[10]

Keaton wasn't the only important person Gabourie found in New York. He also met Evelyn Frances Holitzki, a talented singer and dancer.[11] She was born on September 1, 1895, in Austria and her family emigrated first to Canada, and then to the United States in 1910. She and Gabourie later married.

Even though the critics trounced *Everywoman*, it had quite a run. In September 1912, it played London, where the critics "damned it with faint praise" according to the *New York Times*,[12] and then in June 1913 it spent two weeks in Los Angeles at the Majestic Theater (and again in March 1915). The *L.A. Times* critic noted that "any morality play will be as lifeless as a schoolgirl's charade," but it pleased the big first-night house.[13]

Gabourie must have liked it in L.A., because he came back in 1916,[14] finding a job constructing sets at Inceville, Thomas Ince's Culver City studio.[15] In 1918, when he had to register for the draft, he was working as a stage carpenter for the Fox Film Corporation.[16] He was of medium height and build, and had no disabilities. Next he became the production manager for the small Jesse D. Hampton Company. His projects there included *A Woman of Pleasure*. After two years, he took out a trade ad in *Wid's Yearbook* to find another job.[17]

In 1921 he got a call from the Keaton Studio. According to Rudi Blesh, after Buster broke his leg on the set of the first attempt at filming *The Electric House*, his manager Lou Anger "went out and proselytized the best technical man in Hollywood. He coughed up, even without complaining, the salary Fred Gabouri [sic] demanded."[18] The fact that Gabourie liked to play baseball probably helped him fit right in. His first film with Keaton was *The Playhouse*.

On *The Boat*, his second film at the studio, Gabourie had a run of hard luck. Here's how Blesh recounts Keaton's telling of it:

> He built two separate *Damfinos*, outwardly alike, but intended for two different purposes. One was designed to sink at launching, the other to float. The gremlins that slept at Keaton Studios at night decreed otherwise.

The crew on *The Balloonatic* (1923). From left to right: camera assistant Byron Houck, unknown actress; front row: assistant director Alfred Werker, actress Phyllis Haver, technical director Fred Gabourie, Buster Keaton, director of photography Elgin Lessley; back row: unknown, director Eddie Cline. (*From the collections of the Margaret Herrick Library, Academy of Motion Picture Arts and Sciences.*)

> No. 1, though loaded with scrap iron, refused to sink. Its bottom kept falling out and dumping the iron to the bottom, whereupon the empty shell would shoot up like a cork.
>
> Each time this happened the location rang with laughter, Elgin Lessley and crew, Buster and cast all rolling on the ground. Gabouri [*sic*] sweated and swore. Finally, patience gone, he faced the recalcitrant hulk. "Goddamn your miserable waterlogged soul, you're going to sink!" He gave up on the scrap iron, fastened steel cables below the waterline, ran them to a winch that was turned by a donkey engine, and No. 1 sank by main force. All hands cheered.
>
> Gabe relaxed. But the gremlins didn't. No. 2, built to float, was determined to sink. "This can't happen to me," said Gabouri, although it already had. All through the voyage, No. 2 kept taking on water and listing, until finally a crew had to stay below decks manning jury-rigged pumps.
>
> "It's your ordeal by water," Buster said.[19]

Poor Fred Gabourie was a typical Keaton protagonist for a few days. This story proves the truth of Keaton's films: The universe is cruel and perverse, so all you can do is keep trying different ingenious solutions to problems. Maybe you'll get some laughs.

Gabourie's relationship with boats later improved. On loan to First National Pictures, he designed and executed the ships for the 1924 version of *The Sea Hawk*. While he was looking for out-of-commission clippers for that project, he found the *Buford*, the ocean liner that inspired and starred in *The Navigator*. It behaved itself throughout the film shoot.

While shooting the river rapids scene for *Our Hospitality*, a wire holding Keaton broke and he was swept downriver.[20] The crew finally found him on the bank. Gabourie blamed himself and offered to resign. Blesh wrote that Buster put a wet arm around his shoulder and said, "You'll never make another mistake." And he didn't.

Gabourie was in charge of lots of workers, materials, and money. A Sacramento newspaper reported on his plans when he arrived to construct the sets for *Steamboat Bill, Jr.* He brought 18 men and planned to hire about 100 more carpenters, electricians, and laborers. The total cost was budgeted at $40,000. He was also smart enough to tell the paper that it would be no more interesting than watching a crew of men build a garage. "There really will be nothing to see, and besides that we don't want any mobs around, because the quicker we get the set up the quicker we'll start shooting and then there'll be plenty of action."[21]

Plenty of action, indeed. For the most famous scene in *Steamboat Bill, Jr.*, when Keaton wanted a house front to fall down, barely missing him, everyone on the crew but Gabourie argued against it.[22] Writer Clyde Bruckman threatened to quit. But Keaton and Gabourie knew it would work (he had two whole inches of clearance, after all), and it did.

Keaton described all of the problems they overcame for that one shot:

> First I had them build the framework of this building and make sure that the hinges were all firm and solid. It was a tall V-shaped roof, so that we could make this window up in the roof exceptionally high. An average second story window would be about 12 feet, but we're up about 18 feet. Then you lay the framework down on the ground, and build the window round me. We built the window so that I had a clearance of two inches on each shoulder, and the top missed my head by two inches and the bottom my heels by two inches. We mark that ground out and drive big nails where my two heels are going to be. Then you put that house back up in position while they finish building it. They put the front on, painted it, and made the jagged edge where it tore away from the main building; and then we went in and fixed the interiors so that you're looking at a house that the front has blown off. Then we put up our wind machines with the big Liberty motors. We had six of them and they are pretty powerful; they could lift a truck right off the road. Now we had to make sure we were getting

our foreground and background wind effect, but that no current ever hit the front of that building when it started to fall, because if the wind warps her she's not going to fall where we want her, and I'm standing right out front. But it's a one-take scene and we got it that way. You don't do those things twice.[23]

Even though Keaton's projects kept Gabourie busy, he was occasionally loaned out. In addition to working on *The Sea Hawk*, he was the technical director on the Jackie Coogan comedy *Circus Days* (1923), directed by Eddie Cline, and art director on a dog melodrama, *Wild Justice* (1925). Gabourie proved his ability on all sorts of films.

So perhaps what happened in 1928 after Keaton moved to MGM was not too surprising. As Keaton wrote in his autobiography, "MGM even stole Fred Gabourie, my technical director, from me after I made just one picture on the lot. Before long he was head of the studio's whole technical department."[24] He supervised 33 construction foremen in every sort of craft and over 500 men.[25] The department was on a 24-hour schedule, and at the busiest times they were working on a dozen different productions at once. Judge Gabourie said that his father loved working for MGM, and although he had numerous offers to work for other studios, he never gave them a second thought.[26]

Fred and Evelyn Gabourie had two children. They adopted Mary, born September 30, 1912, who later married Joseph Dietrick; he was an MGM film editor who worked on comedy shorts, including the Pete Smith Specialty series. Mary Dietrick died on March 5, 1970.[27] Fred Gabourie, Jr. was born in 1922.[28] He worked as a laborer, a nurseryman, and as a special effects propmaker.[29] By the 1950s he had become an actor and a stuntman, working on such films as *Yukon Vengeance* and *Yaqui Drums* as well as the TV show *Gunsmoke*.[30] In 1959, he left show business to go to law school, passing the California Bar, and by 1965 he was practicing law.[31] In 1976 he became the first Native American judge appointed in California.[32] In 1980 he moved to Idaho, and currently he is chief judge for the Kootenai Tribe of Idaho and a justice for the Northwest Regional Tribal Council of Appeals.

Fred Gabourie, Sr. died March 1, 1951, at age of 69.[33] His death certificate lists "chronic myocarditis," an all-purpose phrase for the ill effects of both hypertension and coronary artery disease. He was buried at the Calvary Cemetery in East Los Angeles. Evelyn Gabourie survived him for many years. She died on June 8, 1969, also from heart trouble.[34]

As the reference book *Art Directors in Cinema* said, "Gabourie was responsible for some of the most inventively comic sets in all of cinema: his complicated, mechanical designs for boats and ships of all sizes, automobiles, aircraft and other devices give the Rube Goldberg cartoon drawings of equally elaborate and inept machinery a run for their money."[35] But his contributions went beyond art direction. When writing about Fred Gabourie during the filming of *The General* in 1926, the *Cottage Grove Sentinel* said, "[A] description of his job would require almost an entire issue of a newspaper."[36] Judge Gabourie has said that his father really liked working for Buster, and they were great friends socially and professionally.[37] He was Keaton's right-hand man.

Census Records

1871 Census of Canada, Hastings East, Hungerford, Ontario, Page 20–21, Family 70, Francis Meareau household, jpeg image (Online: The Generations Network, Inc., 2010) [Digital scan of original records in the Library and Archives Canada, Ottawa], subscription database, http://www.ancestry.com, accessed 12 December 2010.

1881 Census of Canada, Hastings East, Hungerford, Ontario, Page 65, Family 285, Frederick Gabourie household, jpeg image (Online: The Generations Network, Inc., 2010) [Digital scan of original records in the Library and Archives Canada, Ottawa], subscription database, http://www.ancestry.com, accessed 12 December 2010.

1910 U.S. Federal Census (Population Schedule), Detroit Ward 10, Wayne, Michigan, ED 147, Sheet 1A, Dwelling 9, Family 10, Frederick Gabourie household, jpeg image (Online: The Generations Network, Inc., 2009) [Digital scan of original records in the National Archives, Washington, D.C.], subscription database, http://www.ancestry.com, accessed 11 December 2010.

1920 U.S. Federal Census (Population Schedule), Los Angeles Assembly District 63, Los Angeles, California ED157, Sheet 17A, Dwelling 25, Family 422, Fred Gabourie household, jpeg image (Online: The Generations Network, Inc., 2009) [Digital scan of original records in the National Archives, Washington, D.C.], subscription database, http://www.ancestry.com, accessed 10 December 2010.

1920 U.S. Federal Census (Population Schedule), Los Angeles Assembly District 61, Los Angeles, California ED 106, Sheet 9A, Dwelling 248, Family 268, Fred G. Gabourie household, jpeg image (Online: The Generations Network, Inc., 2009) [Digital scan of original records in the National Archives, Washington, D.C.], subscription database, http://www.ancestry.com, accessed 10 December 2010.

1940 U.S. Federal Census (Population Schedule), Los Angeles Assembly District 56, Los Angeles, California, ED 60–101, Sheet 6A, Family 186, Fred Gabourie household, jpeg image (Online: FamilySearch Historical Collections, 2012) [Digital scan of original records in the National Archives, Washington, D.C.], https://www.familysearch.org, accessed 21 July 2012.

Bert E. Jackson

Keaton property and location manager Bert Jackson is most famous for finding the Cottage Grove, Oregon, location, when Keaton's company needed a railroad for *The General*.

Bert E. Jackson was born on September 6, 1889, in Cleveland, Ohio. His father Edwin had emigrated to the United States from England in 1863; Edwin worked in an oil refinery, and then later became a berry farmer. Bert's mother Catherine came from the Isle of Man in 1870. Jackson had two older sisters, Esther (born in 1875) and Catherine (1877), an older brother, Edwin (1879), and a younger sister, Mabel (1892).

Nothing is known about his younger years, but when Jackson registered for the draft in 1917, he was a foreman at New York Motion Picture Corporation,[1] which was part of the Triangle Corporation (Roscoe Arbuckle's early employer). He had blue eyes and brown hair, and was beginning to bald. Because he was married (he and Ruth L. Meyers McDonald wed on January 9, 1917[2]), he didn't have to serve. Ruth was born in Michigan; her parents were Adolph and Marian "Minnie" Meyers, and she had an older sister, Mary Dorothy, and a younger brother, Adolph. Her father was a Swiss-born watchmaker and bicycle repairman.

Because neither location nor property managers appeared in film credits then, it's impossible to know exactly when he started working for Keaton—it could have been anywhere between 1918 and 1923. After reading about the budget-busting *Cleopatra* in 1961, Keaton told a story about filmmaking's early days:

> About 1918, people were touched at seeing a man in overalls climbing over a fence, placing flowers on a grave. They said, "Poor man, he probably spent his last dime for those flowers for a dear friend." It was our prop man, Bert Jackson, who'd stolen the flowers from the grave to use in a scene—and was putting them back.[3]

The first evidence of Jackson working on the crew of a Keaton film was that his name is on the list of the football team in 1923's *Three Ages*; he appears on the North Side team. The same year, he was listed in the Los Angeles city directory as "Property man Buster Keaton." In 1925 a syndicated article said that Jackson had "materially aided" the production of *Seven Chances*.[4]

According to the *Cottage Grove Sentinel*, Jackson found the town in 1926, and recommended filming *The General* there. The paper even published a short sketch of him:

> A busy man who doesn't observe union hours is Bert Jackson, location manager and chief property man.... It is part of his job to be ready to furnish on a moment's notice a coop of chickens, a lazy dog, a brick building, a 75-foot trestle or a safety pin, all to be true to period. Always he delivers the goods, or has one or more of his assistants do so for him. Once in a while, Bert plays a part in a picture just for exercise. He is in *Battling Butler*, Buster's latest picture about to be released.[5]

Unfortunately, the paper didn't say what part he played.

When Keaton went to MGM, Jackson became an electrician and lamp operator there, and stayed for 24 years.[6]

Ruth Jackson, diagnosed with tuberculosis in 1928, died on September 13, 1929, of heart failure.[7] Bert Jackson's mother-in-law Minnie ran a boarding house and he continued to live there after his first wife's death. In the mid–1930s he married Mary, Ruth's older sister, who worked as a tie maker.

Jackson died following a heart attack on February 16, 1964, at the Motion Picture Home in Woodland Hills, California.[8] He was buried at the Abbey of the Psalms Mausoleum in the Hollywood Memorial Park Cemetery. His second wife died one year later of Laenne's cirrhosis and was buried next to him.[9]

Census Records

1880 U.S. Federal Census (Population Schedule), Cleveland, Cuyahoga, Ohio, ED 45, Sheet 70, Dwelling 48, Family 49, Edwin Jackson household, jpeg image (Online: The Generations Network, Inc., 2009) [Digital scan of original records in the National Archives, Washington, D.C.], subscription database, http://www.ancestry.com, accessed 1 December 2010.

1900 U.S. Federal Census (Population Schedule), Cripple Creek, Teller, Colorado ED 128, Sheet 7B, Dwelling 44, Family 45, Edward Meyers household, jpeg image (Online: The Generations Network, Inc., 2009) [Digital scan of original records in the National Archives, Washington, D.C.], subscription database, http://www.ancestry.com, accessed 3 April 2011.

1910 U.S. Federal Census (Population Schedule), Strongsville, Cuyahoga, Ohio, ED 45, Sheet 2A, Dwelling 24, Family 24, Edwin Jackson household, jpeg image (Online: The Generations Network, Inc., 2009) [Digital scan of original records in the National Archives, Washington, D.C.], subscription database, http://www.ancestry.com, accessed 1 December 2010. 1910 U.S. Federal Census (Population Schedule), Salt Lake City Ward 2, Salt Lake, Utah, 0118, Sheet 6A, Dwelling 117, Family 140, Edward Meyers household, jpeg image (Online: The Generations Network, Inc., 2009) [Digital scan of original records in the National Archives, Washington, D.C.], subscription database, http://www.ancestry.com, accessed 3 April 2011.

1920 U.S. Federal Census (Population Schedule), Glendale, Los Angeles, California, ED 22, Sheet 14A, Dwelling 212, Family 217, Earl B. [sic] Jackson household, jpeg image (Online: The Generations Network, Inc., 2009) [Digital scan of original records in the National Archives, Washington, D.C.], subscription database, http://www.ancestry.com, accessed 1 December 2010.

1920 U.S. Federal Census (Population Schedule), Glendale, Los Angeles, California, ED 22 16 January 1920, Sheet 14A, Dwelling 324, Family 336, Ruth L. Jackson household, jpeg image (Online: The Generations Network, Inc., 2009) [Digital scan of original records in the National Archives, Washington, D.C.], subscription database, http://www.ancestry.com, accessed 1 December 2010.

1930 U.S. Federal Census (Population Schedule), Los Angeles City, Los Angeles, California, ED 15, Sheet 13A, Dwelling 368, Family 340, Minnie S. Meyers household, jpeg image (Online: The Generations Network, Inc., 2009) [Digital scan of original records in the National Archives, Washington, D.C.], subscription database, http://www.ancestry.com, accessed 1 December 2010.

1940 U.S. Federal Census (Population Schedule), Beverly Hills, Los Angeles, California, ED 19–58, Sheet 14A, Family 545, Bert E. Jackson household, jpeg image (Online: FamilySearch Historical Collections, 2012) [Digital scan of original records in the National Archives, Washington, D.C.], https://www.familysearch.org, accessed 21 July 2012.

J. Sherman Kell

Keaton's crew came from all walks of life, but only one had been a railroad man: J. Sherman Kell, the assistant editor on *The General*, who had worked as a conductor for the Illinois Central Railroad for more than a decade.[1] It's a shame the editing room conversation about trains wasn't recorded.

John Sherman Kell was born on May 18, 1884, in Stevenson, a small township in Marion County, southern Illinois. His parents were farmers Orville V. and Daisy M. Jennings Kell, who also had a daughter, Daisy, in 1892.

In 1900, Kell and his sister were living in Centralia, Illinois, working on the family farm of their maternal grandmother, Amanda Jennings, in the wake of their mother's death. His father had remarried and started another family in Haines, Illinois.

Sherman Kell married Ethel Vivian Garner, who was from Louisiana, in 1909[2]; she was twenty and he was twenty-five. By the time of the next census, in 1910, he was employed as a conductor on the Illinois Central Railroad. The ICRR was known as the Main Line of Mid-America because its main route connected Chicago and New Orleans. He and Ethel were then living in Mattoon, Illinois, a small railroad hub where two lines crossed the main line.[3]

When he registered for the draft on September 12, 1918, he was still a conductor,[4] but they had moved 60 miles to Clinton, Illinois, a larger hub where six lines met.[5] He was 34 years old, with brown eyes and brown hair, and of medium height and build.

The 1920 census found the family still in Clinton. By then, the Kells had two daughters, Madelyn (born in 1913) and Eileen (born in 1915). Then they did something surprising: In 1921, Kell left his steady job with the railroad and the family moved to Los Angeles. The ICRR didn't have layoffs or labor unrest that year, so perhaps the Kells just wanted change and adventure. They took a risk, but he quickly found work as a film inspector.⁶ Ethel Kell soon had another baby, Jay. By the next year, Sherman Kell had been promoted to film cutter.⁷

Keaton hired him in 1925; a syndicated article listed him as a person who "materially aided" on *Seven Chances*.⁸ Kell wasn't listed in the credits for the next two films, *Go West* and *Battling Butler*, but neither was any other editor, so it's possible that he worked on them. At that time, film cutters were rarely listed in movie credits. According to the *AFI Catalog*, he was the editor on *The General*, *College* and *Steamboat Bill, Jr.*

Keaton described to Kevin Brownlow how they worked: "Father Sherman, we called him. He looked like a priest. He broke the film down and put it in the racks. I'd say, 'Give me that long shot of the ballroom.' He'd get that out. 'Give me the close-up now of the butler announcing the arrival of his lordship.' As I cut them, he's there splicing them together. Running them onto a reel as fast as I hand them to him."⁹

The *AFI Catalog* has only one other credit for Kell: *The Gun Runner* (1928) from Tiffany-Stahl Productions, which was affiliated with MGM, the studio Keaton was then under contract to. Despite his lack of credits, however, he gave his profession as film cutter in the City Directory every year, as well as on his voter registration. In the 1940 census, his occupation was listed as film editor. In 1942, when he registered for the "old man's draft" during World War II, he was working for the Samuel Goldwyn Studio in Hollywood.¹⁰

In 1927 the Kells had moved to North Hollywood, where they remained. On May 18, 1951, he died at age 67 after a series of strokes following several years of hypertension and arteriosclerosis.¹¹ He was buried in the Valhalla Cemetery in Burbank, California. Ethel Kell died on July 26, 1961.¹²

Census Records

1880 U.S. Federal Census (Population Schedule), Stevenson Township, Marion, Illinois, ED 115, Page 5, Dwelling 48, Family 48, Orval V. Kell [sic] household, jpeg image (Online: The Generations Network, Inc., 2007) [Digital scan of original records in the National Archives, Washington, D.C.], subscription database, http://www.ancestry.com, accessed 9 May 2007.

1900 U.S. Federal Census (Population Schedule), Centrailia Township, Marion, Illinois, ED 18, Sheet 13, Dwelling 246, Family 273, Amanda Jennings household, jpeg image (Online: The Generations Network, Inc., 2007) [Digital scan of original records in the National Archives, Washington, D.C.], subscription database, http://www.ancestry.com, accessed 9 May 2007.

1900 U.S. Federal Census (Population Schedule), Haines Township, Marion, Illinois, ED 22, Sheet 13, Dwelling 250, Family 256, James Hill household, jpeg image (Online: The Generations Network, Inc., 2007) [Digital scan of original records in the National Archives, Washington, D.C.], subscription database, http://www.ancestry.com, accessed 9 May 2007.

1910 U.S. Federal Census (Population Schedule), Mattoon Ward 7, Coles, Illinois, ED 63, Sheet 4A, Dwelling 72, Family 82, John S. Kell household, jpeg image (Online: The Generations Network, Inc., 2006) [Digital scan of original records in the National Archives, Washington, D.C.], subscription database, http://www.ancestry.com, accessed 19 August 2006.

1910 U.S. Federal Census (Population Schedule), Haines Township, Marion, Illinois, ED 141, Sheet 12A, Dwelling 232, Family 235, Orville V. Kell household, jpeg image (Online: The Generations Network, Inc., 2007) [Digital scan of original records in the National Archives, Washington, D.C.], subscription database, http://www.ancestry.com, accessed 15 May 2007.

1920 U.S. Federal Census (Population Schedule), Brookside, Clinton, Illinois ED 5, Sheet 14B, Dwelling 321, Family 323, Sherman Kell household, jpeg image (Online: The Generations Network, Inc., 2006) [Digital scan of original records in the National Archives, Washington, D.C.], subscription database, http://www.ancestry.com, accessed 9 August 2006.

1930 U.S. Federal Census (Population Schedule), Los Angeles City, Los Angeles, California, ED 612, Sheet 33A, Dwelling 346, Family 350, John S. Kell household, jpeg image (Online: The Generations Network, Inc., 2007) [Digital scan of original records in the National Archives, Washington, D.C.], subscription database, http://www.ancestry.com, accessed 8 August 2007.

1940 U.S. Federal Census (Population Schedule), Los Angeles Assembly District 42, Los Angeles, California, ED 60–1308, Sheet 7B, Family 184, J. Sherman Kell household, jpeg image (Online: FamilySearch Historical Collections, 2012) [Digital scan of original records in the National Archives, Washington, D.C.], https://www.familysearch.org, accessed 21 July 2012.

Ernie Orsatti

According to Rudi Blesh, a sportswriter once joked that Buster Keaton's employment application looked like this:

Are you a good actor?   yes [ ] no [ ]
Are you a good baseball player? yes [ ] no [ ]
Passing grade 50 Percent[1]

Ernie Orsatti would have aced the second part of the exam. After he worked for Keaton as a prop assistant and stuntman, he went on to play nine seasons for the St. Louis Cardinals, including four trips to the World Series and two World Championships. His lifetime pro battling average was .306.[2] But there was more to his life than movies and baseball.

Ernest Ralph Orsatti was born on September 8, 1902, in Los Angeles, the sixth child of Morris and Mary Manze Orsatti, who moved to the United States from Italy. It appears that the family was wealthy, because although his father gave his occupation as "tailor" on the 1900 census, by 1904 he was a vice-president of the International Savings and Exchange Bank.[3] He also owned the International Steamship and Railroad Agency.[4]

Mary Orsatti took care of their large family, which included Jesse (born 1890), Frank (born 1893), Carmen (born 1894), Estella (born 1897), and Alfred (born 1901). They had one more son, Victor, in 1905. The couple divorced in 1920 after 31 years of marriage; Mrs. Orsatti named Gertrude Cushing as co-respondent in the divorce suit.[5]

Ernie Orsatti had always been interested in movies, and he hung around the studios as a kid.[6] He attended Manual Arts High School,[7] but when he was old enough, he mixed working as a prop man with playing sandlot baseball. One of the studios he went to was Keaton's.

It's now hard to know exactly what he did in which Keaton films. Blesh says that Orsatti was part of the group that found Keaton after he'd been swept down the river in *Our Hospitality*.[8] He was the assistant prop man on *Sherlock Jr.*, according to Keaton in a 1958 interview.[9] Keaton also mentioned in his autobiography that Orsatti quickly twisted off his (Keaton's) diving helmet when he almost choked on cigarette smoke during the *Navigator* shoot.[10] Orsatti shows up in a crew photo for *Spite Marriage*.[11]

According to a *Sporting News* article written in 1929, he doubled for Keaton in *The Navigator* and *Seven Chances*[12]; at 5 foot 7 inches and 154 pounds he would have been about the right size. However, a later *Sporting News* profile says that "possibly it was only movie publicity that credited Ernie Orsatti with doubling for Buster Keaton in films. Ernie didn't do that—he only worked for Buster as a property man at one time."[13] But his main responsibility seems to have been as first baseman for Keaton's baseball team.

During the time Orsatti worked for Keaton, his father, Morris, was convicted of attempting to bribe a federal Prohibition agent, offering an average of $2,000 per month to H.H. Dolley to suppress evidence, reduce charges and use his influence to get cases dismissed.[14] Morris intended to collect the money from the bootleggers after they were charged, and give it to Dolley. But on July 12, 1922, after his first payment of $750 to fix three cases, he was arrested.[15] Since few prosperous 50-year-old businessmen suddenly joined the mob when Prohibition became official in January 1920, it seems probable that he'd been involved with organized crime for some time. He tried to claim he was a victim of entrapment,[16] but the jury found him guilty on all 21 counts[17] and he was sentenced to 20 years in prison and a $2,100 fine.[18] Although he appealed his conviction all the way to the U.S. Supreme Court, every court upheld it.[19] Morris even asked President Coolidge for clemency, but he was denied.[20] Eventually, his sentence was commuted to eight years,[21] and he served nearly three years at the McNeil Island Prison, a Federal penitentiary on Puget Sound in Washington State.[22] Paroled in 1928,[23] he became a bail bondsman and insurance agent.[24] He died in 1949.[25]

Ernie Orsatti was such a good ballplayer that Mike Donlin, a ballplayer-turned-actor who also worked for Keaton, asked Buster to tell him that he belonged in pro baseball.[26] In 1924, Orsatti was hired by the Vernon Tigers, a Pacific Coast League team owned by Keaton mentor Roscoe Arbuckle. Orsatti became an outfielder who batted and threw left. He played only six games for Vernon, and then he was sent to the San Francisco Seals, and finally on to Cedar Rapids, where Branch Rickey, who was working for the front office of the St. Louis Cardinals, saw him and bought his contract. In the 1926 season, the Cards sent him to their farm teams in Syracuse, San Antonio, Houston and Omaha. He started the 1927 season in Houston, but the Cards called him up to the majors in the fall. His peppy outfielding and .315 batting average helped them *almost* win the pennant against the Philadelphia Athletics.[27]

In 1928, Rickey sent him to Minneapolis to practice his skills at first base. But the Cards needed him again. Ray O'Neil, a St. Louis Union Train Station redcap supervisor, recalled the day he showed up, August 19, 1928: "The team had gone into a batting slump and had sent an emergency call to Minneapolis for Ernie Orsatti, a young outfielder whose bat was expected to save the Redbirds.... [A] group of us met the incoming train at 2:30 p.m. just half an hour before game time and trundled Orsatti into a cab and ordered the driver to rush him to Sportsman's Park. Fortunately, it was raining and the game was delayed until 3:20. Orsatti put on a uniform and, without a warm-up practice, entered the line-up, and facing Carl Hubbell and the Giants, smashed a homer, double, and single."[28] Orsatti would then help his team beat the Giants (Keaton's favorite team when he was a child) for the National League championship. The World Series didn't turn out so well for them that year, however: The Yankees swept it in four games. The Cards did decide to make Orsatti a regular team member.

Between seasons, on January 21, 1929, he married Martha Von Utsey, a 19-year-old from San Antonio.[29] They separated on February 5, 1933.[30] In his divorce suit he said that her nagging and quarrelling put him off his game. He told the *Los Angeles Times* "You can't go out there and knock the old apple around when you got other troubles. I lost 14 or 15 pounds and it affected my playing."[31] Another difficulty might have been their living arrangements: According to the 1930 census, they were in the same house as his mother, sister Carmen, and brother Victor. The divorce was granted on February 16, 1934, and she got a property settlement of $1,300.

Despite his claim, Orsatti didn't actually play all that badly while he was married. His batting average for those years was .315.[32] He did, however, have problems with injuries, "playing a considerable part of the season [1932] with his hands taped up, frequently suffering from a twisted or swollen ankle, but always fighting."[33] Many of his injuries were caused by his daredevil catches. The *Sporting News* went on to say, "Orsatti's work has always been spectacular and this season is no exception."[34]

In addition to his increasing fame as a baseball player, Orsatti was also known as a snappy dresser: "[R]ookies' eyes would bulge when Orsatti reported at spring training camp, with his rainbow sweaters, his ties which challenged the very fauna and flora of Florida, his two-toned and three-toned shoes and brilliant socks."[35] Eclectic, he also collected opera records, particularly those of famous tenor Enrico Caruso,[36] and he was considered a great cook. According to his brother Victor, "his roast beef was excellent and his quail and pheasant were superb. But his specialty was Italian dishes, spaghetti and meatballs, lasagna, chicken cacciatore, pastas, a delicious antipasto and, of course, minestrone soup."[37] In 1933, he even inspired poetry:

> A liner sets sail, a few feet fair;
> It's labeled a three-base clout.
> But Lightning Ernie is waiting there
> And the "triple" becomes an out.
> Add this to his prowess at the plate,
> And a peg like a Browning gun
> And you'll know why the pride of the Golden State
> Is the Cardinals' favorite son.[38]

The rest of the team also played pretty well and they soon became famous as the Gashouse Gang. In 1930, they took another trip to the World Series but lost to the Philadelphia Athletics, four games to two. The following year they were able to get their revenge, beating the A's in seven games.

Even while becoming a star baseball player, Orsatti didn't forget the movies. A sportswriter reported in 1934, "Ernie Orsatti is writing a moving picture play. It's about baseball, love and gangsters, and it's going to be a musical if and when it gets to the screen. Ernie knows what it takes and may turn out to be the first ballplayer-playwright."[39] His screenwriting career was not to be, although he helped with the baseball scenes for *Death on the Diamond*, a 1934 mystery in which a rookie pitcher (Robert Young) helps the Cardinals win the pennant ... even though someone murders three players.[40]

Orsatti played hard, but didn't take it too seriously. Baseball historian Robert E. Hood, in his book *The Gashouse Gang*, tells this story: On a road trip, manager and second baseman Frankie Frisch decided to run a bed check. He called Orsatti. But Orsatti had an arrangement with the hotel's telephone operator to transfer his calls to a nightclub. When the phone rang at the club, he answered in a sleepy voice. After he told Frisch that the noise in the background was the radio, he hung up and ordered another round of drinks. Hood said he wasn't a big drinker, but he loved a good time.[41]

Nineteen thirty-four was the year in baseball that everybody remembered. The Gashouse Gang[42] was fully assembled; the colorful group with an "all-out" style of playing included pitcher Dizzy Dean, his brother Paul (aka "Daffy"), Pepper Martin, Joe Medwick and Leo Durocher (Orsatti was the best man at Durocher's wedding that year).[43] They were known for their "clever pre-game pepper drill and the phantom infield drill in which they hammed it up without a ball,"[44] a routine that sounded similar to the kind of gag baseball playing Keaton had been doing since childhood and would continue to do in Hollywood charity baseball games of the 1930s and '40s. The team didn't take the pennant from the New York Giants until the final day of the season.[45] The Series also went down to the wire, but the Cardinals routed the Detroit Tigers in Game 7, 11–0. The superstar Dean brothers got most of the attention.

Despite hopeful predictions, 1935 was an anticlimax.[46] They finished second in their league. Management decided that it was time to make some changes. They tried to send Orsatti back to the minors, but he wasn't interested.[47] They also refused to sell his contract to another team. So he quit baseball. On February 21, 1936, he sent a telegram to the St. Louis *Post Dispatch*: "Most definitely given up baseball and want you to hear it directly from me. For St. Louis fans, I am now vice-president of Orsatti & Co., artists representative, Hollywood, California."[48]

Three of his brothers owned the Orsatti Agency, which represented actors, executives, producers, directors, writers and radio talent. Their clients included Sonja Henie, Margaret O'Brien, Betty Grable, Judy Garland, Edward G. Robinson, Laurel and Hardy, Preston Sturges and Frank Capra.[49] Ernie's brother Frank started the business in the late 1920s, after an indictment for income tax evasion convinced him to get out of bootlegging (his friend Louis B. Mayer paid his large fine to the tax commission).[50] Frank originally had two other partners, Milton Bren and Herman Weber, but he bought them out and replaced them with his brothers Victor and Al. (The other brother, Jesse, owned a restaurant.[51])

Ernie Orsatti occasionally denied reports that he was going to remarry, first with Barbara Ebner, a "pretty St. Louis miss,"[52] later with Linda Parker, a film actress (she had small parts in *The Unholy Three* and *Naughty Marietta*).[53] His sister Estella said that he was "a real charmer with the ladies."[54]

On September 24, 1938, he did remarry.[55] His bride was Inez Gorman, "a descendant of nine generations of Gormans of Gloucester, Massachusetts, all of who made their living from the sea,"[56] but her father supervised public school music in Adams, Massachusetts.[57] She was a soprano with the Cincinnati Symphony Orchestra when, in 1936, Darryl Zanuck of 20th Century–Fox saw her photo and a short article about her in *Time* magazine. *Time* called her "one of the comeliest young women who has ever made her operatic debut."[58] Zanuck signed her to a contract to make a film called *Love Flight* with Lawrence Tibbett, a star with the Metropolitan Opera.[59] Otto Preminger's directorial debut, the film got made as *Under Your Spell*, but for some reason Gorman didn't appear in it. Despite spending $2,400 to eliminate "tooth shadows" that appeared during a screen test,[60] she was replaced by Wendy Barrie; no explanation was given in the trades or the *Los Angeles Times*.[61] Before marrying Orsatti, Gorman had been married to James Stagliano, a French horn player with the Los Angeles Symphony (he later spent 26 years as the principal horn of the Boston Symphony).[62] Before too long, the Orsattis "dated Doc Stork" as the *L.A. Times* had it.[63] Ernie Jr. was born in 1940 and Frank in 1942.

Besides working at the agency, Orsatti had other business interests. In 1938, he helped to start a West Coast pro hockey minor league[64] which included six teams in Hollywood, Los Angeles, San Francisco, Oakland, San Diego and Long Beach.[65] He was the executive vice-president of the Hollywood Planets hockey team. They played at the Tropical Ice Gardens in Westwood Village. The team made its debut on January 29, 1939.[66] But after February 15, not a word about the team can be found in the newspapers. Hockey history books and encyclopedias are silent on the West Coast League; apparently it went bankrupt and ended.

Orsatti wasn't through with sports yet. In a 1937 charity baseball game that pitted a team of Leading Men against the Cinema Comedians, Joe E. Brown pulled out a Howitzer and "shot" Orsatti when he tried to steal second base. "The game was mercifully brought to a close after two hours of horseplay had finished only four innings," reported the *L.A. Times*. The Comedians won, 7–6.[67] The next year, Orsatti formed a team, the Filmsters, including his former boss, Buster Keaton, which played exhibition games, including one against wrestlers.[68]

In 1939, Ernie Orsatti decided to return to pro ball. At that point, his contract belonged to the Sacramento Solons, a Cardinal farm team, but after some wrangling and a payment of an undisclosed sum (the *L.A. Times* reported it was around $4,000),[69] Branch Rickey released him to play for a new Pacific Coast League team, the Hollywood Stars.[70] He arrived in time for the team's first game on May 2, 1939. Many celebrities attended.[71] Louise Brooks, Lou Anger, Harold Lloyd, Joe E. Brown, Jack Benny, Gary Cooper, Bing Crosby and Walt Disney all turned out, and Keaton was there of course, sharing a box with Orsatti's wife Inez. Rudy Vallee took 16mm films of the game. The Stars lost to the Seattle Rainiers, 9–5.[72] The "Twinks" played at Gilmore Field on Beverly Boulevard and Fairfax Avenue, which is now occupied by CBS Television City.

By July 30, 1939, the Stars had released Orsatti.[73] He signed with the Columbus Red Birds in the American Association (a minor league) and played with them for a few weeks, racking up a .375 average,[74] after which he quit the pros again. Later, he said that he "was afraid that his legs would not hold up."[75]

Throughout this time, Inez continued to work as an actress and singer. Among her appearances was a part in *Topsy and Eva*.[76] She spent the 1944 summer season in the stock company of the St. Louis Municipal Opera,[77] and she performed "Sing Hallelujah" and "One Night of Love" on the Nelson Eddy radio show in 1945.[78] In the early 1950s, she worked at MGM, singing with Ezio Pinza in *Strictly Dishonorable*, and she was a vocal coach and played the studio head's wife, Mrs. Simpson, in *Singin' in the Rain*.

In 1947, Orsatti opened a shop with his two brothers-in-law. He'd promised to go into business with them when they returned from serving in World War II. Ernie Orsatti's Oddity Shop and Florist, on Sunset Boulevard near Beverly Hills, sold flowers and knickknacks, many of which he'd made himself. He said, "I always had a hankering for making little things that fit into homes and offices. And I had been making things so long for my friends that I figured maybe I could develop a business out of the hobby."[79] Despite his new business venture, Orsatti didn't forget baseball: The business cards were decorated with two Cardinals perched on a bat. It quietly went out of business sometime later.

The 1950s brought many changes for Orsatti. His brother Frank had died in 1947[80] and his brother Al in 1949,[81] so brother Victor had taken over the talent agency. In the middle of the decade, Victor closed the agency and became a film producer (*Apache Territory*, *Flight to Hong Kong*), forming a company with Rory Calhoun.[82] Ernie Orsatti's wife Inez ended their marriage in February of 1952.[83] He got custody of their sons, although she had visitation rights on weekends and in the summers.[84] She married Roy A. Pierson in June 1952 and died in Los Angeles on December 6, 1986.[85]

In mid–November of 1956, Ernie Orsatti suffered a heart attack.[86] The notice in *Sporting News* gave his current employer as the Norton Electronic Wholesale Mart.

But still he kept up with baseball. In 1950, he had played in a three-inning old-timers game, with former Cards playing against former Giants (the Giants won, 2 to 1),[87] and he attended several Gashouse Gang reunions, where his former compatriots kidded him about his weight: Gus Mancuso, former Cards catcher, said, "Ernie used to double for Buster Keaton. Now he can triple for him."[88] Throughout, he was always ready to offer his opinion about baseball. In a 1947 profile, he reminisced, "We really played for keeps then. Almost anything went. If a pitcher tried to dust you off, it was up to you to drive it back down his throat at the first chance. From what I read, the boys played more like sissies last season."[89] In 1964, he predicted (correctly) that the Cards would beat the Yankees in the World Series, because the Cards had home field advantage, and their stadium, Sportsman's Park, had one of the roughest sun fields in all of baseball, which was something the New York team wasn't used to.[90]

In the late 1950s, he married Joyce Ritchie and they moved to Canoga Park in the San Fernando Valley. By 1958 he was working as a bail bondsman for the Nardoni Bond and Insurance Company.[91] A few years later, he started his own bail bonds business with his wife, close to the Van Nuys courthouse.[92] Fred Gabourie's son Fred, then an attorney, used the company's services for his clients.[93] Joyce Orsatti kept the bail bonds business going at least until the early 1980s.[94]

Ernie Orsatti died on September 4, 1968, from a heart attack, just four days before his 66th birthday.[95] He was buried in the San Fernando Mission Cemetery.

His two sons joined the film industry. His eldest, Ernie F. Orsatti, has been a stuntman, stunt coordinator and actor since 1968, working on such films as *Pleasantville*, *Big Momma's House* and *In Good Company*, as well as the television shows *Picket Fences* and *The D.A.*[96] He was also the second unit director for several films, including *Black Knight* and *Doctor Doolittle*. Ernie married stuntwoman-model Lynda Farrell in 1974 and his son, Noon Orsatti, is also a stuntman. Frank Orsatti drifted toward baseball, and was drafted by the Cardinals in the early 1960s; an injury ended his baseball career.[97] Later he joined for the Merchant Marines, then returned to Los Angeles in 1968. He began *his* career as a stuntman on *Planet of the Apes*, and followed with dozens of feature films, including *Con Air*, *Star Trek 5* and the second and third *Lethal Weapon* films. In addition, he was Arnold Schwarzenegger's double in *The Terminator* and Bill Bixby's for the TV series *The Incredible Hulk*. He married Julie Ann Steinberg in 1988, and they had two daughters. He died on December 23, 2004, of respiratory failure.

Census Records

1900 U.S. Federal Census (Population Schedule), Los Angeles Ward 2, Los Angeles, California, ED 11, Sheet 6A, Dwelling 76, Family 81, Morris Orsatti household, jpeg image (Online: The Generations Network, Inc., 2009) [Digital scan of original records in the National Archives, Washington, D.C.], subscription database, http://www.ancestry.com, accessed 27 December 2010.

1910 U.S. Federal Census (Population Schedule), Los Angeles Assembly District 75, Los Angeles, California, ED 81, Sheet 9A-B, Dwelling 242, Family 244, Morris Orsatti household, jpeg image (Online: The Generations Network, Inc., 2009) [Digital scan of original records in the National Archives, Washington, D.C.], subscription database, http://www.ancestry.com, accessed 27 December 2010.

1920 U.S. Federal Census (Population Schedule), Los Angeles Assembly District 75, Los Angeles, California, ED 458, Sheet 1B, Dwelling 115, Family 32, Morris Orsatti household, jpeg image (Online: The Generations Network, Inc., 2009) [Digital scan of original records in the National Archives, Washington, D.C.], subscription database, http://www.ancestry.com, accessed 27 December 2010.

1930 U.S. Federal Census (Population Schedule), Beverly Hills, Los Angeles, California, ED 825, Sheet 13B, Dwelling 317, Family 368, Mary Orsatti household, jpeg image (Online: The Generations Network, Inc., 2009) [Digital scan of original records in the National Archives, Washington, D.C.], subscription database, http://www.ancestry.com, accessed 27 December 2010.

1940 U.S. Federal Census (Population Schedule), Los Angeles Assembly District 59, Los Angeles, California, ED 60–193, Sheet 17A, Family 510, Ernest R. Orsatti household, jpeg image (Online: FamilySearch Historical Collections, 2012) [Digital scan of original records in the National Archives, Washington, D.C.], https://www.familysearch.org, accessed 21 July 2012.

Costume Designers

Most of Keaton's independent films list no credits for the costume designer, but there were three exceptions. For the huge undertaking that was *The General*, the names of the whole costume and makeup department are known: Bennie Hubbel, J.K. Pitcarin, and Fred C. Ryle. (Not much other information is available about them; Ryle did go on to have a 30-year career as a makeup artist.) Walter Israel was the costumer for *Our Hospitality* and Clare West the costumer for *Sherlock Jr.* Both of them were already working for Joseph Schenck, designing for Buster's sisters-in-law Norma and Constance Talmadge.

WALTER ISRAEL

Walter Jay Israel was born on August 4, 1882, in San Francisco, California. His father came from the area that was part of Germany in 1910 and became part of Poland after World War I (Posen, West Prussia, and some areas of Upper Silesia). His mother, Sabrina, came from England.

In 1910, Walter was a 27-year-old clothing salesman living in a lodging house, still in San Francisco. His future wife, Ethel Elizabeth Wahlicht, was working as a seamstress in a San Francisco theater. Her parents, August and Mary Schiller Wahlicht, had immigrated from Poland and Germany. The couple married on December 15, 1912, in Los Angeles.[1] She may have inspired him to become a costume designer, because by January 1914 he was working for the Fischer Costuming Company.[2] One of his early jobs was designing costumes for a stage production of *A Midsummer Night's Dream*, presented by a women's club in May 1916.[3]

When Walter registered for the draft on September 11, 1918, he was listed as a merchant for a costume company.[4] His draft registration card states that he was of medium height and build, with dark eyes and brown hair. By January 1920, both he and his wife were employed as theatrical costumers, and they were living with Ethel's mother, sister Elsie, and her son Philip just west of downtown Los Angeles.

By 1922, Walter had branched out into designing costumes for films. His first credit was for *Oliver Twist*, which starred Jackie Coogan. The *L.A. Times* called him as a craftsman who works unseen in pictures, a "silent cog."[5]

In 1923, the *New York Times* reported that Israel was in charge of First National's costume department; he designed the costumes for Norma Talmadge's *Within the Law*.[6] So when Keaton needed period costumes for *Our Hospitality*, it made sense that Israel was asked to design them.[7] After that picture, he started work on Talmadge's *Ashes of Vengeance*; *Camera!* reported that he spent $60,000 on the costumes.[8] He left the film in the middle and Clare West finished the ten-reel drama set in 16th century France.

Israel's last credits were also period films, *The Sea Hawk* (1924—Fred Gabourie was the technical director) and *Abraham Lincoln* (1930, directed by D.W. Griffith). Helen Rose, later an Academy Award–winning costume designer, worked with him on *Lincoln*. In her autobiography she said he was "a walking encyclopedia on period costumes ... Walter was an odd fellow, full of changeable moods. One day he would tell me how talented I was and how far I would go, and the next day he would remember how mean his mother or his aunt had been to him as a boy, and he would hate all women. He would then take out his frustrations on every woman in sight, including his patient wife and me."[9]

On the 1930 census, his occupation was listed "department store proprietor," but it wasn't an ordinary store. He owned Hollywood Costumes, one of the few suppliers of costumes to movie studios and stage productions. He and Ethel continued in the costume business for the rest of their careers. In 1936, with the help of 50 dressmakers and tailors, they made 500 Italian Renaissance–style costumes for *Everyman*, a spectacle staged at the Hollywood Bowl.[10] He told the draft board in 1942 that he was retired,[11] but he still turned up in theatrical credit lists after that. The *L.A. Times* commented on his designs for *Rose Marie* in 1945: "Walter Israel's fashion interpretation of the melody expressed his creative skill in a group of beautiful costumes that transformed the beginning of the second act into a thrilling style show. His artistry in the use of unusual color combinations was outstanding."[12]

He also designed costumes for several stage musicals, including *The Red Mill* and *The Desert Song* (both 1945) on Broadway in New York, and *The Three Musketeers* (1947), *Carousel* (1953), and *The Great Waltz* (1953) in Los Angeles.[13]

Walter Israel lived a long life, dying on January 6, 1970, aged 87, of cardio respiratory collapse following leukemia.[14] He was cremated and buried at sea. Ethel Israel died on March 2, 1974, five days after suffering a stroke.[15] She was also cremated.

Clare West

The other credited costumer for Keaton about whom information is available was Clare West. She was possibly the first full-time specialist costume designer employed by a studio, according to film historian Pat Kirkham.[16] She designed everything from period costumes to contemporary art deco fantasy gowns. *Woman's Home Companion* writer Anne Walker called her "an etcher in costuming, working in fine and subtle lines. She sees individual roles, individual players, individual scenes in detail."[17]

Clare Belle Smith was born on January 30, 1879, in Lathrop, Missouri, a small town 40 miles northeast of Kansas City. Her parents, Abraham C. and Jennie Smalley Smith, were farmers. She had six brothers and sisters: William (born in 1868), Edwin (1870), Blanche (1872), Llewellyn (1874), Lester (1875) and Harry (1885).

She married Otis Oscar Hunley on August 20, 1898, in Cameron, Missouri[18] and they moved to Billings, Montana, where Hunley worked as a store cashier. They had a son, Maxwell Otis Hunley, on March 22, 1900. It was a short marriage; their divorce records aren't available, but he married Ora L. Jones on March 21, 1903.[19] Otis and Ora Hunley named their daughter Claire (born in 1907), so it seems like the divorce was amicable. Maxwell Hunley became a rare book dealer with his own store in Beverly Hills. He died on December 18, 1990.[20]

In 1903 West married Marshall Elmer Carriere in Tulare, California,[21] and they had two sons, Leonard in 1907 and Lester in 1910. The 1910 census found them in Hamilton, Montana, where Marshall worked as a musician. She filed for divorce from him in September 1911.[22] Leonard became an artist who specialized in sandblasted glass designs[23] and Lester became a carpenter.[24]

There are no records of how she became a fashion designer. She probably moved to Los Angeles because other family members were already there.[25] She later told an interviewer that she sold sketches to fashion magazines "when she was still wearing her hair in a braid," graduated from college, and went to Paris to study fashion.[26] None of that can be independently verified, and it seems improbable. It's most likely that she went to work as a seamstress and worked her way up.

Her first film job was in the costume department for *Birth of a Nation* in 1915.[27] She stayed with D.W. Griffith's company for *Intolerance* in 1916, helping to design the hundreds of costumes for Babylonian, Hugonaut, Biblical and modern times.

Impressed by her work, Cecil B. DeMille hired her to create Gloria Swanson's stunning outfits for *Male and Female* (1919), *Why Change Your Wife?* (1919) and *The Affairs of Anatole* (1921), contributing to Swanson's reputation as a "clothes horse." In a later interview, West said, "Gloria was wearing the most exotic gowns and wraps she has ever worn. And I'm sure that she could make the most far-fetched creation in the world seem entirely logical."[28]

She also worked on DeMille's 1923 epic *The Ten Commandments*. Such a big production got big publicity; the *Los Angeles Times* reported that she used 33,000 yards of cloth for more than 3,000 costumes.[29] She went to Paris for some of that material,[30] and said on her return, "The American motion picture has become virtually the dictator of the world's fashions.... Our designers, especially those whose work is reflected on the screen, are months ahead of those of Paris and London."[31]

In September 1923, she took on an additional job: designing for First National Studio.[32] *Ashes of Vengeance* (1923) seems to have been her first assignment, but 1924 was her busiest year. She designed costumes for

Norma Talmadge's *Song of Love* and *Secrets*, as well as her sister's *The Goldfish* (about which Constance Talmadge said, "They've got me all dolled up like a Christmas tree"[33]), dressed Barbara La Marr in *The White Moth*, Colleen Moore in *Flirting with Love* and Nita Naldi in *Blood and Sand*. And she also designed the costumes for *Sherlock Jr.*

Keaton's film wasn't a fashion showcase, so she probably was mostly responsible for Kathryn McGuire's gowns in *Hearts and Pearls*, the film-within-the-film. It doesn't seem to have made much of an impression on her; in an interview she did only a few months after the film, she didn't mention working on it. She did describe her working methods: "I make a sketch first—an idea of what I have in mind—something that expresses to me the character I have read of in the script, as she would be interpreted by the girl who is to play the part. Then I buy the materials, take out the manikin that belongs to the girl concerned, drape the fabric on it—and cut!"[34]

West went back to work for DeMille in 1925. Her last two credits were for his *The Golden Bed* and *The Road to Yesterday*. In December 1925, *Variety* reported that she was opening her own *modiste* shop in downtown Los Angeles.[35] She continued to design clothes. The 1930 census listed her as a dress designer for a department store, living in a lodging house, and in 1940 the Los Angeles City Directory listed her as a designer for Patricia Perkins, Inc., a ladies evening wear manufacturer.

Clare West died on March 13, 1961, in Ontario, California, after a heart attack, at age 82.[36] In 2003, the Costume Designers Guild inducted her into their Hall of Fame along with Natacha Rambova and Mitchell Leisen.[37] They recognized her as one of the industry's first designers.

One day, if more records are discovered, we may find out about the other "silent cogs" in Keaton's wardrobe department.

Further Information

Inaccurate biographical information has been previously published about Clare West. For example, the contributor to the IMDB mistook her for Clare Frances Whitney Prindle, who was born in Kansas in 1889. Prindle was living in Gooding, Idaho with her husband Elmer in 1920, when West was busy working for DeMille. Prindle died in 1980, Ally Acker in *Reel Women* also gave this as West's death date; she might have been similarly confused.

Census Records

Israel:
1910 U.S. Federal Census (Population Schedule), San Francisco Assembly District 38, San Francisco, California, ED 197, Sheet 6A, Dwelling 85, Family 112, Mary

M. Walicht household, jpeg image (Online: The Generations Network, Inc., 2007) [Digital scan of original records in the National Archives, Washington, D.C.], subscription database, http://www.ancestry.com, accessed 4 May 2007.

1910 U.S. Federal Census (Population Schedule), San Francisco Assembly District 44, San Francisco, California, ED 305, Sheet 7B, Dwelling 19, Family 20, George L. Smith household, jpeg image (Online: The Generations Network, Inc., 2007) [Digital scan of original records in the National Archives, Washington, D.C.], subscription database, http://www.ancestry.com, accessed 14 April 2007.

1920 U.S. Federal Census (Population Schedule), Los Angeles Assembly District 63, Los Angeles, California, ED 182, Sheet 15A, Dwelling 384, Family 385, Walter Israel household, jpeg image (Online: The Generations Network, Inc., 2007) [Digital scan of original records in the National Archives, Washington, D.C.], subscription database, http://www.ancestry.com, accessed 4 May 2007.

1930 U.S. Federal Census (Population Schedule), Los Angeles, Los Angeles, California, ED 330, Sheet 4A, Dwelling 61, Family 62, Walter J. Israel household, jpeg image (Online: The Generations Network, Inc., 2007) [Digital scan of original records in the National Archives, Washington, D.C.], subscription database, http://www.ancestry.com, accessed 14 April 2007.

1940 U.S. Federal Census (Population Schedule), Los Angeles Assembly District 55, Los Angeles, California, ED 60–767, Sheet 11A, Family 341, Walter J. Israel household, jpeg image (Online: FamilySearch Historical Collections, 2012) [Digital scan of original records in the National Archives, Washington, D.C.], https://www.familysearch.org, accessed 21 July 2012.

West:

1880 U.S. Federal Census (Population Schedule), Lathrop Township, Clinton, Missouri, ED 110, Sheet 2, Dwelling 15, Family 15, Abraham C. Smith household, jpeg image (Online: The Generations Network, Inc., 2007) [Digital scan of original records in the National Archives, Washington, D.C.], subscription database, http://www.ancestry.com, accessed 24 November 2013.

1900 U.S. Federal Census (Population Schedule), North Billings, Yellowstone, Montana, ED 197, Sheet 16B, Dwelling 268, Family 291, Otis O. Hunley household, jpeg image (Online: The Generations Network, Inc., 2007) [Digital scan of original records in the National Archives, Washington, D.C.], subscription database, http://www.ancestry.com, accessed 24 November 2013.

1910 U.S. Federal Census (Population Schedule), Hamilton Ward 1, Ravalli, Montana, ED 86, Sheet 7A, Dwelling 104, Family 121, Marshall E. Carriere household, jpeg image (Online: The Generations Network, Inc., 2007) [Digital scan of original records in the National Archives, Washington, D.C.], subscription database, http://www.ancestry.com, accessed 24 November 2013.

1910 U.S. Federal Census (Population Schedule), Los Angeles Assembly District 73, Los Angeles, California, ED 192, Sheet 9B, Dwelling 261, Family 273, Otis O. Hunley household, jpeg image (Online: The Generations Network, Inc., 2007) [Digital scan of original records in the National Archives, Washington, D.C.], subscription database, http://www.ancestry.com, accessed 24 November 2013.

1930 U.S. Federal Census (Population Schedule), Los Angeles Assembly District 60, Los Angeles, California, ED 728, Sheet 54A, Dwelling 14, Family 18, William Sellwenne household, jpeg image (Online: The Generations Network, Inc., 2007) [Digital scan of original records in the National Archives, Washington, D.C.], subscription database, http://www.ancestry.com, accessed 27 March 2007.

1940 U.S. Federal Census (Population Schedule), Los Angeles Assembly District 57, Los Angeles, California, ED 60–115, Sheet 11A, Family 261, Leonard B. Carriere household, jpeg image (Online: FamilySearch Historical Collections, 2012) [Digital scan of original records in the National Archives, Washington, D.C.], https://www.familysearch.org, accessed 3 December 2013.

"Clare West," 8 February 1923 Passenger List, S.S. President Adams, passenger, line 93. (Online: The Generations Network, Inc., 2008) [Digital scan of original records in the National Archives, Washington, D.C.], subscription database, http://www.ancestry.com, accessed 12 January 2008.

West, Clare S. Passport application no. 238864. (22 December 1922) (Online: The Generations Network, Inc., 2013) [Digital scan of original records in the National Archives, Washington, D.C.], subscription database, http://www.ancestry.com, accessed 23 November 2013.

Arbuckle's Crew

Some crew members started working with Buster Keaton before he had an independent studio, but others only stayed long enough to be part of Roscoe Arbuckle's crew. They were still part of Keaton's filmmaking education. Undoubtedly, more people worked on the films, but credits were sparse in the 1910s and these are the few whose names were connected with them.

The most important one was cameraman Frank Williams. It was only after Williams introduced Keaton to the camera that Keaton agreed to try acting in film. Williams stayed for two more shorts, then left to work on his invention, the traveling matte shot. George Peters took over the job and photographed the next nine two-reelers.

There were two writers in the credits beside Arbuckle. Joseph Roach co-wrote the stories of the first four films that Keaton appeared in. Herbert Warren was the scenario editor for the first eleven Arbuckle-Keaton collaborations.

There isn't enough information available for entries about two staff members. Harry Williams' name didn't appear in the credits, but according to a *Los Angeles Herald* article he was on the set of *The Garage* writing gags with Jean Havez in 1919.[1] Like Havez, he was a songwriter-turned-film writer. He wrote the lyrics for the hits "In the Shade of the Old Apple Tree," "Mickey" and "Won't You Come Over to My House?" He first worked in films as a gag man for Mack Sennett, then he became a director.[2] He went on to direct the Hall Room Boys, Fox Sunshine Comedies, and some shorts featuring Snooky, a chimpanzee. He died on May 15, 1922, of septicemia in Oakland, California at age 43.[3]

Paul Conlon was also on Arbuckle's staff, as the press representative. He had been a reporter at the *Los Angeles Times*.[4] He went on to a long career in publicity. He left Schenck's company in late 1918 to be William

S. Hart's publicist.[5] After Hart retired, Conlon became a freelance publicity manager.[6] He died on January 30, 1961, in Los Angeles.[7]

Natalie Talmadge, Arbuckle's script supervisor, was obviously important too, but her marriage to Keaton is covered in his biographies.

George Peters

George Peters, the photographer of nine Arbuckle-Keaton shorts, was born October 27, 1891, in Chicago. He first worked as a sports page photographer, taking pictures of airplane flights and auto and horse races. According to *Moving Picture World*, his work appeared in the *Chicago Tribune*, the *New York Journal*, and the *Denver Post*. (Their claim that he took the best photos of the sinking of the *Maine* was certainly wrong as he was only seven years old when it went down.[1]) In 1910, at age 19, he transferred his photographic talents to moving pictures and went to work for the Selig Polyscope company in Chicago.[2] (Roscoe Arbuckle also made films for Selig at the time, but not in Chicago.) His credits, just like those of other pioneer movie cameramen, are hard to find, but he appears to have worked for many companies, including the American Film Manufacturing Company, Biograph, Popular Plays and Players, Majestic and Lewis Selznick.[3] He also joined the Static Club, the cameraman's social club.[4]

By 1916, he was "as well known as a professional aviator as he [was] as an expert cameraman," according to the *New York Dramatic Mirror*.[5] Some of his most daring photographic exploits included following an express train over a dangerous stretch of track through the mountains and flying over a steamer far out in Lake Michigan. This was in the early days of aviation when getting into a plane was risky. The *Mirror* also said

A trade ad from the *Motion Picture Studio Directory and Trade Annual*, 1918, featuring Roscoe Arbuckle's staff.

that he was the first man to make motion pictures from an airplane, although that hasn't been independently confirmed. The first aerial still was taken only a few years earlier, in 1909 by Wilbur Wright. Certainly, this ability to film action and the fact that he was a bit of a daredevil would work well for him filming comedies for Arbuckle and Keaton.

During this period, Peters moved to New York City, where he became a cameraman for Keystone in Fort Lee, New Jersey.[6] Arbuckle also worked at the same studio, so it's certainly possible they might have met at that time. In May 1917, when Comique's cameraman Frank D. Williams left to get married and start his own lab, Peters was there to take over. His first short with them was *His Wedding Night*. He shot their last three East Coast films: *Oh Doctor*, *Coney Island*, and *A Country Hero*.

When the company moved to Long Beach, California, in October, he came along. There his fearlessness was put to good use, with the train shots in *Out West* and the roller coaster shots in *The Cook*. He did the double-exposure trick shot in *Moonshine* in which tens of revenue agents pile out of a car. *The Bell Boy* and *Good Night, Nurse* were also his work.

His wife, Christine La Manna Peters, came along with him to California, and their son John Theodore (usually called Jack) was born in Long Beach on February 26, 1918. According to Peters' grandson Michael, family lore says that she didn't like California and thought he had a drinking problem, so she returned to New York City.[7] The 1920 census found all three of them living with her mother and stepfather in Manhattan, but by 1930, Peters had left and the rest of the family had moved to the Bronx.

After *The Cook*, there were changes in Arbuckle's company: Keaton was drafted into the Army, and Arbuckle moved them to a studio in Edendale. No crew credits for Arbuckle's next films are available, so it's not known if Peters stayed with them. However, in 1919, he was at Triangle's West Coast studio (Triangle had absorbed Keystone) where he shot two features, *Taxi* and *Upside Down*.

In December 1920, he was elected president of the Motion Picture Photographers' Association in New York.[8] It was a membership-by-invitation-only society, like the American Society of Cinematographers in Los Angeles, so to be included in the organization, much less to become its president, was a high honor.

After he left Triangle, he continued the uncertain life of a freelance cameraman. In late 1921, he was hired to photograph all of the feature films for Affiliated Distributors. When its president, Charles C. Burr, came down with such serious pneumonia that he had to recuperate in Florida, the company temporarily stopped making films and Peters was again out of a job. (In 1926 when their current cameraman Charles Gilson needed a vacation, Peters was brought back to work for them again.[9]) While at Affiliated, Peters completed *The Brown Derby*, and shot *Stepping Along* and *All Aboard*, vehicles for the popular comic Johnnie Hines. Other career highlights included *Serenade* (1921), directed by Raoul Walsh with art direction by William Cameron Menzies; *The Bandolero* (1924), which was partially shot in Spain and Cuba; and *The Adventurous Sex* (1925) with Clara Bow.

Peters' life did not end well. Possibly because of his drinking problems, his later films were made at low-budget independent studios. His final film was *Convict's Code*, shot for Monogram in 1930. A few years later, police found him unconscious on the street and took him to a hospital. He died in Los Angeles on October 18, 1935, just a few days short of his 44th birthday, and was buried at the Hollywood Memorial Park Cemetery.[10] The *Los Angeles Times* reported the cause of death was a heart attack, but his death certificate says acute alcoholism.[11]

Census Records

1920 U.S. Federal Census (Population Schedule), Manhattan Assembly District 9, New York, New York, ED 685, Sheet 20B and 22B, Dwelling 29, Family 254, Lawrence H. McDermott household, jpeg image (Online: The Generations Network, Inc., 2009) [Digital scan of original records in the National Archives, Washington, D.C.], subscription database, http://www.ancestry.com, accessed 12 October 2010.

1930 U.S. Federal Census (Population Schedule), Bronx, New York, New York, ED 603, Sheet 9B, Dwelling 31, Family 81E, Christine Peters household, jpeg image (Online: The Generations Network, Inc., 2009) [Digital scan of original records in the National Archives, Washington, D.C.], subscription database, http://www.ancestry.com, accessed 12 October 2010.

Peters, George W. *World War I Draft Registration Cards, 1917–1918* (5 June 1918) (Online: The Generations Network, Inc., 2004) [Digital scan of original records in the National Archives, Washington, D.C.], subscription database, http://www.ancestry.com, accessed 20 November 2004.

Joseph Anthony Roach

Joseph Anthony Roach co-wrote the first four films in which Keaton appeared. He was born in St. Louis, Missouri, on June 17, 1886; his parents were William John and Mary Doyle Roach. Joseph was an only child who, at the time of the 1900 census, was living with his mother in St. Louis and boarding with a bookkeeper's family. Fourteen-year-old Roach was supporting his mother and himself by working as an office boy. By 1910, he was still in St. Louis, but his mother was now also gone and he was living with his aunt, Katie Foley, and working as a moving pictures operator, or what later would be called a projectionist.

Perhaps threading all of those films through his projectors made him dream of writing pictures himself. By 1914 he'd moved to Chicago and was working for Essanay Studios, writing several short dramas such as *Eyes That See Not* and *Twice into the Light.* Soon he had married one of Essanay's leading ladies, Ruth Stonehouse, who would appear in more than 150 short films for the studio. The *New York Dramatic Mirror* reported that they tried to elope to Milwaukee, but Wisconsin state law mandated that they needed five days' residency before they could wed. So they took the train to St. Louis and got married there.[1]

The couple left Chicago in 1916, headed for opposite coasts, with Stonehouse off to Universal Studios in Los Angeles to act and direct, and Roach moving to New York City. He wrote a comedy for Fox Films, *Melting Millions*, and then he went to work with Roscoe Arbuckle, with whom he co-wrote the stories for five two-reelers: *The Butcher Boy, A Reckless Romeo, The Rough House, His Wedding Night,* and *Oh Doctor!* (Jean Havez also worked on the latter.) Keaton co-starred in all but *Romeo*.

Roach joined his wife in Los Angeles in 1917. He wrote *The Curse of Eve* for the Corona Cinema Corporation, and then he went to work for Triangle.[2] In November he, like Keaton, got drafted.[3] His draft registration said he was a photoplay writer, of medium height and build, with blue eyes and brown hair.[4] It also said that he had no dependents, even though he was married. Perhaps because his wife was a successful actress, he didn't consider her a dependent. When Ruth Stonehouse threw a going-away party for him at an ice-skating rink, *L.A. Times* gossip columnist Grace Kingsley said Roach "was heard to remark that the variety of party Ruth chose to give him he considered a chilly farewell."[5]

Roach served from November 1917 to August 1918, and rose to the rank of sergeant. According to *Camera!* magazine, he "stopped one German bullet and was the victim of a gas test at Calais,"[6] but the article was misinformed; his military records state that he spent the war training soldiers at Camp Lewis in Washington state.[7]

After Roach returned to Los Angeles, he was hired by Fox Studios, where he wrote a variety of screenplays, including the comedies *The Rebellious Bride* (1919) and *Tin Pan Alley* (1919), the Westerns *The Cyclone* (1920) with Tom Mix and Colleen Moore, and the crime drama *Black Shadows* (1920).

By December of 1919, his marriage had completely deteriorated and the couple separated, ending up in divorce court in February 1921. Stonehouse stated that Roach "said he was tired of having women tell him when to come to meals and what to do. He said he wanted to live in a hotel."[8] Another witness called him "an artistic swearer ... Mr. Roach made a song of it."[9]

Ruth Stonehouse continued to act until 1928, when she married Felix Hughes, a vocal instructor[10] who also happened to be Howard Hughes' uncle. From that point forward, she devoted her time to her garden and to the Children's Home Society.[11] She died on May 12, 1941.[12]

Following his divorce, Roach apparently had a career interruption, because his next credited film didn't come out until 1924. It was another Western, *Fighting for Justice*, for J. Joseph Sameth Productions. He spent the rest of his career writing Westerns, including *Somewhere in Sonora* (1933), an early John Wayne film. He also wrote some serials for Pathé, including *Melting Millions* (1927) and *The Black Book* (1929). His final credit *Ferocious Pal* was released in 1934. By the time he registered for the 1942 "old man's draft," he was unemployed.[13]

He married Theresa Humphries in 1925, when she was 21 and he was 38. She died on May 30, 1941, of bronchial pneumonia and liver insufficiency due to sub-acute cirrhosis. She also suffered from Korsakoff's syndrome. In other words, she died of alcoholism. She was only 37. She was buried at Inglewood Cemetery, Los Angeles.[14]

Joseph Roach died at the Veteran's Administration hospital in West Los Angeles on April 15, 1945. Alcohol also killed him; he died of Laennec's cirrhosis of the liver. It was exacerbated by diabetes. He was buried at the nearby VA cemetery.[15]

Census Records

1900 U.S. Federal Census (Population Schedule), St. Louis Ward 5, St. Louis, Missouri, ED 348, Sheet 13, Dwelling 171, Family 359, Alfred McCabe household, jpeg image (Online: The Generations Network, Inc., 2007) [Digital scan of original records in the National Archives, Washington, D.C.], subscription database, http://www.ancestry.com, accessed 16 May 2007.

1910 U.S. Federal Census (Population Schedule), St. Louis Ward 16, St. Louis, Missouri, ED 250, Sheet 15B, Dwelling 142, Family 327, Katie Foley household, jpeg image (Online: The Generations Network, Inc., 2007) [Digital scan of original records in the National Archives, Washington, D.C.], subscription database, http://www.ancestry.com, accessed 16 May 2007.

1920 U.S. Federal Census (Population Schedule), Cahuenga Township, Los Angeles, California, ED 509, Sheet 23A, Dwelling 145, Family 148, Joseph A. Roach household, jpeg image (Online: The Generations Network, Inc., 2007) [Digital scan of original records in the National Archives, Washington, D.C.], subscription database, http://www.ancestry.com, accessed 16 May 2007.

1930 U.S. Federal Census (Population Schedule), Beverly Hills, Los Angeles, California, ED 83, Sheet 1A, Dwelling 2, Family 10, Joseph A. Roach household, jpeg image (Online: The Generations Network, Inc., 2007) [Digital scan of original records in the National Archives, Washington, D.C.], subscription database, http://www.ancestry.com, accessed 16 May 2007.

1940 U.S. Federal Census (Population Schedule), Los Angeles Assembly District 56, Los Angeles, California, ED 60–98, Sheet 2B, Family 66, Joseph Roach household, jpeg image (Online: FamilySearch Historical Collections, 2012) [Digital scan of original records in the National Archives, Washington, D.C.], https://www.familysearch.org, accessed 14 July 2012.

Herbert Warren

Herbert Warren was Roscoe Arbuckle's scenario editor-writer on the 11 films he made with Buster Keaton between 1917 and 1918. He was born on September 28, 1879, in Philadelphia, Pennsylvania. No information is available on his early life; it's possible that he changed his name to Herbert Warren when he went into show business. According to his 1918 draft registration, he was stout, with brown hair and brown eyes.[1]

He started touring the vaudeville circuit with the Valerie Bergere Company in 1907. Bergere was a successful stage actress, best known for her role of Cio-Cio-San in famous producer-director David Belasco's production of *Madame Butterfly*.[2] Bergere and Warren presented one-act plays like *Billie's First Love* and *A Bowery Camille*.[3] About the latter, *Variety* said, "There are few acts in vaudeville that flash any harder working couple than Miss Bergere and Herbert Warren. They did some brilliant acting and thereby made the offering impressive and effective. The act would be a joke in other hands than theirs."[4] Warren also wrote one-acts, including *Don't Walk in Your Sleep*.[5] After ten years of working together, Warren and Bergere were married on September 24, 1917.[6]

A few months earlier, he had taken his talents to the movies. His first film credit was as the scenario editor on *The Butcher Boy*, which was Buster Keaton's first film and the beginning of the Keaton-Arbuckle collaboration. When Arbuckle's Comique company moved to the Los Angeles area later in 1917, Warren came along, and he stayed there through *The Cook*, the last film Keaton made with them before he was conscripted into the Army.

A *Moving Picture World* article said that Warren left Arbuckle in 1918 to make pictures on his own. He planned to travel to New York to sign up "a noted comedienne, whose name he does not divulge"[7] and return to

Los Angeles to produce pictures. It seems that nothing came of that. By November he was back touring with his wife in *Little Cherry Blossom*.[8] He told the *Cleveland Plain Dealer* that they were touring for only a brief time, and they planned to go west and "take up the photoplay as a real proposition." For whatever reason, that didn't happen.[9]

Warren had a long career as an actor; from 1925 to 1927 he toured the vaudeville circuit in comedies like *Mahatma*. In 1929, he played a detective in the film *House of Secrets*, and the same year began acting in Broadway plays, working fairly consistently through 1937. Some of the plays in which he appeared were *Light Wines and Beer*, *The Honor Code* and *The Guest Room*. He also acted in several Vitaphone shorts in the early 1930s, including *How've You Bean* with his former employer, Roscoe Arbuckle, who was making a comeback on screen in 1933.

Valerie Bergere died on September 16, 1938. For a while, he continued to act—at least that's the profession he included in the 1939 Los Angeles City Directory. The last known record for him was his registration for the 1942 "old man's draft." At that time, he was working for Marketville, Incorporated, in Los Angeles.[10] There is no known record of his death. It's possible that he went back to using his real name after he retired as an actor, so the obituary might have been under that name, still unknown.

Census Records

1930 U.S. Federal Census (Population Schedule), Manhattan, New York, New York, ED 396, Sheet 17B, Dwelling 12, Family 254, Herbert Warren household, jpeg image (Online: The Generations Network, Inc., 2007) [Digital scan of original records in the National Archives, Washington, D.C.], subscription database, http://www.ancestry.com, accessed 16 April 2007.

1930 U.S. Federal Census (Population Schedule), Manhattan, New York, New York, ED 400, Sheet 28A, Dwelling 1, Family 70, Herbert Warren household, jpeg image (Online: The Generations Network, Inc., 2007) [Digital scan of original records in the National Archives, Washington, D.C.], subscription database, http://www.ancestry.com, accessed 16 April 2007.

Frank D. Williams

"The first thing I did was make friends with the cameraman."
—Buster Keaton, in a 1960 interview
with Herbert Feinstein[1]

March 19, 1917, was quite a day for Buster Keaton. On that spring day, he met his future mentor Roscoe Arbuckle, met his future wife Natalie

Talmadge, and perhaps most important, he met the movie camera. The man who introduced the man to the machine was Frank D. Williams. And although that meeting was momentous, it isn't why Williams has a place in film history books. No, he's there because he put a brontosaurus on London streets and King Kong on Skull Island. He's the man who invented the traveling matte shot, an essential technique for modern filmmaking, and still in use today.

Frank Douglas Williams was born on March 21, 1893, in Nashville, Missouri, a small town in the Ozarks region. His parents James H. Williams and Lucinda Bowles Williams were farmers. He told *Moving Picture World* in 1917 that he studied electrical engineering in Pittsburgh and then he began his film career with the Martin Brothers of Omaha, Nebraska, making commercial films and travelogues of Yellowstone Park.[2] After that, he said, he worked abroad with Pathé for four years. However, he said he was 32 years old when he was actually 24, so whatever he said might need to be taken with a grain of salt. In all probability, he lied about his age because it made him appear to be more experienced. The account he gave Cal York of *Photoplay* in 1926 seems more plausible: In that article, he claimed that he started as a cameraman at Essanay the year he finished school, 1908.[3] Fifteen years old, he "knew just enough about a camera to turn a crank." In 1912, he became a cameraman at Mack Sennett's Keystone Studio.[4]

By an odd coincidence, he not only shot Buster Keaton's first appearance on film, but also Charlie Chaplin's, with *Making a Living*, filmed in early January 1914. Williams is credited with appearing onscreen in Chaplin's second film, *Kid Auto Races in Venice*, as the beleaguered cameraman who wants to film a race and not a Little Tramp. Despite the rumor, however, Williams was a tall man, and the actor playing the cameraman was short, so it's unlikely to have been Williams.

Williams was an early member of the Static Club, a social organization for cameramen, serving on the group's Board of Directors in 1915.[5] During a race between cameramen and actors in San Pedro, California, where the Port of Los Angeles is located, he reportedly he fell overboard when the camera boat collided with the actors' boat. According to *Static Flashes*, the club's newsletter, he "related his thrilling escape from a watery end in a serio-comic manner, and is ready for new and daring deeds."[6]

In 1914, Williams left Keystone to join Ford Sterling's company at Universal Studios, but he returned to Sennett when Sterling stopped production.[7] He also worked with director Henry "Pathe" Lehrman at the L-KO Kompany, and was on the staff at Reliance-Majestic Studio.[8] (Perhaps this was what he meant when he told people he "worked for Pathe.") Then in 1917, Roscoe Arbuckle formed his own company and hired Williams as his cameraman.[9] They set up shop at 318 East 48th Street in Manhattan, calling the company Comique Films. The stage was set for Keaton's entrance.

On March 19, so goes the story, studio manager Lou Anger ran into Keaton on the street and talked him into visiting the studio.[10] Anger then introduced him to Arbuckle, who asked him to do a bit in the next scene of *The Butcher Boy*, but Keaton reportedly turned him down. Arbuckle invited him to stay and see how they worked, then called for a 20-minute break, during which he asked Keaton what he wanted to see first. The camera, Keaton replied. So the two went over to Frank Williams.

Keaton and Arbuckle must have been persuasive, because most cameramen wouldn't let a stranger (even worse, an actor) get anywhere near their equipment. But according to York in *Photoplay*, Williams was "shy, rather diffident in speech, he makes everything he does look easy. When he comes on a set, his quiet presence is scarcely noticed, and cameramen and technical experts go on spluttering and arguing, and when he is finally appealed to, he settles the problem so simply that everyone wonders why he didn't think of it himself."[11] He sounds like Keaton himself. Maybe that's why Williams let Keaton, as Rudi Blesh put it, all but climb inside the camera, inspecting the gears, sprockets, and shutter. Then Keaton looked at the lights and the cutting room, and watched some dailies. Blesh continued, "This, he saw, was for him. As the last frame of the last rush faded on the screen, he stood up in the darkness. The 20-minute break had been nearly an hour. 'Let's do that scene,' he said."[12] And that's how Keaton became a filmmaker.

Williams shot the first three Comique films: *The Butcher Boy*, *A Reckless Romeo* and *The Rough House*. But being a cameraman was only his day job. In his spare hours, he had been working on his traveling matte idea since 1912, usually in the bathroom of wherever he was living.[13] In 1916, he filed his first patent application for the process.[14] In 1917, Adolph Zukor of Paramount gave him space in his lab to work on it, but Williams couldn't overcome the problems of inaccurate cameras and printers and crude film stocks.[15] But then he had a breakthrough: He built his own printer, accurate to one ten-thousandth of an inch, used a motor-cranked camera and a better grade of film, and it worked. He was granted a patent on the process and he opened his own film lab. The idea was slow to catch on, so to support his lab he shot films for Sessue Hayakawa after he left Arbuckle.

Stationary mattes had been used in filmmaking since the earliest days; it was a technique borrowed from still photography, the same method that Keaton cameraman Elgin Lessley used to get multiple Busters in *The Playhouse*. Actors were filmed with part of the negative blocked and left unexposed, and then the film was re-wound and another image was shot on the unexposed area. The two images formed a composite. However, actors had to stay within a set portion of the image. With the Williams Process, the whole background could be replaced, and the actor could move freely.

Cinefex, in a 1982 article on effects pioneer Willis O'Brien, described the process:

> In its earliest form, the Williams technique involved the photography of foreground action against a white or black background. By overexposure and intensification on high-contrast stock, a silhouette matte would be prepared which could then be printed in bi-pack with the original background negative, producing a positive image with the foreground subject area left unexposed. This positive would then be run through the printer once again, thereby printing the foreground subject into the silhouette window left in the background.[16]

The first Williams shots to gain wide attention were in *Beyond the Rocks* (1922), in which his techniques helped Rudolph Valentino rescue Gloria Swanson from a mountain crag. Even more spectacular scenes were in *The Lost World* (1925), when the process allowed dinosaurs to roam London. The destruction of Pontius Pilate's palace in *Ben-Hur* (1925) was also Williams' work, as were the battle scenes in *The Big Parade* (1925). The process wasn't cheap. His work in *The Big Parade* cost $70,000, while a storm at sea that included a ship crushed by an ice floe for *The Barrier* (1926) cost $85,000.[17] It almost makes the $42,000 Keaton spent on crashing the *Texas* into the river for *The General* seem like a bargain—no wonder Keaton decided to not to use miniatures and composite work.

When Williams left Arbuckle's crew, he also got married. Mildred E. Hansen, 21, of Los Angeles was the bride, and the wedding took place at the Little Church Around the Corner in New York City on May 19, 1917.[18] They had a daughter, Barbara Jane.

In 1927 the *Los Angeles Times* summed up Williams' personal life with the headline "Film Inventor Piles Up Woes."[19] Mildred sued him for divorce, charging that he was paying attention to other women.[20] He resisted the suit, saying that she continually nagged him and had declared that anybody who married a person connected with the movies was a fool. The court battle was long, because the sides disagreed on Williams' assets—

she said they were worth more than $580,000, while he claimed he was $30,000 in debt. An independent auditor reported that he was worth $94,000, not including the value of his patents.[21]

Williams didn't help matters by slugging one of Mildred's witnesses in the courthouse hallway.[22] He claimed self-defense and received a 90-day suspended sentence. Then an anonymous telephone tip led police to a large cache of liquor in a closet at Mrs. Williams' apartment.[23] During her trial on that charge, Deputy City Prosecutor Harry Margid accused her husband of arranging the tip, because it smacked of a deliberate plot to discredit her divorce action. She told the jury that her husband had bought the liquor and she hadn't touched it since he'd moved out two years earlier. She was quickly acquitted and Frank Williams was arrested. He was later found guilty and fined $100.[24] At that point, he stopped fighting the divorce. An interlocutory judgment was entered on May 11, 1928, and it was finalized on January 9, 1930.[25]

Williams married Porter Lee, and they had four children: Frank Jr., Lucinda, Melinda, and Brenda.[26] Back at work, he continued to improve his process, eventually getting six patents, five for the process and a sixth for a tank that allowed better underwater photography. In 1932, he introduced a double matting process. That year, in an article he wrote for *International Photographer* magazine, he noted that the old process sometimes caused transparencies and visible matte lines, and it took from one to six weeks to complete.[27] The improved process corrected those defects and was more efficient. It was ready in time to contribute to 1933's *King Kong*. One of its most memorable uses was the scene in which the huge village gates swing open and Kong appears in the 60-foot high opening.

Even with Williams' technical innovations, the business had its ups and downs. His lab survived bankruptcy in 1932[28] and an explosion and fire that caused $50,000 worth of damage in 1938.[29] Ultimately, there were three Williams Labs. The first was at 6225 Santa Monica Blvd. (near Vine, two and a half blocks from Keaton's studio), which is now home to several stores. In 1924, the company moved two and a half miles west to 8111 Santa Monica Blvd. (just west of Fairfax), which is now a park. Then, in 1941, the company moved back to its old neighborhood, 1040 N. McCadden Place (one block east of Highland), a site that is now the parking lot for the Eastman Kodak company. At the lab, his staff did more than just Williams shots: They developed negatives, dailies and release prints, and rented out cutting rooms and negative vault space.[30]

Williams also kept his lawyers busy. In 1928, he sued Samuel Goldwyn Productions for failure to pay for work he'd done on the *Potash and Perl-*

mutter series.[31] In 1943, he sued the International Alliance of Theatrical Stage Employees (IATSE) for failure to supply technicians, but he dropped the case after receiving permission to train apprentices.[32] He filed another suit against the union in 1945, after it briefly shuttered his business with a strike (he'd refused to hire a union projectionist).[33] And finally, in 1948, he filed suit against the Southern California Camellia Society because they'd expelled him.[34] He charged that he was kicked out after asking state authorities to investigate seedlings being taken from the Huntington Library Garden, and claimed that the expulsion had impaired his health so much that he couldn't attend to laboratory business.

Sadly, it probably wasn't his rift with the Camellia Society that was impairing his work. It was alcohol. In 1955, the lab was sold to Mickey Kaplan, a real estate developer.[35] Kaplan operated it for a year under the supervision of George Seid, who had run both the Columbia and Universal film labs. But a year later, Seid died of a heart attack and the lab was out of business.[36]

In 1959, Williams' chronic drinking problem had become so bad that he was diagnosed with Korsakoff's Syndrome and confined to Camarillo State Mental Hospital in Ventura County, California.[37] Korsakoff's Syndrome is characterized by confusion, severely impaired memory of recent events, and inability to learn new skills. He died at the hospital of hypertensive cardiovascular disease on October 16, 1961, aged 68, and was buried at the Hollywood Memorial Park Cemetery (now called Hollywood Forever), just half a block from his first lab.

Census Records

1800 U.S. Federal Census (Population Schedule), Post Oak, Johnson, Missouri, ED 106, Sheet 37, Dwelling 320, Family 329, James H. Williams household, jpeg image (Online: The Generations Network, Inc., 2009) [Digital scan of original records in the National Archives, Washington, D.C.], subscription database, http://www.ancestry.com, accessed 6 November 2010.

1920 U.S. Federal Census (Population Schedule), Los Angeles Assembly District 64, Los Angeles, California ED 225, Sheet 20B, Dwelling 2, Family 244, Frank D. Williams household, jpeg image (Online: The Generations Network, Inc., 2007) [Digital scan of original records in the National Archives, Washington, D.C.], subscription database, http://www.ancestry.com, accessed 27 May 2007.

1930 U.S. Federal Census (Population Schedule), Beverly Hills Township, Los Angeles, California, ED 832, Sheet 9B, Dwelling 29, Family 29, Frank D. Williams household, jpeg image (Online: The Generations Network, Inc., 2007) [Digital scan of original records in the National Archives, Washington, D.C.], subscription database, http://www.ancestry.com, accessed 22 May 2007.

1940 U.S. Federal Census (Population Schedule), Beverly Hills Township, Los Angeles, California, ED 19–63, Sheet 6B, Family 165, Frank D. Williams household, jpeg image (Online: FamilySearch Historical Collections, 2012) [Digital scan of original records in the National Archives, Washington, D.C.], https://www.familysearch.org, accessed 14 July 2012.

Williams, Frank D. *World War I Draft Registration Cards, 1917–1918* (5 June 1917) (Online: The Generations Network, Inc., 2007) [Digital scan of original records in the National Archives, Washington, D.C.], subscription database, http://www.ancestry.com, accessed 22 May 2007.

Source Notes

Preface

1. Buster Keaton with Charles Samuels, *My Wonderful World of Slapstick* (New York: Doubleday, 1960), 129–130.
2. John Gillett and James Blue, "Keaton at Venice," *Sight and Sound* (Winter 65/66), 27.
3. Luke McKernan, "Searching for Mary Murillo," *The Bioscope*, 5 November 2009, http://bioscopic.wordpress.com/?s=murillo, accessed 19 January 2012.

Camera and Electrical Departments

1. Gillett and Blue, "Keaton at Venice," 27.
2. Karl Brown, *Adventures with D.W. Griffith* (New York: Farrar, Straus, and Giroux, 1973), 12.
3. "Pulse of the Studio," *Camera!*, 5 August 1922, 11; 2 September 1922, 11.
4. "Buster Keaton's Again Victorious," *Los Angeles Times*, 25 February 1924, http://pqasb.pqarchiver.com/latimes/search.html
5. "Character Actress is Given Role," *Los Angeles Times*, 29 June 1923, http://pqasb.pqarchiver.com/latimes/search.html
6. Harry D. Brown, "The Importance of the Studio Electrician," *American Cinematographer* (August 1922), 7.

DAL CLAWSON

1. Lawrence Dallin Clawson, *World War I Draft Registration Cards, 1917–1918* (8 September 1918) (Online: The Generations Network, Inc., 2007) [Digital scan of original records in the National Archives, Washington, D.C.], subscription database, http://www.ancestry.com, accessed 3 August 2007.
2. "Dr. Clawson," *Daughters of Utah Pioneers Obituary Scrapbook* (Online: The Generations Network, Inc., 2007), subscription database, http://www.ancestry.com, accessed 28 September 2007.
3. "Lawrence Dallin Clawson," http://www/familysearch.org, accessed 27 September 2007.
4. "Lawrence Dallin Clawson," *Daughters of Utah Pioneers Obituary Scrapbook* (Online: The Generations Network, Inc., 2007), subscription database, http://www.ancestry.com, accessed 28 September 2007; "About Dallin," *Cyrus E. Dallin Art Museum*, http://dallin.org/?page_id=19, accessed 29 January 2013.

5. Salt Lake City Directories, 1903–1913.
6. "Clawson Works Out New Photographical Effects," *Static Flashes*, 19 June 1915, 2.
7. Salt Lake City Directories, 1910–1913.
8. Raymond Fielding, *The American Newsreel* (Norman: University of Oklahoma Press, 1972), 85.
9. Minutes of the Static Club of America, Inc. 1913.
10. Lawrence Dallin Clawson, *World War I Draft Registration Cards, 1917–1918* (8 September 1918) (Online: The Generations Network, Inc., 2007) [Digital scan of original records in the National Archives, Washington, D.C.], subscription database, http://www.ancestry.com, accessed 3 August 2007.
11. Dal Clawson, *Motion Picture Studio Directory and Trade Annual*, 1920, 331.
12. Ibid.
13. "Clawson Heads Walsh Cameramen," *Moving Picture World*, 5 June 1920, 1342.
14. "Newsy Notes," *New York Dramatic Mirror*, 1 September 1915, 1809.
15. "Back to God's Country," *Canadian Film Encyclopedia*, http://tiff.net/CANADIANFILMENCYCLOPEDIA/content/films/back-to-gods-country, accessed 10 June 2011.
16. "Camera Spread Terror in China," *Los Angeles Times*, 11 March 1923, http://pqasb.pqarchiver.com/latimes/search.html
17. "L. Dal Clawson," *American Cinematographer*, 1 February 1922, 35.
18. "Mrs. Dal Clawson Dies," *Moving Picture World*, 31 July 1920, 615.
19. Lawrence Dallin Clawson, Birth certificate (21 July 1921), informational copy from New Jersey State Bureau of Vital Statistics.
20. "Lawrence Clawson," 1928 Passenger List, S.S. Berengaria, lines 26–27. (Online: The Generations Network, Inc., 2007) [Digital scan of original records in the National Archives, Washington, D.C.], subscription database, http://www.ancestry.com, accessed 3 August 2007.
21. *The Day Buster Smiled* (Cottage Grove, OR: Historical Society, 1998), 48.
22. "Dal Clawson," *Internet Movie Database*, http://www.imdb.com/name/nm0165469/, accessed 3 August 2007.
23. "Pathe Camera Man Weds," *New York Times*, 20 March 1929, http://query.nytimes.com/search/sitesearch
24. "Lawrence Clawson, *New York Times*, 20 July 1937, http://query.nytimes.com/search/sitesearch
25. Ibid.; Dal Clawson, Death certificate (18 July 1937), informational copy from New Jersey State Bureau of Vital Statistics.
26. Lawrence Dallin Clawson Jr., *Social Security Death Index* (30 November 2002) (Online: The Generations Network, Inc., 2009) [Digital scan of original records in the Master File, Social Security Administration, Washington, D.C.], subscription database, http://www.ancestry.com, accessed 20 September 2010.

Elmer Ellsworth

1. His draft registration and death certificate give this date, but the 1900 census says he was born in November 1899. He might have fudged the date, preferring to be born in the 20th Century.
2. "E.E. Ellsworth, Retired Miller, Dies at age of 91," *Los Angeles Times*, 29 April 1951, http://pqasb.pqarchiver.com/latimes/search.html
3. Los Angeles City Directories, 1913–1942.
4. Elmer Emery Ellsworth, *World War I Draft Registration Cards, 1917–1918* (12

September 1918) (Online: The Generations Network, Inc., 2007) [Digital scan of original records in the National Archives, Washington, D.C.], subscription database, http://www.ancestry.com, accessed 30 April 2007.

5. Los Angeles City Directories, 1920–1926.
6. AFI Catalog of Films, accessed 3 November 2010.
7. *The Day Buster Smiled*, 48.
8. Stephen Lodge, "David Janssen," AuthorsDen.com, 19 May 2007, http://www.authorsden.com/visit/viewarticle.asp?AuthorID=12206&id=29889, accessed 4 November 2010.
9. Los Angeles City Directory, 1927.
10. Los Angeles City Directory, 1928.
11. Los Angeles City Directory, 1929.
12. "Elmer Ellsworth," *Variety*, 16 April 1969, 69.
13. Lodge, "David Janssen," AuthorsDen.com, 19 May 2007.
14. "Ellsworth Retiring from Costumer Post," *Variety*, 14 May 1963, 3.
15. "Dolores Del Rio Stand-in for her Stand-in's Bridal," *Variety*, 28 March 1934, 3; Los Angeles City Directory, 1935.
16. Dolores Carmen Ellsworth, *California Birth Index, 1905–1995* (September 1934) (Online: The Generations Network, Inc., 2007) [Digital scan of original records in the State of California Department of Health Services Center for Health Statistics, Sacramento, CA], subscription database, http://www.ancestry.com, accessed 22 May 2007.
17. Carmen Roux Ellsworth, Death certificate no. 1953 8903110 (24 August 1942), informational copy from Los Angeles County Registrar-Recorder/County Clerk.
18. "Funeral Today for Carmen Roux, Former Actress," *Los Angeles Daily News*, 27 August 1942, 11.
19. Elmer E. Ellsworth, Death certificate no. 7097 014443 (5 April 1969), informational copy from Los Angeles County Registrar-Recorder/County Clerk.
20. Bob Ellsworth, "Costume and Design," *Los Angeles Times*, 12 June 1986, http://pqasb.pqarchiver.com/latimes/search.html

BERT HAINES

1. Los Angeles City Directories, 1908.
2. Herbert Marcus Haines, *World War I Draft Registration Cards, 1917–1918* (5 June 1918) (Online: The Generations Network, Inc., 2007) [Digital scan of original records in the National Archives, Washington, D.C.], subscription database, http://www.ancestry.com, accessed 27 March 2007.
3. Herbert M. Haines, Military Personnel Records, National Personnel Records Center, St. Louis, MO, retrieved 12 October 2007.
4. 32nd Red Arrow Veteran Association, "32nd Division in the World War part 2," http://www.32nd-division.org/history/ww1/32-ww1a.html, revised 8 October 2005.
5. Herbert M. Haines, *California County Marriages, 1850–1952* (31 July 1919) (Online: FamilySearch Historical Collections, 2011) [Digital copies of originals housed in the clerks' offices of the district courts in various counties throughout California. FHL microfilm, Family History Library, Salt Lake City, Utah], https://www.familysearch.org, accessed 16 January 2012.
6. Los Angeles City Directories, 1922–1924.
7. "Keatons Wallop 'em Indoors Now," *Los Angeles Times*, 18 January 1921, http://pqasb.pqarchiver.com/latimes/search.html
8. Ibid.

9. *The Day Buster Smiled*, 48.
10. AFI Catalog of Films, accessed 21 September 2010.
11. Herbert Marcus Haines, Death certificate no. 3911 9025808 (19 June 1991), informational copy from Los Angeles County Registrar-Recorder/County Clerk.
12. "Metro's Legions Chase Golfing Glory," *Variety*, 22 June 1936, 10.
13. "Robert Z. Leonard Directed *Maytime*," *Variety*, 3 March 1937, 8.
14. "Gumshoe Cupid Pulls the Wool O'er Dad's Eyes," *Los Angeles Times*, 31 August 1911. http://pqasb.pqarchiver.com/latimes/search.html
15. "Divorces Mate Who 'Worked at Night at Office,'" *Los Angeles Times*, 30 July 1924, http://pqasb.pqarchiver.com/latimes/search.html
16. Olga McCoy Haines, Death certificate no. 7097 020464 (9 May 1966), informational copy from Los Angeles County Registrar-Recorder/County Clerk.
17. Herbert Marcus Haines, Death certificate.

Wayne "Denver" Harmon

1. Columbus City Directory, 1892–1911.
2. Ibid.
3. Fred J. Balshofer and Arthur C. Miller, *One Reel a Week* (Berkeley: University of California Press, 1967), 144. 4. "Begin Filming 'The Third Eye,'" *Los Angeles Times*, 17 August 1919, http://pqasb.pqarchiver.com/latimes/search.html
5. AFI Catalog of Films, accessed 21 September 2010.
6. Los Angeles City Directory, 1921.
7. "The Men Who Light the Pictures," *American Cinematographer*, 1 April 1922, 23.
8. *The Day Buster Smiled*.
9. "Personnel of Studios: Columbia Studio," *Film Daily Yearbook* (New York: Film Daily, 1929), 557.
10. Edward Bernds, *Mr. Bernds Goes to Hollywood* (Lanham, MD: Scarecrow Press, 1999), 267.
11. Ibid., 168–9.
12. Los Angeles City Directories, 1915–1942.
13. "Intention to Marry," *Los Angeles Times*, 20 March 1929, http://pqasb.pqarchiver.com/latimes/search.html; Wayne L. Harmon, *California County Marriages, 1850–1952* (23 March 1929) (Online: FamilySearch Historical Collections, 2011) [Digital copies of originals housed in the clerks' offices of the district courts in various counties throughout California. FHL microfilm, Family History Library, Salt Lake City, Utah], https://www.familysearch.org, accessed 3 February 2013.
14. "Pair Exchange Wedding Vows," *Los Angeles Times*, 12 July 1939, http://pqasb.pqarchiver.com/latimes/search.html
15. *Film Daily Yearbook*
16. "Denver Harmon," *Variety*, 3 February 1959, 4.
17. Wayne Lowell Harmon, Death certificate no. 7053 2213 (1 February 1959), informational copy from Los Angeles County Registrar-Recorder/County Clerk.
18. Birdie May Harmon, Death certificate no. 0190 054760 (23 November 1982), informational copy from Los Angeles County Registrar-Recorder/County Clerk.

Byron Houck

1. Office of the Registrar, University of Oregon, Portland, OR, letter to author, 4 February 2013.

2. "Byron Houck," *Baseball Reference*, http://www.baseball-reference.com/players/h/houckby01.shtml, accessed 30 September 2010.

3. Ibid.

4. Norman L. Macht, "Byron Houck," *Baseball Library*, http://www.baseballlibrary.com/ballplayers/player.php?name=Byron_Houck_1891, accessed 30 September 2010.

5. "Houck Won't Go to Orioles," *New York Times*, 20 May 1914, http://query.nytimes.com/search/sitesearch

6. "Feds Hit Houck Hard," *New York Times*, 23 May 1914, http://query.nytimes.com/search/sitesearch

7. Morris Miller, "Sports Snap Shots," *Janesville Daily Gazette*, 23 March 1916, http://www.newspaperarchive.com

8. "Beavers Sign Houck," *Bakersfield Morning Echo*, 2 March 1916, 7; "Beavers Beat Angels Twice," *Los Angeles Times*, 5 September 1916, http://pqasb.pqarchiver.com/latimes/search.html

9. Byron Simon Houck, *World War I Draft Registration Cards, 1917–1918* (5 June 1918) (Online: The Generations Network, Inc., 2007) [Digital scan of original records in the National Archives, Washington, D.C.], subscription database, http://www.ancestry.com, accessed 12 April 2007.

10. "Byron Houck," *Baseball Reference*.

11. "Vernon Buys Byron Houck," *Los Angeles Times*, 3 February 1919, http://pqasb.pqarchiver.com/latimes/search.html

12. Reed Heustis, "Madman Runs Fat Arbuckle's Studio—Sure, It's Lou Anger." *Los Angeles Evening Herald*, 3 November 1919, part 2, 1, 32.

13. "Oaks Swamp Essick's Lads," *Los Angeles Times*, 8 June 1920, http://pqasb.pqarchiver.com/latimes/search.html

14. Harry A. Williams, "Artificial Delivery to be Eradicated from Baseball," *Los Angeles Times*, 27 January 1920, http://pqasb.pqarchiver.com/latimes/search.html

15. Ed O'Malley, "Tigers Clamp Jaws on Suds," *Los Angeles Times*, 3 September 1920, http://pqasb.pqarchiver.com/latimes/search.html

16. Harry A. Williams, "Houck to Crank Camera," *Los Angeles Times*, 24 December 1920, http://pqasb.pqarchiver.com/latimes/search.html

17. "Tigers Drop Byron Houck," *Los Angeles Times*, 10 July 1922, http://pqasb.pqarchiver.com/latimes/search.html

18. Harry A. Williams, "Poor Portland Again Dented," *Los Angeles Times*, 25 June 1922, http://pqasb.pqarchiver.com/latimes/search.html

19. "Hubbard Outheaves Houck of All-Stars," *Los Angeles Times*, 3 January 1921, http://pqasb.pqarchiver.com/latimes/search.html

20. "Keatons Wallop 'em Indoors Now," *Los Angeles Times*, 18 January 1921, http://pqasb.pqarchiver.com/latimes/search.html

21. "Byron Houck Given Release by Tigers," *Oakland Tribune*, 10 July 1923, http://www.newspaperarchive.com.

22. Kittye B. Houck, Death certificate no. 23 012058 2842 (26 March 1923), informational copy from Los Angeles County Registrar-Recorder/County Clerk.

23. Mary Eunice McCarthy, *Hands of Hollywood* (Hollywood, CA: Photoplay Research Bureau, 1929), 66–67.

24. *The Day Buster Smiled*, 48.

25. "Buster Keaton Goes Down to Sea in a Diving Suit," *Lethbridge Daily Herald*, 14 March 1925, http://www.newspaperarchive.com

26. "'Throw Out the Lifeline' Save the Cameramen," *Lethbridge Daily Herald*, 16 March 1925, http://www.newspaperarchive.com

27. Los Angeles City Directory, 1928.

28. Byron S. Houck, *California County Marriages, 1850–1952* (26 October 1927) (Online: FamilySearch Historical Collections, 2011) [Digital copies of originals housed in the clerks' offices of the district courts in various counties throughout California. FHL microfilm, Family History Library, Salt Lake City, Utah], https://www.familysearch.org, accessed 3 February 2013.

29. Mrs. Rose Houck, *Index to Register of Voters, Los Angeles County, California, 1928* (Online: The Generations Network, Inc., 2009) [Digital scan of original records in the California State Library. Sacramento, California], subscription database, http://www.ancestry.com, accessed 30 September 2010; Rose Houck, Death certificate no. 4400 205 (16 February 1976), informational copy from Santa Cruz County Recorder.

30. Edward Lawrence, "Dave Martin Spurns 'Pro' Career," *Los Angeles Times*, 14 February 1932, http://pqasb.pqarchiver.com/latimes/search.html; Bob Ray, "Angels Battle Stars, Old-Timers Perform in Baseball Charity Bill," *Los Angeles Times*, 8 October 1933, http://pqasb.pqarchiver.com/latimes/search.html; Bob Ray, "Old-Timers on Parade Next Sunday," *Los Angeles Times*, 20 June 1937, http://pqasb.pqarchiver.com/latimes/search.html.

31. Los Angeles City Directory, 1936.

32. Byron Simon Houck, Death certificate no. 4400 707 (17 June 1969), informational copy from Santa Cruz County Recorder.

33. Rose Houck, Death certificate.

34. Byron Simon Houck, Death certificate.

35. Rose Houck, Death certificate.

Dev Jennings

1. *The Day Buster Smiled*, 6.

2. Nobel Warrum, *Utah Since Statehood* (Salt Lake City: S. J. Clarke, 1919), 614–617.

3. Orson F. Whitney, *Utah History* (Online: The Generations Network, Inc., 2009), subscription database, http://www.ancestry.com, accessed 1 July 2006.

4. Joseph D. Jennings, University of Utah School Records, Office of the Registrar, Salt Lake City, Utah, retrieved 19 July 2006; Henry Gordon Jennings, University of Utah School Records. Office of the Registrar, Salt Lake City, Utah, retrieved 19 July 2006.

5. Kevin Brownlow, *The Parade's Gone By ...* (Berkeley: University of California Press, 1968), 485.

6. Salt Lake City Directory, 1906.

7. "Kisses Children Adieu Then Takes Her Life," *Los Angeles Herald*, 7 Dec. 1910.

8. Ellen Jennings, Death certificate no. 4363 (6 December 1910), informational copy from Los Angeles County Registrar-Recorder/County Clerk.

9. Salt Lake City Directory, 1911.

10. Warrum, *Utah Since Statehood*, 617; Salt Lake City Directory 1916.

11. Joseph A. Jennings, Death certificate no. 1901 1724 (29 June 1943), informational copy from Los Angeles County Registrar-Recorder/County Clerk.

12. Los Angeles City Directory, 1911.

13. "Three Utahns Going Strong in Chosen Vocations at that Coveted Field, Hollywood," *Salt Lake Tribune*, 16 September 1928, http://www.newspaperarchive.com

14. *The Day Buster Smiled*, 48.

15. Joseph D. Jennings, *California County Marriages, 1850–1952* (4 July 1914) (Online: FamilySearch Historical Collections, 2011) [Digital copies of originals housed in the clerks' offices of the district courts in various counties throughout

California. FHL microfilm, Family History Library, Salt Lake City, Utah], https://www.familysearch.org, accessed 16 January 2012.

16. *Souvenir: Picture Player Camera Man's Ball under the Auspices of the Static Club of America*, 16 January 1914, 2.

17. Ibid.

18. "Static Club Officers, Directors, and Members," *Static Flashes*, 23 January 1915, 2.

19. "Doings of the Men Who Make the Movies," *Static Flashes*, 20 February 1915, 1.

20. *Minutes of the Static Club of America, Inc.* 1915.

21. "Static Club News Notes," *Static Flashes*, 19 June 1915, 8.

22. "Story of Achievement and Development," *Static Flashes*, 22 May 1915, 6.

23. H. Lyman Broening, "How It Happened: a Brief Review of the Beginnings of the American Society of Cinematographers," *American Cinematographer*, 1 November 1921, 13.

24. "Film Industry Pioneer Dies," *Los Angeles Times*, 14 March 1952. http://pqasb.pqarchiver.com/latimes/search.html; "H. Gordon Jennings, Won Five 'Oscars,' 56." *New York Times*, 13 January 1953, http://query.nytimes.com/search/sitesearch

25. Joseph Devereux Jennings, *World War I Draft Registration Cards, 1917–1918* (3 October 1918) (Online: The Generations Network, Inc., 2006) [Digital scan of original records in the National Archives, Washington, D.C.], subscription database, http://www.ancestry.com, accessed 1 July 2006.

26. "Badly Burned," *Salt Lake Herald*, 9 April 1892, 5.

27. Keaton and Samuels, *My Wonderful World of Slapstick*, 120.

28. "Pedestrian Loses $406," *Los Angeles Times*, 20 July 1922, http://pqasb.pqarchiver.com/latimes/search.html

29. "Photographer Gets Thrill in Steel Picture," *Los Angeles Times*, 1 November 1925, http://pqasb.pqarchiver.com/latimes/search.html

30. Kevin Brownlow, *The Parade's Gone By...* (Berkeley: University of California Press, 1968), 491.

31. Jim Kline, *The Complete Films of Buster Keaton* (New York: Carol Publishing Group, 1993), 115.

32. "Best-Shot Films 1894–1949," *American Cinematographer*, March 1999, 120.

33. Bob, e-mail message to Buster Keaton Fans Yahoo Group, message 20772, 30 January 2012.

34. Joseph Debereux [sic] Jennings, *California County Marriages, 1850–1952* (6 June 1925) (Online: FamilySearch Historical Collections, 2011) [Digital copies of originals housed in the clerks' offices of the district courts in various counties throughout California. FHL microfilm, Family History Library, Salt Lake City, Utah], https://www.familysearch.org, accessed 3 February 2013.

35. "Gloom Thick and Dark at Coffee Dan's," *San Francisco Chronicle*, 17 December 1917, http://proquest.umi.com

36. San Francisco City Directories, 1920–1923; Los Angeles City Directory, 1923.

37. Adele Jennings, Death certificate no. 3801 1788 (10 March 1929), informational copy from San Francisco Office of Vital Records.

38. "Best-Shot Films 1894–1949," *American Cinematographer*, March 1999, 124.

39. J.D. Jennings, "How Miniatures are Photographed," *American Cinematographer*, June 1934, 60.

40. Academy of Motion Picture Arts and Sciences, "Official Academy Awards Database."

41. R.M. Hayes, *Trick Cinematography: The Oscar Special Effects Movies* (Jefferson, NC: McFarland, 1986), 28.

42. Joseph Devereux Jennings, Death certificate no. 1901 4972 (12 March 1952), informational copy from Los Angeles County Registrar-Recorder/County Clerk.

GORDON JENNINGS

1. Henry G. Jennings, *Utah, Military Records, 1861–1970*. (Online: The Generations Network, Inc., 2011) [Digital scan of original records in the Utah State Archives, Salt Lake City, Utah], subscription database, http://www.ancestry.com, accessed 12 June 2011.
2. Nobel Warrum, *Utah Since Statehood* (Salt Lake City: S. J. Clarke, 1919), 614–617.
3. John Grayson, "Ex-Utahans Win Movie Fame," *Salt Lake Tribune*, 23 March 1947, http://www.newspaperarchive.com
4. Grady Johnson, "Special Photographic Effects' Magic," *American Cinematographer*, December 1947, 459.
5. "Pulse of the Studio," *Camera!*, 30 June 1923, 17.
6. John Bengtson, *Silent Echoes* (Santa Monica, CA: Santa Monica Press, 2000), 133.
7. "Inventions to Revolutionize Cinema Making," *Los Angeles Times*, 12 January 1924, http://pqasb.pqarchiver.com/latimes/search.html
8. Johnson, "Special Photographic Effects' Magic," 459.
9. Academy of Motion Picture Arts and Sciences, "Official Academy Awards Database," http://awardsdatabase.oscars.org/ampas_awards/BasicSearchInput.jsp, accessed 5 July 2006.
10. Henry Gordon Jennings, Lewis L. Mellor, William F. Rudolph, and Arthur Smith, 1934, Tilt and panning head for motion picture camera tripods, U.S. Patent 1,971,486, filed 18 February 1933, issued 28 August 1934; Henry Gordon Jennings, Paul K. Lerpee, and Arthur Zaugg, 1936, Means for producing special effects in motion picture photography. U.S. Patent 2,051,526, filed 13 August 1934, issued 18 August 1936; Gilbert L. Stancliff, Jr. and Henry Gordon Jennings, 1953, Control of camera-subject motion in motion-picture photography, U.S. Patent 2,648,252, filed 17 September 1948, issued 11 August 1953.
11. "Patented Title Machine," *Variety*, 18 November 1925, 36.
12. "Jennings Gets Tricky," *Variety*, 8 April 1931, 5.
13. "Paramount's Semi-Final," *Variety*, 26 December 1928, 35.
14. AFI Catalog of Films, accessed 10 September 2010.
15. Gordon Jennings. "Special-Effects and Montage for *Cleopatra*," *American Cinematographer*, December 1934, 350.
16. Ibid.
17. Patricia D. Netzley, *Encyclopedia of Movie Special Effects* (Phoenix, AZ: Oryx Press, 2000), 233; Kenneth Von Gunden and Stuart H. Stock, "War of the Worlds," *Twenty All-Time Great Science Fiction Films* (New York: Arlington House, 1982), 240.
18. "Men From Mars Blast City Hall to Pieces," *Los Angeles Times*, 9 May 1952, http://pqasb.pqarchiver.com/latimes/search.html
19. Johnson, "Special Photographic Effects' Magic," 431. 20. Cecil B. DeMille, *Autobiography* (Englewood Cliffs, NJ: Prentice-Hall), 1959, 272.
21. "A.S.C. Members on Parade," *American Cinematographer*, April 1937, 140.
22. "A.S.C. Members on Parade," *American Cinematographer*, May 1937, 195; "A.S.C. Members on Parade," *American Cinematographer*, August 1937, 326.
23. "Bing Crosby Cops Golf Title in Lakeside Studio Tournament," *Los Angeles Times*, 13 June 1938, http://pqasb.pqarchiver.com/latimes/search.html

24. Ibid.

25. "A.S.C. Golf Tournament Huge Success," *American Cinematographer*, May 1934, 8, 24.

26. "Intention to Marry," *Los Angeles Times*, 13 June 1929, http://pqasb.pqarchiver.com/latimes/search.html

27. "Chatter," *Variety*, 14 October 1933, 2.

28. "Ruggerio Will Defend Title," *Los Angeles Times*, 9 June 1938, http://pqasb.pqarchiver.com/latimes/search.html

29. Academy of Motion Picture Arts and Sciences, "Official Academy Awards Database."

30. R.M. Hayes, *Trick Cinematography: The Oscar Special Effects Movies* (Jefferson, NC: McFarland, 1986), 28.

31. Henry Gordon Jennings, Death certificate no. 1901 609 (11 January 1953), informational copy from Los Angeles County Registrar-Recorder/County Clerk.

32. "Gordon Jennings Rites," *Variety*, 14 January 1953, 11.

33. "Camp Fire Unit has New Board," *Los Angeles Times*, 16 February 1965, http://pqasb.pqarchiver.com/latimes/search.html; "Old Picture Will Spice Church Fete," *Los Angeles Times*, 3 May 1964, http://pqasb.pqarchiver.com/latimes/search.html

34. Florence A. Jennings, Death certificate no. 3000 06698 (21 July 1982), informational copy from Los Angeles County Registrar-Recorder/County Clerk.

35. John Jennings, Unpublished interview with Marion Meade, conducted 29 May 1990, Special Collections, University of Iowa Library.

36. Philip K. Scheuer, "Chakiris of Sharks in 'Day of the Damned,'" *Los Angeles Times*, 12 December 1961, http://pqasb.pqarchiver.com/latimes/search.html

37. John D. Jennings, *California Death Index, 1940–1997* (1 January 1992) (Online: The Generations Network, Inc., 2012) [Digital scan of original records in the State of California Department of Health Services Center for Health Statistics, Sacramento, CA], subscription database, http://www.ancestry.com, accessed 25 August 2012.

REGGIE LANNING

1. "Congress," *Ghost Towns*, http://www.ghosttowns.com/states/az/congress.html, accessed 28 August 2007.

2. Los Angeles City Directory, 1911.

3. Los Angeles City Directory, 1914.

4. Los Angeles City Directory, 1917.

5. Reggie Lanning, *World War I Draft Registration Cards, 1917–1918* (3 October 1918) (Online: The Generations Network, Inc., 2007) [Digital scan of original records in the National Archives, Washington, D.C.], subscription database, http://www.ancestry.com, accessed 12 April 2007.

6. Terry McClure, National Personnel Records Center, St. Louis, MO, letter to author, 12 October 2007.

7. "California, Death Index, 1905–1939," jpeg image (Online: FamilySearch Historical Collections, 2012) [Digital scan of original records in the Office of the State Register, Sacramento, California,] https://www.familysearch.org, accessed 1 February 2013.

8. Reggie Lanning, *California County Marriages, 1850–1952* (23 September 1923) (Online: FamilySearch Historical Collections, 2011) [Digital copies of originals housed in the clerks' offices of the district courts in various counties throughout California. FHL microfilm, Family History Library, Salt Lake City, Utah], https://www.familysearch.org, accessed 3 February 2013.

9. Sharon Leota Lanning, *California Birth Index, 1905–1995* (August 1936) (Online: The Generations Network, Inc., 2009) [Digital scan of original records in the State of California Department of Health Services Center for Health Statistics, Sacramento, CA], subscription database, http://www.ancestry.com, accessed 20 September 2010.
   10. Los Angeles City Directory, 1921.
   11. "Chatter," *Variety*, 7 July 1948, 2.
   12. Rob Wagner, *Film Folk* (New York: Century, 1918), 117.
   13. "300 Important Cameramen Becoming Recognized as Photographic Marvels," *Variety*, 4 January 1928, 6, 13.
   14. "Three Clubs Enter League," *Los Angeles Times*, 16 August 1934, http://pqasb.pqarchiver.com/latimes/search.html
   15. Bill Witney, *In a Door, Into a Fight, Out a Door, Into a Chase: Moviemaking Remembered by the Guy at the Door* (Jefferson, NC: McFarland, 1996), 284.
   16. Jim Harmon and Donald Glut, *The Great Movie Serials: Their Sound and Fury* (Garden City, NY: Doubleday, 1972), 25. 17. Roy Kinnard, *Fifty Years of Serial Thrills* (Metuchen, NJ: Scarecrow Press, 1983), 69.
   18. "A.S.C. Golf Tournament Huge Success," *American Cinematographer*, May 1934, 8, 24.
   19. Reggie Thomas Lanning, Death certificate no. 7053 049457 (6 December 1965), informational copy from Los Angeles County Registrar-Recorder/County Clerk.
   20. Ibid.
   21. Eileen Juanita Lanning, Death certificate no. 3915 6003578 (29 December 1991), informational copy from Ventura County Clerk-Recorder.

Elgin Lessley

   1. Kevin Brownlow and David Gill, *A Hard Act to Follow*, volume 2, Thames Television PLC, 1987.
   2. Colorado Springs, Colorado City, and Manitou City Directory, 1904–1905.
   3. "New Members," *Camera Craft*, January 1910, 40.
   4. "Our Illustrations," *Photo-era Magazine*, July 1910, 40–41.
   5. "Our Monthly Competition," *American Photography*, August 1910, 478.
   6. *Early Morning Shadows*, *Photo-era Magazine*, September 1910, 139.
   7. "Changes of address," *Camera Craft*, December 1910, 466.
   8. Los Angeles City Directory, 1911.
   9. Elgin Lessley, *World War I Draft Registration Cards, 1917–1918* (12 September 1918) (Online: The Generations Network, Inc., 2009) [Digital scan of original records in the National Archives, Washington, D.C.], subscription database, http://www.ancestry.com, accessed 29 August 2010.
   10. "Who's Who in *Long Pants*," *Motion Picture World*, 22 January 1927, 265.
   11. Paul Hammond, *Marvelous Melies* (New York: St. Martin's Press, 1975), 48–49; 66–67; 72–78.
   12. "A Breaking Wave," *Popular Photography*, November 1912, 59.
   13. Gaston Méliès, *Le voyage autour du monde de la G. Méliès Manufacturing Company: Juillet 1912–mai 1913*, Paris: les Amis de Georges Méliès, 1988.
   14. "Elgin Lessley," 1913 Passenger List, Toyo Kisen Kaisha, saloon passenger, line 76. (Online: The Generations Network, Inc., 2009) [Digital scan of original records in the National Archives, Washington, D.C.], subscription database, http://www.ancestry.com, accessed 2 August 2010.
   15. Elgin Lessley, *California County Marriages, 1850–1952* (17 November 1914)

(Online: FamilySearch Historical Collections, 2011) [Digital copies of originals housed in the clerks' offices of the district courts in various counties throughout California. FHL microfilm, Family History Library, Salt Lake City, Utah], https://www.familysearch.org, accessed 3 February 2013.

16. Frederick T. Schultz, *Colorado Statewide Divorce Index, 1900–1930* (2 April 1907) (Online: FamilySearch Historical Collections, 2011) [Digital copies of originals housed in the Division of Vital Statistics, Department of Health, Colorado State Archives, Denver, Colorado], https://www.familysearch.org, accessed 28 January 2013.

17. "Static Club Officers, Directors, and Members," *Static Flashes*, 23 January 1915, 2.

18. Marilyn Slater, "Elgin Lessley," *Looking for Mabel*, http://www.freewebs.com/looking-for-mabel/elginlessley.htm, accessed 16 August 2010.

19. Wil Rex, "Behind the Scenes with Fatty and Mabel," *Picture Play*, April 1916, 47.

20. *Minutes of the Static Club of America, Inc.*, 1916.

21. Brent E. Walker, *Mack Sennett's Fun Factory* (Jefferson, NC: McFarland, 2010), 524.

22. Ibee., "Her Decision," *Variety*, 24, May 1918, 46.

23. Rudi Blesh, *Keaton* (New York: Macmillan, 1966), 152.

24. Blesh, *Keaton*, 168.

25. Keaton and Samuels, *My Wonderful World of Slapstick*, 170.

26. Robert Franklin and Joan Franklin, "Interview with Buster Keaton," in Kevin B. Sweeney, *Buster Keaton Interviews* (Jackson, MS: University Press of Mississippi, 2007), 90.

27. Kevin Brownlow, *The Parade's Gone By...* (Berkeley: University of California Press, 1968), 487.

28. Mordaunt Hall. "The Screen," New York *Times*, 26 May 1924, http://query.nytimes.com/search/sitesearch

29. "Keaton's Bill for Expenses Rouses Anger," *Los Angeles Times*, 25 November 1923. http://pqasb.pqarchiver.com/latimes/search.html

30. Brownlow, *Parade*, 494.

31. William Schelly. *Harry Langdon*, Metuchen, N.J.: Scarecrow Press, 1982, 56.

32. "Who's Who in *Long Pants*," *Moving Picture World*, 22 January 1927, 265.

33. Los Angeles City Directory, 1925.

34. "Womens' Black Eyes Unnatural, Man Pays Fine," *Los Angeles Times*, 11 March 1926. http://pqasb.pqarchiver.com/latimes/search.html

35. Blanche Lessley, Death certificate no. 10822 (28 September 1931), informational copy from Los Angeles County Registrar-Recorder/County Clerk.

36. "Chancy Olmstead," Find A Grave Memorial #11252879, Arapahoe County, Colorado. http://www.findagrave.com, accessed 19 January 2013. 37. Elgin Lessley, Death certificate no. 1901–2375 (8 February 1944), informational copy from Los Angeles County Registrar-Recorder/County Clerk.

38. Louis J. Acierno, *The History of Cardiology* (Pearl River, NY: Parthenon Publishing Group, 1994), 77.

39. "That All May be Represented." *International Photographer*, June 1930, 76.

40. Los Angeles City Directories, 1929–1942.

41. Elgin Lessley, *World War II Draft Registration Cards, 1942* (Online: FamilySearch Historical Collections, 2011) [Digital scan of original records in the National Archives, Washington, D.C.], https://www.familysearch.org, accessed 31 December 2011.

42. "In Memorium," *International Photographer*, March 1944, 28.

43. Elgin Lessley, Death certificate.
44. "Donald J. Ehlers," *Variety*, 4 September 1945, 3.
45. Blesh, 231.

WILLIAM McGANN

1. Office of the Registrar, University of California, Berkeley, CA, letter to author, 25 May 2007.
2. "William M. McGann," *American Cinematographer*, 1 February 1922, 25; Los Angeles City Directory, 1913.
3. Ibid.
4. William M. McGann, *World War I Draft Registration Cards, 1917–1918* (5 June 1918) (Online: The Generations Network, Inc., 2007) [Digital scan of original records in the National Archives, Washington, D.C.], subscription database, http://www.ancestry.com, accessed 14 April 2007.
5. William McGann, Military Personnel Records, National Personnel Records Center, St. Louis, MO, retrieved 13 June 2007.
6. "William M. McGann," *American Cinematographer*, 1 February 1922, 25.
7. "Foy will Film Phony History," *Film Tribune*, 26 January 1924, 1.
8. "Warners End Production of Three Pictures," *Los Angeles Times*, 17 November 1929, http://pqasb.pqarchiver.com/latimes/search.html
9. "Three Films Planned for Star," *Los Angeles Times*, 24 July 1930, http://pqasb.pqarchiver.com/latimes/search.html
10. "William McGann," *Variety Obituaries, 1905–1986* (New York: Garland, 1988).
11. William M. McGann, *California County Marriages, 1850–1952* (6 December 1918) (Online: FamilySearch Historical Collections, 2011) [Digital copies of originals housed in the clerks' offices of the district courts in various counties throughout California. FHL microfilm, Family History Library, Salt Lake City, Utah], https://www.familysearch.org, accessed 16 January 2012.
12. "Roberta McGann," 1922 Passenger List, S.S. Maui, line 18. (Online: The Generations Network, Inc., 2009) [Digital scan of original records in the National Archives, Washington, D.C.], subscription database, http://www.ancestry.com, accessed 24 September 2010.
13. William M. McGann, *California County Marriages, 1850–1952* (8 June 1929) (Online: FamilySearch Historical Collections, 2011) [Digital copies of originals housed in the clerks' offices of the district courts in various counties throughout California. FHL microfilm, Family History Library, Salt Lake City, Utah], https://www.familysearch.org, accessed 19 February 2013.
14. "Divorcee Denies Triangle Charges," *Los Angeles Times*, 2 October 1946, http://pqasb.pqarchiver.com/latimes/search.html
15. "Film Director's Estranged Wife Kidnap Victim," *Los Angeles Times*, 5 November 1960, http://pqasb.pqarchiver.com/latimes/search.html
16. William McGann, Death certificate no. 0190–049836 (11 November 1977), informational copy from Los Angeles County Registrar-Recorder/County Clerk.

WILLIAM PILTZ

1. William Jacob Piltz, Death certificate no. 1310 17013 (2 November 1944), informational copy from Los Angeles County Registrar-Recorder/County Clerk; "William Piltz," *Variety*, 6 November 1944, 19.
2. Los Angeles City Directory, 1914.

3. *Souvenir: Picture Player Camera Man's Ball under the Auspices of the Static Club of America*, 16 January 1914, 95.
4. "Static Club May Dance Proves Notable Social Opening Event," *Static Flashes*, 5 June 1915, 2.
5. "Static Club Officers, Directors, and Members," *Static Flashes*, 23 January 1915, 2.
6. "Wm. J. Piltz," *Static Flashes*, 10 July 1915, 2.
7. "Billy Piltz with L-KO Kompany," *Static Flashes*, 6 March 1915, 2.
8. Ibid.
9. "Doing Things at the L-KO Studios," *Static Flashes*, 10 April 1915, 8.
10. William Jacob Piltz, *World War I Draft Registration Cards, 1917–1918* (5 September 1918) (Online: The Generations Network, Inc., 2007) [Digital scan of original records in the National Archives, Washington, D.C.], subscription database, http://www.ancestry.com, accessed 28 September 2007.
11. "Pulse of the Studios," *Camera!*, 23 February 1919; 5 June 1920.
12. *The Day Buster Smiled*, 48.
13. Los Angeles City Directory, 1932.
14. Los Angeles City Directories, 1909, 1915.
15. Los Angeles City Directory, 1932.
16. William Jacob Piltz, Death certificate.
17. Fern L. Petrie, Death certificate no. 7097–038252 (11 September 1969), informational copy from Los Angeles County Registrar-Recorder/County Clerk.

Co-Directors

1. Gillett and Blue, "Keaton at Venice," 27.
2. Kevin Brownlow, *Parade's Gone By...* (Berkeley: University of California Press, 1968), 491.
3. "Pulse of the Studio," *Camera!*, 1 December 1923, 16.
4. Keaton and Samuels, *My Wonderful World of Slapstick*, 194.
5. "Marion Davies' Red Mill," *Variety*, 7 October 1925, 38.
6. "Fatty Arbuckle Directing Marion Davies in Film," *Variety*, 3 March 1926, 1.
7. David Yallop, *The Day the Laughter Stopped* (New York: St. Martin's Press, 1976), 278.
8. Kevin Brownlow and David Gill, "The *Sherlock Junior* Question," *Pacific Film Archive*, http://cinefiles.bampfa.berkeley.edu/cinefiles/DocDetail?docId=13654, accessed 21 August 2011.
9. "McDermott With Buster," *Los Angeles Times*, 11 September 1924, http://pqasb.pqarchiver.com/latimes/search.html
10. "McDermott Quits as Keaton's Director," *Variety*, 24 September 1924, 21.
11. "Fun Is Serious," *Los Angeles Times*, 10 May 1925, http://pqasb.pqarchiver.com/latimes/search.html
12. Keaton and Samuels, *My Wonderful World of Slapstick*, 132–133.
13. "Keaton Directing Himself," *Variety*, 14 April 1926, 25.
14. Rudi Blesh, *Keaton* (New York: Macmillan, 1966), 150.
15. Brownlow, *Parade's Gone By*, 491.
16. Keaton and Samuels, *My Wonderful World of Slapstick*, 203.

John Blystone

1. "Free-for-all Tricks Taught,'" *Los Angeles Times*, 2 September 1936, http://pqasb.pqarchiver.com/latimes/search.html
2. Georgette Ballweg (Office of the Registrar), University of Wisconsin-Madison, e-mail to author, 18 May 2011.
3. Lee Shippey, "Lee Side o'L.A.," *Los Angeles Times*, 22 February 1936, http://pqasb.pqarchiver.com/latimes/search.html
4. *Souvenir: Picture Player Camera Man's Ball under the Auspices of the Static Club of America*, 16 January 1914, 98.
5. "Behind the Screen," *Washington Times*, 10 July 1914, 10.
6. Glenn Mitchell, *A-Z of Silent Film Comedy* (London: BT Batsford, 1998), 127.
7. Kristin Gilpatrick, *Famous Wisconsin Film Stars* (Oregon, WI: Badger Books, 2002), 149.
8. "Life's Gentler Side," *Los Angeles Times*, 9 July 1915, http://pqasb.pqarchiver.com/latimes/search.html
9. "Lehrman Engages Jack Blystone," *Moving Picture World*, December 21 1918, 1324.
10. "Names New Film Staff," *Los Angeles Times*, 25 May 1923, http://pqasb.pqarchiver.com/latimes/search.html
11. Kevin Brownlow, "Buster Keaton," in Kevin B. Sweeney, *Buster Keaton Interviews* (Jackson, MS: University Press of Mississippi, 2007), 210–211.
12. "Signs Fox Contract," *Moving Picture World*, 21 July 1923, 243.
13. "Quirks of Directors," *New York Times*, 3 June 1934, http://query.nytimes.com/search/sitesearch
14. "Jack Blystone has Reins for 'Captain Lash,'" *Los Angeles Times*, 28 October 1928, http://pqasb.pqarchiver.com/latimes/search.html
15. Edwin Schallert, "Movietone in Great Triumph," *Los Angeles Times*, 26 September 1928, http://pqasb.pqarchiver.com/latimes/search.html
16. "Pity the Director," *New York Evening Post*, 5 May 1934. John Blystone, Clipping file, Billy Rose Theater Collection, New York Public Library for the Performing Arts.
17. "Blystone to Be Director of 'Tol'able David,'" *Los Angeles Times*, 9 August 1930, http://pqasb.pqarchiver.com/latimes/search.html
18. "Blystone Boasts Unusual Record," *Los Angeles Times*, 25 October 1935, http://pqasb.pqarchiver.com/latimes/search.html
19. "John Blystone will Direct 'Woman's Touch,'" *Los Angeles Times*, 11 February 1937, http://pqasb.pqarchiver.com/latimes/search.html
20. Randy Skretvedt, *Laurel and Hardy: The Magic Behind the Movies* (Beverly Hills, CA: Moonstone Press), 1987, 343.
21. "Director Plans Vacation Tour," *Los Angeles Times*, 8 February 1936, http://pqasb.pqarchiver.com/latimes/search.html; "Director Returns," *Los Angeles Times*, 2 October 1936, http://pqasb.pqarchiver.com/latimes/search.html
22. John Gilman Blystone, Death certificate no. 38–048645 (6 August 1938), informational copy from Los Angeles County Registrar-Recorder/County Clerk.
23. "John G. Blystone." *Variety Obituaries, 1905–1986* (New York: Garland, 1988); "Blystone, Film Director, Dies," *Los Angeles Times*, 7 August 1938, http://pqasb.pqarchiver.com/latimes/search.html
24. Gwendolyn Davis Blystone, *California Death Index* (27 November 1978) (Online: The Generations Network, Inc., 2010) [Digital scan of original records in the State of California Department of Health Services, Center for Health Statistics,

Sacramento.], subscription database, http://www.ancestry.com/, accessed 29 May 2011.

25. "Francine Blystone Wed in Evening Ceremony," *Los Angeles Times*, 25 August 1939, http://pqasb.pqarchiver.com/latimes/search.html

26. "Chatterbox," *Los Angeles Times*, 20 February 1942, http://pqasb.pqarchiver.com/latimes/search.html

27. "Betty Blystone," *Los Angeles Times*, 29 October 1939, http://pqasb.pqarchiver.com/latimes/search.html

EDDIE CLINE

1. "Lesser Signs Edward Cline, Comedy Expert," *Los Angeles Times*, 31 January 1923, http://pqasb.pqarchiver.com/latimes/search.html

2. Markku Salmi, "Eddie Cline," *Film Dope*, April 1975, 33.

3. Los Angeles City Directories, 1905–1920.

4. Bill Henry, "By the Way," *Los Angeles Times*, 8 October 1951, http://pqasb.pqarchiver.com/latimes/search.html

5. Bill Henry, "By the Way," *Los Angeles Times*, 26 October 1949, http://pqasb.pqarchiver.com/latimes/search.html

6. "Rosary to be Recited Tonight for Eddie Cline," *Los Angeles Times*, 24 May 1961, http://pqasb.pqarchiver.com/latimes/search.html

7. "Active Workers in Comedy," *Los Angeles Herald*, 16 January 1910, 3.

8. "*A Certain Party* an Amusing Farce," *New York Times*, 25 April 1911, http://query.nytimes.com/search/sitesearch

9. Los Angeles City Directory, 1911.

10. "Love Marathon Keeps Sorority on Tiptoe," *Los Angeles Times*, 2 June 1913, http://pqasb.pqarchiver.com/latimes/search.html

11. Los Angeles City Directory, 1915.

12. Edward Francis Cline, *California County Marriages, 1850–1952* (6 March 1916) (Online: FamilySearch Historical Collections, 2011) [Digital copies of originals housed in the clerks' offices of the district courts in various counties throughout California. FHL microfilm, Family History Library, Salt Lake City, Utah], https://www.familysearch.org, accessed 16 January 2012.

13. Elena Boland, "Memories of Slapstick Comedy Days Recalled," *Los Angeles Times*, 17 November 1929, http://pqasb.pqarchiver.com/latimes/search.html

14. Los Angeles City Directory, 1914.

15. Boland, "Memories," *Los Angeles Times*, 17 November 1929.

16. Edward F. Cline, "What's Become of the Keystone Kops?" *Los Angeles Times*, 10 July 1938, http://pqasb.pqarchiver.com/latimes/search.html

17. Ibid.

18. James Agee, "Comedy's Greatest Era," *Life*, 5 September 1949, 72.

19. Hal Hall, "Credit President Hoover," *American Cinematographer*, July 1930, 14.

20. Mack Sennett, as told to Cameron Shipp, *King of Comedy* (Garden City, NY: Doubleday, 1954), 167.

21. Brent E. Walker, *Mack Sennett's Fun Factory* (Jefferson, NC: McFarland, 2010), 20.

22. Patricia Cline, Birth certificate no. 6125 (5 September 1918), informational copy from Los Angeles County Registrar-Recorder/County Clerk.

23. Minnie Elizabeth Cline, Death certificate no. 5217 (15 September 1918), informational copy from Los Angeles County Registrar-Recorder/County Clerk.

24. Patricia Cline, Birth certificate.

25. Edward Francis Cline, *California County Marriages, 1850–1952* (2 June 1919) (Online: FamilySearch Historical Collections, 2011) [Digital copies of originals housed in the clerks' offices of the district courts in various counties throughout California. FHL microfilm, Family History Library, Salt Lake City, Utah], https://www.familysearch.org, accessed 16 January 2012.

26. Harry Burns, "Chit, Chat, and Chatter," *Camera!*, 25 October 1919, 7.

27. "Buster Keaton Nine Trounces Larry Semon's," *Los Angeles Times*, 24 October 1921, http://pqasb.pqarchiver.com/latimes/search.html; "Buster Keatons Win Sixth Straight," *Los Angeles Times*, 17 April 1923. http://pqasb.pqarchiver.com/latimes/search.html

28. "Movie Director Like Peerless Sedan Limousine," *Los Angeles Times*, 10 July 1921, http://pqasb.pqarchiver.com/latimes/search.html

29. "Radio Fishing Wild Life," *Los Angeles Times*, 14 February 1926, http://pqasb.pqarchiver.com/latimes/search.html

30. Rudi Blesh, *Keaton* (New York: Macmillan, 1966), 150.

31. "Making Comedy is No Cinch," *Los Angeles Times*, 10 December 1922, http://pqasb.pqarchiver.com/latimes/search.html

32. Robert de Roos, "The Biggest Laugh in Movie History," *Coronet*, August 1959, 98–99. 33. "Lesser Signs Edward Cline, Comedy Expert," *Los Angeles Times*, 31 January 1923, http://pqasb.pqarchiver.com/latimes/search.html; "Who's Who and What's What in Filmland this Week," *Camera!*, 3 February 1923, 14.

34. "Ed Cline with Principal," *Moving Picture World*, 17 February 1923, 693.

35. "Brief Story on Rise of Edward F. Cline," *Moving Picture World*, 6 October 1923, 505.

36. Raymond McKee, "Along New York's Rialto," *Camera!*, 12 May 1923, 6.

37. "Noted Author Is Here on Visit," *Camera!*, 15 September 1923, 15.

38. Gerry Chudleigh, "The Winning of Barbara Worth," *Harold Bell Wright*, http://gchudleigh.com/barbmv1926.htm

39. "Actress's Father Is Lost at Sea," *Los Angeles Times*, 8 January 1925, http://pqasb.pqarchiver.com/latimes/search.html

40. "Charlie Ray to Have Big Roles," *Los Angeles Times*, 19 October 1926, http://pqasb.pqarchiver.com/latimes/search.html

41. "Goldwyn and Wife to go East," *Los Angeles Times*, 24 November 1926, http://pqasb.pqarchiver.com/latimes/search.html

42. "Hollywood Photographic Section," *Moving Picture World*, 8 October 1927, 358.

43. "Fox Buys Story for Star," *Los Angeles Times*, 18 August 1927, http://pqasb.pqarchiver.com/latimes/search.html

44. "Fred Niblo Returns to MGM," *Los Angeles Times*, 17 February 1928, http://pqasb.pqarchiver.com/latimes/search.html

45. Hall, "Credit President Hoover," 14.

46. Braven Dyer, "Sheiks Lose Billy Gray," *Los Angeles Times*, 20 February 1942, http://pqasb.pqarchiver.com/latimes/search.html

47. Jack Curnow, "7500 Fans See Film Stars in Golf Benefit," *Los Angeles Times*, 5 April 1943, http://pqasb.pqarchiver.com/latimes/search.html

48. Bill Henry, "By the Way," *Los Angeles Times*, 8 October 1951, http://pqasb.pqarchiver.com/latimes/search.html

49. "Knowledge Proved a Handicap This Time," *Los Angeles Times*, 17 April 1924, http://pqasb.pqarchiver.com/latimes/search.html

50. "Australian Cricket Team Triumphs Over Hollywood, 182–164," *Los Angeles Times*, 29 August 1932, http://pqasb.pqarchiver.com/latimes/search.html

51. Hall, "Credit President Hoover," 14.

52. Walker, *Mack Sennett's Fun Factory*, 559.

53. "Plenty of Music on This Party," *Los Angeles Times*, 22 March 1925, http://pqasb.pqarchiver.com/latimes/search.html

54. Ed Watz, *Wheeler and Woolsey: The Comic Duo and Their Films 1929–1937* (Jefferson, NC: McFarland, 1994), 106.

55. "Picture Director Plays Early Bird," *Los Angeles Times*, 9 March 1924, http://pqasb.pqarchiver.com/latimes/search.html

56. "Brief Story on Rise of Edward F. Cline," 505.

57. Watz, *Wheeler and Woolsey*, 282.

58. Hedda Hopper "Hedda Hopper's Hollywood," *Los Angeles Times*, 20 March 1942, http://pqasb.pqarchiver.com/latimes/search.html

59. David Bruskin, *White Brothers Oral History*, Directors Guild of America (Metuchen, N.J.: Scarecrow Press, 1990), 30.

60. Ibid., 29.

61. Watz, *Wheeler and Woolsey*, 105.

62. Pauline Kael, *5001 Nights at the Movies* (New York: H. Holt, 1991), 481.

63. James Curtis, *W.C. Fields: A Biography* (New York: Knopf, 2003), 384.

64. Ibid., 402.

65. "My Little Chickadee," *Newsweek*, 26 February 1940, 30.

66. "Jimmy Fidler in Hollywood," *Los Angeles Times*, 13 November 1939, http://pqasb.pqarchiver.com/latimes/search.html

67. Curtis, *W.C. Fields*, 410.

68. Edwin F. Schallert, "Mae West, Fields Team in Comedy of Old West," *Los Angeles Times*, 7 February 1940, http://pqasb.pqarchiver.com/latimes/search.html

69. "Vows Taken in Nevada," *Los Angeles Times*, 4 February 1940, http://pqasb.pqarchiver.com/latimes/search.html

70. "James Bain Manager of Elmhurst Gold Club," *Los Angeles Times*, 26 August 1941, http://pqasb.pqarchiver.com/latimes/search.html; "Jim Bain," *Denver Post*, 15 July 2009, http://www.denverpost.com/obituaries

71. "Elizabeth N. Bain," Find a Grave Memorial #41102331, Jefferson County, Colorado, http://www.findagrave.com, accessed 28 November 2010.

72. Philip K. Scheuer, "Town Called Hollywood," *Los Angeles Times*, 31 March 1940, http://pqasb.pqarchiver.com/latimes/search.html

73. "Villain Still Pursued Her," *Variety*, 23 July 1940, 3.

74. Jim Kline, *Complete Films of Buster Keaton* (New York: Carol Publishing Group, 1993), 178.

75. Curtis, *W.C. Fields*, 423.

76. Ibid., 428.

77. Ibid., 448.

78. "Sheriff's Auxiliary Deputies Sworn In," *Los Angeles Times*, 8 June 1942, http://pqasb.pqarchiver.com/latimes/search.html

79. Lewis Nichols, "Laffing Room Only," *New York Times*, 25 December 1944, http://query.nytimes.com/search/sitesearch

80. Brooks Atkinson, "Heads or Tails," *New York Times*, 3 May 1947, http://query.nytimes.com/search/sitesearch

81. Watz, *Wheeler and Woolsey*, 309–10.

82. Kevin Brownlow, *The Parade's Gone By...* (Berkeley: University of California Press, 1968), 478.

83. "Eddie Cline Takes That Tele Plunge," *Variety*, 8 September 1949, 1.

84. Beatrice Cinci Cline, Death certificate no. 1953 11788 (24 August 1949), informational copy from Los Angeles County Registrar-Recorder/County Clerk.

85. Jordan Young, *City Slickers: An Illustrated Biography* (Beverly Hills, CA: Disharmony Books, 1982), 60.

86. Rudi Blesh, *Keaton* (New York: Macmillan, 1966), 365.

87. Edward Francis Cline, Death certificate no. 7053 10521 (22 May 1961), informational copy from Los Angeles County Registrar-Recorder/County Clerk.

88. Edwin F. Schallert, "Comedians in War with Gangsters," *Los Angeles Times*, 25 December 1930, http://pqasb.pqarchiver.com/latimes/search.html

89. "Film Folk Aspire to Comedies," *Los Angeles Times*, 29 March 1925, http://pqasb.pqarchiver.com/latimes/search.html

90. Cline, "What's Become of the Keystone Kops?," *Los Angeles Times*.

Donald Crisp

1. George William Crisp, *Baptisms in the Parish of St. James the Great* (27 August 1882), *London, England, Births and Baptisms, 1813–1906* (Online: The Generations Network, Inc., 2007) [Digital scan of original records in the Board of Guardian Records, 1834–1906 and Church of England Parish Registers, 1754–1906. London Metropolitan Archives, London], subscription database, http://www.ancestry.com, accessed 16 February 2012.

2. Emma Marsh (Archives Assistant). Bodleian Library, Oxford, England, e-mail to author, 16 February 2007.

3. "Wm. George Crisp," 1906 Passenger List, S.S. Carmania, line 9. (Online: The Generations Network, Inc., 2007) [Digital scan of original records in the National Archives, Washington, D.C.], subscription database, http://www.ancestry.com, accessed 16 February 2007.

4. "Donald Crisp," MGM Studio Publicity Department, 21 June 1957. Clippings file, Margaret Herrick Library, Academy of Motion Pictures Arts and Sciences, Los Angeles, CA.

5. "Donald Crisp," Paramount Studio Publicity Department, 20 May 1947. Clippings file, Margaret Herrick Library, Academy of Motion Pictures Arts and Sciences, Los Angeles, CA.

6. "Biography of Donald Crisp," 20th Century–Fox Studio Publicity Department, 21 June 1941. Clippings file, Margaret Herrick Library, Academy of Motion Pictures Arts and Sciences, Los Angeles, CA.

7. Ibid.

8. Ibid.

9. Nathaniel Benchley, "Donald Crisp's Career: It Took 135 Films to Land an Oscar," *New York Herald Tribune*, 7 June 1942. Clippings file. Margaret Herrick Library, Academy of Motion Pictures Arts and Sciences, Los Angeles, CA.

10. "Donald Crisp," *Internet Broadway Database*, http://www.ibdb.com/person.php?id=36704, accessed 23 September 2011.

11. "Current Bills," *Los Angeles Herald*, 21 November 1909, 2. 12. British Film Institute, "Film Index International," http://fii.chadwyck.com/home, accessed 5 October 2006.

13. "Donald Crisp," *Internet Broadway Database*, http://www.ibdb.com/person.php?id=36704, accessed 23 September 2011.

14. "Biography of Donald Crisp," Paramount Studio Publicity Department, May 1947. Clippings file, Margaret Herrick Library, Academy of Motion Pictures Arts and Sciences, Los Angeles, CA.

15. "Wedding in 'The Little Millionaire," *New York Times*, 30 December 1911, http://query.nytimes.com/search/sitesearch

16. "Mrs. Donald Crisp," Ypsilanti Michigan newspaper clipping, 1913, from Kelly Brown's collection, sent to the author 1 March 2010. (Thanks, Kelly!)

17. Brown, *Adventures with D.W. Griffith*, 57.

18. "Some 'Class' to This Mob," *Moving Picture World*, 12 December 1914, 1538.
19. Richard Schickel, *D.W. Griffith: An American Life* (New York: Simon & Schuster, 1984), 392.
20. Donald W. Crisp, *California County Marriages, 1850–1952* (15 December 1917) (Online: FamilySearch Historical Collections, 2011) [Digital copies of originals housed in the clerks' offices of the district courts in various counties throughout California. FHL microfilm, Family History Library, Salt Lake City, Utah], https://www.familysearch.org, accessed 16 January 2012.
21. "Wife Says Film Lover Is Brutal," *Los Angeles Times*, 18 October 1921, http://pqasb.pqarchiver.com/latimes/search.html
22. "Mrs. Crisp Wins Divorce," *Los Angeles Times*, 19 May 1923, http://pqasb.pqarchiver.com/latimes/search.html
23. Read Kendall, "Around and About in Hollywood," *Los Angeles Times*, 11 July 1936, http://pqasb.pqarchiver.com/latimes/search.html
24. Sumner Smith, "Donald Crisp, Veteran Director, Actor, Will Pioneer in England and India," *Moving Picture World*, 11 September 1920, 193.
25. "South Africa Familiar Soil to Director," *Los Angeles Times*, 9 December 1923, http://pqasb.pqarchiver.com/latimes/search.html
26. Kevin Brownlow, "Buster Keaton" in Kevin B. Sweeney, *Buster Keaton Interviews* (Jackson, MS: University Press of Mississippi, 2007), 202.
27. Christopher Bishop, "The Great Stone Face," *Film Quarterly*, Fall 1958, 21.
28. Kevin Brownlow, *The Parade's Gone By* (Berkeley: University of California Press, 1968), 489.
29. "Inside Stuff on Pictures," *Variety*, 27 August 1924, 26.
30. Crisp, Donald. *U.S. Naturalization Record Indexes, 1791–1992* (Online: The Generations Network, Inc., 2011) [Digital scan of original records in the National Archives, Washington, D.C.], subscription database, http://www.ancestry.com, accessed 29 September 2011.
31. Ted Thackery Jr., "Oscar Winner Donald Crisp Dies," *Los Angeles Times*, 27 May 1974, http://pqasb.pqarchiver.com/latimes/search.html
32. Donald Crisp, "We Lost So Much Dignity as We Came of Age," *Films and Filming*, December 1960, 7, 41; "Donald Crisp," Clippings file, Margaret Herrick Library, Academy of Motion Pictures Arts and Sciences, Los Angeles, CA.
33. "Jane Murfin Married," *New York Times*, 16 August 1932, http://query.nytimes.com/search/sitesearch
34. "Jane Murfin," *Variety*, 17 August 1955, 71.
35. Ibid.
36. "Donald Crisp, Producer," *Moving Picture World*, 29 April 1916, 1947.
37. Smith, "Donald Crisp," *Moving Picture World*, 11 September 1920, 193.
38. "One Italian as Director is Vignola," *Los Angeles Times*, 27 July 1924, http://pqasb.pqarchiver.com/latimes/search.html
39. "Crisp Acts in Movie Studio He Once Owned," Paramount Studio Publicity Department, 1930. Clippings file, Margaret Herrick Library, Academy of Motion Pictures Arts and Sciences, Los Angeles, CA.
40. "Jane Murfin Married," *New York Times*, 16 August 1932, http://query.nytimes.com/search/sitesearch
41. Edwin Schallert, "Pageant of the Film World," *Los Angeles Times*, 20 February 1936, http://pqasb.pqarchiver.com/latimes/search.html
42. Hedda Hopper, "Hedda Hopper's Hollywood," *Los Angeles Times*, 12 March 1938, http://pqasb.pqarchiver.com/latimes/search.html
43. E.V. Durling, "On the Side with E.V. Durling," *Los Angeles Times*, 17 December 1938, http://pqasb.pqarchiver.com/latimes/search.html

44. Bosley Crowther, "Dollars and Sense," *New York Times*, 23 July 1939, http://query.nytimes.com/search/sitesearch

45. "Donald Crisp," Paramount Studio Publicity Department, 20 May 1947. Clippings file, Margaret Herrick Library.

46. "Donald Crisp," MGM Studio Publicity Department, 21 June 1957. Clippings file, Margaret Herrick Library.

47. Grace Kingsley, "Real Soldiers in the Reels," *Los Angeles Times*, 13 December 1914, http://pqasb.pqarchiver.com/latimes/search.html

48. "Donald Crisp," Paramount Studio Publicity Department, 20 May 1947. Clippings file, Margaret Herrick Library.

49. Ibid.

50. "South Africa Familiar Soil to Director," *Los Angeles Times*, 9 December 1923, http://pqasb.pqarchiver.com/latimes/search.html

51. "Crisp Acts in Movie Studio He Once Owned," Paramount Studio Publicity Department, 1930. Clipping file, Margaret Herrick Library.

52. Irving Johnson, "Donald Crisp," *World Telegram*, 23 June 1942. Clipping file, Billy Rose Theater Collection, New York Public Library for the Performing Arts, retrieved 7 February 2012.

53. "Motion-Picture Folk Turn Coupon Clippers," *Los Angeles Times*, 30 June 1929, http://pqasb.pqarchiver.com/latimes/search.html

54. Wayne B. Cave, "Liners to Bear Saintly Titles," *Los Angeles Times*, 28 October 1931, http://pqasb.pqarchiver.com/latimes/search.html

55. Read Kendall, "Around and About in Hollywood," *Los Angeles Times*, 14 January 1938, http://pqasb.pqarchiver.com/latimes/search.html

56. Bosley Crowther, "Dollars and Sense," *New York Times*, 23 July 1939, http://query.nytimes.com/search/sitesearch

57. Gerald D. Nash, *A.P. Giannini and the Bank of America* (Norman OK: University of Oklahoma Press, 1992), 119.

58. "Jane Murfin Crisp, Film Writer, Taken by Death," *Los Angeles Times*, 11 August 1955, http://pqasb.pqarchiver.com/latimes/search.html

59. Jane Murfin Crisp, Death certificate no. 7053 14094 (10 August 1955), informational copy from Los Angeles County Registrar-Recorder/County Clerk.

60. Hedda Hopper, "Novelist-General Sells Story to 20th," *Los Angeles Times*, 15 August 1955, http://pqasb.pqarchiver.com/latimes/search.html

61. Benchley, "Donald Crisp's Career," *New York Herald Tribune*, 7 June 1942. 62. "Donald Crisp to Make 375th Film of Career," *Los Angeles Times*, 27 May 1956, http://pqasb.pqarchiver.com/latimes/search.html

63. Hedda Hopper, "Crisp Remaining Active in Films," *Los Angeles Times*, 6 September 1961, http://pqasb.pqarchiver.com/latimes/search.html

64. Al Bine, "Donald Crisp: 32 Years of Life with Oscar," *Los Angeles Herald Examiner*, 25 March 1973. Clippings file. Margaret Herrick Library, Academy of Motion Pictures Arts and Sciences, Los Angeles, CA.

65. Donald Crisp, Death certificate no. 0190 023918 (25 May 1974), informational copy from Los Angeles County Registrar-Recorder/County Clerk.

66. Rayment was Crisp's sister Eliza's grandson. His mother, Ivy Rayment, was Eliza's daughter.

67. Gordon Currie, "Donald Crisp: The Secret Sassenach," *The Scotsman*, 9 February 2001, 9.

68. "Hollywood Scot a Secret Cockney," *Scottish Daily Record*, 9 February 2001, p. 23

JAMES HORNE

1. Kevin Brownlow, *The Parade's Gone By ...* (Berkeley: University of California Press, 1968), 491.
2. Richard Koszarski, *Hollywood Directors, 1914–1940* (New York: Oxford University Press, 1976), 29.
3. "Once-Noted Actress Dies," *Los Angeles Times*, 26 August 1927, http://pqasb.pqarchiver.com/latimes/search.html
4. Marilyn Ann Moss, *Giant: George Stevens, a Life on Film* (Madison, WI: University of Wisconsin Press, 2004), 8.
5. "Died," *Morning Call*, 17 October 1894, 10.
6. "Horne a Product of Stage," *Moving Picture World*, 7 October 1916, 88.
7. "James Horne," *Internet Broadway Database*, http://www.ibdb.com/person php?id=45604, accessed 30 January 2007.
8. James Horne, "James Horne's Own Story," *Photoplay*, February 1916, 112.
9. "Horne a Product of Stage," *Moving Picture World*, 7 October 1916, 88.
10. Pearl Gaddis, "The Girl Who Rode Across the Continent—Cleo Ridgely," *Motion Picture Classic*, August 1916, 33.
11. Robert Birchard, *Cecil B. DeMille's Hollywood* (Lexington, KY: University of Kentucky Press, 2004), 72.
12. "Cleo Ridgely Wins Divorce," *Chicago Daily Tribune*, 8 December 1916, 18.
13. "Ridgelys at Grecian," *El Paso Herald*, 16 September 1913, 5; "Ridgelys Make a Big Hit at Lowell," *Bisbee Daily Review*, 7 October 1913, 5.
14. "Cleo Ridgely Wins Divorce," *Chicago Daily Tribune*, 8 December 1916, 18.
15. "Cleo Ridgley Engaged by Lasky," *Moving Picture World*, 17 July 1915, 499.
16. Gaddis, "Cleo Ridgely," *Motion Picture Classic*, August 1916, 33.
17. "105 Pounds of Director Lands 125 Pounds of Tuna," *Moving Picture World*, 16 August 1919, 978.
18. James Horne, "James Horne's Own Story," In Richard Koszarski, *Hollywood directors, 1914–1940* (New York: Oxford University Press, 1976), 30.
19. "Rex Troupe, Five Comedy Units, in Roach Line-Up," *Los Angeles Times*, 18 July 1925, http://pqasb.pqarchiver.com/latimes/search.html
20. Horne, "James Horne's Own Story," 30.
21. George C. Pratt, C. "'Anything Can Happen—And Generally Did': Buster Keaton on his Silent Film Career," in Kevin B. Sweeney, *Buster Keaton Interviews* (Jackson, MS: University Press of Mississippi, 2007), 33–35.
22. Robert Edwards, "James W. Horne," *Find a Grave*, http://www.findagrave.com/cgi-bin/fg.cgi?page=gr&GRid=12354, accessed 8 June 2011.
23. "James W. Horne, Director, Dies," *Los Angeles Times*, 30 June 1942, http://pqasb.pqarchiver.com/latimes/search.html
24. James Wesley Horne, Death certificate no. 1901 9372 (29 June 1942), informational copy from Los Angeles County Registrar-Recorder/County Clerk.
25. Cleo Ridgely Horne, Death certificate no. 7034 15065 (18 August 1962), informational copy from Los Angeles County Registrar-Recorder/County Clerk.
26. Bruce Weber, "Jim Horne, a Familiar Face in Ads from the 1950s, Dies at 91," *New York Times*, 25 January 2009, http://query.nytimes.com/search/sitesearch
27. James Wesley Horne, *California County Marriages, 1850–1952* (8 September 1948) (Online: FamilySearch Historical Collections, 2011) [Digital copies of originals housed in the clerks' offices of the district courts in various counties throughout California. FHL microfilm, Family History Library, Salt Lake City, Utah], https://www.familysearch.org, accessed 3 February 2013.

28. "Jackie Cooper Weds Actress June Horne," *Los Angeles Times*, 12 December 1944, http://pqasb.pqarchiver.com/latimes/search.html

29. "Actress Obtains Divorce from Jackie Cooper," *Los Angeles Times*, 5 November 1949, http://pqasb.pqarchiver.com/latimes/search.html

30. "Jackie Cooper's Ex-Wife Rewed," *Los Angeles Times*, 26 August 1953, http://pqasb.pqarchiver.com/latimes/search.html

31. June Jessamine Horne, *California Death Index, 1940–1975* (17 September 1993) (Online: The Generations Network, Inc., 2011) [Digital scan of original records in the State of California Department of Health Services Center for Health Statistics, Sacramento, CA], subscription database, http://www.ancestry.com/, accessed 30 March 2012.

CHARLES RIESNER

1. Dean Riesner, "Dean Riesner, 1918–2002," Wendagowww, http://wendago.com/2004/05/11/dean-reisner-1918–2002/, accessed 5 September 2011.

2. "Living Example of Predestination," *Los Angeles Times*, 13 July 1924, http://pqasb.pqarchiver.com/latimes/search.html

3. Ibid.

4. Riesner, "Dean Riesner, 1918–2002," Wendago.com

5. "Athletics on Northside," *Minneapolis Journal*, 25 December 1906, 5.

6. Charles F. Riesner, *Minnesota Marriages, 1849–1950* (5 June 1908) (Online: FamilySearch Historical Collections, 2011) [Index based on the International Genealogical Index, Genealogical Society of Utah, Salt Lake City, UT, FHL digital index. Family History Library, Salt Lake City, UT], https://www.familysearch.org, accessed 9 February 2012.

7. "Amusements," *Salt Lake Tribune*, 28 October 1914, 11.

8. "Amusements," *San Antonio Light*, 13 March 1915, 5.

9. Riesner, "Dean Riesner, 1918–2002," Wendago.com

10. Charles F. Riesner, *Illinois, Cook County Marriages, 1871–1920* (30 October 1917) (Online: FamilySearch Historical Collections, 2011) [from Illinois Department of Public Health. "Marriage Records, 1871—present." Division of Vital Records, Springfield. FHL microfilm. Family History Library, Salt Lake City, Utah], https://www.familysearch.org, accessed 9 February 2012.

11. Kalton C. Lahue and Terry Brewer, *Kops and Custards: The Legend of Keystone Films* (Norman, OK: University of Oklahoma Press, 1967), 89.

12. Charles Francis Riesner, *World War I Draft Registration Cards, 1917–1918* (5 June 1918) (Online: The Generations Network, Inc., 2006) [Digital scan of original records in the National Archives, Washington, D.C.], subscription database, http://www.ancestry.com, accessed 14 October 2006. 13. C. Francis Riesner, Benny Davis, and Billy Bakette, "Goodbye Broadway, Hello France" (New York: Leo Feist, 1917).

14. "Notes," *Variety*, 15 August 1919, 10.

15. "One Actor Who Dislikes Idea of Fan Letters," *Los Angeles Times*, 3 April 1924, http://pqasb.pqarchiver.com/latimes/search.html

16. Mel Gussow, *Don't Say Yes Until I Finish Talking; a Biography of Darryl F. Zanuck* (Garden City, N.Y.: Doubleday, 1971), 28.

17. "News of the Film World," *Variety*, 18 July 1919, 41.

18. Brent E. Walker, *Mack Sennett's Fun Factory* (Jefferson, NC: McFarland, 2010), 577.

19. "Living Example of Predestination," *Los Angeles Times*.

20. Kevin Brownlow and David Gill, *Unknown Chaplin*, Thames Television PLC, 1983

21. "Pulse of the Studios," *Camera!*, 25 August 1923, 18.
22. "Incorporate for 'Dinky' Dean," *Camera!*, 5 January 1924, 9.
23. Riesner, "Dean Riesner, 1918–2002," Wendagowww
24. Lisa K. Stein, *Syd Chaplin: A Biography* (Jefferson, NC: McFarland, 2011), 152.
25. Keaton and Samuels, *My Wonderful World of Slapstick*, 203.
26. Charles F. Riesner, "Getting People to Laugh Is Serious Business," in Ira Price, *A Hundred Million Movie-Goers Must Be Right* (Cleveland, OH: Movie Appreciation Press, 1938), 115–140.
27. Kevin Brownlow and David Gill, *A Hard Act to Follow*, Thames Television PLC, 1987.
28. Rudi Blesh, *Keaton* (New York: Macmillan, 1966), 293.
29. Ibid.
30. Kevin Brownlow, "Buster Keaton," in Kevin B. Sweeney, *Buster Keaton Interviews* (Jackson, MS: University Press of Mississippi, 2007), 186.
31. "Effects of Mrs. Post to Be Sold," *Los Angeles Times*, 30 June 1930, http://pqasb.pqarchiver.com/latimes/search.html
32. "Beach Home of Mrs. Post Purchased," *Los Angeles Times*, 19 March 1931, http://pqasb.pqarchiver.com/latimes/search.html
33. "A Permanent 'Set,'" *Los Angeles Times*, 2 April 1933, http://pqasb.pqarchiver.com/latimes/search.html
34. "Beloved Vagabonds to Meet at Laguna," *Los Angeles Times*, 14 October 1936, http://pqasb.pqarchiver.com/latimes/search.html
35. "Church Calls Colony Leader," *Los Angeles Times*, 27 October 1938, http://pqasb.pqarchiver.com/latimes/search.html
36. Read.Kendall, "Around and About in Hollywood," *Los Angeles Times*, 19 May 1938, http://pqasb.qarchiver.com/latimes/search.html
37. "Film Director Opens Sports Goods Shop," *Toledo News-Bee*, 14 November 1931, 5.
38. "Hurrah!," *Variety*, 12 January 1932, 22.
39. "Chuck Riesner's Book Off Press," *Los Angeles Times*, 1 March 1938, http://pqasb.pqarchiver.com/latimes/search.html
40. Riesner, "Getting People to Laugh Is Serious Business," 115–140.
41. Hopper, Hedda. "Hedda Hopper's Hollywood," *Los Angeles Times*, 16 April 1941, http://pqasb.pqarchiver.com/latimes/search.html
42. "Film Threat for England Belittled," *Los Angeles Times*, 15 October 1936, http://pqasb.pqarchiver.com/latimes/search.html
43. Hedda Hopper, "Looking at Hollywood," *Los Angeles Times*, 4 March 1947, http://pqasb.pqarchiver.com/latimes/search.html
44. "Riesner Revives Local 'Scentest' for Ad Tie-Ins," *Variety*, 8 February 1956, 7, 20.
45. "Director's Wife Dies in Laguna," *Los Angeles Times*, 3 March 1947, http://pqasb.pqarchiver.com/latimes/search.html
46. "Film Director Riesner Weds," *Los Angeles Times*, 25 April 1948, http://pqasb.pqarchiver.com/latimes/search.html
47. "Licenses Issued," *Oakland Tribune*, 7 September 1956, 45.
48. Charles Francis Riesner, Death certificate no. 8009 5694 (24 September 1962), informational copy from San Diego County Registrar-Recorder/County Clerk.
49. Riesner, "Dean Riesner, 1918–2002," Wendagowww
50. Michael Carlson, "Dean Riesner," *Guardian*, 30 August 2002, http://www.guardian.co.uk/news/2002/aug/30/guardianobituaries.filmnews?INTCMP=SRCH

Malcolm St. Clair

1. Andrew Sarris, *The American Cinema: Directors and Directions 1929–1968* (New York: Dutton, 1968), 235.
2. "The Ten Best Directors," *Film Daily Year Book*, 1927, 19; "The Ten Best Directors," *Film Daily Year Book*, 1928, 21.
3. William K. Everson, "Foreword," in Ruth Anne Dwyer, *Malcolm St. Clair: His Films, 1915–1948* (Lanham, MD: Scarecrow Press, 1996), xxvii.
4. Ruth Anne Dwyer, *Malcolm St. Clair: His Films, 1915–1948* (Lanham, MD: Scarecrow Press, 1996), 44.
5. "Found! The Most Modest Man of Movies," *Los Angeles Times*, 10 February 1929, http://pqasb.pqarchiver.com/latimes/search.html
6. Dwyer, *Malcolm St. Clair*, 3.
7. "Norman St. Clair, Artist, Dead," *New York Times*, 8 March 1912, http://query.nytimes.com/search/sitesearch
8. George Geltzer, "Mal. St. Clair," *Films in Review*, February 1954, 56.
9. "St. Clair Shows Deft Touch," *Los Angeles Times*, 1 May 1927, http://pqasb.pqarchiver.com/latimes/search.html
10. Ruth Waterbury, "Sex—With a Sense of Humor," *Photoplay*, September 1926, 112.
11. Peter Milne, "The Keystone Kop Who Became a Director," *Motion Picture Classic*, Oct. 1926, 34–35, 81.
12. "'Slim' Makes Good," *Los Angeles Times*, 30 September 1917, http://pqasb.pqarchiver.com/latimes/search.html
13. Geltzer, "Mal. St. Clair," 56.
14. "He Directs Them Now, Drew First," *Los Angeles Times*, 19 February 1928, http://pqasb.pqarchiver.com/latimes/search.html
15. Dwyer, *Malcolm St. Clair*, 147.
16. St. Clair, Malcolm Oswald. *World War I Draft Registration Cards, 1917–1918* (5 June 1918) (Online: The Generations Network, Inc., 2011) [Digital scan of original records in the National Archives, Washington, D.C.], subscription database, http://www.ancestry.com, accessed 18 June 2011.
17. Allene Talmey, *Doug and Mary and Others* (New York: Macy-Masius, 1927), 107–8.
18. Waterbury, "Sex—With a Sense of Humor," 112.
19. Leonard Mosley, *Zanuck: The Rise and Fall of Hollywood's Last Tycoon* (Boston: Little, Brown, 1984), 56.
20. Grace Kingsley, "Flashes. Metro Plans Schedule," *Los Angeles Times*, 1 September 1921, http://pqasb.pqarchiver.com/latimes/search.html
21. "Keaton Signs St. Clair," *Moving Picture World*, 26 February 1921, 1070.
22. Jim Kline, *Complete Films of Buster Keaton* (New York: Carol Publishing Group, 1993), 68.
23. Ibid., 79. His remarks were not based on the version of *The Blacksmith* discovered in 2013; he might have re-evaluated it since then.
24. Dwyer, *Malcolm St. Clair*, 45.
25. Mosley, *Zanuck*, 68.
26. "Fighting Blood," *Variety*, 18 October 1923, 23.
27. Dwyer, *Malcolm St. Clair*, 80.
28. Ibid.
29. Mosley, *Zanuck*, 68.
30. Peter Milne, "The Keystone Kop," 35.
31. Waterbury, "Sex—With a Sense of Humor," 42.

32. Dwyer, *Malcolm St. Clair*, 100–101.
33. Waterbury, "Sex—With a Sense of Humor," 42.
34. William K. Everson, *American Silent Film* (New York: Da Capo Press, 1998), 268–9.
35. Allene Talmey, *Doug and Mary and Others* (New York: Macy-Masius, 1927), 104.
36. "Best Films of the Year," *Film Daily Year Book*, 1927, 17.
37. Barry Paris, *Louise Brooks* (New York: Knopf, 1989), 134.
38. Ibid., 206.
39. Ibid., 183.
40. Ibid., 212.
41. Ibid., 155.
42. "Found! The Most Modest Man," 10 February 1929.
43. Dwyer, *Malcolm St. Clair*, 127.
44. Geltzer, "Mal. St. Clair," 56.
45. "'Side Street' Entertains," *New York Times*, 9 September 1929, http://query.nytimes.com/search/sitesearch
46. Grace Kingsley, "Richard Dix Film Chosen," *Los Angeles Times*, 19 March 1931, http://pqasb.pqarchiver.com/latimes/search.html
47. Philip K. Scheuer, "Old-Times of Silents Return," *Los Angeles Times*, 25 September 1932, http://pqasb.pqarchiver.com/latimes/search.html
48. Dwyer, *Malcolm St. Clair*, 144.
49. Read Kendall, "Around and About in Hollywood," *Los Angeles Times*, 23 August 1934, http://pqasb.pqarchiver.com/latimes/search.html
50. Cordelia St. Clair, *California Death Index* (12 June 1981) (Online: The Generations Network, Inc., 2010) [Digital scan of original records in the State of California Department of Health Services Center for Health Statistics, Sacramento, CA], subscription database, http://www.ancestry.com/, accessed 10 April 2010.
51. Kline, *Complete Films of Buster Keaton*, 173.
52. Mal St. Clair, Clipping file, Billy Rose Theater Collection, New York Public Library for the Performing Arts.
53. Edward M. Murray, 1893, Ladder, U.S. Patent 499028, filed 9 November 1892, and issued 6 June 1893.
54. Simon Louvish, *Stan and Ollie, the Roots of Comedy: The Double Life of Laurel and Hardy*, London: Faber, 2001, 409.
55. Ibid., 413.
56. Malcolm St. Clair, Death certificate no. 1904 695 (1 June 1952), informational copy from Los Angeles County Registrar-Recorder/County Clerk.
57. "St. Clair, Ex-Film Director, Dies," *Los Angeles Times*, 3 June 1952, http://pqasb.pqarchiver.com/latimes/search.html
58. Margaret A. St. Clair, *Social Security Death Index* (October 1988) (Online: The Generations Network, Inc., 2006) [Digital scan of original records in the Master File, Social Security Administration, Washington, D.C.], subscription database, http://www.ancestry.com, accessed 14 October 2006.

EDWARD SEDGWICK

1. Galveston, Texas City Directories, 1888–91 (Online: The Generations Network, Inc., 2000) [Digital scan of *Morrison and Fourmy's General Directory of the City of Galveston, 1888–1889, 1890–91*. Galveston, TX: Morrison and Fourmy Co., 1889, 1891.], subscription database, http://www.ancestry.com, accessed 12 September 2011.

2. Edward Hutson, Unpublished interview with Marion Meade, conducted September 1990, Special Collections, University of Iowa Library.

3. "Edward Sedgwick," MGM Studio Publicity Department, 1927, Clipping file, Billy Rose Theater Collection, New York Public Library for the Performing Arts, retrieved 31 January 2012.

4. Ibid.

5. "Orpheum Theater," *Pensacola Journal*, 11 October 1908, 8; "Five Sedgwicks to Present 'The White Squaw,'" *Daily Progress*, 15 February 1909; "Grand," *Evening Independent*, 25 October 1909, 5.

6. "Amusements," *Galveston Daily News*, 19 November 1910, 5.

7. "Football vs. Films," *Los Angeles Times*, 25 November 1928, http://pqasb.pqarchiver.com/latimes/search.html

8. "Star Plays Baseball Hero," *Los Angeles Times*, 5 November 1926, http://pqasb.pqarchiver.com/latimes/search.html

9. Robert Grau, *The Theater of Science* (New York: Broadway Publishing, 1914), 372–3.

10. John Baxter, *King Vidor* (New York: Simon & Schuster, 1976), 5.

11. Edward Martin Sedgwick, *World War I Draft Registration Cards, 1917–1918* (5 June 1917) (Online: The Generations Network, Inc., 2006) [Digital scan of original records in the National Archives, Washington, D.C.], subscription database, http://www.ancestry.com, accessed 11 September 2006.

12. "Mrs. Sedgwick Asks Divorce," *Los Angeles Times*, 22 August 1933, http://pqasb.pqarchiver.com/latimes/search.html; "News from the Dailies," *Variety*, 29 August 1933, 58.

13. Mary Sedgwick, 1930 Passenger List, S.S. City of Los Angeles, sailing from Honolulu, Hawaii, 5 August 1930, line 2. (Online: The Generations Network, Inc., 2011) subscription database, http://www.ancestry.com, accessed 3 February 2012.

14. "Who's Who in 'Slide, Kelly, Slide,'" *Moving Picture World*, 2 April 1927, 477.

15. "Ed. Sedgwick Joins the Lubin Co.," *Moving Picture World*, 28 March 1914, 1682.

16. Hans J. Wollstein, "Josie Sedgwick," *All Movie Guide*, http://www.answers.com/topic/josie-sedgwick, accessed 21 May 2007.

17. "Eileen Sedgwick," *Weekly Variety*, 6 May 1991, 349; Hans J. Wollstein, "Eileen Sedgwick," *All Movie Guide*, http://www.answers.com/topic/eileen-sedgwick, accessed 21 May 2007.

18. Los Angeles City Directories, 1921.

19. "Signs Sedgwick for Gibson," *Moving Picture World*, 7 April 1923, 673.

20. "Who's Who in 'Slide, Kelly, Slide,'" *Moving Picture World*, 2 April 1927, 477.

21. Tom Dupree, "Phantom of the Opera," in *George Lucas' Blockbusting*, Alex Ben Block and Lucy Autry Wilson, ed. (New York: HarperCollins, 2010), 99.

22. "Directors Need Variety," *Los Angeles Times*, 30 November 1924, http://pqasb.pqarchiver.com/latimes/search.html

23. Ibid.

24. "Sedgwick Plans One of the Largest Western Films," *Los Angeles Times*, 31 May 1925, http://pqasb.pqarchiver.com/latimes/search.html

25. "Ed Sedgwick Joins MGM," *Moving Picture World*, 3 April 1926, 334.

26. Marquis Busby, "Life of Cadets Depicted," *Los Angeles Times*, 13 January 1928, http://pqasb.pqarchiver.com/latimes/search.html

27. Grace Kingsley, "MGM Director for Keaton," *Los Angeles Times*, 26 January 1928, http://pqasb.pqarchiver.com/latimes/search.html

28. "Reunion Note," *Los Angeles Times*, 11 February 1928, http://pqasb.pqarchiver.com/latimes/search.html

29. "Keaton Rents Residence as a Dressing Room," *Los Angeles Times*, 15 April 1928, http://pqasb.pqarchiver.com/latimes/search.html
30. Rudi Blesh, *Keaton* (New York: Macmillan, 1966), 303–4
31. "Production Manager Turns Actor for Each of His Films," *Los Angeles Times*, 12 March 1933, http://pqasb.pqarchiver.com/latimes/search.html
32. Keaton and Samuels, *My Wonderful World of Slapstick*, 211.
33. Ibid., 212–13.
34. "Who's Who in 'Slide, Kelly, Slide,' *Moving Picture World*, 2 April 1927, 477.
35. "Constance Talmadge Weds Netcher Today," *Los Angeles Times*, 8 May 1929, http://pqasb.pqarchiver.com/latimes/search.html
36. "Mrs. Sedgwick Asks Divorce," *Los Angeles Times*, 22 August 1933, http://pqasb.pqarchiver.com/latimes/search.html
37. Edward M. Sedgwick and Ebba A. Havez, Marriage certificate no. 10957 (3 September 1933), copy from Los Angeles County Registrar-Recorder/County Clerk; "Sedgwick-Havez Rite Performed," *Los Angeles Times*, 4 September 1933, http://pqasb.pqarchiver.com/latimes/search.html
38. Simon Louvish, *Stan and Ollie, the Roots of Comedy: The Double Life of Laurel and Hardy* (London: Faber, 2001), 408.
39. Philip Scheuer, "Embroidery, Contraptions Spur Keaton's Comicality," *Los Angeles Times*, 3 February 1946, http://pqasb.pqarchiver.com/latimes/search.html
40. Walter Ames, "Death of Ed Sedgwick Casts Gloom Over 'Lucy' Lot," *Los Angeles Times*, 8 May 1953, http://pqasb.pqarchiver.com/latimes/search.html
41. Stefan Kanfer, *Ball of Fire: The Tumultuous Life and Comic Art of Lucille Ball* (New York: Alfred A. Knopf, 2003). 51.
42. Ibid., 62.
43. Kathleen Brady, *Lucille* (New York: Billboard Books, 2001), 49.
44. Kanfer, *Ball of Fire*, 114; "Edward Sedgwick, Film Director, 60," *New York Times*, 8 May 1953, http://query.nytimes.com/search/sitesearch
45. Edward Martin Sedgwick, Death certificate no. 1901 8324 (7 May 1953), informational copy from Los Angeles County Registrar-Recorder/County Clerk.
46. Hollywood Chamber of Commerce, "History of the Walk of Fame," *Hollywood Walk of Fame*, http://www.walkoffame.com/pages/history, accessed 20 September 2011.
47. Ebba Sedgwick, Death certificate no. 0190 028004 (18 June 1982), informational copy from Los Angeles County Registrar-Recorder/County Clerk.

Assistant Directors

1. Additionally, *Camera's* "Pulse of the Studios" chart wasn't complete. From September 1920 to February 1921, Keaton's productions were listed under Metro Studio, but they disappeared completely from March 1921 to July 1922, articles about Keaton ran in the rest of the magazine; it's unknown why they left him out of "Pulse." In August 1922 his productions reappeared under Keaton Studio.
2. Irene Burns, "Pity the Assistant Director!," *Motion Picture Classic*, October 1926, 55.
3. "Pulse of the Studio," *Camera!*, 23 October 1920, 11.
4. Keaton and Samuels, *My Wonderful World of Slapstick*, 168.
5. "Buster Keaton in *Seven Chances*," *Davenport Democrat and Leader*, 17 May 1925, 18.
6. *Film Daily Year Book* (New York: Film Daily, 1927), 405.
7. Alfred Louis Werker, *World War I Draft Registration Cards, 1917–1918* (5 June 1917) (Online: The Generations Network, Inc., 2008) [Digital scan of original records

in the National Archives, Washington, D.C.], subscription database, http://www.ancestry.com, accessed 9 May 2008.

8. Alfred Louis Werker, Death certificate no. 3000 05597 (28 July 1975), informational copy from Los Angeles County Registrar-Recorder/County Clerk.
9. "You Can't Fool 'Em," *Van Wert Daily Bulletin*, 3 February 1921, 3.
10. "Coast Picture News," *Variety*, 14 July 1922, 41.
11. Alfred Louis Werker, Passport application no. 228065,(24 October 1922) (Online: The Generations Network, Inc., 2010) [Digital scan of original records in the National Archives, Washington, D.C.], subscription database, http://www.ancestry.com, accessed 13 March 2011.
12. "Alfred Werker," 1923 Passenger List, S.S. Minnewaska (23 November 1923). (Online: The Generations Network, Inc., 2010) [Digital scan of original records in the National Archives, Washington, D.C.], subscription database, http://www.ancestry.com, accessed 13 March 2011.
13. "New Film Era Lets Younger Talent Show," *Los Angeles Times*, 17 May 1929, http://pqasb.pqarchiver.com/latimes/search.html
14. Alfred Louis Werker, Death certificate no. 3000 05597 (28 July 1975), informational copy from Los Angeles County Registrar-Recorder/County Clerk.
15. Frances Allen Werker, Death certificate no. 0190 057990 (11 December 1982), informational copy from Los Angeles County Registrar-Recorder/County Clerk.
16. "Coast Picture News," *Variety*, 31 October 1919, 56.
17. "Pulse of the Studio," *Camera!*, 6 January 1923, 17.
18. Rudi Blesh, *Keaton* (New York: Macmillan, 1966), 233.
19. John L. Collins, Death certificate no. 0190–053547 (25 November 1981), informational copy from Los Angeles County Registrar-Recorder/County Clerk.
20. "Pulse of the Studio," *Camera!*, 4 August 1923, 16.
21. *The Day Buster Smiled*, 48.
22. "Political Skit Pleases Patrons of the Unique," *Los Angeles Herald*, 4 February 1908, 6.
23. "'Cinderella' Draws Capacity Audiences," *Los Angeles Herald*, 19 January 1909, 5.
24. "Good Pantomime at the Auditorium," *Los Angeles Herald*, 3 February 1909, 5.
25. "Current Bills at Local Playhouses," *Los Angeles Herald*, 14 February 1909, 6.
26. "Amusements," *Bisbee Daily Review*, 17 June 1909, 5; "Amusements: Orpheum." *Bisbee Daily Review*, 26 October 1909, 5.
27. "Amusements: Orpheum," *Bisbee Daily Review*, 14 December 1909, 4.
28. "Globe Amusements," *Daily Arizona Silver Belt*, 18 January 1910, 8.
29. "Burlesque on King Dodo Makes Hit at Majestic," *Daily Arizona Silver Belt*, 8 February 1910, 6.
30. "Amusements: Orpheum," *Bisbee Daily Review*, 5 September 1909, 5.
31. Lee Hamilton, "*Man from Boston* Scores Big Hit in Two Performances," *Bisbee Daily Review*, 28 December 1909, 8.
32. "Orpheum: *Finnegan at Coney Island*," *Bisbee Daily Review*, 12 October 1913, 5; "Orpheum: *Ten Bar Rooms in One Night*," *Bisbee Daily Review*, 7 October 1913, 5.
33. "*Swat the Fly* Useful as Well as Humorous," *Bisbee Daily Review*, 9 October 1913, 5.
34. Brent E. Walker, *Mack Sennett's Fun Factory* (Jefferson, NC: McFarland, 2010), 593–4.
35. "Walter Reed," *Camera!*, 20 April 1918, 5.
36. "Famous Irish Comedian with Arbuckle," *Moving Picture World*, 2 March 1918, 1231.

37. Walter Chapman Reed, *World War I Draft Registration Cards, 1917–1918* (6 September 1918) (Online: The Generations Network, Inc., 2007) [Digital scan of original records in the National Archives, Washington, D.C.], subscription database, http://www.ancestry.com, accessed 4 August 2010.
38. "Pulse of the Studio," *Camera!*, 1 December 1923, 17.
39. Walter Reed, Death certificate no. 1901 8383 (27 May 1943), informational copy from Los Angeles County Registrar-Recorder/County Clerk.
40. "American's New Bill an Attractive One," *San Francisco Chronicle*, 11 April 1910, http://www.sfgate.com/cgi-bin/qws/as/main
41. "Chutes Theater Has Popular Entertainers," *San Francisco Call*, 15 August 1910, 4.
42. "Drama," *Los Angeles Times*, 18 April 1916, http://pqasb.pqarchiver.com/latimes/search.html
43. Sanford Rothenberg, *World War I Draft Registration Cards, 1917–1918* (5 June 1917) (Online: The Generations Network, Inc., 2006) [Digital scan of original records in the National Archives, Washington, D.C.], subscription database, http://www.ancestry.com, accessed 14 October 2006.
44. Sanford Lewton Rothenberg, Military Personnel Records. National Personnel Records Center, St. Louis, MO, retrieved 25 January 2007.
45. "Frisco Notes," *Variety*, 23 May 1919, 21.
46. "Coast Picture News," *Variety*, 30 June 1922, 34.
47. "Dainty Winters Girl Honored by Film Men as Yolo's Prettiest," *Woodland Democrat*, 22 July 1927, 1.
48. Brent E. Walker, *Mack Sennett's Fun Factory* (Jefferson, NC: McFarland, 2010), 422, 425, 428.
49. "'Cynara' Will Be Produced," *Los Angeles Times*, 23 December 1931, http://pqasb.pqarchiver.com/latimes/search.html
50. Jimmie Fidler, "In Hollywood," *Los Angeles Times*, 20 July 1939, http://pqasb.pqarchiver.com/latimes/search.html
51. Sanford Lewton Roth, Death certificate no. 1901 16661 (4 November 1943), informational copy from Los Angeles County Registrar-Recorder/County Clerk.

Writers

1. Keaton and Samuels, *My Wonderful World of Slapstick*, 130–131.
2. Ibid., 131.
3. "Like their Music," *Camera*, 15 September 1923, 13.
4. "Keaton Stops Work," *Variety*, 3 December 1924, 22.
5. Keaton and Samuels, *My Wonderful World of Slapstick*, 132.
6. Kevin Brownlow, "Buster Keaton," in Kevin B. Sweeney, *Buster Keaton Interviews* (Jackson, MS: University Press of Mississippi, 2007), 176.
7. "Byron Morgan," *Variety*, 29 May 1963, 9.
8. "Studio Shutdown Denied," *Los Angeles Times*, 3 February 1928, http://pqasb.pqarchiver.com/latimes/search.html; "Sedgwick's on Buster's MGM," *Variety*, 25 January 1928, 27; "Keaton's 'Snapshots' First, *Variety*, 8 January 1928, 14.
9. "Still Revising Keaton's," *Variety*, 7 March 1928, 12.

AL BOASBERG

1. Arthur Ungar, "Al Boasberg Does an 'Off to Buffalo'; Gagsters Will Miss His Ready Wit," *Variety*, 23 June 1937, 2.

2. The 1900 and 1910 censuses give his birth year as 1892, but his draft registration and death certificate make it 1891. Most likely the earlier sources are correct.
3. Ben Schwartz, "The Gag Man: Being a Discourse on Al Boasberg, Professional Jokesmith, His Manner, and Method," In: *The Film Comedy Reader*, Gregg Rickman, ed. (New York: Limelight Editions, 2001), 69.
4. *The Day Buster Smiled*, 45.
5. Ungar, "Al Boasberg," *Variety*, 23 June 1937, 2.
6. "Gagster," *New Yorker*, 10 September 1932, 12–13.
7. Ibid.
8. Albert Boasberg, *New York County Marriages, 1908–1935* (21 July 1916) (Online: FamilySearch Historical Collections, 2011) [Digital copies of originals housed in the clerks' offices of the district courts in various counties throughout New York. FHL microfilm, Family History Library, Salt Lake City, Utah], https://www.familysearch.org, accessed 30 January 2012.
9. Hilda Boasberg, Passport application no. 195008. (19 June 1922) (Online: The Generations Network, Inc., 2010) [Digital scan of original records in the National Archives, Washington, D.C.], subscription database, http://www.ancestry.com, accessed 11 January 2012.
10. Albert Issac Boasberg, *World War I Draft Registration Cards, 1917–1918* (5 June 1918) (Online: The Generations Network, Inc., 2007) [Digital scan of original records in the National Archives, Washington, D.C.], subscription database, http://www.ancestry.com, accessed 27 March 2007.
11. "Returns Home, Wife Gone," *Variety*, 20 May 1925, 42.
12. Ungar, "Al Boasberg," *Variety*, 23 June 1937, 2.
13. "Boasberg Joins R-C Pictures," *Moving Picture World*, 6 May 1922, 56.
14. Ungar, "Al Boasberg," *Variety*, 23 June 1937, 2.
15. Schwartz, "The Gag Man," 71.
16. Schwartz, "The Gag Man," 77.
17. "Keaton's Next is Prize-Fight Comedy Feature," *Los Angeles Times*, 16 December 1925, http://pqasb.pqarchiver.com/latimes/search.html
18. Schwartz, "The Gag Man," 78.
19. *The Day Buster Smiled*, 45.
20. Ibid., 25.
21. "Al Boasberg Acting When Not Clowning," *Variety*, 1 June 1926, 12.
22. Tracy Doyle, "That Stovepipe Hat: The Story of *The General's* Abandoned Sequence," *The Great Stone Face*, v. 1, 17–23.
23. *The Day Buster Smiled*, 28.
24. Ibid., 23.
25. Max Wilk, *The Wit and Wisdom of Hollywood* (New York: Atheneum, 1971), 60.
26. "Boasberg Leaves Keaton," *Variety*, 25 August 1926, 9.
27. Keaton and Samuels, *My Wonderful World of Slapstick*, 131.
28. "F.P. Signs Boasberg," *Moving Picture World*, 19 February 1927, 1.
29. "Al Writes a Nasty Title," *Moving Picture World*, 25 June 1927, 573.
30. "Lamb Chops," *George Burns and Gracie Allen*, http://georgegracie.wordpress.com/2009/07/06/lamb-chops/, accessed 12 January 2012.
31. Myrna Nye, "Society of Cinemaland," *Los Angeles Times*, 21 November 1926, http://pqasb.pqarchiver.com/latimes/search.html
32. "Scenarist and Wife Separate," *Los Angeles Times*, 30 April 1927, http://pqasb.pqarchiver.com/latimes/search.html
33. "Al Boasberg to Marry in East," *Los Angeles Times*, 7 September 1927, http://pqasb.pqarchiver.com/latimes/search.html

34. "Mammoth Shrine Theater Opens," *Los Angeles Times*, 19 August 1928, http://pqasb.pqarchiver.com/latimes/search.html
35. Ungar, "Al Boasberg," *Variety*, 23 June 1937, 2.
36. Schwartz, "The Gag Man," 82.
37. Bob Hope and Pete Martin, *Bob Hope's Own Story: Have Tux, Will Travel* (New York: Pocket Books, 1956), 92.
38. Arthur Marx, *Life with Groucho* (New York: Simon & Schuster, 1954), 191–192.
39. Schwartz, "The Gag Man," 88.
40. Ibid.," 88–89.
41. Ungar, "Al Boasberg," *Variety*, 23 June 1937, 2.
42. Leonard Maltin, *The Great Movie Shorts* (New York: Crown, 1972), 116.
43. Marx, *Life with Groucho*, 192–3; Joe Adamson, *Groucho, Harpo, Chico, and Sometimes Zeppo* (New York: Simon & Schuster, 1973), 274.
44. Adamson, *Groucho, Harpo, Chico, and Sometimes Zeppo*, 319–321; Schwartz, "The Gag Man," 97–98.
45. Ungar, "Al Boasberg," *Variety*, 23 June 1937, 2.
46. "Film and Radio Writer Dies," *Los Angeles Times*, 19 June 1937, http://pqasb.pqarchiver.com/latimes/search.html; Albert I. Boasberg, Death certificate no. 1916 6870 (17 June 1937), informational copy from Los Angeles County Registrar-Recorder/County Clerk.
47. "Death Denies Author Pleasure of a Valley Home," *Van Nuys News*, 21 June 1937, 1.
48. Buffalo International Film Festival, "Al Boasberg Comedy Award," http://buffalofilmfestival.com/festivalinformation/alboasbergaward.html, accessed 16 January 2012.

CLYDE BRUCKMAN

1. Leonard Maltin, *The Great Movie Shorts* (New York: Crown, 1972), 6.
2. There's a discrepancy in his birth date. According to the 1900 Federal Census, his 1917 draft registration and a 1930 ship passenger record, he was born on June 30. But his death certificate lists it as 30 September and some secondary sources have used that date. His second wife was the informant on the certificate, and it was probably just a mistake.
3. "Widely Known Man Takes Life," *San Bernardino Daily Sun*, 8 November 1912, 4.
4. Ibid.
5. "Death Rather Than Insanity," *Los Angeles Times*, 8 November 1912, http://pqasb.pqarchiver.com/latimes/search.html
6. "The Bruckman Rites This Afternoon," *San Bernardino Daily Sun*, 9 November 1912, 2.
7. "Hundreds Pay Tribute to the Dead," *San Bernardino Daily Sun*, 10 November 1912, 2.
8. Clyde Bruckman, "Peculiarities of Batters," Los *Angeles Times*, 6 April 1914, http://pqasb.pqarchiver.com/latimes/search.html
9. C.A. Bruckman, "Vernon Tigers Picked to Run Among the First 3," *Los Angeles Examiner*, 31 March 1918, section 2, 1.
10. Clyde A. Bruckman, *California County Marriages, 1850–1952* (29 July 1916) (Online: FamilySearch Historical Collections, 2011) [Digital copies of originals housed in the clerks' offices of the district courts in various counties throughout California. FHL microfilm, Family History Library, Salt Lake City, Utah], https://www.familysearch.org, accessed 16 January 2012.

11. "Clyde Bruckman," *Camera!*, 2 February 1919, 13.
12. Clyde A. Bruckman, "Reverse English," *Saturday Evening Post*, 21 October 1916, 16.
13. Ibid., 17.
14. Ibid.
15. Ibid.
16. Ibid., 74.
17. Ibid.
18. Ibid.
19. Clyde A. Bruckman, "Joe Gum," *Saturday Evening Post*, 5 May 1917, 57–58.
20. Ibid., 57.
21. Ibid., 58.
22. Ibid., 61.
23. Ibid.
24. Ibid., 63.
25. "Lyons and Moran Increase Staff," *Moving Picture World*, 15 February 1919, 887.
26. Hans J. Wollstein, "Eddie Lyons," AllRovi.com, http://www.allrovi.com/name/eddie-lyons-p185333, accessed 8 November 2011.
27. Rob Pinsel, "Bruckman, Clyde," *Film Reference*, http://www.filmreference.com/Writers-and-Production-Artists-Bo-Ce/Bruckman-Clyde.html, accessed 8 November 2011.
28. Bruckman, "Reverse English," 57.
29. Ibid., 58.
30. Ibid., 70.
31. "Scribes Throw It into the Boobs," *Los Angeles Times*, 9 September 1919, http://pqasb.pqarchiver.com/latimes/search.html
32. Davide Turconi, Robert Farr, and Joe Moore, "Monty Banks Filmography," http://www.slapsticon.org/mugshots/banksfilmo.htm, accessed 8 November 2011.
33. C.A. Bruckman, "The Open Season for Grandmothers' Funerals Starts Today," *Los Angeles Examiner*, 5 April 1921, section 2, 3.
34. Fred Schader, "Coast Film Notes," *Variety*, 15 April 1921, 41.
35. Rudi Blesh, *Keaton* (New York: Macmillan, 1966), 148.
36. Ibid., 163–164.
37. Kevin Brownlow, "Buster Keaton," in Kevin B. Sweeney, *Buster Keaton Interviews* (Jackson, MS: University Press of Mississippi, 2007), 176.
38. Blesh, *Keaton*, 149.
39. "Humorists All at Sea," *Los Angeles Times*, 25 May 1924, http://pqasb.pqarchiver.com/latimes/search.html
40. "Keaton Stops Work," *Variety*, 3 December 1924, 22.
41. "At the Isis Theatre," *Kokomo Daily Tribune*, 11 September 1926, 11.
42. *The Day Buster Smiled*, 2.
43. Ibid., 44.
44. "Bruckman Again to Direct Banks," *Moving Picture World*, 29 January 1927, 355.
45. Keaton and Samuels, *My Wonderful World of Slapstick*, 211.
46. Joseph Adamson III, "Clyde Bruckman," in *Dictionary of Literary Biography, Volume 26: American Screenwriters*. Edited by Robert E. Morsberger, Stephen O. Lesser, and Randall Clark. (New York: Gale, 1984).
47. "Lloyd's First Talkie Beset with Tribulation," *Los Angeles Times*, 22 September 1929, http://pqasb.pqarchiver.com/latimes/search.html
48. "Mrs. Bruckman's Last Rites Set for Tomorrow, *Los Angeles Times*, 9 October

1931, http://pqasb.pqarchiver.com/latimes/search.html; Lola M. Bruckman, Death certificate no. 1901 11182 (8 October 1931), informational copy from Los Angeles County Registrar-Recorder/County Clerk.

49. Hurbert I. Cohen, "The Serious Business of Being Funny: an Interview with Harold Lloyd," In: Lloyd, Harold. *An American Comedy* (New York: Dover, 1971), 131.

50. Leonard Maltin, *The Great Movie Shorts* (New York: Crown, 1972), 82. 51. Ted Okuda and Edward Watz, *Two Reel Hollywood Film Comedies* (Jefferson, NC: McFarland, 1986), 202–203.

52. Maltin, *Movie Shorts*, 157.

53. Ibid.

54. Brent Seguine, "Clyde Bruckman's Stooge Repose," *Three Stooges Journal*, Winter 1999, 9–10.

55. Brent Seguine, "Clyde Bruckman's Stooge Repose," *Three Stooges Journal*, Winter 1999, 10.

56. Miss Gladys M. Prevost, *Index to Great Register of Orange County, California, 1926* (Online: The Generations Network, Inc., 2009) [Digital scan of original records in the California State Library. Sacramento, California], subscription database, http://www.ancestry.com, accessed 30 September 2010; Mrs. Gladys M. Bruckman, *Index to Register of Voters, Los Angeles County, California, 1936* (Online: The Generations Network, Inc., 2009) [Digital scan of original records in the California State Library. Sacramento, California], subscription database, http://www.ancestry.com, accessed 30 September 2010.

57. "Beverly Hills Property," *Los Angeles Times*, 22 January 1935, http://pqasb.pqarchiver.com/latimes/search.html

58. "Beverly Hills Property," *Los Angeles Times*, 7 April 1941, http://pqasb.pqarchiver.com/latimes/search.html

59. "Furniture at Auction," *Los Angeles Times*, 27 April 1941, http://pqasb.pqarchiver.com/latimes/search.html

60. Adamson, *Dictionary of American Literary Biography*.

61. "Harold Lloyd Corp. Sues Universal for $1,700,000," *Los Angeles Times*, 5 April 1945, http://pqasb.pqarchiver.com/latimes/search.html

62. "Lloyd Testifies about Asserted Sequence Theft," *Los Angeles Times*, 13 September 1945, http://pqasb.pqarchiver.com/latimes/search.html

63. "Two Lloyd Corp. Suits Over Films Settled," *Los Angeles Times*, 11 November 1947, http://pqasb.pqarchiver.com/latimes/search.html

64. "Harold Lloyd Award Upheld by Court," Los Angeles Times, 13 May 1947, http://pqasb.pqarchiver.com/latimes/search.html

65. "Two Lloyd Corp.," *Los Angeles Times*, 11 November 1947. 66. Thomas F. Brady, "Hollywood 'Don'ts,'" *New York Times*, 16 November 1947, http://query.nytimes.com/search/sitesearch

67. "Lloyd Sues Columbia on 2 Films," *New York Times*, 8 March 1946, http://query.nytimes.com/search/sitesearch

68. Brady, "Hollywood 'Don'ts,'" *New York Times*, 16 November 1947.

69. Okuda and Watz, *Two Reel Hollywood Film Comedies*, 204.

70. Seguine, Brent. "Clyde Bruckman's Stooge Repose," *Three Stooges Journal*, Spring 200, 7.

71. David N. Bruskin, *The White Brothers: Jack, Jules & Sam White* (Hollywood, CA: Directors Guild of America; Metuchen, NJ: Scarecrow Press, 1990), 227.

72. "Bruckman, Film Writer, Ends His Life," *Los Angeles Times*, 5 January 1955, http://pqasb.pqarchiver.com/latimes/search.html

73. "Borrow Gun, Kills Himself," *Daily Chronicle*, 5 January 1955, 12. Joe Adamson

has discovered that Bruckman's note has three dates: 26 December, 3 January and January 4. He believes that Bruckman considered suicide on the 26th and 3rd before he ended his life on the 4th. (Joe Adamson, *Keaton Chronicle*, forthcoming issue.)

74. Clyde Adolf Bruckman, Death certificate no. 7080 437 (4 January 1955), informational copy from Los Angeles County Registrar-Recorder/County Clerk.

75. Gladys Marie Bruckman, Death certificate no. 50 1049 (9 June 1983), informational copy from Stanislaus County Clerk-Recorder.

76. In the acknowledgments, Blesh also said he interviewed Eddie Cline, but he doesn't quote him directly.

77. Blesh, *Keaton*, 149–150.

78. Brownlow, "Buster Keaton," 176.

RAYMOND CANNON

1. Gene Kira, *The Unforgettable Sea of Cortez: Baja California's Golden Age, 1947–1977: The Life and Writings of Ray Cannon* (Torrance, CA: Cortez Publications, 1999), 12–13.

2. Ibid.

3. "Cannon, Raymond," *Motion Picture Almanac* (New York: Quigley Publishing, 1934), 118.

4. Kira, *The Unforgettable Sea of Cortez*, 3.

5. Ibid., 13.

6. *Motion Picture Almanac*, 118.

7. "Selig Company Provides Start for Director," *Los Angeles Times*, 2 September 1930, http://pqasb.pqarchiver.com/latimes/search.html

8. "Cannon, Ulises T." *Index to Register of Voters, Los Angeles County, California, 1916* (Online: The Generations Network, Inc., 2009) [Digital scan of original records in the California State Library. Sacramento, California], subscription database, http://www.ancestry.com, accessed 19 September 2009.

9. Ulises Tildman Cannon, *World War I Draft Registration Cards, 1917–1918* (5 June 1917) (Online: The Generations Network, Inc., 2007) [Digital scan of original records in the National Archives, Washington, D.C.], subscription database, http://www.ancestry.com, accessed 2 April 2007.

10. "Motion Picture Industry is Centering Around Hollywood and Sunset," *Camera!*, 11 May 1918, 8.

11. "Items Gathered In and Around the Studios," *Camera!*, 11 May 1918, 2.

12. Masthead, *Camera!*, 30 June 1918, 4.

13. "Casting Column," *Camera!*, 16 June 1918, 6.

14. "Staff Changes," *Camera!*, 6 December 1919, 4.

15. "It is with great sorrow...," *Camera!*, 6 March 1920, 3.

16. "Beginning with this week's issue...," *Camera!*, 18 June 1921, 15.

17. Masthead, *Camera!*, 13 May 1922; 20 May 1922, 3.

18. Masthead, *Camera!*, 5 January 1924, 12.

19. Raymond Cannon, *California County Marriages, 1850–1952* (9 February 1920) (Online: FamilySearch Historical Collections, 2011) [Digital copies of originals housed in the clerks' offices of the district courts in various counties throughout California. FHL microfilm, Family History Library, Salt Lake City, Utah], https://www.familysearch.org, accessed 3 February 2013.

20. "John Alden's Act Emulated," *Los Angeles Times*, 17 May 1931, http://pqasb.pqarchiver.com/latimes/search.html; "People in Films," *New York Times*, 15 May 1938, http://query.nytimes.com/search/sitesearch

21. "Fanchon Royer [Advertisement]," *Camera!*, 15 June 1919, 15.

22. Masthead, *Camera!*, 24 January 1920, 4; 31 January 1920, 4.
23. Masthead, *Camera!*, 25 September 1920, 5.
24. "To You," *Camera!*, 20 May 1922, 3.
25. "John Alden's Act Emulated," *Los Angeles Times*, 17 May 1931.
26. Grace Kingsley, "Background New York Docks," *Los Angeles Times*, 27 April 1928, http://pqasb.pqarchiver.com/latimes/search.html
27. "Pulse of the Studios," *Camera!*, 6 January 1923, 17.
28. "Pulse of the Studios," *Camera!*, 15 January 1923, 17.
29. "Writer Works Up Imaginative Tale," *Los Angeles Times*, 1 June 1924, http://pqasb.pqarchiver.com/latimes/search.html; "High Altitude Humor," *Los Angeles Times*, 25 February 1925, http://pqasb.pqarchiver.com/latimes/search.html
30. Mordaunt Hall, "A Timid Mountain Climber," *New York Times*, 9 March 1925, http://query.nytimes.com/search/sitesearch
31. "High Altitude Humor," *Los Angeles Times*, 25 February 1925.
32. "Cannon Does Drama," *Los Angeles Times*, 27 April 1925, http://pqasb.pqarchiver.com/latimes/search.html
33. "All Studios of Schenck to Be Busy," *Los Angeles Times*, 17 May 1925, http://pqasb.pqarchiver.com/latimes/search.html
34. Grace Kingsley, "Flashes," *Los Angeles Times*, 19 September 1925, http://pqasb.pqarchiver.com/latimes/search.html
35. Whitney Williams, "*Taxi, Taxi* Amusing Comedy Fare," *Los Angeles Times*, 12 September 1926, http://pqasb.pqarchiver.com/latimes/search.html
36. "Cannon Penciling for Met," *Variety*, 2 March 1927, 15.
37. "Coast Film Notes," *Variety*, 4 August 1927, 26.
38. "Writer to Build Swiss Design," *Los Angeles Times*, 7 November 1926, http://pqasb.pqarchiver.com/latimes/search.html
39. Grace Kingsley, "Newlywed Housewarming," 9 October 1927, http://pqasb.pqarchiver.com/latimes/search.html
40. Kingsley, "Background New York Docks," *Los Angeles Times*, 27 April 1928.
41. "Life's Like That," *Film Index International*, http://fii.chadwyck.com/home, accessed 1 December 2007.
42. "Cannon Starts Production," *Los Angeles Times*, 24 August 1928, http://pqasb.pqarchiver.com/latimes/search.html
43. "Fanchon Royer Scores in Tilt," *Los Angeles Times*, 28 August 1937, http://pqasb.pqarchiver.com/latimes/search.html
44. Grace Kingsley, "'Trade Horn' Actors Teamed," *Los Angeles Times*, 15 January 1932, http://pqasb.pqarchiver.com/latimes/search.html
45. "Film Man's Mexican Divorce Attacked in Support Suit," *Los Angeles Times*, 22 February 1940, http://pqasb.pqarchiver.com/latimes/search.html
46. Kira, *The Unforgettable Sea of Cortez*, 19.
47. "Carla Laemmle," *Classic Horror Players Directory*, http://myweb.evnet.edu/~u0e53/carlalaemmle.html, accessed 4 May 2007.
48. Rick Atkins, *Among the Rugged Peaks* (Baltimore, MD: Midnight Marquee Press, 2009), 99.
49. Ibid., 111.
50. "New Chinese Cultural Club Formed," *Los Angeles Times*, 6 January 1939, http://pqasb.pqarchiver.com/latimes/search.html
51. Atkins, *Among the Rugged Peaks*, 83.
52. "'Her Majesty The Prince' to Open Tonight at Music Box," *Los Angeles Times*, 10 May 1936, http://pqasb.pqarchiver.com/latimes/search.html
53. Kira, *The Unforgettable Sea of Cortez*, 23.
54. Atkins, *Among the Rugged Peaks*, 118.

55. Kira, *The Unforgettable Sea of Cortez*, 345.
56. "Carla Laemmle," *Classic Horror Players Directory*.
57. Raymond Cannon, Death certificate no. 0190 026516 (7 June 1977), informational copy from Los Angeles County Registrar-Recorder/County Clerk.
58. Kira, *The Unforgettable Sea of Cortez*, 345.

Bryan Foy

1. One of 'Little Foys' Succumbs," *Los Angeles Times*, 21 April 1977, http://pqasb.pqarchiver.com/latimes/search.html
2. Eddie Foy and Alvin F. Harlow, *Clowning Through Life* (New York: Dutton, 1928), 315–316.
3. Anthony Slide, "Eddie Foy," in *The Vaudevillians* (Westport, CT: Greenwood Press, 1994), 57.
4. Damon Runyon, "The Brighter Side," *Daily Mirror*, 25 November 1941, 10, Bryan Foy clipping file, Billy Rose Theater Collection, New York Public Library for the Performing Arts, retrieved 31 January 2012.
5. "Nine Foys Keystoning with Sennett," *Moving Picture World*, 28 August 1915, 1488.
6. Brent E. Walker, *Mack Sennett's Fun Factory* (Jefferson, NC: McFarland, 2010), 59.
7. "Eddie Foy's a Favorite Fool," *The Triangle*, 11 March 1916, 6.
8. Bryan Robert Foy, Military Personnel Records, National Personnel Records Center, St. Louis, MO, retrieved 21 June 2007.
9. Sidney Skolsky, "Tin Types," 16 June 1938, Bryan Foy clipping file, Billy Rose Theater Collection, New York Public Library for the Performing Arts, retrieved 31 January 2012.
10. "Mrs. Madeline Morando Foy," *New York Times*, 15 June 1918, http://query.nytimes.com/search/sitesearch
11. Frank Cullen, with Florence Hackman and Donald McNeilly, *Vaudeville Old & New* (New York: Routledge, 2007), 410.
12. "Foy Family Sketch," *Variety*, 16 August 1912, 5.
13. "Notes," *Variety*, 15 August 1919, 10.
14. Stewart D. Travis, *No Applause Just Throw Money* (New York: Faber and Faber, 2005), 209.
15. Marquis Busby, "It Started as a Two-Reeler," *Los Angeles Times*, 29 July 1928, http://pqasb.pqarchiver.com/latimes/search.html
16. "'Gallagher' Author Loses Royalty Suit," *Evening World*, 11 August 1922, 9.
17. "Requiem Mass for Mrs. Vivian Foy of Encino on Tuesday," *Van Nuys News*, 8 December 1949, 22.
18. Grace Kingsley, "Recalling the Good Old Days," *Los Angeles Times*, 9 August 1931, http://pqasb.pqarchiver.com/latimes/search.html
19. "Los Angeles," *Variety*, 9 October 1919, 64.
20. "Vaudeville," *Variety*, 24 January 1920, 6; "Vaudeville," *Variety*, 9 April 1920, 6.
21. "News of the Film World," *Variety*, 18 July 1919, 41.
22. "The Hollywood Photographic Section," *Moving Picture World*, 20 August 1927, 517.
23. "Pickups by the Staff," *Camera!*, 18 March 1922, 16.
24. "Bryan Foy Promoted to Be Director," *Moving Picture World*, 15 September 1923, 280.
25. "News Section," *Camera!*, 1 December 1923, 14.
26. "Foy Will Film Phony History," *Film Tribune*, 26 January 1924, 1.

27. "Keaton's Collegiate Film," *Variety*, 9 February 1927, 9.
28. "Six Added to Roster of Writers," *Los Angeles Times*, 13 February 1927, http://pqasb.pqarchiver.com/latimes/search.html
29. Grace Kingsley, "DeMille Loans Star to MGM," *Los Angeles Times*, 3 February 1927, http://pqasb.pqarchiver.com/latimes/search.html
30. Grace Kingsley, "Bryan Foy Going to New York," *Los Angeles Times*, 25 October 1928, http://pqasb.pqarchiver.com/latimes/search.html
31. "Foy, Bryan," *Motion Picture News Blue Book* (New York: Motion Picture News, 1929), 95.
32. Edwin Schallert, "*Jazz Singer* Is a Landmark," *Los Angeles Times*, 30 December 1927, http://pqasb.pqarchiver.com/latimes/search.html
33. Marquis Busby, "It Started as a Two-Reeler," *Los Angeles Times*, 29 July 1928, http://pqasb.pqarchiver.com/latimes/search.html
34. Les Rowley, "Vitaphone Variety," *International Photographer*, June 1930, 165.
35. "Short Subject Producers," *Film Daily Yearbook of Motion Pictures* (New York: Film and Television Daily, 1932), 640.
36. Leonard Maltin, *The Great Movie Shorts* (New York: Crown, 1972), 190–191.
37. Joseph McBride, "Bryan Foy, Rajah of "B" Pics," *Variety*, 27 April 1977, 30.
38. Richard Maltby, *Harmless Entertainment* (Metuchen, NJ: Scarecrow, 1983), 27.
39. McBride, "Bryan Foy," *Variety*, 27 April 1977, 30.
40. Thomas M. Pryor, "Reluctant Monarch," *New York Times*, 2 December 1945, http://query.nytimes.com/search/sitesearch
41. Philip K. Scheuer, "Bryan Foy Sets Dizzy Pace in New Key Post," *Los Angeles Times*, 18 August 1946, http://pqasb.pqarchiver.com/latimes/search.html
42. Edwin Schallert, "Bryan Foy Alters Setup," *Los Angeles Times* 7 April 1948, http://pqasb.pqarchiver.com/latimes/search.html; Thomas F. Brady, "Bryan Foy in Deal with Warner Bros," *New York Times*, 29 March 1949, http://query.nytimes.com/search/sitesearch
43. Vivian C. Foy, Death certificate no. 1901–19422 (4 December 1949), informational copy from Los Angeles County Registrar-Recorder/County Clerk.
44. "Edelman's Top Spot at Producers Guild," *Variety*, 19 May 1965, 27.
45. Joseph McBride, "Requiem Mass Tomorrow for Pioneer Pic-Maker Bryan Foy," *Variety*, 22 April 1977, 16.
46. Bryan Foy, Death certificate no. 0190–019799 (20 April 1977), informational copy from Los Angeles County Registrar-Recorder/County Clerk.
47. McBride, "Bryan Foy, Rajah of "B" Pics," *Variety*, 27 April 1977, 30.
48. Bryan Foy, Death certificate.

TOMMY GRAY

1. Thomas J. Gray, Clipping file, Billy Rose Theater Collection, New York Public Library for the Performing Arts, retrieved 7 February 2012.
2. Emily Wortis Leider, *Becoming Mae West* (New York: Farrar, Straus, Giroux, 1997), 71.
3. "Thomas J. Gray," *Variety*, 20 December 1912, 139.
4. Thomas J. Gray, "Tommy's Tattles," *Variety*, 31 May 1913, 7.
5. "Funny Writer an Actor," *Variety*, 26 August 1911, 8.
6. "Tommy Gray, Actor," *Variety*, 8 January 1915, 17.
7. "Vaudeville," *Variety*, 15 January 1915, 5.
8. Stephen R. Webb, "Klever Komedies in the Great War: One Studio's Contribution to the War Effort," *Film History* (3) 1989:106.
9. Thomas J. Gray, *World War I Draft Registration Cards, 1917–1918* (5 June

1918) (Online: The Generations Network, Inc., 2010) [Digital scan of original records in the National Archives, Washington, D.C.], subscription database, http://www.ancestry.com, accessed 7 January 2010.

10. Albert Bushnell Hart (ed.), *Harper's Pictorial Library of the World War*, v.7.(New York: Harper & Brothers, 1920), 340.

11. "Tommy Gray," *Variety*, 3 December 1924, 11.

12. Edwin Shallert, "Comedy Melo at the Majestic," *Los Angeles Times*, 26 July 1920, http://pqasb.pqarchiver.com/latimes/search.html

13. Leider, *Becoming Mae West*, 110.

14. "Tommy Gray Peps Them Up," *Los Angeles Times*, 23 June 1923, http://pqasb.pqarchiver.com/latimes/search.html

15. Thomas Joseph Gray, Passport application no. 129345. (13 January 1921) (Online: The Generations Network, Inc., 2010) [Digital scan of original records in the National Archives, Washington, D.C.], subscription database, http://www.ancestry.com, accessed 7 January 2010.

16. Buster Keaton, "Tommy Gray Hits Beach and Floor," *Variety*, 16 December 1921, 8.

17. Thomas J. Gray, "Tommy's Tattles," *Variety*, 17 March 1922, 12.

18. Thomas J. Gray, "Tommy's Tattles," *Variety*, 3 March 1922, 12.

19. Thomas J. Gray, "Tommy's Tattles," *Variety*, 20 January 1922, 6.

20. Thomas J. Gray, "Tommy's Tattles," *Variety*, 27 January 1922, 10.

21. Thomas J. Gray, "Tommy's Tattles," *Variety*, 3 March 1922, 12.

22. "Largest Staff," *Los Angeles Times*, 14 January 1923, http://pqasb.pqarchiver.com/latimes/search.html

23. "Universal Gets Signatures of Famed Authors," *Los Angeles Times*, 15 March 1923, http://pqasb.pqarchiver.com/latimes/search.html

24. "In Lloyd Company," *Los Angeles Times*, 11 October 1923, http://pqasb.pqarchiver.com/latimes/search.html

25. Annette M. D'Agostino, *Harold Lloyd Encyclopedia* (Jefferson, NC: McFarland, 2004), 137.

26. "Tommy Gray," *Variety*, 3 December 1924, 11.

27. Thomas J. Gray, "Tommy's Tattles," *Variety*, 5 November 1924, 8.

28. "Thomas J. Gray Dead," *New York Times*, 1 December 1924, http://query.nytimes.com/search/sitesearch

Carl Harbaugh

1. Kevin Brownlow, "Buster Keaton," In: *Buster Keaton Interviews*, edited by Kevin B. Sweeny (Jackson: University Press of Mississippi, 2007), 175.

2. "Noted Friend of Stage Folk Dies at 92," *Los Angeles Times*, 30 April 1958, http://pqasb.pqarchiver.com/latimes/search.html

3. "Smith and Ongley to Act," *New York Times*, 13 December 1908, http://query.nytimes.com/search/sitesearch

4. Arthur L. Robb, "The Signal," *Variety*, 14 October 1911, 23.

5. "How Chicago Dramatic Critics View New Play *The Greyhound*," *Indianapolis Star*, 18 January 1912, 6.

6. "Last Night at the Theaters," *Washington Post*, 11 February 1913, 9; "Amusements," *Waterloo Times Tribune*, 27 September 1912, 7.

7. "The Bludgeon Is Dull," *New York Times*, 9 September 1914, http://query.nytimes.com/search/sitesearch

8. "Woman Killed; 6 Persons Hurt While Coasting," *Baltimore Sun*, 13 January 1922, 20.

9. "Mary Pickford to Begin Swamp Film," *Los Angeles Times*, 6 August 1925, http://pqasb.pqarchiver.com/latimes/search.html

10. Randy Skretvedt, *Laurel and Hardy: The Magic Behind the Movies* (Beverly Hills, CA: Past Times Publishing, 1996), 83.

11. "Dainty Winters Girl Honored by Film Men as Yolo's Prettiest," *Woodland Democrat*, 22 July 1927, 1.

12. Carl Harbaugh, *World War II Draft Registration Cards, 1942* (Online: FamilySearch Historical Collections, 2011) [Digital scan of original records in the National Archives, Washington, D.C.], https://www.familysearch.org, accessed 19 January 2012.

13. Carl Harbaugh, Death certificate no. 7053 5023 (26 February 1960), informational copy from Los Angeles County Registrar-Recorder/County Clerk.

JEAN HAVEZ

1. Kevin Brownlow, "Buster Keaton," in Kevin B. Sweeney, *Buster Keaton Interviews* (Jackson, MS: University Press of Mississippi, 2007), 176.

2. Jean Constant Havez, Johns Hopkins University Records, Ferdinand Hamburger, Jr. Archives, Baltimore, Maryland, retrieved February 2010.

3. H.L. Mencken, *Newspaper Days, 1899–1906* (New York: Knopf, 1955), 71. (Mencken used the old name for the paper; the *Evening News* changed its name to the *Daily News* in 1876, then to simply the *News* in 1892.)

4. Daniel I. McNamara, ed., *ASCAP Biographical Dictionary of Composers, Authors, and Publishers* (New York: Thomas Y. Crowell, 1948), 164.

5. Mencken, *Newspaper Days*, 71–72.

6. "Great Baseball Battle," *Baltimore Sun*, 3 May 1902, 6.

7. "A Literary Partnership," *Variety*, 5 November 1910, 15.

8. Jean Havez and Leo Donnelly, "The Fun Factory," *Green Book Album*, January 1912, 130.

9. Ibid., 133.

10. Ibid., 134.

11. Ibid., 129.

12. "The Girl from Brighton," *New York Times*, 1 September 1912, http://query.nytimes.com/search/sitesearch

13. McNamera, *ASCAP*, 164.

14. Brent E. Walker, *Mack Sennett's Fun Factory* (Jefferson, NC: McFarland, 2010), 326, 327, 333.

15. "Jolo." "A Dash of Courage," *Variety*, 26 May 1916, 20.

16. "Cup for Miss Cunningham," *New York Times*, 23 March 1915, http://query.nytimes.com/search/sitesearch.

17. Grace Kingsley, "At the Stage Door," *Los Angeles Times*, 18 October 1915, http://pqasb.pqarchiver.com/latimes/search.html

18. "Jean Havez Sues for Separation," *New York Times*, 17 August 1917, http://query.nytimes.com/search/sitesearch.

19. "'Marble Bride' Says She Can be Human If Man Is 'Boss,'" *Washington Times*, 9 September 1917, 2.

20. "Jean Havez Married Again," *Variety*, 3 May 1918, 7.

21. Jean Constant Havez, *World War I Draft Registration Cards, 1917–1918* (5 June 1918) (Online: The Generations Network, Inc., 2007) [Digital scan of original records in the National Archives, Washington, D.C.], subscription database, http://www.ancestry.com, accessed 27 March 2007.

22. "Ebba Ahl." 1896 Passenger List, S.S. Hebla, second cabin passenger, line 14.

(Online: The Generations Network, Inc., 2007) [Digital scan of original records in the National Archives, Washington, D.C.], subscription database, http://www.ancestry.com, accessed 4 August 2007.
    23. "*My Home Town Girl*," *Elyria Evening Telegram*, 23 January 1917, 6.
    24. "Marriages," *Variety*, 10 May 1918, 40.
    25. "Dramatic Play at the Majestic," *Los Angeles Times*, 24 November 1919, http://pqasb.pqarchiver.com/latimes/search.html
    26. Grace Kingsley, "Trixie Sparkles," *Los Angeles Times*, 25 November 1919, http://pqasb.pqarchiver.com/latimes/search.html
    27. "Rialto's Variety," *Los Angeles Times*, 10 September 1920, http://pqasb.pqarchiver.com/latimes/search.html.
    28. "Jean Havez Writing Scenarios," *Variety*, 21 March 1919, 56.
    29. "Havez Writes Scripts for Keaton," *Moving Picture World*, 15 May 1920, 938.
    30. Rudi Blesh, *Keaton* (New York: Macmillan, 1966, 163.
    31. "Addition to Lloyd Scenario Staff," *Camera!*, 11 June 1921, 6.
    32. "Where to Find People You Know," *Camera!*, 2 December 1922, 6.
    33. Jean C. Havez, Passport application no. 193145 (17 June 1922) (Online: The Generations Network, Inc., 2010) [Digital scan of original records in the National Archives, Washington, D.C.], subscription database, http://www.ancestry.com, accessed 31 October 2011.
    34. "Jean Havez." 1922 Passenger List, S.S. Olympic (23 August 1922). (Online: The Generations Network, Inc., 2010) [Digital scan of original records in the National Archives, Washington, D.C.], subscription database, http://www.ancestry.com, accessed 1 November 2011.
    35. Blesh, *Keaton*, 221.
    36. Con., "Our Hospitality," *Variety*, 13 December 1923, 22.
    37. Blesh, *Keaton*, 252.
    38. "Keaton Stops Work," *Variety*, 3 December 1924, 22.
    39. Blesh, *Keaton*, 260–261.
    40. Jean Havez, Death certificate no. 1676 (12 February 1925), informational copy from Los Angeles County Registrar-Recorder/County Clerk.

Lew Lipton

    1. "Lipton, Lew," *Motion Picture Almanac* (New York: Quigley Publishing, 1934), 360.
    2. Kristen Boddy (Alumni Assistant), Art Institute of Chicago, Illinois, e-mail to author, 14 May 2010.
    3. "Coast Picture News," *Variety*, 18 June 1920, 21.
    4. Los Angeles City Directories, 1921.
    5. Jack Stinnett, "New Yorker at Large," *The Register* (Sandusky, Ohio), 20 July 1937, 4.
    6. "Film Capital Production Notes," *Camera!*, 9 August 1922, 4.
    7. "Pulse of the Studios," *Camera!*, 6 January 1923, 18.
    8. "Pulse of the Studios," *Camera!*, 25 August 1923, 18.
    9. "*Baby Mine* All New," *Variety*, 21 September 1927, 12.
    10. "Lipton Supervising Comedies," *Variety*, 2 November 1927, 16.
    11. Keaton and Samuels, *My Wonderful World of Slapstick*, 211.
    12. Grace Kingsley, "Howard Hughes to Produce New Flyer," *Los Angeles Times*, 2 May 1930, http://pqasb.pqarchiver.com/latimes/search.html
    13. "Here and Elsewhere," *Los Angeles Times*, 10 May 1931, http://pqasb.pqarchiver.com/latimes/search.html

14. "Buster Keaton Confirms His Contract to Make 6 Talkies," *St. Petersburg Times*, 4 June 1933, 2.
15. "St. Petersburg Has Ambitions," *Bakersfield Californian*, 9 June 1933, 6.
16. "Comedian's Wife Here," *El Paso Herald Post*, 15 June 1933, 1.
17. "Why Buster Keaton Came to Florida," *Evening Independent*, 29 July 1933, 6.
18. Keaton and Samuels, *My Wonderful World of Slapstick*, 244–245.
19. "Keaton Will Not Return to City to Make Movies," *St. Petersburg Times*, 14 August 1933, 1.
20. Christopher Carmen, "The Florida Fiasco," *Keaton Chronicle*, Autumn 1994, 3.
21. "News of the Screen," *New York Times*, 27 November 1936, http://query.nytimes.com/search/sitesearch.
22. Jack Stinnett, "New Yorker at Large," *The Register* (Sandusky, Ohio), 20 July 1937, 4.
23. "Two Transactions Reported by Feminine Realty Company," *Los Angeles Times*, 17 May 1942, http://pqasb.pqarchiver.com/latimes/search.html
24. "Tommy Warner Jr. Takes Actress as a Third Wife," *Los Angeles Times*, 16 January 1946, http://pqasb.pqarchiver.com/latimes/search.html
25. "Estranged Wife Contests Will of Tommy Warner," *Los Angeles Times*, 24 November 1955, http://pqasb.pqarchiver.com/latimes/search.html
26. "Plot Laid to Vengeance," *Los Angeles Times*, 7 January 1943, http://pqasb.pqarchiver.com/latimes/search.html
27. "Two Acquitted on Charges in Mayer Case," *Los Angeles Times*, 11 January 1943, http://pqasb.pqarchiver.com/latimes/search.html
28. Lew Lipton and Ralph Murphy, *Lambs Will Gamble*, Unpublished play, New York Public Library Performing Arts Division.
29. Patricia Tobias, E-mail message to Buster Keaton Fans Yahoo listserv, 8 December 2007.
30. "'Truckline Café' to Quit Next Week," *New York Times*, 1 March 1946, http://query.nytimes.com/search/sitesearch.
31. "Eleven New Plays to Bow This Month," *New York Times*, 4 May 1946, http://query.nytimes.com/search/sitesearch.
32. William T. Leonard, *Broadway Bound: A Guide to Show that Died Aborning* (Metuchen, NJ: Scarecrow, 1983), 251.
33. Ibid.
34. "Closing the Books on the 1945–46 Campaign," *New York Times*, 2 June 1946, http://query.nytimes.com/search/sitesearch.
35. "Rites Set for Ruth Lipton, Real Estate Broker," *Los Angeles Times*, 1 September 1977, http://pqasb.pqarchiver.com/latimes/search.html
36. Ruth Lipton, Death certificate no. 0190 037342 (29 August 1977), informational copy from Los Angeles County Registrar-Recorder/County Clerk.
37. "Aaroe Joins Ruth Lipton Office," *Los Angeles Times*, 25 June 1977, http://pqasb.pqarchiver.com/latimes/search.html
38. Rex Lipton, Death certificate no. 387 9048637 (3 November 1987), informational copy from Los Angeles County Registrar-Recorder/County Clerk.

Joseph Mitchell

1. "Theatrical Week," *New York Times*, 20 September 1891, 13.
2. "Notable First Nights," *Boston Daily Globe*, 6 October 1891, 2.
3. "Attractions This Week," *Salt Lake City Daily Tribune*, 3 January 1892, 7.
4. "*The Stowaway*," *Boston Daily Globe*, 30 April 1894, 6.
5. "General Mention," *New York Times*, 15 December 1885, 5; "Entertainment,"

Piqua Daily Call, 30 March 1886, 2; "Amusement Points," *Boston Daily Globe*, 5 November 1889, 8; "New Palace Theater," *Boston Daily Globe*, 23 September 1900, 19.

6. "Amusements," *Logansport Journal* (Indiana), 3 January 1906, 7.
7. "Rush," "Quinn and Mitchell," *Variety*, 9 March 1907, 8.
8. "Vaudeville: Keith's," *Evening Public Ledger* (Philadelphia, PA), 31 August 1915, 5.
9. "Two Old Teams Spilt," *Variety*, 28 June 1918, 6.
10. "Vaudeville," *Variety*, 18 December 1909, 7.
11. "Pulse of the Studios." *Camera!*, 4 September 1920, 13.
12. "Joe Mitchell," *Camera!*, 21 May 1921, 9.
13. "Where to Find People You Know," *Camera!*, 2 July 1921, 6.
14. "Keaton Stops Work," *Variety*, 3 December 1924, 22.
15. Joseph Albert Mitchell, Death certificate no. 1901 6724 (21 April 1950), informational copy from Los Angeles County Registrar-Recorder/County Clerk.

Lex Neal

1. "Edward Jolly and Winifred Wild [advertisement]," *Variety*, 24 July 1909, 18.
2. "Lyric," *Ft. Wayne Daily News*, 18 December 1909, 4.
3. "Cris.," "Jolly, Wild & Co.," *Variety*, 5 February 1910, 35.
4. "Orpheum Theatre," *Salt Lake Herald-Republican*, 15 May 1910, 8.
5. Grace Kingsley, "Arnold Daly and G.B Shaw," *Los Angeles Times*, 6 October 1914, http://pqasb.pqarchiver.com/latimes/search.html
6. "Theaters: At the Orpheum," *Ogden Standard*, 16 October 1914, 3.
7. Rudi Blesh, *Keaton* (New York: Macmillan), 1966, 71.
8. Keaton and Samuels, *My Wonderful World of Slapstick*, 71–72.
9. Marc Okkonen and Ron Pesch, *Buster Keaton and the Muskegon Connection: The Actor's Colony at Bluffton, 1908–1938* (Muskegon, MI: Muskegon Chronicle, 1995), 34.
10. "Lyric—Vaudeville," *Indianapolis Star*, 12 January 1915, 15.
11. Lex Neal, *World War I Draft Registration Cards, 1917–1918* (5 June 1917) (Online: The Generations Network, Inc., 2007) [Digital scan of original records in the National Archives, Washington, D.C.], subscription database, http://www.ancestry.com, accessed 27 May 2007.
12. Lex Neal, Military Personnel Records. National Personnel Records Center, St. Louis, MO, retrieved 18 December 2006.
13. "Young Musicians Top Princess Bill," *San Antonio Evening News*, 24 March 1921, 3.
14. Fred Schader, "Coast Film Notes," *Variety*, March 11, 1921, 33.
15. "Pulse of the Studios," *Camera!*, 12 November 1921, 13. 16. "Warner Engages Neal," *Moving Picture World*, 16 September 1922, 200. 17. Harry Burns, "Chatter About Southland Folks," *Camera!*, 5 August 1922, 8.
18. Grace Kingsley, "Flashes," *Los Angeles Times*, 15 November 1923, http://pqasb.pqarchiver.com/latimes/search.html
19. "Fun Is Serious," *Los Angeles Times*, 10 May 1925, http://pqasb.pqarchiver.com/latimes/search.html
20. Keaton and Samuels, *My Wonderful World of Slapstick*, 132.
21. Ibid., 135.
22. Jack Dragga, "Filmography," In Marion Meade, *Buster Keaton: Cut to the Chase* (New York: HarperCollins, 1995), 360; Jim Kline, *Complete Films of Buster Keaton* (New York: Carol Publishing Group, 1993), 107.
23. "Keaton Directing Himself," *Variety*, 14 April 1926, 25.

24. "Keaton's Next Is Prize-Fight Comedy Feature," *Los Angeles Times*, 16 December 1925, http://pqasb.pqarchiver.com/latimes/search.html
25. Ibid.
26. "Los Angeles," *Variety*, 11 August 1926, 62.
27. Keaton and Samuels, *My Wonderful World of Slapstick*, 135–137.
28. "Marriages," *Variety*, 8 February 1928, 30.
29. Lex Neal, *California County Marriages, 1850–1952* (7 April 1931) (Online: FamilySearch Historical Collections, 2011) [Digital copies of originals housed in the clerks' offices of the district courts in various counties throughout California. FHL microfilm, Family History Library, Salt Lake City, Utah], https://www.familysearch.org, accessed 3 February 2013.
30. "Paramount Assigns Neal," *Los Angeles Times*, 25 September 1932, http://pqasb.pqarchiver.com/latimes/search.html
31. "Film Previews," *Variety*, 6 January 1933, 3.
32. Lex Neal, Death certificate no. 1901 8993 (4 July 1940), informational copy from Los Angeles County Registrar-Recorder/County Clerk. His former fiancée Yvonne Howell Stevens was the informant.

CHARLES SMITH

1. Robert Grau, *Forty Years Observation of Music and the Drama* (New York: Broadway Publishing, 1909), 23.
2. Ibid.
3. Frank J. Wilstach, "What They Used to Laugh At," *New York Times*, 15 July 1923, http://query.nytimes.com/search/sitesearch. A slightly longer version of this sketch can be found in the Smith and Campbell clipping file, Billy Rose Theater Collection, New York Public Library for the Performing Arts.
4. "The Playhouses," *Los Angeles Times*, 14 September 1897, http://pqasb.pqarchiver.com/latimes/search.html
5. "The Playhouses," *Los Angeles Times*, 21 September 1897, http://pqasb.pqarchiver.com/latimes/search.html
6. "The Playhouses," *Los Angeles Times*, 8 November 1898, http://pqasb.pqarchiver.com/latimes/search.html
7. "About the Players," *Woodland Daily Democrat*, 5 January 1904, 1.
8. Edward Le Roy Rice, *Monarchs of Minstrels, from "Daddy" Rice to Date* (New York: Kenny Publishing, 1911), 334.
9. Grau, *Forty Years Observation*, 24.
10. "Keaton Famous at Seven," *Los Angeles Times*, 20 July 1924, http://pqasb.pqarchiver.com/latimes/search.html
11. 'Dash.,' "Smith and Campbell," *Variety*, 20 February 1909, 15.
12. "Charles H. Smith," *Variety*, 24 March 1916, 9.
13. "Who Is Roland West?," *New York Times*, 22 September 1918, http://query.nytimes.com/search/sitesearch
14. "The Unknown Purple," *Internet Broadway Database*, http://www.ibdb.com/production.php?id=8745, accessed 1 February 2010.
15. "Ibee.," "Our Boys," *Variety*, 3 May 1918, 18.
16. Al Boasberg, "Famous Old Timers Meet in Keaton Troop," in *The Day Buster Smiled*, 24–25.
17. "New Evidence Indicates Murder of Thelma Todd," *Salt Lake Tribute*, 20 December 1935, 12.
18. "Todd Death Tests Made," *Los Angeles Times*, 23 December 1935, http://pqasb.pqarchiver.com/latimes/search.html

19. "Mother Believes Screen Star's Death Accidental," *Los Angeles Examiner*, 20 December 1935, 8.
20. "Jury Told of Party," *Los Angeles Times*, 24 December 1935, http://pqasb.pqarchiver.com/latimes/search.html
21. Charles Henry Smith, Death certificate no. 1901 10095 (11 July 1942), informational copy from Los Angeles County Registrar-Recorder/County Clerk.

Paul Gerald Smith

1. Paul Gerald Smith, "The Story of an Egg," Clipping file, Billy Rose Theater Collection, New York Public Library for the Performing Arts, retrieved 24 January 2012.
2. Paul Gerald Smith III, "Paul Gerald Smith," *Vaudeville Times*, Summer 2001, 16.
3. Ibid.
4. Ibid.
5. Smith, "The Story of an Egg," Clipping file, Billy Rose Theater Collection, New York Public Library.
6. Ibid.
7. Paul G. Smith, *Illinois, Cook County Marriages, 1871–1920* (22 October 1919) (Online: FamilySearch Historical Collections, 2011) [FHL microfilm, Family History Library, Salt Lake City, Utah], https://www.familysearch.org, accessed 3 February 2013.
8. Paul Gerald Smith III, "Paul Gerald Smith," *Vaudeville Times*, 17.
9. Ibid.
10. "Paul Gerald Smith," *Internet Broadway Database*, http://www.ibdb.com/person.php?id=8041, accessed 24 January 2010.
11. "Keaton's Next Is Prize-Fight Comedy Feature," *Los Angeles Times*, 16 December 1925, http://pqasb.pqarchiver.com/latimes/search.html
12. "Butterfly," *Sheboygan Press*, 19 February 1927, 18.
13. "Paul G. Smith Back; Had Tilt with Keaton," *Variety*, 30 June 1926, 20.
14. "Paul Gerald Smith," *Internet Broadway Database*.
15. Paul Gerald Smith, "Smithereens," *Rob Wagner's Script*, 22 August 1931, 24; 9 November 1940, 14.
16. Paul Gerald Smith, Death certificate no. 8009 2336 (4 April 1968), informational copy from San Diego County Assessor/Recorder/County Clerk.
17. Mary Alice Smith, Death certificate no. 8009 7438 (2 October 1969), informational copy from San Diego County Assessor/Recorder/County Clerk.

Lou Anger

1. "Henry Dixon," *Variety*, 12 May 1943, 54.
2. "Vaudeville," *Variety*, 18 December 1909, 7.
3. George M. Young, "Lou Anger, The German Soldier," *Variety*, 3 October 1908, 13.
4. "Hilarity Is Its Keynote," *Los Angeles Times*, 20 January 1914, http://pqasb.pqarchiver.com/latimes/search.html
5. "The Gay Hussars," *New York Telegraph*, 20 May 1910, Louis Anger clipping file, Billy Rose Theater Collection, New York Public Library for the Performing Arts.
6. "Lou Anger Married," *Variety*, 25 June 1910, 4.
7. "Sophye Barnard," *Internet Broadway Database*, http://www.ibdb.com/person.php?id=30934, accessed 9 February 2011.

8. "New Plays in Vaudeville," *New York Times*, 26 March 1912, http://query.nytimes.com/search/sitesearch
9. "Hilarity Is Its Keynote," Los *Angeles Times*, 20 January 1914, http://pqasb.pqarchiver.com/latimes/search.html
10. "Lou Anger," *Internet Broadway Database*, http://www.ibdb.com/person.php?id=29954, accessed 9 February 2011.
11. "Lou Anger at Bushwick," *Brooklyn Daily Eagle*, 22 September 1914, Louis Anger clipping file, Billy Rose Theater Collection, New York Public Library for the Performing Arts.
12. "Louis Anger, Sophye Barnard," Passenger List, Lusitania, sailed from Liverpool to New York 19 September 1913, line 6–7. (Online: The Generations Network, Inc., 2007) [Digital scan of original records in the National Archives, Washington, D.C.], subscription database, http://www.ancestry.com, accessed 27 March 2007.
13. "Philadelphia: Keith's," *Variety*, 17 September 1915, 35.
14. "Vaudeville: Keith's," *Evening Public Ledger*, 14 September 1915, 8.
15. William Hamilton Cline, "Olden Theater Days Recalled," *Los Angeles Times*, 13 October 1929, http://pqasb.pqarchiver.com/latimes/search.html
16. "Lou Anger Dies at 65," *Variety*, 22 May 1946, 1, 14.
17. Douglas Gomery, "Schenck, Joseph M." *American National Biography Online*. http://www.anb.org/, accessed 18 February 2011.
18. Stuart Oderman, *Roscoe "Fatty" Arbuckle: A Biography of the Silent Film Comedian, 1887–1933* (Jefferson, NC: McFarland, 1994), 88–90.
19. Rudi Blesh, *Keaton* (New York: Macmillan, 1966), 85–87.
20. "Arbuckle on the Coast," *Variety*, 7 September 1917, 27.
21. Reed Heustis, "Madman Runs Fat Arbuckle's Studio—Sure, It's Lou Anger," *Los Angeles Herald*, 3 November 1919, part 2, 1.
22. Keaton and Samuels, *My Wonderful World of Slapstick*, 278–280.
23. "Vernon Deal Seems Certain," *Los Angeles Times*, 2 May 1919, http://pqasb.pqarchiver.com/latimes/search.html
24. "Vernon Buys Byron Houck," *Los Angeles Times*, 3 February 1919, http://pqasb.pqarchiver.com/latimes/search.html
25. "Sophye Barnard," *Internet Broadway Database*.
26. E.V. Durling, "On the Side," *Los Angeles Times*, 10 March 1936, http://pqasb.pqarchiver.com/latimes/search.html
27. "Sophye Barnard," *Theatre Magazine*, April 1918, Sophye Barnard clipping file, Billy Rose Theater Collection, New York Public Library for the Performing Arts.
28. "Pulse of the Studios," *Camera!*, 4 September 1920, 13; 2 October 1920, 13.
29. Blesh, *Keaton*, 109.
30. "Keaton's Bill for Expenses Rouses Anger," *Los Angeles Times*, 25 November 1923, http://pqasb.pqarchiver.com/latimes/search.html
31. Blesh, *Keaton*, 156–160.
32. "Clyde Cook Is Cast for Mack Story," *Los Angeles Times*, 16 May 1923, http://pqasb.pqarchiver.com/latimes/search.html
33. "Anger's Corp.—Schenck's?," *Variety*, 8 February 1923, 46.
34. Blesh, Keaton, 284.
35. "Schenck Heads United Studios," *Los Angeles Times*, 1 February 1923, http://pqasb.pqarchiver.com/latimes/search.html
36. "Lou Anger Leaving U.A.," *Variety*, 22 August 1928, 7.
37. "Loan to Bioff Get Study," *Los Angeles Times*, 2 December 1939, http://pqasb.pqarchiver.com/latimes/search.html
38. "Roosevelt Hostelry Ready Soon," *Los Angeles Times*, Nov. 28, 1926, http://pqasb.pqarchiver.com/latimes/search.html; "Lou Anger," *Variety*, 24 May 1946, 6;

"Many Designated as Concert Aids," *Los Angeles Times*, 8 March 1936, http://pqasb.pqarchiver.com/latimes/search.html

39. E.V. During, "On the Side," *Los Angeles Times*, 28 August 1938, http://pqasb.pqarchiver.com/latimes/search.html

40. Louis Anger, Death certificate no. 1901 8679 (21 May 1946), informational copy from Los Angeles County Registrar-Recorder/County Clerk.

41. "NINDS Dermatomyositis Information Page," National Institute of Neurological Disorders and Stroke, National Institutes of Health, http://www.ninds.nih.gov/disorders/dermatomyositis/dermatomyositis.htm, accessed 10 February 2010.

42. "Lou Anger," *Variety*, 24 May 1946, 6; "Lou Anger Dies; Pioneered in Film Industry," *Los Angeles Times*, 22 May 1946, http://pqasb.pqarchiver.com/latimes/search.html; "Lou Anger," *New York Times*, 22 May 1946, http://query.nytimes.com/search/sitesearch

43. "Lou Anger Will Filed," *Los Angeles Times*, 13 June 1946, 1946, http://pqasb.pqarchiver.com/latimes/search.html

44. Virginia Horn, "Over Fifty Club Going Like Sixty After Fun for the Elderly," *Los Angeles Times*, 20 December 1965, http://pqasb.pqarchiver.com/latimes/search.html

45. Sophye Barnard Anger, Death certificate no. 1901 8679 (16 December 1965), informational copy from San Diego County Assessor/Recorder/County Clerk.

46. "Kid Your Audience, New Orpheum Maxim," *Los Angeles Times*, 18 January 1921, http://pqasb.pqarchiver.com/latimes/search.html; Bill Henry, "By the Way," *Los Angeles Times*, 5 August 1945, http://pqasb.pqarchiver.com/latimes/search.html

HARRY BRAND

1. Pam Munter, "Birdwell, Brand, and Strickling: The Secret Keepers," *Classic Images*, July 2005, 12.

2. Ibid., 12.

3. Harry Brand, *World War I Draft Registration Cards, 1917–1918* (5 June 1918) (Online: The Generations Network, Inc., 2007) [Digital scan of original records in the National Archives, Washington, D.C.], subscription database, http://www.ancestry.com, accessed 2 April 2007.

4. "Harry Brand," *Variety*, 1 March 1989, 83; "In the Public Schools," *Los Angeles Times*, 9 March 1913, http://pqasb.pqarchiver.com/latimes/search.html

5. Herb Stein, "Harry Brand Another Brilliant Publicist?," *Morning Telegraph* (New York), 9 May 1959, 2.

6. Los Angeles City Directory, 1915.

7. "First Round Is Completed," *Los Angeles Times*, 14 June 1915, http://pqasb.pqarchiver.com/latimes/search.html

8. Brand, *World War I Draft Registration Cards*.

9. "Fournier Signs Angels Contract," *Los Angeles Times*, 19 March 1919, http://pqasb.pqarchiver.com/latimes/search.html

10. "Baseball Scribes Look Like Winners," *Los Angeles Times*, 8 September 1919, http://pqasb.pqarchiver.com/latimes/search.html

11. Stein, "Harry Brand," *Morning Telegraph* (New York), 9 May 1959, 2.

12. "Brand Mayor's Secretary," *Los Angeles Times*, 30 March 1921, http://pqasb.pqarchiver.com/latimes/search.html

13. Harry Brand, *Index to Register of Voters, Los Angeles County, California, 1922–1954* (Online: The Generations Network, Inc., 2009) [Digital scan of original records in the California State Library. Sacramento, California], subscription database, http://www.ancestry.com, accessed 5 October 2010.

14. "Actor Finds a Two-Headed Scorpion," *Camera!*, 24 February 1923, 11.
15. "What Did Baby Say?," *Camera!*, 30 June 1923, 16.
16. Harry A. Williams, "Sport Shrapnel," *Los Angeles Times*, 21 August 1922, http://pqasb.pqarchiver.com/latimes/search.html
17. "Fooling Old-Timers," *Camera!*, 7 July 1923, 7.
18. "Ex-Leader Welcomed by WAMPAS," *Los Angeles Times*, 7 October 1925, http://pqasb.pqarchiver.com/latimes/search.html
19. "Brand, Keaton Gen. Mgr.," *Variety*, 3 November 1926, 19.
20. Rudi Blesh, *Keaton* (New York: Macmillan, 1966), 284.
21. Ibid., 285.
22. Ibid., 286.
23. "Camera Pair Completes Trip," *Los Angeles Times*, 25 November 1928, http://pqasb.pqarchiver.com/latimes/search.html
24. Frederica Sagor Maas, *The Shocking Miss Pilgrim* (Lexington, KY, 1999), 143.
25. Braven Dyer, "Practice Won for Diegel," *Los Angeles Times*, 8 December 1929, http://pqasb.pqarchiver.com/latimes/search.html
26. Maas, 145.
27. Kyle Crichton, *Total Recoil* (New York: Doubleday, 1960), 85–86.
28. Paul Lowry, "Rabbit Punches," *Los Angeles Times*, 29 November 1931, 6, http://pqasb.pqarchiver.com/latimes/search.html
29. Tino Balio, *Grand Design: Hollywood as a Modern Business Enterprise 1930–1939* (Berkeley, CA: University of California Press, 1995), 169.
30. "Publicity Man Takes Bride," *Los Angeles Times*, 1 July 1933, http://pqasb.pqarchiver.com/latimes/search.html
31. "A.W. Morris, Brokerage Firm Head, Dies at 72," *Los Angeles Times*, 22 August 1951, http://pqasb.pqarchiver.com/latimes/search.html
32. Wedding to Be Event of March," *Los Angeles Times*, 23 January 1927, http://pqasb.pqarchiver.com/latimes/search.html
33. Jody Jacobs, "Nostalgia Night at the Grove," *Los Angeles Times*, 22 August 1971, http://pqasb.pqarchiver.com/latimes/search.html
34. Dennis McLellan and Myrna Oliver, "Sybil Brand, 104; Fought for Jailed Women," *Los Angeles Times*, 19 February 2004, http://pqasb.pqarchiver.com/latimes/search.html
35. Burt A. Folkart, "Last of Old-Time Hollywood Press Agents Ex-Studio Publicist Harry Brand Dies," *Los Angeles Times*, 23 February 1989, http://pqasb.pqarchiver.com/latimes/search.html
36. Bennet Cerf, "Babes in Hollywood," *Los Angeles Times*, 23 March 1952, http://pqasb.pqarchiver.com/latimes/search.html
37. "Singer Marries Hotel Employee," *Los Angeles Times*, 16 October 1935, http://pqasb.pqarchiver.com/latimes/search.html; "Atty. Norman Brand Wed in Home of Judge," *Los Angeles Times*, 2 December 1956, http://pqasb.pqarchiver.com/latimes/search.html
38. "Harry Brand," *Variety*, 1 March 1989, 83.
39. Maggie Savoy, "The Can-Do Lady Who Does It All," *Los Angeles Times*, 16 February 1969, http://pqasb.pqarchiver.com/latimes/search.html
40. Ibid.
41. Harry Robert Brand, Death certificate no. 389 90 0802 (22 February 1989), informational copy from Los Angeles County Registrar-Recorder/County Clerk.
42. "George Brand," *Variety*, 10 May 1989, 129.
43. Sybil Brand, Death certificate no. 32004 9007985 (17 February 2004), informational copy from Los Angeles County Registrar-Recorder/County Clerk.

CHRYSTINE FRANCIS

1. Tacoma City Directory, 1911.
2. "Mrs. R.V. Grace," *Tacoma News Tribune*, 16 February 1952, 2.
3. Los Angeles City Directory, 1921.
4. "Morosco's Success Draws a Crowd," *Oakland Tribune*, 26 December 1922, 11.
5. "Opinions on Short Subjects," *Motion Picture News*, 30 January 1926, 590.
6. Isabel Stuyvesant, "Society of Cinemaland," *Los Angeles Times*, 13 September 1925, http://pqasb.pqarchiver.com/latimes/search.html; "Scrapping Mate Ideal of 'Fatty,'" *Los Angeles Times*, 5 October 1929, http://pqasb.pqarchiver.com/latimes/search.html.
7. *The Day Buster Smiled*, 30.
8. McCarthy, Mary Eunice. *Hands of Hollywood* (Hollywood, CA: Photoplay Research Bureau, 1929), 36.
9. *The Day Buster Smiled*, 30.
10. Dick Grace, *Visibility Unlimited* (New York: Longmans, Green, 1950), 87–90.
11. Ibid., 206.
12. "Coming Marriages," *Billboard*, 15 February 1930, 95; Grace Kingsley, "And Joy," *Los Angeles Times*, 16 March 1930, http://pqasb.pqarchiver.com/latimes/search.html
13. "Stunt Flyer Weds Secretary," *Los Angeles Times*, 11 June 1938, http://pqasb.pqarchiver.com/latimes/search.html.
14. Dick Grace, *Visibility Unlimited*, 211.
15. Louella O. Parsons, "'Applejack' Role Slated for Benny," *Charleston Gazette*, 13 June 1938, 12.
16. Dick Grace, *I Am Still Alive* (New York: Rand McNally, 1931), 19.
17. Ibid., 21.
18. Dick Grace, *Visibility Unlimited*, 98.
19. Ibid., 96
20. Ibid., 178, 205.
21. Ibid., 188.
22. "Mrs. R.V. Grace," *Tacoma News Tribune*, 16 February 1952, 2.
23. Richard V. Grace, *California Death Index, 1940–1997* (25 June 1965) (Online: The Generations Network, Inc., 2012) [Digital scan of original records in the State of California Department of Health Services Center for Health Statistics, Sacramento, CA], subscription database, http://www.ancestry.com, accessed 1 November 2013.

FRED GABOURIE

1. Keaton and Samuels, *My Wonderful World of Slapstick*, 204–5.
2. His death certificate says he was born in 1881, but his draft registration says 1879. I'm using the date he gave himself.
3. Fred W. Gabourie, letter to author, sent 17 January 2004.
4. Fred Gabourie, Military Personnel Records. National Personnel Records Center, St. Louis, MO, retrieved June 2003.
5. Department of Military and Veterans Affairs, Michigan, "The Spanish American War," http://www.michigan.gov/dmva/0,1607,7-126-2360_3003_3009-17032-,00.html, accessed 12/20/2010.
6. Gabourie, Military Personnel Records.

7. Fred W. Gabourie, letter to author, sent 17 January 2004.
8. "Success in Hollywood," *Los Angeles Times*, 15 October 1939, http://pqasb.pqarchiver.com/latimes/search.html
9. "Walter Browne's Play, 'Everywoman,' Pictorially Lovely and Elaborately Produced," *New York Times*, 10 February 1911, http://query.nytimes.com/search/site search
10. Fred W. Gabourie, letter to author, sent 17 January 2004.
11. Ibid.
12. "*Everywoman* In London," *New York Times*, 13 September 1912, http://query.nytimes.com/search/sitesearch
13. "*Everywoman* At Majestic," *Los Angeles Times*, 1 March 1915, http://pqasb.pqarchiver.com/latimes/search.html
14. Fred Gabourie, *Index to Register of Voters, Los Angeles County, California, 1916* (Online: The Generations Network, Inc., 2009) [Digital scan of original records in the California State Library. Sacramento, California], subscription database, http://www.ancestry.com, accessed 20 December 2010.
15. Fred W. Gabourie, letter to author, sent 17 January 2004.
16. Fred Gabourie, *World War I Draft Registration Cards, 1917–1918* (6 September 1918) (Online: The Generations Network, Inc., 2007) [Digital scan of original records in the National Archives, Washington, D.C.], subscription database, http://www.ancestry.com, accessed 12 November 2003.
17. "Fred Gabourie, Art Director," *Wid's Yearbook, 1920–21*, 479.
18. Rudi Blesh, *Keaton* (New York: Macmillan, 1966), 154.
19. Ibid., 195–6.
20. Ibid., 234.
21. "Technical Crew at Work on Buster Keaton Sets," n.d. Fred W. Gabourie's files.
22. Ibid., 290.
23. John Gillett and James Blue, "Keaton at Venice," in Kevin B. Sweeney, *Buster Keaton Interviews* (Jackson, MS: University Press of Mississippi, 2007), 226–227.
24. Keaton and Samuels, *My Wonderful World of Slapstick*, 205.
25. "Studio Construction Experts Make Film Dreams Come True," *M.G.M. Studio News*, 1 no. 6 (25 December 1933).
26. Fred W. Gabourie, letter to author, sent 17 January 2004.
27. Mary Barbara Dietrick, Death certificate no.7097 009144 (5 March 1970), informational copy from Los Angeles County Registrar-Recorder/County Clerk.
28. Fred W. Gabourie, *California Birth Index, 1905–1995* (October 1922) (Online: The Generations Network, Inc., 2007) [Digital scan of original records in the State of California Department of Health Services Center for Health Statistics, Sacramento, CA], subscription database, http://www.ancestry.com/, accessed 21 July 2007.
29. Fred W. Gabourie, letter to author, sent 17 January 2004.
30. Leslie Lieber, "TV's Big Boom in Brawls," *Los Angeles Times*, 15 March 1959, http://pqasb.pqarchiver.com/latimes/search.html
31. Fred W. Gabourie, letter to author, sent 17 January 2004.
32. "California's First Indian Judge Named; Other Vacancies Filled," *Los Angeles Times*, 18 January 1976, http://pqasb.pqarchiver.com/latimes/search.html
33. Fred Gabourie, Death certificate no. 1901 3891 (1 March 1951), informational copy from Los Angeles County Registrar-Recorder/County Clerk.
34. Evelyn Frances Gabourie, Death certificate no. 7097 025005 (8 June 1969), informational copy from Los Angeles County Registrar-Recorder/County Clerk.
35. Michael L. Stephens, *Art Directors in Cinema: A Worldwide Biographical Dictionary* (Jefferson, NC: McFarland, 1998), 112.

36. *The Day Buster Smiled*, 44.
37. Fred W. Gabourie, letter to author, sent 17 January 2004.

BERT E. JACKSON

1. Bert Jackson, *World War I Draft Registration Cards, 1917–1918* (5 June 1918) (Online: The Generations Network, Inc., 2009) [Digital scan of original records in the National Archives, Washington, D.C.], subscription database, http://www.ancestry.com, accessed 1 December 2010.
2. Bert Jackson, *California County Marriages, 1850–1952* (9 January 1917) (Online: FamilySearch Historical Collections, 2011) [Digital copies of originals housed in the clerks' offices of the district courts in various counties throughout California. FHL microfilm, Family History Library, Salt Lake City, Utah], https://www.familysearch.org, accessed 16 January 2012.
3. Earl Wilson, "Judy Blubbers Like a Baby at Stage Debut of Daughter, 15," *Long Beach Press Telegram*, 26 July 1961, B-13.
4. "Buster Keaton in *Seven Chances*," *Davenport Democrat and Leader*, 17 May 1925, 18.
5. *The Day Buster Smiled*, 44.
6. Burt [sic] E. Jackson, Death certificate no. 7053 3633 (18 February 1964), informational copy from Los Angeles County Registrar-Recorder/County Clerk.
7. Ruth Lillian Jackson, Death certificate no. 1901 9893 (13 September 1929), informational copy from Los Angeles County Registrar-Recorder/County Clerk.
8. Burt [sic] E. Jackson, death certificate.
9. Mary Dorothy Jackson, Death certificate no. 7053 18271 (4 May 1965), informational copy from Los Angeles County Registrar-Recorder/County Clerk.

J. SHERMAN KELL

1. Dev Jennings was a manufacturers' agent for the Southern Pacific Railroad, but he didn't work on the trains.
2. John Sherman Kell, *Illinois County Marriages, 1810–1934* (1909) (Online: FamilySearch Historical Collections, 2011) [Digital copies of originals housed in the clerks' offices of the district courts in various counties throughout California. FHL microfilm, Family History Library, Salt Lake City, Utah], https://www.familysearch.org, accessed 12 May 2012.
3. Alan R. Lind, *From the Lakes to the Gulf: The Illinois Central Railroad Story: An Illustrated History of the Main Line of Mid-America* (Park Forest, IL: Transport History Press, 1993), 50.
4. John Sherman Kell, *World War I Draft Registration Cards, 1917–1918* (12 September 1918) (Online: The Generations Network, Inc., 2007) [Digital scan of original records in the National Archives, Washington, D.C.], subscription database, http://www.ancestry.com, accessed 27 March 2007.
5. Lind, *From the Lakes to the Gulf*, 50.
6. Los Angeles City Directory, 1921.
7. Los Angeles City Directory, 1922.
8. "Buster Keaton in *Seven Chances*," *Davenport Democrat and Leader*, 17 May 1925, 18.
9. Kevin Brownlow, *The Parade's Gone By...* (Berkeley: University of California Press, 1968), 484–5.
10. John Sherman Kell, *World War II Draft Registration Cards, 1942* (Online: FamilySearch Historical Collections, 2011) [Digital scan of original records in the

National Archives, Washington, D.C.], https://www.familysearch.org, accessed 31 December 2011.

11. Kell, John Sherman. Death certificate no. 1917297 12699 (26 August 1951), informational copy from Los Angeles County Registrar-Recorder/County Clerk.

12. Kell, Ethel V. *California Death Index* (26 July 1961) (Online: The Generations Network, Inc., 2010) [Digital scan of original records in the State of California Department of Health Services, Center for Health Statistics, Sacramento], subscription database, http://www.ancestry.com, accessed 2 January 2011.

ERNIE ORSATTI

1. Rudi Blesh, *Keaton* (New York: Macmillan, 1966), 148.
2. "Ernie Orsatti," *Baseball Reference*, http://www.baseball-reference.com/players/o/orsater01.shtml, accessed 20 September 2003.
3. "Bank for Foreigners," *Los Angeles Times*, 21 September 1904, http://pqasb.pqarchiver.com/latimes/search.html
4. "Money Flows to Sufferers," *Los Angeles Times*, 1 January 1909, http://pqasb.pqarchiver.com/latimes/search.html
5. "Asks Support Without Him," *Los Angeles Times*, 24 June 1920, http://pqasb.pqarchiver.com/latimes/search.html
6. "Steals Show from Martin," *Sporting News*, 18 August 1932, http://www.paperofrecord.com/search.asp
7. Robert E. Hood, *The Gashouse Gang* (New York: Morrow, 1976), 99.
8. Rudi Blesh, *Keaton* (New York: Macmillan, 1966), 233.
9. Bishop, Christopher. "An Interview with Buster Keaton," *Film Quarterly*, Fall 1958, 22.
10. Keaton and Samuels, *My Wonderful World of Slapstick*, 169.
11. Eleanor Keaton and Jeffrey Vance, *Buster Keaton Remembered* (New York: Harry N. Abrams, 2001), 172.
12. "Fanning with Lanigan," *Sporting News*, 3 January 1929, http://www.paperofrecord.com/search.asp
13. "Steals Show from Martin," *Sporting News*, 18 August 1932, http://www.paperofrecord.com/search.asp
14. "Assert Briber Has Confessed," *Los Angeles Times*, 14 July 1922, http://pqasb.pqarchiver.com/latimes/search.html
15. "Hold Suspects in Liquor Ring," *Los Angeles Times*, 13 July 1922, http://pqasb.pqarchiver.com/latimes/search.html
16. "Orsatti Plans Novel Defense," *Los Angeles Times*, 20 July 1922, http://pqasb.pqarchiver.com/latimes/search.html
17. "Federal Court to be Busy," *Los Angeles Times*, 4 November 1923, http://pqasb.pqarchiver.com/latimes/search.html
18. "Twenty Years for Orsatti," *Los Angeles Times*, 6 November 1923, http://pqasb.pqarchiver.com/latimes/search.html
19. "Orsatti Loses Probation Plea," *Los Angeles Times*, 21 August 1925, http://pqasb.pqarchiver.com/latimes/search.html
20. "Morris Orsatti Seeks Probation on Bribe Charges," *Los Angeles Times*, 9 August 1925, http://pqasb.pqarchiver.com/latimes/search.html
21. "Morris Orsatti Out on Parole," *Los Angeles Times*, 28 August 1928, http://pqasb.pqarchiver.com/latimes/search.html
22. Morris Orsatti, Prisoner no. 5414 (4 September 1925), McNeil Island Penitentiary Records of Prisoners Received. (Online: The Generations Network, Inc., 2009) [Digital scan of original records in the Records of the Bureau of Prisons, Na-

tional Archives, Washington, D.C.], subscription database, http://www.ancestry.com/, accessed 20 September 2010.

23. "Morris Orsatti Out on Parole," *Los Angeles Times*, 28 August 1928.

24. Los Angeles City Directories, 1932–1942.

25. "Deaths, Funeral Announcements," *Los Angeles Times*, 20 August 1949, http://pqasb.pqarchiver.com/latimes/search.html

26. "Steals Show from Martin," *Sporting News*, 18 August 1932, http://www.paperofrecord.com/search.asp

27. Murray, Feg. "Another Walloping Wop," *Los Angeles Times*, 16 January 1929, http://pqasb.pqarchiver.com/latimes/search.html. It's interesting that the sports reporters never mentioned his family's legal entanglements. Either they were polite, or they didn't read the other sections of the paper.

28. "Red Caps Rushed New Hitter to Cards to Help Him Deliver," *Sporting News*, 10 January 1962. http://www.paperofrecord.com/search.asp

29. Ernest Ralph Orsatti, *California County Marriages, 1850–1952* (21 January 1929) (Online: FamilySearch Historical Collections, 2011) [Digital copies of originals housed in the clerks' offices of the district courts in various counties throughout California. FHL microfilm, Family History Library, Salt Lake City, Utah], https://www.familysearch.org, accessed 3 February 2013.

30. "Orsatti, Cardinal Player, Sues Wife," *Los Angeles Times*, 8 February 1934, http://pqasb.pqarchiver.com/latimes/search.html

31. "League Fielder Tells Woes and Wins Divorce," *Los Angeles Times*, 17 February 1934, http://pqasb.pqarchiver.com/latimes/search.html

32. "Ernie Orsatti," *Baseball Reference*, http://www.baseball-reference.com/players/o/orsater01.shtml, accessed 20 September 2003.

33. Steals Show...," *Sporting News*, 18 August 1932. 34. Ibid.

35. "Orsatti's Hollywood Hues Dazzled Gashouse Gang," *Sporting News*, 5 February 1947, http://www.paperofrecord.com/search.asp

36. Robert E. Hood, *The Gashouse Gang* (New York: Morrow, 1976), 100.

37. Ibid.

38. Pat Patten, "Snapshots of the Stars," *Sporting News*, 9 March 1933, http://www.paperofrecord.com/search.asp

39. J.G. Taylor Spark, "Three and One," *Sporting News*, 7 June 1934, http://www.paperofrecord.com/search.asp

40. Sanderson Beck, "Death on the Diamond," *Movie Mirrors*, 1999, http://www.san.beck.org/MM/1934/DeathOnDiamond.html, accessed 29 December 2010.

41. Hood, *The Gashouse Gang*, 99.

42. The name Gashouse Gang was given to them by Chicago sportswriter Warren Brown because "a team that plays the game for all it's worth can't keep uniforms clean through a three-week trip," said Frankie Frisch. (Hood, *The Gashouse Gang*, 143.)

43. J.G. Taylor Spark, "Three and One," *Sporting News*, 7 June 1934, http://www.paperofrecord.com/search.asp

44. "What Would Diz Earn Today?," *Sporting News*, 10 August 1974, http://www.paperofrecord.com/search.asp

45. "Cardinals Timeline," *St. Louis Cardinals*, http://stlouis.cardinals.mlb.com/stl/history/timeline.jsp, accessed 18 February 2005.

46. "St. Louis Cardinals Considered Heavy Favorites to Repeat in National Loop," *Los Angeles Times*, 3 March 1935, http://pqasb.pqarchiver.com/latimes/search.html

47. "What the Waivers Say to Redbirds," *Sporting News*, 19 December 1935, http://www.paperofrecord.com/search.asp

48. Dick Farrington, "Brownie Big Shots Backfire on Terms," *Sporting News*, 27 February 1936, http://www.paperofrecord.com/search.asp

49. Philip K. Scheuer, "Agent Vic Orsatti Becomes Producer of Own Movies," *Los Angeles Times*, 30 June 1957, http://pqasb.pqarchiver.com/latimes/search.html

50. "Income Tax Liens Filed on Orsatti," *Los Angeles Times*, 27 August 1925, http://pqasb.pqarchiver.com/latimes/search.html; "Fourteen Named in True Bills," *Los Angeles Times*, 4 May 1928, http://pqasb.pqarchiver.com/latimes/search.html; Samuel Marx, *Mayer and Thalberg, the Make Believe Saints* (New York: Random House, 1975), 141.

51. "Frank Orsatti," *Variety*, 21 May 1947, 10.

52. J.G. Taylor Spark, "Three and One," *Sporting News*, 7 June 1934, http://www.paperofrecord.com/search.asp

53. "Ernie Orsatti," *Sporting News*, 7 February 1935, http://www.paperofrecord.com/search.asp

54. Hood, *The Gashouse Gang*, 99.

55. Ernest Ralph Orsatti, *California County Marriages, 1850–1952* (24 September 1938) (Online: FamilySearch Historical Collections, 2011) [Digital copies of originals housed in the clerks' offices of the district courts in various counties throughout California. FHL microfilm, Family History Library, Salt Lake City, Utah], https://www.familysearch.org, accessed 3 February 2013.

56. "Change in Locale," *Los Angeles Times*, 17 December 1942, http://pqasb.pqarchiver.com/latimes/search.html

57. "Music," *Time Magazine*, 30 March 1936, 65.

58. Ibid.

59. Read Kendall, "Around and About in Hollywood," *Los Angeles Times*, 29 June 1936, http://pqasb.pqarchiver.com/latimes/search.html

60. Ibid.

61. Edwin Schallert, "Wendy Barrie, Ratoff Set for 'Love Flight,'" *Los Angeles Times*, 31 July 1936, http://pqasb.pqarchiver.com/latimes/search.html

62. "Singer Seeks Nuptial License," *Los Angeles Times*, 21 September 1938, http://pqasb.pqarchiver.com/latimes/search.html; "James Stagliano, 1912–1987," *International Horn Society Online*, http://www.hornsociety.org/ihs-people/honoraries/67-james-stagliano-1912-1987, accessed 28 May 2011.

63. Jimmie Fidler, "In Hollywood," *Los Angeles Times*, 18 January 1940, http://pqasb.pqarchiver.com/latimes/search.html

64. "Puck Stars Open Practice," *Los Angeles Times*, 4 December 1938, http://pqasb.pqarchiver.com/latimes/search.html

65. "Ice Hockey League Formed," *Los Angeles Times*, 13 December 1938, http://pqasb.pqarchiver.com/latimes/search.html

66. "Pro Hockey to Open Here on Jan. 29," *Los Angeles Times*, 8 January 1939, http://pqasb.pqarchiver.com/latimes/search.html

67. Bill Henry, "Comics Win 'Ball Game,'" *Los Angeles Times*, 18 July 1937, http://pqasb.pqarchiver.com/latimes/search.html

68. Kendall, Read. "Around and About in Hollywood," *Los Angeles Times*, 12 May 1938, http://pqasb.pqarchiver.com/latimes/search.html

69. "Stars Finally Obtain Orsatti," *Los Angeles Times*, 10 April 1939, http://pqasb.pqarchiver.com/latimes/search.html

70. Bob Ray, "Reinstatement of Orsatti Paves Way for Purchase by Hollywood Club," *Los Angeles Times*, 14 March 1939, http://pqasb.pqarchiver.com/latimes/search.html; Bob Hunter, "Orsatti and Brandt Join Stars on Eve of Opener," *Sporting News*, 30 March 1939, http://www.paperofrecord.com/search.asp

71. Read Kendall, "Movie Celebrities Attend Opening of Gilmore Field," *Los Angeles Times*, 3 May 1939, http://pqasb.pqarchiver.com/latimes/search.html

72. Jeff Hause, "Hollywood Stars: A History," *Sports Hollywood*, http://www.sportshollywood.com/hollywoodstars.html, accessed 30 December 2010.

73. Bob Ray, "Sports X-Ray," *Los Angeles Times*, 30 July 1939, http://pqasb.pqarchiver.com/latimes/search.html

74. Bob Ray, "Sports X-Ray," *Los Angeles Times*, 13 August 1939, http://pqasb.pqarchiver.com/latimes/search.html

75. "Handy Orsatti Capitalizes on Hobby in Opening His Beverly Hills Business," *Sporting News*, 5 February 1947, http://www.paperofrecord.com/search.asp

76. "Duncans to Star Tonight," *Los Angeles Times*, 26 October 1942, http://pqasb.pqarchiver.com/latimes/search.html

77. "Inez Orsatti," *Variety*, 26 April 1944, 6.

78. Jerry Haendiges, "Jerry's Vintage Radio Logs," *The Vintage Radio Place*S2008 http://www.otrsite.com/radiolog/index.html, accessed 31 December 2010.

79. "Handy Orsatti..," *Sporting News*, 5 February 1947. 80. "Frank Orsatti," *Variety*, 21 May 1947, 10.

81. "Al Orsatti," *Variety*, 13 July 1949, 1.

82. Philip K. Scheuer, "Agent Vic Orsatti Becomes Producer of Own Movies," *Los Angeles Times*, 30 June 1957, http://pqasb.pqarchiver.com/latimes/search.html

83. "Opera Singer Sues Hollywood Talent Agent for Divorce," *Los Angeles Times*, 2 February 1952, http://pqasb.pqarchiver.com/latimes/search.html

84. "Singer Divorces Silent Husband," *Los Angeles Times*, 27 February 1952, http://pqasb.pqarchiver.com/latimes/search.html

85. "Vic Orsatti's Ex-Wife Weds," *Los Angeles Times*, 27 June 1952, http://pqasb.pqarchiver.com/latimes/search.html; "Inez Pierson," *Variety*, 11 December 1986, 27.

86. "Ernie Orsatti in Hospital," *Sporting News*, 26 December 1956, http://www.paperofrecord.com/search.asp

87. "Old Heroes Battle at Coogan's Bluff," *New York Times*, 31 July 1950, http://query.nytimes.com/search/sitesearch

88. "Hefty Orsatti Gets Needle from Quipster Mancuso," *Sporting News*, 17 August 1960, http://www.paperofrecord.com/search.asp

89. "Handy Orsatti..," *Sporting News*, 5 February 1947.

90. Stan Mandel, "Ex-Gashouse Gang Member Picks Cards," *Los Angeles Times*, 7 October 1964, http://pqasb.pqarchiver.com/latimes/search.html

91. Los Angeles City Directories, 1958.

92. Mandel, Stan. "Opinion Divided on Night Court," *Los Angeles Times*, 9 May 1965, http://pqasb.pqarchiver.com/latimes/search.html

93. Fred W. Gabourie, Unpublished, undated interview with Marion Meade, Special Collections, University of Iowa Library.

94. Los Angeles City Directories, 1982.

95. Ernest Ralph Orsatti, Death certificate no. 70970035745 (4 September 1968), informational copy from Los Angeles County Registrar-Recorder/County Clerk.

96. Lynda Farrell, "Biography for Ernie F. Orsatti," *Internet Movie Database*, http://www.imdb.com/name/nm0650683/bio, accessed 18 May 2004.

97. "Frank Orsatti, Actor, Stuntman," *Variety*, 12 January 2005, http://www.variety.com

Costume Designers

1. Walter J. Israel, *California County Marriages, 1850–1952* (15 December 1912) (Online: FamilySearch Historical Collections, 2011) [Digital copies of originals housed in the clerks' offices of the district courts in various counties throughout California. FHL microfilm, Family History Library, Salt Lake City, Utah], https://www.familysearch.org, accessed 16 January 2012.

2. *Souvenir: Picture Player Camera Man's Ball Under the Auspices of the Static Club of America*, 16 January 1914.
3. "Women's Work, Women's Clubs," *Los Angeles Times*, 11 May 1916, http://pqasb.pqarchiver.com/latimes/search.html
4. Walter Jay Israel, *World War I Draft Registration Cards, 1917–1918* (11 September 1918) (Online: The Generations Network, Inc., 2007) [Digital scan of original records in the National Archives, Washington, D.C.], subscription database, http://www.ancestry.com, accessed 5 May 2007.
5. "Many Crafts Work Unseen in Good Picture," *Los Angeles Times*, 8 April 1923, http://pqasb.pqarchiver.com/latimes/search.html
6. "Screen," *New York Times*, 25 March 1923, http://query.nytimes.com/search/sitesearch
7. 1923 was quite a year for period films in Joseph Schenck's company, First National. Constance Talmadge's *Dangerous Maid*, set in 17th Century England, came out in the same month (12/1923) as *Our Hospitality*. There is no costume credit for it.
8. "Schenck Spends $80,000 in Furniture and Costumes for Norma's New Film," *Camera!*, 31 March 1923, 10.
9. Helen Rose, *"Just Make Them Beautiful"*: The Many Worlds of a Designing Woman *(Santa Monica, CA: Dennis-Landman Publishers, 1976)*, 30.
10. "Color to Rule Play Start," *Los Angeles Times*, 5 September 1936, http://pqasb.pqarchiver.com/latimes/search.html
11. Walter Jay Israel, *World War II Draft Registration Cards, 1942* (Online: FamilySearch Historical Collections, 2011) [Digital scan of original records in the National Archives, Washington, D.C.], https://www.familysearch.org, accessed 19 January 2012.
12. "Rose Marie Gown Shop Styles Allure," *Los Angeles Times*, 8 July 1945, http://pqasb.pqarchiver.com/latimes/search.html
13. "More Shows Asked for Men Overseas," *New York Times*, 20 April 1945; Burns Mantle, *Best Plays of 1945–46* (New York: Dodd, Mead, 1946), 398; "Opera Costumes Heavily Insured, *Los Angeles Times*, 19 June 1947; "Rehearsals Under Way for Civic Light Opera, *Los Angeles Times*, 17 April 1953; "Costumes to be Feature of 'Great Waltz,'" *Los Angeles Times*, 22 May 1953.
14. Walter Jay Israel, Death certificate no. 7097 001083 (6 January 1970), informational copy from Los Angeles County Registrar-Recorder/County Clerk.
15. Ethel W. Israel, Death certificate no. 0190 008232 (2 March 1974), informational copy from Los Angeles County Registrar-Recorder/County Clerk.
16. Pat Kirkham, ed., *Women Designers in the U.S.A. 1900–2000* (New Haven, CT: Yale University Press, 2000), 249–50.
17. Anne Walker, "Dressing the Movies," *Women's Home Companion*, May 1921, 24.
18. Clare Smith, *Missouri Marriage Records, 1805–2002* (24 August 1898) (Online: The Generations Network, Inc., 2013) [Digital scan of original records in the Missouri State Archives. Jefferson City, Missouri], subscription database, http://www.ancestry.com, accessed 1 December 2013.
19. Otis Hunley, *Missouri Marriage Records, 1805–2002* (21 March 1903) (Online: The Generations Network, Inc., 2013) [Digital scan of original records in the Missouri State Archives. Jefferson City, Missouri], subscription database, http://www.ancestry.com, accessed 1 December 2013.
20. "Maxwell O. Hunley," *Los Angeles Times*, 21 December 1990, http://pqasb.pqarchiver.com/latimes/search.html
21. Marriage Record for Marshall Carriere and Clara Hunley, http://www.rootsweb.ancestry.com, accessed 1 December 2013.

22. "City and County," *Bakersfield Morning Echo*, 29 September 1911, 8.
23. Los Angeles City Directory, 1942.
24. Sacramento City Directory, 1929.
25. "Abram C. Smith," *U.S. National Homes for Disabled Volunteer Soldiers, 1866–1938* (Online: The Generations Network, Inc., 2007) [Digital scan of original records of the Department of Veterans Affairs in the National Archives, Washington, D.C.], subscription database, http://www.ancestry.com, accessed 1 December 2013.
26. Walker, *Women's Home Companion*, 24.
27. Edward Maeder and David Ehrenstein, "Filmography," in Edward Maeder, *Hollywood and History Costume Design in Film* (New York: Thames and Hudson, 1987), 220.
28. Adele Witely Fletcher, "Clare West, Costumer to the Stars, Tells Tales Out of School," *Movie Weekly*, 29 November 1924, 27.
29. "Decalogue Cast Made Real Army," *Los Angeles Times*, 17 January 1924, http://pqasb.pqarchiver.com/latimes/search.html
30. "Seek Data for Great Film Idea," *Los Angeles Times*, 21 December 1922, http://pqasb.pqarchiver.com/latimes/search.html
31. "Copied from Films," *Moving Picture World*, 3 March 1923, 33.
32. "Coast Brevities," *Film Daily*, 9 September 1923, 15.
33. "Constance Dazzles in Her New Production," *Los Angeles Times*, January 12, 1924, http://pqasb.pqarchiver.com/latimes/search.html
34. Alice Tildesley, "A Creator of Personalities," *Movie Weekly*, 24 May 1924, 11, 31.
35. "Clare West," *Variety*, 9 December 1925, 56.
36. Clare B. West, Death certificate no. 3607–338 (13 March 1961), informational copy from San Bernardino County Registrar-Recorder/County Clerk.
37. Costume Designers' Guild, "Hall of Fame Award," http://www.costumedesignersguild.com/aw-archive/aw-cat.asp?awardtype=3, accessed 27 February 2011.

Arbuckle's Crew

1. Reed Heustis, "Madman Runs Fat Arbuckle's Studio—Sure, It's Lou Anger," *Los Angeles Herald*, 3 November 1919, part 2, 1, 32.
2. Brent E. Walker, *Mack Sennett's Fun Factory* (Jefferson, NC: McFarland, 2010), 585.
3. Harry Williams, Death certificate no. 1209 (15 May 1922), informational copy from Alameda County Recorder.
4. Paul Hubert Conlon, *World War I Draft Registration Cards, 1917–1918* (4 June 1917) (Online: The Generations Network, Inc., 2012) [Digital scan of original records in the National Archives, Washington, D.C.], subscription database, http://www.ancestry.com, accessed 23 December 2012.
5. Ronald L. Davis, *William S. Hart: Projecting the American West* (Norman: University of Oklahoma Press, 2003), 124.
6. Paul Hubert Conlon, *World War II Draft Registration Cards, 1942* (Online: FamilySearch Historical Collections, 2012) [Digital scan of original records in the National Archives, Washington, D.C.], https://www.familysearch.org, accessed 23 December 2012.
7. Paul H. Conlon, *California Death Index, 1940–1997* (30 January 1961) (Online: The Generations Network, Inc., 2012) [Digital scan of original records in the State of California Department of Health Services Center for Health Statistics, Sacramento, CA], subscription database, http://www.ancestry.com, accessed 25 August 2012.

GEORGE PETERS

1. "Aviator Peters with Metro," *Moving Picture World*, 5 February 1916, 763.
2. "George W. Peters Joins American Forces," *Moving Picture World*, 8 June 1912, 946.
3. "Peters to Photograph Burr Feature Productions in 1922," *Moving Picture World*, 31 December 1921, 1096.
4. *Souvenir: Picture Player Camera Man's Ball Under the Auspices of the Static Club of America*, 16 January 1914.
5. "Up in the Air Again," *New York Dramatic Mirror*, 29 January 1916, 54.
6. "Aviator Peters with Metro," *Moving Picture World*, 5 February 1916, 763.
7. Michael Peters, e-mail message to author, 11 November 2004.
8. "Screen People and Plays," *New York Times*, 19 December 1920, http://query.nytimes.com/search/sitesearch
9. "New Cameraman Shooting Hines' 'The Brown Derby,'" *Moving Picture World*. 1 May 1926, 41.
10. George W. Peters, Death certificate no. 13098 (18 October 1935), informational copy from Los Angeles County Registrar-Recorder/County Clerk.
11. "Rites Arranged for Cameraman," *Los Angeles Times*, 24 October 1935, http://pqasb.pqarchiver.com/latimes/search.html

JOSEPH ANTHONY ROACH

1. "An Essanay Elopement," *New York Dramatic Mirror*, 4 February 1914, 30.
2. Grace Kingsley, "Studio," *Los Angeles Times*, 4 February 1917, http://pqasb.pqarchiver.com/latimes/search.html
3. "Roach on 24-Hour Notice," *Moving Picture World*, 27 October 1917, 544.
4. Joseph Anthony Roach, *World War I Draft Registration Cards, 1917–1918* (Online: The Generations Network, Inc., 2007) [Digital scan of original records in the National Archives, Washington, D.C.], subscription database, http://www.ancestry.com, accessed 16 May 2007.
5. Grace Kingsley, "Quinns' Theater System Is on Private Capital," *Los Angeles Times*, 21 October 1917, http://pqasb.pqarchiver.com/latimes/search.html
6. "Where to Find People You Know," *Camera!*, 5 January 1919, 3.
7. Joseph A. Roach, Military Personnel Records. National Personnel Records Center, St. Louis, MO, retrieved 2 August 2007.
8. "Cinema Writer Made Artistic Song of Oaths," *Los Angeles Times*, 10 February 1921, http://pqasb.pqarchiver.com/latimes/search.html
9. Ibid.
10. "Brother of Writer Wed to Actress," *Los Angeles Times*, 26 January 1928, http://pqasb.pqarchiver.com/latimes/search.html
11. Marion Q. Toy, "Expresses Herself," *Los Angeles Times*, 20 December 1931, http://pqasb.pqarchiver.com/latimes/search.html
12. "Mrs. Felix Hughes," *Los Angeles Times*, 14 May 1941, http://pqasb.pqarchiver.com/latimes/search.html
13. Joseph A. Roach, *World War II Draft Registration Cards, 1942* (Online: FamilySearch Historical Collections, 2011) [Digital scan of original records in the National Archives, Washington, D.C.], https://www.familysearch.org, accessed 19 January 2012.
14. Theresa Roach, Death certificate no. 1901 7681 (30 May 1941), informational copy from Los Angeles County Registrar-Recorder/County Clerk.
15. Joseph Anthony Roach, Death certificate no. 1992 5139282 (15 April 1945), informational copy from Los Angeles County Registrar-Recorder/County Clerk.

Herbert Warren

1. Herbert Warren, *World War I Draft Registration Cards, 1917–1918* (12 September 1918) (Online: The Generations Network, Inc., 2007) [Digital scan of original records in the National Archives, Washington, D.C.], subscription database, http://www.ancestry.com, accessed 16 April 2007.
2. "Collected for the Curious," *Washington Post*, 22 July 1906, 4.
3. "Orpheum Theater," *Deseret Evening News*, 27 November 1909, 16.
4. "Fifth Avenue," *Variety*, 31 October 1913, 2.
5. "Show Reviews," *Variety*, 26 November 1915, 17.
6. "Valerie Bergere Weds Herbert Warren; Both Leave for Coast," (3 November 1917) in Herbert Warren Clipping file, Billy Rose Theater Collection, New York Public Library for the Performing Arts, retrieved 19 January 2012.
7. "Warren to Make Pictures," *Moving Picture World*, 21 September 1918, 1709.
8. "Royal," *Variety*, 8 November 1918, 21.
9. Herbert Warren Clipping file, Billy Rose Theater Collection, New York Public Library for the Performing Arts, retrieved 19 January 2012.
10. Herbert Warren, *World War II Draft Registration Cards, 1942* (Online: FamilySearch Historical Collections, 2011) [Digital scan of original records in the National Archives, Washington, D.C.], https://www.familysearch.org, accessed 19 January 2012.

Frank D. Williams

1. Herbert Feinstein, "Buster Keaton: An Interview," in Kevin B. Sweeney, *Buster Keaton Interviews* (Jackson, MS: University Press of Mississippi, 2007), 129.
2. "Cameraman Williams an Old-Timer," *Moving Picture World*, 26 May 1917, 1295.
3. Cal York, "How They Do It!," *Photoplay*, April 1926, 30.
4. York, "How They Do It!," *Photoplay*, 30.
5. "Static Club Officers, Directors, and Members," *Static Flashes*. 23 January 1915, 2.
6. "L-KO Kompany," *Static Flashes*. 13 March 1915, 3.
7. Brent E. Walker, *Mack Sennett's Fun Factory* (Jefferson, NC: McFarland, 2010), 583.
Wendy Warwick White, *Ford Sterling: The Life and Films* (Jefferson, NC: McFarland, 2007), 38.
8. "Frank D. Williams," *Static Flashes*, 3 April 1915, 2.
9. "Cameraman Williams an Old-Timer," *Moving Picture World*, 26 May 1917, 1295.
10. Rudi Blesh, *Keaton* (New York: Macmillan, 1966), p. 88
11. York, "How They Do It!," *Photoplay*, April 1926, 29–30.
12. Blesh, *Keaton*, 88.
13. York, "How They Do It!," *Photoplay*, 30.
14. Frank D. Williams, 1916, Method of Taking Motion Pictures. U.S. Patent 1,273,435 filed 22 May 1916, and issued 23 July 1918.
15. York, "How They Do It!," *Photoplay*, 31.
16. Don Shay, "Willis O'Brien—Creator of the Impossible," *Cinefex*, January 1982, 38.
17. York, "How They Do It!," *Photoplay*, 114.
18. "Cupid Gets 'Fatty' Arbuckle's Cameraman," *Moving Picture World*, 2 June 1917, 1445.

19. "Film Inventor Piles Up Woes," *Los Angeles Times*, 21 December 1927, http://pqasb.pqarchiver.com/latimes/search.html

20. "Inventor's Wife Asks Bonds Cut," *Los Angeles Times*, 8 December 1927, http://pqasb.pqarchiver.com/latimes/search.html

21. "Inventor's Case Hinges on Patents," *Los Angeles Times*, 14 December 1927, http://pqasb.pqarchiver.com/latimes/search.html; "Warn Inventor in Divorce on Fist Fight," *Los Angeles Evening Herald*, 9 December 1927, B1. 22. "Fight Enlivens Divorce Trial," *Los Angeles Times*, 9 December 1927, http://pqasb.pqarchiver.com/latimes/search.html

23. "Liquor Witness Arrested," *Los Angeles Times*, 16 December 1927, http://pqasb.pqarchiver.com/latimes/search.html

24. "Husband Finds Tables Turned," *Los Angeles Times*, 18 January 1928, http://pqasb.pqarchiver.com/latimes/search.html

25. *Williams v. Williams* D-47208 (Los Angeles County Superior Court 1930),

26. "Frank D. Williams," *Los Angeles Times*, 19 October 1961. http://pqasb.pqarchiver.com/latimes/search.html

27. Frank D. Williams, "Inventor Describes New Process," *International Photographer*, September 1932, 10.

28. "Turnbull Denies Prejudice," *Los Angeles Times*, 6 April 1932, http://pqasb.pqarchiver.com/latimes/search.html

29. "Officials Seek Film Fire Cause," *Los Angeles Times*, 29 November 1938, http://pqasb.pqarchiver.com/latimes/search.html

30. "Innovation in New Williams Laboratory," *American Cinematographer*, March 1941, 110–111, 134.

31. "Matte Process Suit Against Films Deferred," *Los Angeles Times*, 29 June 1928, http://pqasb.pqarchiver.com/latimes/search.html

32. "Film Unionists Named in Suit," *Los Angeles Times*, 23 January 1943, http://pqasb.pqarchiver.com/latimes/search.html; "Suit Against Union Dropped," *Los Angeles Times*, 10 October 1943, http://pqasb.pqarchiver.com/latimes/search.html

33. "Union Injunction Asked," *Los Angeles Times*, 18 September 1945, http://pqasb.pqarchiver.com/latimes/search.html; "Laboratory Sues Union," *Los Angeles Times*, 29 June 1946, http://pqasb.pqarchiver.com/latimes/search.html

34. "Expelled Collector Files $250,000 Action Against Camellia Society," *Los Angeles Times*, 16 August 1948, http://pqasb.pqarchiver.com/latimes/search.html

35. "Williams Laboratory," *International Motion Picture Almanac* (New York: Quigley, 1953–56).

36. "George Seid," *Los Angeles Times*, 28 November 1956, http://pqasb.pqarchiver.com/latimes/search.html

37. Frank Douglas Williams, Death certificate no. 5600 1333 (16 October 1961), informational copy from Ventura County Recorder.

Bibliography

American Film Institute. "AFI Catalog of Films." http://www.afi.com/members/catalog/.
Bengtson, John. *Silent Echoes: Discovering Early Hollywood Through the Films of Buster Keaton.* Santa Monica, CA: Santa Monica Press, 2000.
Bishop, Christopher. "The Great Stone Face." *Film Quarterly*, Fall 1958, 10–15.
Bishop, Christopher. "An Interview with Buster Keaton." *Film Quarterly*, Fall 1958, 15–22.
Blesh, Rudi. *Keaton.* New York: Macmillan, 1966.
Brownlow, Kevin. "The D.W. Griffith of Comedy." In *Projections 4½*, John Boorman and Walter Donohue, eds. London: Faber and Faber, 1995.
Brownlow, Kevin. *The Parade's Gone By...* Berkeley: University of California Press, 1968.
Brownlow, Kevin, and David Gill. *A Hard Act to Follow.* Thames Television PLC, 1987.
Dardis, Tom. *Keaton: The Man Who Wouldn't Lie Down.* New York: Scribner's, 1979.
The Day Buster Smiled. Cottage Grove, OR: Historical Society, 1998.
Dwyer, Ruth Anne. *Malcolm St. Clair: His Films, 1915–1948.* Lanham, MD: Scarecrow, 1996.
Gillett, John, and James Blue. "Keaton at Venice." *Sight and Sound*, Winter 65/66, 26–30.
Keaton, Buster, with Charles Samuels. *My Wonderful World of Slapstick.* New York: Doubleday, 1960.
Keaton, Eleanor, and Jeffrey Vance. *Buster Keaton Remembered.* New York: Harry N. Abrams, 2001.
Keaton Chronicle. (Quarterly newsletter of The Damfinos, the International Buster Keaton Society.) Winter 1993–Autumn 2013.
Kira, Gene. *The Unforgettable Sea of Cortez: Baja California's Golden Age, 1947–1977: The Life and Writings of Ray Cannon.* Torrance, CA: Cortez Publications, 1999.
Kline, Jim. *Complete Films of Buster Keaton.* New York: Carol Publishing Group, 1993.
Los Angeles City Directories, 1901–1942.
Meade, Marion. *Buster Keaton: Cut to the Chase.* New York: HarperCollins, 1995.

Neibaur, James L. *Arbuckle and Keaton: Their 14 Film Collaborations.* Jefferson, NC: McFarland, 2007.

Oderman, Stuart. *Roscoe "Fatty" Arbuckle: A Biography of the Silent Film Comedian, 1887–1933.* Jefferson, NC: McFarland, 1994.

Schwartz, Ben. "The Gag Man: Being a Discourse on Al Boasberg, Professional Jokesmith, His Manner, and Method." In *The Film Comedy Reader*, Gregg Rickman, ed. New York: Limelight Editions, 2001, 68–104.

Skretvedt, Randy. *Laurel and Hardy: The Magic Behind the Movies.* Beverly Hills, CA: Past Times Publishing, 1996.

Smith, Paul Gerald, III. "Paul Gerald Smith." *Vaudeville Times*, Summer 2001, 16–20.

Souvenir: Picture Player Camera Man's Ball Under the Auspices of the Static Club of America. January 16, 1914.

Sweeney, Kevin B. *Buster Keaton Interviews.* Jackson: University Press of Mississippi, 2007.

Vazzana, Eugene Michael. *Silent Film Necrology.* Jefferson, NC: McFarland, 2001.

Walker, Brent E. *Mack Sennett's Fun Factory.* Jefferson, NC: McFarland, 2010.

Wead, George, and George Lellis. *The Film Career of Buster Keaton.* Pleasantville, NY: Redgrave Publishing, 1977.

Yallop, David A. *The Day the Laughter Stopped.* New York: St. Martin's Press, 1976.

Index

Numbers in ***bold italics*** indicate pages with photographs.

A-Haunting We Will Go 114
Abbott and Costello 95, 140
Aberfeldy, Scotland 75, 78, 80, 83
Abie's Irish Rose 195
Abraham Lincoln 216
Academy awards 31, 34–5, 37, 38, 50, 81, 82, 83
actors, theatrical 62, 76, 77, 85, 91–2, 106–7, 116–8, 143–4, 153, 156, 169, 183–4, 195, 228–9
Adams, Jimmy 170
Adamson, Joe 138, 139
Adler, Felix 140
Adventures of Kathlyn 143
Adventures of Robin Hood (1938) 13
Adventures of Sherlock Holmes 114
The Adventurous Sex 225
advertising writers 160, 180
Aerial Joyride 118
Affiliated Distributors 224–5
After Business Hours 101
Ahl, Ebba 110–1, 162
Air Raid Wardens 110
Al Boasberg Award 130
Alcazar Theater 85
alcoholism 46–7, 138, 140–1, 224, 225, 227, 234
Alfred Hitchcock Presents 40

Ali Baba and the Forty Thieves 117
All Aboard 225
All Over Town 88
Along Came Ruth 66, 68
American Cinematographer 29, 31, 35, 49, 67
American Photography 41
American Society of Cinematographers (ASC) 10, 28, 36, 37, 39, 49, 224
American Society of Composers, Authors and Publishers (ASCAP) 153,
161
America's Over There Theater League 154
Ames, Walter 111
Andrews Sisters 71
Anger, Adeline 183, 187
Anger, David 183, 187
Anger, Emanuel 183, 187
Anger, Harry 187
Anger, Hermann 183
Anger, Jacob 183, 187
Anger, Lena 183
Anger, Lou 1, 6, 22, 24, 55, 114, 153, 160, 170, 180, 182, 183–8, 191, 195, 198, ***223***, 231
Anger, Samuel 183, 187
Anger, Sophye Barnard 22, 183–4, 185–6, 187
Another Scandal 11
Antics 128
"Any Little Girl" 153
Arbuckle, Roscoe 5, 22–3, 24, 42–3, 55, 104, 117,

118, 122, 161, 162, 165–6, 185, 195, 222–31, ***223***, 224
Are Parents People? 102
Argus Weekly 9
army service *see* military service
Arnez, Desi 111
Art Institute of Chicago 164
Ashes of Vengeance 216, 218
Ashley, Lillian 177, 178
assistant directors' responsibilities 112–3, 121
Astra Film Company 19
At the Circus 121
The Awful Truth 161
Ayers, Lou 138

Babes in the Woods 117
Baby Mine 165
Baby Peggy 66
Back to God's Country 10
Backstage 43, 162
Bacon, Lloyd 120
Badger, Clarence 161
Baer, Bugs 122–3
bail bondsmen 209, 214
Bain, James 70
Baker, Faye 120
Baker, Phil 126
Bakette, Billy 92
Balio, Tino 192
Ball, Lucille 111
The Balloonatic 58
Balloonatics 58
Baltimore City College 159
Baltimore Orioles 22

299

Index

The Bandolero 225
The Bank Dick 71
bankers 82
Banks, Monty 135, 137, 163, 173
Banky, Vilma 66
Bara, Theda 99, 157
Barnard, Sophye 22, 183–4, 185–6, 187
Barnes, Harry 182
The Barrier 232
Barrymore, Maurice 156
baseball 12, 16, 39, 62, 65, 67, 131–4, 135, 160, 179, 190, 198, 207, 209–13
Bashful Bachelor 104
Bashful Jim 137, 149
The Bat Whisperers 178
bathing beauty films 63–4
The Battle of the Century 138
Battleship Potemkin 102
Battling Butler 16, 29, 56, 123, 126, 137, 174, 175, 177, 179, 206
Battling Buttler (play) 123, 180
Be Careful, Dearie 195
Beach Pajamas 165–6
The Beast of the City 120–1
Beau Hunks 88
Beaumont, Harry 120
A Bedroom Blunder 63
Belasco, David 85, 156, 228
Bell, Monta 120
The Bell Boy 224
Bells of Haslemere 169
Beloved Cheater 19
Ben-Hur (1925) 232
Benny, Jack 126, 129, 130
Bergere, Valerie 228–9
Berlin, Irving 91, 126, 162, 180–1
Berlin Correspondent 150
Berman, Pandro 101
Bernds, Edward 19–20
Bernstein, Isadore 108
Better Late than Never 161
The Better 'Ole 93
Beyond the Rocks 232
bicycle repairmen 38
The Big Noise 104
The Big Parade 232
The Big Sleep 50
The Big Store 95, 121

Billie's First Love 228
Biograph Company 75, 76
The Birth of a Nation 62, 77, 218
Bitzer, Billy 6
The Black Book 227
Black Shadows 226
blackface 106, 117, 175–6
The Blacksmith 97, 100
Blesh, Rudi 47, 109, 115, 135, 141, 162, 163, 186, 191, 198–9, 207
Blockheads 60
Blood and Sand 219
The Blot 33
The Bludgeon 156
Blystone, Betty 58, 60
Blystone, Francine 58
Blystone, Francine Oliver 57, 60
Blystone, George, Jr. 57, 60
Blystone, George, Sr. 57
Blystone, Gwendolyn Davis 58, 60
Blystone, Jasper 57, 59–60
Blystone, John 54–5, 57–61, 186
Blystone, Stanley 57, 60
Boasberg, Al 123, 124–30, 150, 174, 177–8, 180
Boasberg, Harriet Freedman 124–5
Boasberg, Herman 124–5
Boasberg, Hilda Levy 125
Boasberg, Nathan 124–5
Boasberg, Rosadel Stadecker 127–8
Boasberg, Roslyn Goldberg 128
The Boat 65, 198–9
The Bohemian Girl 88
The Bomb Boy 157
Bonfils, Helen 167–8
Bonnie Scotland 88
Borzage, Frank 58, 120
The Boss of Little Arcady 67
Bow, Clara 103, 225
A Bowery Camille 228
boxing 65, 91, 92
Boy of Mine 173
Boys and Girls 169
Brabin, Charles 120
Brand, Celia 189
Brand, Edward 189, 193

Brand, George 192, 193
Brand, Harry 17, 24, 44, 56, 85, 87, 93–4, 114, 135, 182, 189–194
Brand, Herman 189, 193
Brand, Jacob 189, 193
Brand, Louis 189
Brand, Sybil Morris 192–3
Brandt, Eddie 72–3
Brewer, Terry 91–2
Brice, Fanny 184
Bride 13 108
Bright Eyes 99
"Bringing Up Father" 72
Broadway 62, 71, 76, 79, 85, 153, 160, 167–8, 177, 179–80, 184, 197–8, 217, 229
Broadway After Dark 120
Broken Blossoms 77, 78
Bronco Twister 66
Brooklyn Federals 22
Brooks, Louise 102–3
Brophy, Edward 109–10
Brown, Joe E. 110
Brown, Karl 6
The Brown Derby 225
Brown Eyes see Go West
Brownie the Dog 149
Browning, Tod 128, 165
Brownlow, Kevin 29, 54, 59, 85, 88, 94, 123–4, 135, 156, 206
Bruckman, Bertha Smith 131
Bruckman, Clyde 43, 56, 65, 69, 103, 122–3, 124, 128, 131–42, *136*, 149, 174, 200
Bruckman, Gladys Prevost 139, 141
Bruckman, Lola Hamblin 132, 137
Bruckman, Rudolph 131
Bryan Foy Productions 150
Bryant, James 178
Bubbles of Trouble 63
Bull Durham (1908) 160
Bulls Eye 87
Burns and Allen 127
Business Is Pleasure 68
The Buster Keaton Show 72, 104, 140
The Butcher Boy 104, 226, 228, 231

Index

California or Bust 127
Calvary Cemetery (California) 151, 201
Calvary Cemetery (New York) 155
Calvert, Catherine 156
Camera! (magazine) 112, 143–4
The Cameraman 1, 30, 38, 39, 40, 46, 56–7, 109–10, 124, 157–8
cameramen's responsibilities 5–6, 16 23, 39
Campbell, Jack 175–7
The Canada Dry Show 129
The Canary Murder Case 103
Cannon, Fanchon Royer 144, 145–6
Cannon, Manuel 143
Cannon, Newton 143
Cannon, Raymond 123, 142–7
Cannon, Sarah Bolinger 143
Cannon, Thornburg 143
Capra, Frank 19, 45
Captain January 66
Carmen 157
Carr, Harry 98
Carriere, Leonard 218
Carriere, Lester 218
Carriere, Marshall 218
Caruso, Enrico 156, 210
Cash and Carry 139
Cavacade Pictures 146
The Celebrated Case 106
Century Film Corporation 58, 93
A Certain Party 62
Change of Heart 59
Chapel of the Pines 17
Chaplin, Charlie 12, 13, 56, 63, 92–3, 230
Chaplin, Sydney 64, 93, 120, 150
Charlie Chan's Chance 60
Chase, Charlie 88, 161
Chasing Through Europe 114, 191
chauffeurs 13, 38, 39
Cheer Up 185
Cheyenne Massacre 86
Chickens 144
China Bound 39
Chips Off the Old Block 150

Christie Company 52
The Church of the Latter-Day Saints 9, 26, 33
Cinderella 117
Circus Days 66, 165, 201
Citizen Kane 14
civil engineers 9, 26
Civilization 10, 28
Clawson, Charlotte Schuer 10
Clawson, Dal 2, 7, **8**, 9–12, 33, 51
Clawson, Elliot 9, 10
Clawson, Hazel Hanson 9, 10
Clawson, Irene Boylan 10
Clawson, Lawrence Dallin, Jr. 10, 11
Clawson, Mary Ann Jones 9
Clawson, Stanley 9
Clear the Decks 178
Cleopatra (1934) 33, 35
clerks, office 179
clerks, store 41, 62, 119, 143, 216
A Clever Dummy 43
The Clever Mrs. Carfax 77
Cline, Beatrice Ives 64, 72
Cline, Betty 64, 70
Cline, Eddie 1, 30, 54, 58, 61–75, 99–100, 114, 127, 128, **136**, 137, 139, 142, 149, 157, 161, 165, 180, **199**, 201
Cline, Francis 62
Cline, Mary Bailey 62
Cline, Minnie Matheis 62, 64
Clune Film Producing Company 77
Clyde, Andy 67
Cobra 29
Coconut Grove 99
co-directors' responsibilities 54–7, 65
Cody, Lew 87
Coffee Dan's 30
Cohan, George M. 66, 76, 77, 101, 156
Cohen, Henry 108
The Cohens and the Kellys in Africa 165
Cohn, Harry 20, 170
Colbert, Claudette 71
College 16, 29, 56, 85, **86**,

88, 124, 148, 149, 156, 157–8, 206
Collins, Catherine Magel 115
Collins, John "Chick" 112, 115–6
Collins, Michael 115
Collins, Pierre 102
Colman, Ronald 66
Columbia Pictures 18, 19, 101, 114, 139, 140, 151, 170
Columbus Red Birds 213
Comique Film Company 43, 228, 231
Coney Island 224
Conklin, Chester 58, 91, 161
Conley, Lige (Lige Crommie) 98
Conlon, Paul 222–3, **223**
Considine, John W. 163
Convict 13 65
Convict's Code 225
Coogan, Jackie 66, 165, 201, 216
The Cook 94, 224, 225
Cook, Clyde 58, 186, 195
The Cook of Canyon Country 77
Cooper, Gay 66
Cooper, Jackie 89
Cops 65, 154
Corona Cinema Corporation 226
costume department's responsibilities 13, 215–9
Cottage Grove, Oregon 11, 12, 13, 137, 202–3
Cottage Grove Sentinel 177, 182
Cotten, Joseph 71
The Country Chairman 60
A Country Hero 224
Cowardice Court 28
Cracked Nuts 71, 128
Crazy House 71
Crichton, Kyle 192
cricket (game) 67
Crisp, Donald 55, 75–84
Crisp, Elizabeth 75
Crisp, Hazel Stark 77–8
Crisp, Helen, Pease 77
Crisp, James 75
Crisp, Jane Murfin 79, 82
Cromwell, Richard 60

Crooked to the End 118
Crosland, Alan 150
The Cruise of the Jasper B 87
Cruze, James 103, 108
Cunningham, Cecil 161
The Curse of Eve 226
The Curses 118
The Cyclone 226

Dallin, Cyrus 9
Dana, Viola 66, 87–8, 137, 178
Daring Youth 173
"Darktown Poker Club" 161
A Dash of Courage 161
Davies, Marion 55
Davis, Benny 92
Davy Crockett, Indian Scout 13
Day, Alice 137
Day, Marceline 66
A Day at the Races 129–30
Daydreams 65
A Days Pleasure 12
Death on the Diamond 210
De Haven, Carter 100, 165
De Haven, Flora Parker 100
del Rio, Dolores 14
del Ruth, Roy 49, 120
De Luxe Annie 177
De Mille, Cecil B. 35, 36, 37, 79, 186, 218, 219
Denny, Reginald 67, 100
Desilu 111
Deslys, Gaby 189
The Devil's Squadron 196
Dietrick, Joseph 201
Dinky Dean Productions 93, 165
Dinwoody, Henry 26
directors' responsibilities 54, 65, 85, 88, 112–3
The Diving Girl 64
Dixie National Pictures 175
Dixon, Henry 183
Dizzy Heights and Daring Hearts 161
Dobson, Alfred 85
Dockstader, Lew 160
Dr. Jack 163

Dr. Jekyll and Mr. Hyde 115
Dog Days 149
A Dog's Life 92
Don Key (Son of Burro) 157
Don Q., Son of Zorro 79
Donlin, Mike 62, 178, 209
Donnelly, Leo 160, 170, 183
Don't Walk In Your Sleep 228
Don't Weaken 99
Doughboys 128
Doyle, Tracy 126
Dracula (1931) 146
draft registration 3
Dragon Seed 82
"Dream On, Little Soldier Boy" 162
The Dude Ranger 68
Dumbo 110
Dunne, Irene 67
Dwyer, Ruth Anne 97–8, 101, 102, 103

The Eagle 29
Eagle-Lion Films 95, 114, 151
Earl, Lew 173
Earl Carroll's Vanities of 1928 180
Eastwood, Clint 96
Easy to Wed 111
Ebner, Barbara 212
editorial assistants' responsibilities 206
Edmunds, Lee 106
Edwards, Snitz 87, 126, 163
Ehlers, Donald 47
Ehlers, Evelyn Hess 47
The Electric House 135, 198
electrical department's responsibilities 7, 19–20
Ellsworth, Carmen Roux 14
Ellsworth, Carrie Kennedy 12
Ellsworth, Dolores 14
Ellsworth, Elmer 7, 12–15
Ellsworth, Robert 14
Ellswoth, Elmer Ellis 12
Eltinge, Julian 88
Elysia, Valley of the Nude 150

engineering studies 9, 26, 33, 57, 107, 230
Epstein, Myer 190
Ernie Orsatti's Oddity Shop 213
Errol, Leon 129, 167
Escort West 13
Essanay Studios 226, 230
Everson, William K. 97, 102
Everybody Dance 95
"Everybody Works But Father" 155, 159, 160
Everyman 217
Everything's Rosie 128, 138
EveryWoman 197–8
Ex-Plumber 118
Eyes of the Forrest 196
Eyes of the World 77
Eyes That See Not 226

The Face of Jesus 37
Fairbanks, Douglas 49, 79
Fairhaven Memorial Park 141
Famous Players-Lasky Studio 19, 77, 87, 165, 170
Fanchon and Marco 162
Fantomas 108
The Farmer's Daughter 191–2
A Fatal Glass of Beer 138
A Favorite Fool 148
Faye, Alice 104
Fazenda, Louise 63
Federal League 22
Feet First 138, 174, 180
Ferocious Pal 227
Fidler, Jimmie 70, 121
"Fido Is a Hot Dog Now" 153
Fielding, Romaine 107
Fields, W.C. 69–70, 71, 94, 138, 161, 174–5
Fighting Blood 100
Fighting for Justice 227
Film Booking Office (FBO) 100–1, 125; *see also* RKO; Robertson-Cole Pictures
Film Dope 61
film laboratory workers 16, 51, 52–3, 205–6, 231–4
Find Your Man 101
Fine Arts Studios 144
Finnegan 117–8

Index

Fireball Fun-for-All 72
Firefly of Tough Luck 113
The First Degree 108
First National Pictures 200
Fischer, Fred 152
Fischer Costuming Company 216
Fisher, John C. 76
The Fisherman 166
fishing writers 143, 146–7
The Five Sedgwicks 106
A Flaming Affair 174
The Flaming Hour 108
Flapper Wives 79
Flirting with Love 219
The Flirty Four-Flushers 157
Florida failed film production 166
Fools for Luck 94
football 62, 65, 67, 106–7, 192
Footloose Widows 49
For Heaven's Sake 137
Ford, John 82
Forest Lawn Cemetery, Buffalo, New York 130
Forest Lawn Cemetery, Hollywood 158
Forest Lawn Memorial Park, Glendale 20, 37, 47, 83, 89, 121, 168, 187
The Forgotten Law 87
The Fortune Hunter 150
Foster, Ed 178
The Fountainhead 50
Fowl Play (1929) 157
Fox, Virginia 99
Fox Film Corporation 10, 28, 49, 55, 56, 57, 59–60, 99, 107–8, 114, 117, 119, 124, 138, 145, 149, 157, 174, 180, 191, 192, 193, 198, 226; see also Twentieth Century–Fox
Fox Sunshine Comedies 58, 64, 149, 222
Foy, Bryan 49, 92, 95, 114, 124, 129, 137, 148–52, 158
Foy, Charles 148–9, 150, 151
Foy, Eddie 148–9
Foy, Eddie, Jr. 148–9, 150, 151
Foy, Irving 148–9, 150, 151

Foy, Madeline 148–9, 150, 151
Foy, Madeline Morando 148
Foy, Mary 148–9, 150, 151
Foy, Mary Jane 149
Foy, Richard 148–9, 150, 151
Foy, Vivian 149, 151
Francis, Chrystine 182, 194–7
Frazee, Edwin 148
Freaks 128
Frederick, Pauline 29
Fredericks, Ann 89
Free and Easy 128
The French Maid 76
The Freshman 140, 155
Friganza, Trixie 153, 162
The Frozen North 65
The Fugitive 13
Fuller Brush Girl 111
"Fun in a Dissecting Room" 106
Funny Face 180
The Funny Mr. Dooley 169, 177

Gabourie, Evelyn Holitzki 198, 201
Gabourie, Frances Meareau 197
Gabourie, Fred 182, 197–202, **199**
Gabourie, Fred, Jr. 197, 201, 214
Gabourie, Frederick 197
Gabourie, Mary 201
gag men vs. writers 122
Gallagher, Ed 149
Gallagher, Jack 146
Galveston, Texas 106, 107
The Garage 43, 162, 222
Gashouse Gang 210–1
Gateway to Hollywood 180
Gaudio, Tony 190
Gay Coney Island 177
The Gay Hussars 183
The General 2, 3, 7, 11, 13, 16, 19, 26, 29–30, 51, 52, 56, 62, 110, 113, 116, 123–4, 126–7, 137, 145, 175, 177, 180, 182, 191, 194, 195, 202, 203, 205, 206, 215, 232
General Productions 158
General Spanky 158

Gentle Julia 60
Gentlemen Prefer Blondes (1928) 102–3
George Washington, Jr. 101
George White Company 120
The German Soldier 160, 170, 183–4
Gibson, Hoot 108
Gilmore, Al 112–3
The Girl Detective 86, 87
The Girl from Brighton 161
The Girl on the Barge 178
Girl Shy 155
Gish, Dorothy 77, 144
Gish, Lillian 144
Glad Rags 137
Go West (1925) 16, 19, 45, 56, 123, 142, 145, 163, 174, 206
Go West (1940) 121
The Goat 65, 97, 100, 162
Going Up 144
The Gold Rush 93
The Golden Bed 219
The Goldfish 219
Goldie Gets Along 103
Goldwyn Studios 29, 47, 60, 66, 157, 206, 233–4
golf 36, 37, 39, 67, 192
Gone with the Wind 13
Good Night, Nurse 224
"Goodbye Broadway, Hello France" 92
Goodrich, William see Arbuckle, Roscoe
Goof on the Roof 140
The Goose Woman 78
Gores, Henrietta 91
Gorman, Inez 212, 213, 214
Grab Bag Bride 43
Grable, Betty 64
Grace, Dick 195–6
The Grand Duchess and the Waiter 102
Grand National Pictures 146
Grandma's Boy 163
Grau, Robert 176
Grauman, Sid 192
Graves, Ralph 137
Gray, Daniel 152
Gray, James 152
Gray, Johnny 174
Gray, Mary 152
Gray, Mollie 152, 155

Index

Gray, Tommy 123, 152–6, 184
The Great Locomotive Chase 137
The Greatest Show on Earth 35
Greenwich Village Follies 180
The Greyhound 156
Griffith, D.W. 42, 55, 76–7, 78, 144, 145, 218
Griffith, Raymond 43, 118, 170
Growing Up with Monsters 146
Guadalcanal Diary 150
Gummerson, Charles 17
The Gun Runner 206
Gypsy Joe 118

Haines, Bert 6–7, 15–8, 29, **86**
Haines, David 15–6
Haines, Dorothy Vidou 16
Haines, Ida Shank 15
Haines, Olga McCoy 17
Haines, William 108–9
Half-Shot Shooters 139
Hall, Mordaunt 44
Hallroom Boys 163, 170, 173, 222
Hamilton, Lloyd 24
Hands Up 87
Harbaugh, Carl 120, 124, 149, 156–9
Harbaugh, Frances Bouis 157
Harbaugh, Harriett 157, 158
Harbaugh, Lewis 156
Harbaugh, Maria Spraul 156, 158
A Hard Act to Follow 94
Hard Luck 1, 65
Hardy, Sam 138
Harmon, Bird Claypool 20
Harmon, Denver Dudley 20n
Harmon, Henry 18
Harmon, Jessie Fermin 18–9
Harmon, Ollie 18, 20
Harmon, Wayne "Denver" 7, 18–21, 87
Harmon, William Zerble 20

Harris, Elmer 162
Harris, Sam 77, 179–80
Harron, Robert 77
Hart, William S. 222–3
The Haunted House 65
Haver, Phyllis **199**
Havez, Alice 159
Havez, Alice, Jr. 159
Havez, Cecil Cunningham 161
Havez, Ebba Ahl 162, 163–4; *see also* Sedgwick, Ebba
Havez, Herbert 159, 160
Havez, Jean 110, 122–3, **136**, 137, 141, 145, 153, 155, 159–64, 170, 173, 222, 226
Havez, Jean, Sr. 159
Hawkes, Howard 103
Hayakawa, Sessue 10, 231
The Hayseed 43, 162
He Did and He Didn't 42–3
Heads or Tails 72
Heads Up 180
Heart Trouble 30, 46
Hearts and Flowers 64
Hearts of Men 49
Hearts of the World 120
Hell's Angels 165
Hell's Highway 121
Her Caveman 43
Her Decision 43
Her Father Said No 127
Her Lucky Night 140
"Her Majesty the Prince" 146
Her Marriage Vow 49
Higgins Family 104
High Stakes 43
Hill, George W. 51
Hired, Tired and Fired 107
His Bread and Butter 63, 100
His Busted Trust 63
His First False Step 91
His Last Laugh 98
His Lesson 77
His Little Widows 153
His Lucky Day 67
His Lying Heart 91
His Naughty Night 135
His Wedding Night 224, 226
Hitchcock, Alfred 40, 78
Hollywood Cavalcade 104

Hollywood Costumes 217
Hollywood Memorial Park Cemetery (Hollywood Forever) 14, 53, 163, 204, 225, 234
Hollywood Planets 212
Hollywood Revue of 1929 94, 120
Hollywood Starmakers 95
Hollywood Stars 213
Hollywood Walk of Fame 111
Holy Cross Cemetery 111, 115, 118, 171, 180–1
The Honeymoon Express 184
Hook, Line and Sinker 68, 73
Hope, Bob 128, 148, 192–3
Hope, Miriam 91, 93, 94–5
Hopper, Hedda 68–9
Horne, Charles Wesley 85
Horne, Cleo Ridgely 86–7, 89
Horne, Edith Woodthorp 85
Horne, James 19, 56, 84–90, **86**, 149, 158–9
Horne, James, Jr. 87, 89
Horne, June 87, 89
Horne, Victoria 89
horse racing 67
Horse Shoes 137
Horseplay 110
Horse's Collars 139
Horton, Edward Everett 145
Hot Water 155
Houck, Arthur 21
Houck, Byron **2**, 6, 16, 21–5, 185, **199**
Houck, Ida Call 21
Houck, Kittye Issacs 22, 23
Houck, Rose Johnson 24, 25
House of Wax 151
How Green Was My Valley 81
How to Fish the Pacific Coast 146
Howell, Alice 58, 174
Howell, Yvonne 174
How've You Bean 229
Hoxie, Jack 108
Hubble, Bennie 215

Index

Hughes, Felix 227
Hughes, Howard 165, 227
Hunley, Maxwell 218
Hunley, Otis 217–8
Hunting Tigers in India 10
Hutson, Clarence 107
Hysterical History Comedies 49, 149

I Can't Give You Anything but Love 180
I Wanted Wings 37
IATSE Motion Picture Costumers Union 14
Ideas 166
If I Had a Million 161
I'll Tell the World 67
Illinois Central Railroad 205
"I'm to Be Shot at Sunrise" 153
Imagine My Embarrassment 145
In Society 140
Ince Studios 10, 27, 28, 42, 107, 143, 198
Ingram, Rex 103
International Photographic Association 41
Intolerance 218
Introduce Me 144–5
The Iron Claw 89
Iroquois Tribe 197
"Isn't She a Brazen Thing" 153
Israel, Ethel Wahlicht 216, 217
Israel, Sabrina 216
Israel, Walter 182, 215–7, 219–20
It's a Great Life 68
"It's an Awfully Easy Way to Make a Living" 153
Ives, Robert 64

Jackson, Bert 182, 202–5
Jackson, Catherine 203
Jackson, Edwin 203
Jackson, Mary Dorothy Meyers 203, 204
Jackson, Ruth Meyers 203, 204
James Ormont Productions 170
The Jazz Singer (1927) 150
Jazzmania 157

Jennings, Adele Badarous 30
Jennings, Cleo Wells 27
Jennings, Dev 2, 6–7, **8**, 9, 10, 12, 16, 19, 25–33, 36, 46, 51, **86**
Jennings, Ellen Dinwoody 26, 27
Jennings, Florence Anderson 36, 37
Jennings, Genevra 33
Jennings, Gordon 6, 26, 30–1, 33–38
Jennings, John 33, 37
Jennings, Joseph 26, 27
Jennings, Mary McClellan 33
Jennings, William 26
Jessel, George 157
Jessie D, Hampton Company 198
jewelers 125, 164
Jezebel 80
Jim's Girl 154
Jitterbugs 104
"Joe Gum" 133–4
Johns Hopkins University 159
Johnson, Henry 191–2
Jolly, Edward 172
Jolson, Al 160, 184
Jones, F. Richard 98
Jones, Spike 72–3
The Jones Family in Hollywood 59, 104
journalists *see* newspaper writers
Joy Street 145

Kalem Company 85–6, 87
Kay-Bee 10
Keaton, Buster 1, **2**, 3, 13, 29–30, 33, 39, 40, 43–4, 49–50, 60, 70–1, 78–9, 82–3, **86**, 93–4, 97–8, 99–100, 103, 104, 106, 109–10, 115, 120, 121, 122, 126–7, 135, **136**, 139, 140, 141, 145, 149, 154–5, 156, 158, 159, 161, 162, 165, 166, 167–8, 170, 172, 173–4, 177, 180, 198–9, **199**, 200–1, 203, 208, 212, 214, **223**, 225, 226, 228, 229–30, 231; on cameramen's responsibilities 5, 25–6; on co-directors' responsibilities 54–7, 65, 85, 88, 137
Keaton, Joe 159, 178, 195
Keaton All-Stars 16
Keep Kool 180
Keep Smiling 137
Kelly, Claude 117
Kell, Daisy Jennings 205
Kell, Eileen 205–6
Kell, Ethel Garner 205–6
Kell, J. Sherman 182, 205–7
Kell, Jay 205–6
Kell, Madelyn 205–6
Kell, Orville 205
Kennedy Productions 166
Kenton, Erle C. 99
Keystone Cops (Keystone Kops) 63, 71, 73, 98
Keystone Studio *see* Triangle-Keystone Film Corporation
Kick In 79
The Kid 92
The Kid Brother 174
King, Henry 29, 66
King Kong (1933) 115, 233
King of the Jungle 175
King Slodo 117
King Vidor 19
Kingsley, Grace 99, 103, 145, 149, 162, 226
Kira, Gene 143, 146
Kit Carson 114
Kit, the Arkansas Traveler 169
Klemperer, Werner 72
Klever Komedies 154
Kline, Jim 71, 100, 104
Kosher Kitty Kelly 87

LaCava, Gregory 68–9
Ladies Must Dance 145
Ladies Night in a Turkish Bath 127
Lady Windermere's Fan 102
Laemmle, Carl 100, 146
Laemmle, Carla 146–7
Laffing Room Only 71–2
Lahue, Kalton 91–2
Lake, Alice **223**
LaMarr, Barbara 219
"Lamb Chops" 127
Lambs Will Gamble 167–8

Lane, Lupino 24, 58
Langdon, Harry 6, 7, 19, 30, 40, 45–6, 88, 137
Lanning, Bessie 38
Lanning, Eileen Christensen 38, 40
Lanning, Nathaniel 38
Lanning, Reggie 7, 38–40
Lanning, Sharon 38
LaRoux, Carmen 14
Lasky Film Company *see* Famous Players-Lasky
Lauder, Harry 119
Laurel, Stan 158; *see also* Laurel and Hardy
Laurel and Hardy 60, 88, 104, 110, 114, 138
The League of Notions 154
The Leather Pushers 100
Leathernecking 67–8, 79
Leave 'Em Laughing 138
Leavy, Gabriel 193
Lehrman-Knockout Kompany (L-KO Kompany) 52, 58, 230–1
Lemon City 170
Leonard, Robert Z. 17, 165
Lesser, Sol 58, 66, 68
Lessley, Blanche Olmstead 42, 46
Lessley, Elgin 1, 5–6, 7, 16, 24, 29, 39, 40–8, 186, **199**, 232
Lessley, Orpha Brooks 40–1
Lessley, Shelton 40–1
Let It Rain 66
Levy, Ed 7
Lew Dockstader's Minstrels 160
Lewis, Jack 7
Liberty Films 39
Life's Like That 145
The Lighthouse by the Sea 101
The Lights of New York 150
Lilac Time 79, 196
Limelight 13
Lipshitz, Esther 164
Lipshitz, Herman *see* Lipton, Lew
Lipshitz, Issac 164
Lipton, Anita (Nora Perry, Nora Warner) 165, 167, 168

Lipton, Channing (Rex) 165, 167, 168
Lipton, Lew 93, 124, 164–8
Lipton, Ruth Colman 165, 166, 167, 168
Little, Jack 182
Little Inch High People 95
The Little Millionaire 77
Little Red Riding Hood 117
Littleton Cemetery 46
Lloyd, Harold 103, 119, 137, 138, 139, 140, 155, 163, 174, 180
location managers' responsibilities 203
Loco Boy Makes Good 140
Lodge, Stephen 14
Long Pants 19, 45
Loos, Anita 102–3
Lord, Marjorie 68
Lorraine of the Lions 108
Los Angeles Express 98
Los Angeles High School 62, 189
Lost: A Cook 98
Lost and Found on a South Sea Island 157
Lost Squadron 196
The Lost World 30, 232
Louisiana Territory 11
Louvish, Simon 104, 110
The Love Cure 85
The Love Nest 114
The Love Thrill 170
Lubin Company 107
Lubitsch, Ernest 97
Lum and Abner 104
Lure of the Circus 107
Lyman, Abe 108
Lyons, Eddie 134

Ma and Pa Kettle Back On the Farm 110
Maas, Frederica Sagor 191–2
Mack, Marion 144, 145
MacLean, Douglas 66, 87, 144–5
MacRae, Henry 10
Madamoiselle Midnight 157
Madison, Mae 50
Making a Living 230
Male and Female 218
Malstrom, Alvin 193

Malstrom, Chrystine Francis 182, 194–7
Malstrom, Gustava 193
Malstrom, Gustave 193
Malstrom, Harriet Schneyer 193
Maltby, Richard 150
Maltin, Leonard 129, 131, 138, 139, 150
The Man from Boston 117
A Man from Wyoming 165
The Man on the Box 120
The Man on the Flying Trapeze 138
The Man with Three Wives 184
Man's Desire 49
Manual Arts High School 208
The Mark of Zorro 49
Marlowe, Francesca 89
Marriage Rows 118
Marx, Arthur 128, 129
Marx Brothers 95, 121, 129–30
Mary of the Movies 144
Mary, Queen of Scotland 80
Mascot Pictures 34
Masked Emotions 191
Mason, Ernie 95
Masons 28, 37
Masquers Club 150
Matrimony 28
Mattox, Martha 144
Mayer, Louis B. 167
Mayhew, Stella 160
McCoy, Olga 17
McDermott, Jack 55–6
McGann, Edna Briggs 48
McGann, Kathryn Glaze 50
McGann, Margaret Clinch 50
McGann, Michael 48
McGann, Roberta Hall 50
McGann, William 6, 48–51, 128
McGuire, Katherine 68, 219
McKee, Raymond 68
McKernan, Luke 3
McNally, John J. 169
Meet the Chump 71
Melies-Star Company 41–2

Melting Millions 226, 227
Mencken, H.L. 160
Menjou, Adolphe, 99, 102, 120
The Merchant of Venice (1914) 9
MGM 39, 56, 57, 82, 94–5, 108, 110–1, 120, 124, 128, 129–30, 165, 173, 179, 184, 191, 197, 201, 204, 206, 226
Midnight Mary 121
A Midsummer Night's Dream 216
military service 16, 33, 49, 78, 81, 89, 114, 115, 120, 148–9
Miller, Arthur C. 19
Million Dollar Legs 69
Mineo, Sal 114
The Misfit 186
Miss Fatty's Seaside Lovers 118
Mr. Dooley and the Land Agent 169–70
"Mr. Gallagher and Mr. Shean" 149
Mitchell, Joseph 122–3, **136**, 137, 160, 169–71, 177, 183
Mitchell, Leo 171
Mitchell, Lorna 83
Mitchell, Margaret 171
Mitchell, Margaret Nicoli 169
Mitchell, Mary 171
Mitchell, Peter 169, 170
Mix, Tom 28, 55, 58, 59, 66, 108, 196, 226
Monogram Pictures 39, 72, 114, 146, 225
Monroe, Marilyn 193
Montana, Bull 136–7
Moonlight and Cactus 71, 180
Moonshine 224
Moore, Colleen 67, 219, 226
Moore, Matt 103
Moore, Owen 77, 103
Moore, Tom 103, 137
Moore, Victor 86, 154
Moran, Lee 134
Morgan, Byron 124
Mormons *see* Church of the Latter-Day Saints
Morosco, Oliver 10

Mother Knows Best 59
Motion Picture Country House and Hospital 40, 50, 83, 118, 204
Motion Picture Photographers' Association 224
Mountain View Mausoleum 104–5
Movie Crazy 138, 140, 174
Munter, Pam 189
Murfin, Jane 79, 82
Murphy, Ralph 167–8
Murray, Charlie 67
Murray, Mae 157
Music Box Revue 126, 180
Muskegon, Michigan 172
My Home Town Girl 162
"My Irish American Rose" 92, 149
My Little Chickadee 69
My Wife's Relations 65, 155
My Wonderful World of Slapstick 56, 122, 165, 173, 174, 200–1
Myrt and Marge 129, 150

Naldi, Nita 29, 219
Nang Sao Suwan (*Miss Suwanna of Siam*) 10
National Velvet 81
Naughty Nanette 178
The Navigator 19, 23–4, 45, 55, 75, 78–9, 82–3, 123, 135–6, 163, 200, 208
Nawn, Tom 178
Neal, Eleanor Horne 174
Neal, Lex 56, 122, 145, 163, 171–5, 177, 180
Neal, Nancy Stokes 172
Neal, William 172
Neal, Willie 172
Ned Wayburn's Town Topics 153
Neighbors 65
Neilan, Marshall 55
Nestor Films 51, 58
The Neutral Soldier 184
"Never Bank on a Travelling Man" 160
Never Give a Sucker and Even Break 71
Never Say Die 144
New York Motion Picture Company 27, 51, 52, 203

newspaper writers 98, 131–2, 135, 143–4, 152–5, 159–60, 164–5, 179, 189, 223; *see also* sports writers
A Night at the Opera 129–30
Nobody 177
nodal point tripod 34
Noisy Neighbors 94
Normand, Mabel 42–3, 63
Nothing but Pleasure 139
Nurmi, Maila 96

Oakwood Memorial Park 40
office boys 226
Oh Brother, Where Art Thou? 129
Oh Doctor 161, 224, 226
Oh What a Nurse! 93
Okuda, Ted 138, 140
Oland Warner 60
The Old Fashioned Way 174–5
Oliver Films 157
Oliver Twist 216
Oliy Scoundrel 118
Olman, Abe 92
Olsen and Johnson 71–2, 88
Olsen's Night Off 103
On Broadway 117
On the Border 49
On the Brink of Ruin 86
On Thin Ice 101
One Week 113
organized crime 208–9
Orsatti, Alfred 208, 211, 213
Orsatti, Carmen 208, 209
Orsatti, Ernie 108–9, 183, 207–15
Orsatti, Ernie, Jr. 212, 213–4
Orsatti, Estella 208, 212
Orsatti, Frank 208, 211, 213
Orsatti, Frank, Jr. 212, 213–5
Orsatti, Inez Gorman 212, 213–4
Orsatti, Jesse 208, 209, 211
Orsatti, Joyce Ritchie 214
Orsatti, Martha Von Utsey 209–10

Index

Orsatti, Mary Manze 207–8, 209
Orsatti, Morris 207, 208–9
Orsatti, Victor 208, 210, 211, 213
Orsatti Agency 211
Oscars *see* Academy awards
O'Sullivan, William 34
The Other Man's Wife 157
"Our Boys" 177
Our Gang 158
Our Hospitality 19, 33–4, 45, 47, 54, 58–9, 115, 116, 123, 135–6, 163, 183, 190, 208, 216
Out West 224
Outside the Law 165

Pabst, G.W. 103
Pacific Coast League 22
Padlocks of 1927 180
Palmer, Doris Murray 95
Paramount Studios 26, 30–1, 35, 39, 53, 95, 101–3, 114, 125, 165, 174–5, 180
Paris, Barry 102
Parker, Bob 6
Parker, Linda 212
patents 35, 231, 233
Patricia Perkins, Inc. 219
Paul Bern Productions 94
Payday 92
Peacock Military Academy 107
Pearce, Peggy 63
Peck's Bad Boy 66
Pedigree Pictures 10
A Perfect Gentleman 137
Perry, Nora 165, 167
The Pest from the West 139
Peter the Great 163
Peters, Christine LaManna 224
Peters, George 222, 223–5, **223**
Peters, Jack 224
A Phantom Husband 43
The Phantom of the Opera 9, 108
Philadelphia Athletics (A's) 21
The Phony Bluff Gold Mine 170

Photo-era Magazine 41
"Pick a Four-Leaf Clover" 92
Pickford, Mary 114, 157
The Pilgrim 93
Piltz, Albert 51
Piltz, Bertha Taker 51, 52
Piltz, Fern Jackson 52
Piltz, Henry 51, 52
Piltz, Otto 51, 52
Piltz, William 7, 51–3
Pioneer Scout 114
Pitcarin, J.K. 215
Pittenger, William 137
Plastered in Paris 191
The Playhouse 43, 54, 65, 162, 198, 232
Plunkett, Walter 13
Polar Baron A 174
Ponjola 78
Pony Express (1924) 195
Pony Express (1925) 108
Poor Mamma 162
Popular Photography 42
Port of Dreams 178
Portland Beavers 22
Potel, Victor 68
practical jokes 174
Price, Vincent 151
Pride and Prejudice (1940) 79
A Prince of a King 93
Principal Players Corporation 66
Professor Beware 139
projectionists 226
property managers' responsibilities 203, 208
"P.T. Barnum, Jr." 172
PT 109 151
The Public Enemy 26, 30
publicists' responsibilities 192
publicity 44–5, 189–93, 222–3
A Punctured Prince 137

Quick Millions 104
Quillan, Eddie 69, 72
Quinn, Paul 169–70

Racing Luck 163, 173
radio fishing 65
radio writers 129–30, 180
Rag Man 66
Ragtime (1927) 170

railroad workers 19, 27, 205
Rainbow Films 99
Ralston, Jobyna 88
Ramona 77
Rayment, John 83
Ready Money 156
real estate agents 167, 168
Reap the Wild Wind 37
The Rebellious Bride 226
A Reckless Romeo 226, 231
The Red Canary 153
The Red Mill 55
The Red Widow 184
Red Wine 145
Reed, Florence 117, 118
Reed, Walter 112, 116–9
Reelcraft Films 99
The Regenerates 113
Regeneration 157
A Regular Fellow 170
Reid, Wallace 124
The Rejuvenation of Aunt Mary 145
Remember When 137
Republic Pictures 39–40, 95, 104; *see also* Monogram Pictures
The Return of Sherlock Holmes 79
"Reverse English" 132–3, 134
Ridgely, Cleo 86–7
Ridgely, Richard 86–7
Riding the Wind 114
Riesner, Anna Costello 91
Riesner, Charles 56, 90–7, 114, 120, 149, 151, 158, 165
Riesner, Dean (Dinky) 91, 93, 94, 95–6
Riesner, Emille Russell 95
Riesner, George 91, 95
Riesner, Henrietta Gores 91
Riesner, Irene Ganzer 95
Riesner, John 91
Riesner, Marie Moorhouse 96
Riesner, Miriam Hope 91, 93, 94–5
Rin-Tin-Tin 49, 100, 101
Ritchie, Adele 95
RKO 60, 101, 103, 104, 114, 125, 127, 129, 165–6, 180; *see also* Foreign

Index

Booking Office (FBO); Robertson-Cole Pictures
Roach, Bert 99
Roach, Hal 60, 87, 88, 98, 108, 156, 157, 158, 180
Roach, Joseph Anthony 162, 222, 225–8
Roach, Mary Doyle 226–7
Roach, Ruth Stonehouse 43, 226, 227
Roach, Theresa Humphries 227
Roach, William 226
The Road to Yesterday 219
Roadhouse Queen 138
Roadside Impresario 77
Rob 'Em Good 137
Rob Wagner's Script 180
Robbins, Elmer 144–5
Roberts, Joe 186, 189
Robertson-Cole Pictures 19, 29, 100, 114, 124, 125, 144; *see also* Foreign Booking Office (FBO); RKO
Robinson, Edward G. 68
Rodgers, Will 60
Rork, Sam E. 78
Rose, Helen 216–7
Rose, (Mr.) 112, 116
Rose Marie 217
Roselotte, Harry 116
Roth, Jean 121
Roth, Sandy 112, 119–21, 158
Rothacker Film Company 149
Rothenberg, Louis 119
Rothenberg, Sarah Wolf 119
Rouged Lips 137
The Rough House 226, 231
Rowe, Madeline 117
A Royal Rogue 43
Royer, Fanchon 144, 145–6
The Runaway Bride 79
Ruth Lipton Agency 167, 168
Ryle, Fred 215

Sacramento Solons 213
Safety First 184
Safety Last! 163
A Sailor-Made Man 163
St. Clair, Ann Fleetwood 98
St. Clair, Aubrey 98, 105
St. Clair, Bernard 98
St. Clair, Cordelia Andrews 99, 103–4
St. Clair, Eric 98, 105
St. Clair, Malcolm 54, 69, 97–105, 138, 174
St. Clair, Margaret Murray 104–5
St. Clair, Norman 98
St. John, Al 43, 54, 55, 61, 62–4, 66, 67, 73, 77, 91–2, 98–9, 100, 118, 120, 137, 138, 148, 149, 156, 158, 161, 170, 185, 189, 222, **223**, 230
St. Louis Browns 22
St. Louis Cardinals 209–11, 213, 214
St. Mary's University 107
salesmen 24, 124, 125, 152, 216; *see also* clerks, store
Salmi, Markku 61
Salt Lake City Cemetery 11
Samurai 146
San Fernando Mission Cemetery 50
Sands of Iwo Jima 39
Sarris, Andrew 97
The Satires of 1920 162
Saturday Evening Post 124, 132–4
Saved by the Belle 14
The Scarecrow 65
The Scarlet Letter (1917) 157
Schenck, Joseph 56, 59, 162, 177, 182, 184–7, 189–91
Schmid, Alfred 47
Schoolhouse Scandal 63
Schultz, Leonard 42, 46
Schwartz, Ben 125–6
script supervisors' responsibilities 195
scrolling titles 34
Sea Fury 13
The Sea Hawk 200, 216
Sea of Cortez 147
Sea Sirens 52
secretaries 195–6
Secrets 219
Sedgwick, Ebba Ahl 110–1
Sedgwick, Edward, Jr. 56–7, 69, 106–12, 124
Sedgwick, Edward, Sr. 106–7
Sedgwick, Eileen 106–7
Sedgwick, Josephine Walker 106–7
Sedgwick, Josie 106–7
Sedgwick, Mary 107
Sedgwick, Rose Adams 107, 110
Seeback, Henry 177
Seitz, George 120
A Self-Made Failure 173
Selig Polyscope Films 223
Sennett, Mack 42, 54, 55, 61, 62–4, 66, 67, 73, 77, 91–2, 98–9, 100, 118, 120, 137, 138, 148, 149, 156, 158, 161, 170, 185, 222, 230
Serenade 225
servo-operated repeating device 35
Seven Chances 19, 24, 55–6, 113, 123, 135–6, 163, 203, 206, 208
Seven Little Foys 148–9
Sh! The Octopus 50, 150
Shadows of Life 9
"Shakey Eyes" 106
She Gets Her Man 140
Shean, Al 149
Shearer, Norma 120
Sherlock Jr. 1, 19, 23, 34, 44–5, 55, 78, 104, 118, 123, 135–6, 163, 208, 216, 219
Sherwood, Robert 56, 123, 173
Ship a Hooey! 158
Shipman, Nell 10
"Show Business" 166
The Show Off 102
Shriners 28, 36
Side Street 103
Sidewalks of New York 180
The Signal 156
Silent Movie Theater 46
The Silver Lining 177
Since You Went Away 71
Singin' in the Rain 115, 213
The Sixth Marine Revue 179
Sjöström, Victor 97
Skretvedt, Randy 158
Sky High 196
The Skyscraper 56, 123, 173

Slide, Kelly, Slide 108–9
Smalley, Phillip 9
The Smart Set 169
Smilin' Through 79
Smith, Abraham 217
Smith, Beatrice 177
Smith, Beatrice Lapla 177
Smith, Carl 180
Smith, Carlton 179
Smith, Charles 123, 169, 174, 175–9, 180
Smith, Dorothy 179
Smith, Edith 177
Smith, Eva McDonagh 179
Smith, Frances 177
Smith, Jean 180
Smith, Jennie Smalley 217
Smith, Lillian Ashley 177, 178
Smith, Mary 180
Smith, Mary Alice Lundgren 180, 181
Smith, Paul Gerald 123, 174, 177, 179–81
Smith, Paul Gerald, Jr. 180
Smith, Sid 170
Smith, Sidney 177
Smith and Campbell 175–7
Snapshots 124; see also *The Cameraman*
So This is London 60
Somebody Lied 149
Somewhere in Sonora 227
Sommes, George 167–8
Song of Love 219
songwriters 149, 152–3, 159, 160–2, 222
So's Your Uncle 140
sound films, transition to 67, 79, 98, 103, 128, 138, 150
South of Dixie 139
A Southern Yankee 110
Sparrows 157
Spawn of the North 31, 33, 37
Speak Easily 178
special effects 31, 33–6, 43, 50
Speedy 174
Spencer's Mountain 83
Spite Marriage 38, 39, 46, 165, 208
sporting goods stores 95

sportswriters 122–3, 131–2, 135, 189
Spring Fever 109
Spring Tonic 138
Spy Smasher 39
Stadium High School 193
Stagliano, James 212
Standcliffe, S.L. 35
Static Club 8, 9, 27, 28, 43, 51–2, 58, 223, 230
Steamboat Bill, Jr. 16, 29, 56, 90, 93–4, 113, 120, 124, 158, 191, 200–1, 206
Steel Preferred 29
Stepping Along 225
Sterling, Ford 63, 91, 102, 135, 230
Stevens, George 88, 174
Stevens, Georgie Cooper 85
Stewart, Billie 173
Stock, Prairie 36
stockbrokers 149
The Stolen Jools 50, 128
A Stolen Life 50
Stonehouse, Ruth 43, 226, 227
Stop! Look! Listen! 91
The Stowaway 169
The Stranger 177
Strictly Dishonorable 213
The Strong Man 19, 45
Strongheart 79
stunt pilots 196
suicide 14, 27, 131, 141
Suicide Fleet 166
Sullivan's Travels 115
The Summer Girls 64
Sutherland, Eddie 69, 103
Swanson, Gloria 43, 218, 232
The Sweepstakes 166
Swingtime Johnny 71, 139
Swiss Miss 60

Talmadge, Constance 110, 216, 219
Talmadge, James 190, 193
Talmadge, Natalie 186, 223, 230–1
Talmadge, Norma 177, 185, 190, 216, 218–9
Talmadge, Richard 87
Talmey, Allene 99
Taxi 224

Taxi Driver series (1928–9) 129
Taxi, Taxi 145
technical directors' responsibilities 197, 199–202
Technicolor 67–8, 79
Teddy the Dog 99
telephone company workers 24, 40, 49
The Telephone Girl 101
television 13, 40, 72–3, 96, 104, 106, 111, 140
Tell Your Children 78
Ten Commandments (1923) 218
Ten Nights Without a Barroom 64
Terror Trail 107
Terry and the Pirates 89
Thalberg, Irving 129–30
That's My Line 165–6
theater support staff 77, 85, 91, 114, 120, 160, 177, 197–8
"There's Lots More Fun..." 162
Thicker Than Water 88
The Third Eye 19, 87
This Is Your Life 73, 82
Thomson, Fred 114
Thorpe, Harry 6, 33
Those Athletic Girls 64
Three Ages 19, 48, 49, 54, 66, 115, 123, 135–6, 152, 155, 203
Three Legionnaires 158
Three Little Beers 139
Three Sappy People 139
Three Stooges 129, 139, 140
Three Wise Saps 140
Through the Breakers 77
Thundering Dawn 13
Ticey 156
Tiffany-Stahl Productions 206
Tiger Shark 151
Tin Hats 108
Tin Pan Alley 226
Todd, Thelma 178
Tol'able David (1930) 60
"Tommy's Tattles" 153–5
Too Busy to Work 60
Too Much Speed 124
The Tough Guy 114
Tourneur, Jacques 120

Index

Training for Husbands 64
Tramp, Tramp, Tramp 45, 102
Traveling Man 165–6
traveling matte shots 230, 231–2, 233
Traveling Saleslady 95
The Treasure of the Sierra Madre 50
Triangle-Keystone Film Corporation 27, 42, 91, 98–9, 107, 113, 148, 161, 163, 203, 224, 230
Trimble, Lawrence 79
A Trip to Chinatown 177
truck drivers 76
True Heart Susie 144
Turpin, Ben 43, 63, 99
Tuttle, Frank 103
Twentieth Century–Fox 104, 107, 150, 192, 193; see also Fox Film Corporation
Twice into the Light 226
Two Fisted Jones 108
"The Two Senators" 106

Uncle Jake 138
"Uncle Quit Work Too" 160
Uncle Tom's Cabin 117, 166
Ungar, Arthur 125, 128
United Artists 186–7, 191
Universal Film Manufacturing Company 12, 19, 27, 49, 57–8, 60, 69–70, 71, 88, 93, 107, 108, 114, 123, 124, 140, 145, 146, 149, 155, 165, 167, 170, 175, 178, 180
University of Oregon Ducks 21
University of Southern California 189
University of Texas 106–7
University of Utah 26, 33
Unknown Chaplin 93
The Unknown Purple 177
Upside Down 224

Valentino, Rudolph 29, 232
Valhalla Memorial Park 60, 206
"Vamping the Vamp" 173
Vamping Venus 30, 67

Vampira 96
vaudevillians 91, 92, 106–7, 109, 116–8, 119, 120, 123, 125–6, 127–8, 148, 153–5, 160–2, 169–70, 172–3, 175–7, 179–80, 183–4, 228–9
Vernon, Doris *see* Ahl, Ebba
Vernon Tigers 22–3, 132, 185, 209
Veteran's Cemetery, Los Angeles 175, 227
Vidor, Florence 102
Vidor, King 97, 107
The Viking 79
Village Vampire 118
The Villain Still Pursued Her 70–1
Visibility Unlimited 196
Vitagraph Company 93
Vitaphone Variety Company 150
von Stroheim, Erich 97, 186

Walker, Brent 64, 148, 161
Walsh, Raoul 10, 157, 158, 225
The War of the Worlds (1953) 33, 35–6, 37
Wark Producing 114
Warner, Thomas, Jr. 167
Warner Bros. Studios 49–50, 95–6, 101, 120, 150, 151, 173, 175, 180
Warren, Herbert 222, **223**, 228–9
Warren, Valerie Bergere 228–9
Watson, William 99
Watz, Ed 68, 138, 140
Way Down South 117
Way Out West 88
The Weaker Vessel 12
Webb, Millard 49
Weber, Lois 9, 33
Wedded Blitz 167
Welcome, Danger 103, 138, 140, 174, 180
Wenzel, Francis 152
Werker, Alfred 113–5, **199**
Werker, Alfred, Jr. 113, 114
Werker, Frances Allen 113, 114
West, Billy 92, 149

West, Clare 182, 216, 217–21
West, Mae 69–70, 153, 154
West, Roland 177, 178
West Point 109
Western Associated Motion Picture Advertisers Society 190–1
Western Costume Company 13
Western Vaudeville Circuit 92
What! No Beer? 110
What Price Beauty? 29
What Price Hollywood? 79
What the Milk Did 156–7
What's Your Hurry 124
Wheel of Life 58
Wheeler and Woolsey 67, 68, 138
When a Man's a Man 66, 68
When Slim Was Home Cured 107
When Worlds Collide 37
"When You Ain't Got No Money..." 160
Where Is My Wife? 135
White, Isabel 162
White, Jules 69, 140
White, Sam 69
The White Moth 219
Why Change Your Wife? 218
Why Leave Home? 145
The Widow from Chicago 68
Wife Tamers 157
Wild, Winifred 172
Wilde, Ted 103
William Lab 233
Williams, Barbara 232
Williams, Bert 153, 160–1
Williams, Brenda 233
Williams, Frank 1, 51, 222, 224, 229–35
Williams, Frank, Jr. 233
Williams, Harry 222
Williams, James 230
Williams, Lucinda 233
Williams, Lucinda Bowles 230
Williams, Melinda 233
Williams, Mildren Hansen 232–3
Williams, Porter Lee 233

Wilnat Films 173
Wings 196
The Winning of Barbara Worth 66
Within the Law 216
Woman Hater 117
Woman in Room 13 29
A Woman of Pleasure 198
The Women 79
Woodlawn Cemetery 30
Woodthorpe, Georgia 85

Wright, Harold Bell 66
writers' responsibilities 122–4, 127, 156, 160
Wuthering Heights 79

X-Files 141

Yallop, David 55
The Yankee Counsel 144
The Yankee Prince 76
The Yankee Way 107–8

Yip, Yip Yaphank 162
You Can't Cheat an Honest Man 69
You Nazty Spy 139
"You Told Me to Go" 108
The Young Don't Cry 114

Zanuck, Darryl 92, 99, 100–1, 104, 192, 212
Ziegfeld Follies 160, 180